BRITTANY & NORMANDY

THE ROUGH GUIDE

KU-409-097

ROUGH GUIDE CREDITS

Series Editor: Mark Ellingham
Editorial: Martin Dunford, John Fisher, Jack Holland, Jonathan Buckley
Production: Susanne Hillen, Kate Berens, Andy Hilliard, Gail Jammy
Typesetting and Design: Greg Ward
Series Design: Andrew Oliver

Thanks to all at Rough Guides, especially Mark Ellingham and Susanne Hillen, for allowing me as complete control over the **production** and **design** of this book as any author can ever have had. Thanks to Kate, Susanne and Andy for proofing and to Jon Dear for the use of his scanner and Linotron.

Continuing thanks also to my friends who helped with the **research** and **writing**; Deborah Jones, Robert Jones, Sandra Jones, Sally Bull, Caroline Wright, Lynn Taylor and Meg Scott.

Thank you for **practical assistance** to Sarah Bensted-Smith and Toby Oliver of Brittany Ferries; to Jean-Paul Dorie in Nantes, Michel Poulain in Bayeux, Philip Rabany in Rouen, and Brian and Rosalie Kirby in Sées; and to Beatrice Jeffries, Pauline Hallam, Isabel Moussu and Dominique Gigante of the French Government Tourist Office in London.

Thanks too to all those who sent in letters about the first edition, including Geoff Hearfield, Colin Wilson, Josie Pearse, L. R. Goodwin, Oona Wesley-Smith, Col G. P. Wood, Norman Rice, Janice Groves, Ginger Brusca and Margaret Adcock.

And a special mention for Kate Baillie and Mark Ellingham, for pointing me in the right direction and for their continued friendly help.

Published by Harrap Columbus, Chelsea House, 26 Market Square, Bromley, Kent BR1 1NA

Typeset in Linotron Univers and Century Old Style.
Printed by Cox & Wyman, Reading, Berks

Small incidental illustrations in Part One and Part Four by Ed Briant
All other illustrations by Deborah Jones

256pp
includes index

British Library Cataloguing in Publication Data
Ward, Greg
Brittany and Normandy: the rough guide
2nd ed.
1. France. Brittany. Visitors' guides 2. France. Normandy. Visitors' guides
   I. Title
   914.4104838
   ISBN 0-7471-0211-2

BRITTANY &
NORMANDY
THE ROUGH GUIDE

written, researched and edited by

GREG WARD

illustrated by Deborah Jones

contributing editor
Kate Baillie

HARRAP-COLUMBUS ■ LONDON

UPDATES: YOU CAN HELP

While this book is based on as much first-hand research as possible, the preparation of its second edition has been greatly aided by the many letters I have received from readers. If you do spot any detail which may have changed since publication – for example, restaurants and hotels come and go, opening hours change, and so on – or find anything which you feel should be included, I would be extremely glad to hear from you. Any comments you might wish to pass on would also be welcome; I would be interested to know how useful you find certain features, such as the "Travel Details" at the end of each chapter, and the maps.

All contributions will be credited in print, and a copy of the next edition (or any other Rough Guide if you prefer) is the reward for the best letters. Please write to:

Greg Ward, The Rough Guides, 149 Kennington Lane, London SE11 4EZ.

CONTENTS

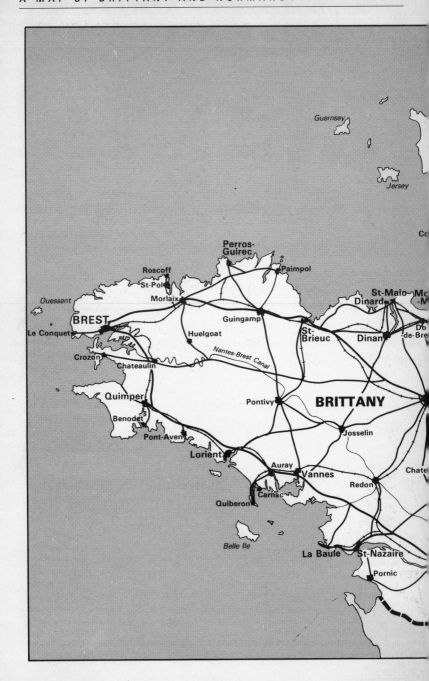

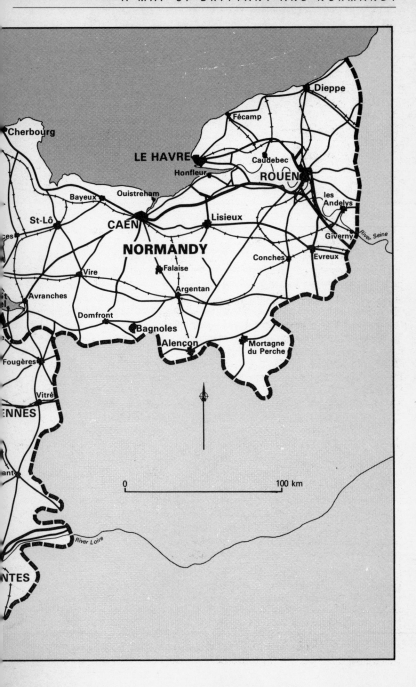

INTRODUCTION

O f all France's strongly individual regions, **Brittany** and **Normandy** are among the most distinct. This sense of separateness – in cultures and peoples, landscapes and histories – is undoubtedly a major aspect of their appeal. Travelling through both regions, you take in much of the best that France has to offer: wild coast and sheltered white sand beaches; sparse heathland and dense forests; medieval ports and evidence of the prehistoric past; and, just as important, abundant seafood and (especially in Normandy) a compelling and exuberant cuisine.

Brittany

Brittany is the more popular of the two regions, with both French and foreign tourists. Its attractions lie most obviously along the **coast**, which, dotted with offshore islands and islets, makes up over a third of France's seaboard. In parts of the north and in the western region of Finistère, it can be nothing but rocks and cliffs, buffeted by the full force of the Atlantic and swept by dangerous currents. But elsewhere, especially in the southern resorts around the Morbihan and La Baule, it is the gentlest, most sheltered of seas, the sands rambling for miles or broken into coves between steep cliff headlands.

The extent of the Breton coastline means that it's always possible to walk alone with the elements. Although in high season it can be hard to find solitude on the sandy beaches or in the small bays with their sun-struck swimmers, there could never be enough visitors to cover all the twists of Finistère's coast. As well as exploring the mainland resorts and seaside villages, it's worth making the time to take in at least one of **the islands**. Boat trips out to these offshore microcosms are one of the most enjoyable features of Brittany. The magical Ile de Bréhat is just a ten-minute crossing from the north coast near Paimpol, while historic Belle-Ile to the south is under an hour from Quiberon. There are island bird sanctuaries, and, off Finistère, the Iles d'Ouessant and Molène are as remote and strange as Orkney or the Shetland Isles.

The **Celtic** elements in Brittany are inextricably linked with it's seafaring past. Anciently the land was known as *Armorica* (in Breton the land of the sea, *ar-mor*), and it was from fishing and shipbuilding, along with occasional bouts of piracy and smuggling, that the people made their living. The harshness of the Breton coast and the poor communications with its interior and with "mainland" France enforced isolation. Christianity took time to establish itself, strongly but idiosyncratically, in a region where Druids survived on the Ile de Sein until Roman times, and it was only in 1532 that the territory lost its independence and became a province of the France. It was a reluctant partner even then, treated virtually as a colony by the national government, who until well into this century found it necessary to suppress the Breton language and traditions. Today, there is something of a reversal, with the **language** and **culture** being rediscovered and reasserted. If you are a Celt – Welsh, Scots or Irish –

you will find shared words, and great appreciation in their use. For everyone, though, the traditions are active, accessible and enjoyable at the various Inter-Celtic **festivals**, the biggest of which takes place at Lorient in early August.

The forests and moors of **inland Brittany** evoke times even before the Celts, with a wealth of **megalithic remains**. At Carnac there are spectacular alignments of menhirs – possibly part of a prehistoric observatory. On Gavrinis, and other islands in the gulf of Morbihan, stand related stones and burial tumuli. Always beautifully sited, they are one of the province's key fascinations. The **forests** of Huelgoat and Paimpont, relics of Brittany's mythic dark ages, are identified with the tales of Merlin, the Fisher King and the Holy Grail. This was the Little Britain of King Arthur's domain, and an other-worldly element still seems entrenched in the land and people.

Normandy

NORMANDY has a less harsh appearance and a more mainstream – and more prosperous – history. It too is a seaboard province, colonised by Norsemen from Scandinavia and colonising in turn; first of all, in the eleventh and twelfth centuries, England, Sicily and parts of the Near East, and later on Canada. It has always had large-scale **ports**: Rouen, on the Seine, is the nearest navigable point to Paris; Dieppe and Le Havre have important transatlantic trade. **Inland**, it is overwhelmingly agricultural – a wonderfully fertile belt of tranquil pastureland, where the chief goal of most visitors will be the restaurants of towns such as Vire and Conches.

The pleasures of the place are perhaps less intense and unique than those of Brittany. Much of the **seaside** is a little overdeveloped. The last French emperor created towards the end of the last century a "Norman Riviera" around Trouville and Deauville, and an air of pretentiousness hangs about their elegant promenades. But the ancient ports – **Honfleur** and **Barfleur** especially – are visual delights, and there are numerous seaside villages with few crowds or affectations. Along the Seine, too, are several idyllic resorts.

Normandy also boasts extraordinary **architectural** treasures, although only the much-restored capital, **Rouen**, has preserved a complete medieval centre. The attractions are more often single buildings than entire towns. Most famous of all is the spectacular *merveille* on the island of **Mont St-Michel**, but there are also the monasteries at Jumièges and Caen; the cathedrals of Bayeux and Coutances; and Richard the Lionheart's castle above the Seine at Les Andelys. And Bayeux has in addition its vivid and astonishing **Tapestry**. Many other great Norman buildings survived into this century, only to be destroyed during the Allied landings in 1944 and the subsequent **Battle of Normandy**, which has its own legacy in a series of war museums, memorials and cemeteries. These are hardly conventional sights, though as part of the fabric of the province, moving and enlightening nonetheless.

Routes

Individual **highlights** are detailed in introductions to each of the specific chapter regions. Dictatorial itineraries aren't given – much of the fun in both provinces is in rambling off on side roads – but the text is structured as logically as possible in continuous routes or definable areas.

Ways of **getting around** are set out on p.13. If you read this before deciding how to travel, think about cycling. Both provinces are ideal, with short distances between towns and attractions, and bikes can be hired at any French railway station. Second to this, cars are probably most functional. Unless you plan to stay within a limited area, public transport can be frustrating.

Climate and time of year

Every French town or district eagerly promotes a *"micro-climat"*, maintaining some meteorological freak that makes it milder or drier or more balmy than its neighbours. On the whole, however, the bulk of Normandy and Brittany follows a fairly set pattern. There is a genuine **summer**, more reliable than in Britain, that begins around mid-June and lasts, in a good year, through to mid-October. **Spring** and **autumn** are mild but sporadically wet. If you come for a week in April or November, it could be spoilt by rain; a fortnight, however, should yield better luck – the rainy spells rarely last more than a couple of days. **Winter** is not too severe, though in western Brittany, especially, it can be damp and very misty on the coast.

Sea temperatures are not Mediterranean, and any greater warmth felt in the Channel waters off the Norman coast as opposed to the South of England is probably more psychological than real. But the south coast of Brittany is a very different matter – consistently warm through the summer months, with no need for you to brace yourself before going into the sea.

The other factor that may affect planning is the **tourist season**. On the coast, this gets going properly around July, reaches a peak during the first two weeks of August and then fades quite swiftly – although you should try to avoid the great *rentrée* at the end of the month, when the roads are jammed with cars returning to Paris. Inland, the season is less defined, though such delights as Monet's gardens at Giverny and the most accessible sections of the Nantes–Brest canal can be crowded out in midsummer. Conversely, the seaside resorts that have grown up irrespective of any town, take on a distinctly ghost-like appearance in the winter months – and are often without any kind of facilities. In summer, at least in August, you may also find smaller hotels in the inland towns closing up as their owners take their own holidays at the seaside.

CLIMATE CHART													
	April		May		June		July		August		Sept		Oct	
	Max °C	Hrs Sun	Max °C	Hrs Sun	Max °C	Hrs Sun	Max °C	Hrs Sun	Max °C	Hrs Sun	Max °C	Hrs Sun	Max °C	Hrs Sun
Brittany														
Brest	13	6.3	16	6.9	19	7.0	20	7.0	21	6.7	19	5.2	16	3.9
Carnac	13	7.3	15	7.8	18	8.5	19	8.5	20	8.1	18	6.6	15	4.7
St Brieuc	13	6.7	15	7.2	18	7.2	20	7.3	20	7.2	19	5.8	16	4.0
Normandy														
Caen	13	6.1	17	7.4	20	7.5	22	7.4	22	7.5	20	5.7	15	4.2
Cherbourg	12	6.0	15	7.3	18	7.1	19	7.2	20	7.2	18	5.5	15	3.7

PART ONE

THE

BASICS

GETTING THERE

FROM BRITAIN

FERRIES

Until such time as the Channel Tunnel finally opens, motorists, cyclists and pedestrians seeking to get directly to Normandy or Brittany can cross the channel by ferry to any of four Norman and two Breton ports. There's also the cheaper but more roundabout alternative of using the ports further east: Calais, Boulogne and Dunkerque. All these services, with specimen 1990 fares, are fully detailed in the box over the page.

Any **travel agent** will have a variety of fares and brochures on offer and should be able to advise on particular needs; it's well worth shopping around for the most competitive deals. Prices vary with the month, day and even hour that you're travelling, how long you're staying, the size of your car, and so on, and the different ferry companies are always offering special fares to outdo their competitors. In particular, since the price structures tend to be geared around one-way rather than return travel, you don't necessarily have to cross over and back from the same port.

NOTE: Although the long-standing dispute over staffing levels has officially been resolved, the National Union of Seamen was at the time of going to press still advising travellers not to use *P&O* sailings from Dover. In addition, the sinking of the *Herald of Free Enterprise* at Zeebrugge is now the subject of proceedings for corporate manslaughter.

If you're just going for a **weekend break**, check out the short-period excursion fares offered by all the companies; usually 60- or 120-hour returns which can cost the same as a single. (more details overleaf). All also carry **children** under four – and (*Irish Continental* excepted) **cycles** – free; children up to thirteen are normally charged half the adult fare. **Booking ahead** is strongly recommended for motorists, certainly in high season; passengers/cyclists can normally just turn up and board, at any time of year.

TRAINS

Travelling by train, you can buy **connecting tickets** from any British station to any French station, via any of the ferry routes. Details and prices (again with various special and seasonal offers) are obtainable from any **British Rail travel centre**. In London, the main office is at Victoria Station (see the box on p.7 for the address, along with those of other rail agents).

To take advantage of combined **discount rail/ferry tickets**, you have a more limited choice. The main options are the under-26 *BIGE* tickets, marketed in Britain by *Eurotrain*. These tickets are valid for two months and can be used (along pre-specified routes) with unlimited stopovers. The routes, however, are geared to long-distance European travel and use only the main ferry crossings. To get to Brittany on a *BIGE* ticket you'd have to travel via Paris to Nantes or Rennes – a very long way round.

Although again designed for long European trips, the ***InterRail*** pass (£155) can also be worth considering. The pass is available to those aged under 26 or over 65 and it allows a month's unlimited travel on all European railways, plus half-price travel in Britain and on (*Sealink*) Channel ferries. If you use the railways extensively, and especially if you're considering side-trips elsewhere in France (or beyond), it could prove good value. Officially the pass is restricted to people resident in Europe for the previous six months – a rule which is designed to exclude North Americans, who are catered for by the more expensive ***EurRail*** pass, available only in North America. In practice, it is possible to find travel agents who won't worry about the proof.

Details and prices of the *SNCF* **France Vacances** pass, almost certainly a better deal if

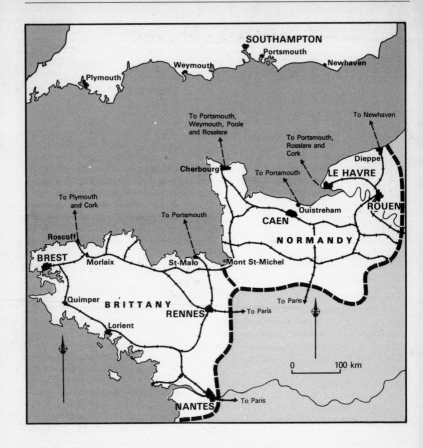

you're just going to Brittany and Normandy, and available for all age groups, are given in the "Air and Rail" box on p.6.

Incidentally, travellers catching ferries from **Portsmouth** should be warned that "Portsmouth Harbour" station is nowhere near the cross-Channel ferry terminals; there is a connecting bus service, but allow plenty of time.

COACHES

You can get a coach from any British town, via London, to **Caen**, **Le Havre**, **St-Malo** or **Roscoff**, and in summer to **Cherbourg** as well. Services are marketed as *Eurolines* by the *National Express* company, and tickets and information are available from any of their offices at regional coach terminals.

The **routes** are:

#112 London–Le Havre (1–2 daily, 11hr, £37 return).

#113 London–Caen (1–2 daily, 12hr, £39 return). Also direct from **Birmingham**, **Oxford** and **Reading**.

#115 London–Cherbourg (1 daily, end May to mid-Sept, 10hr overnight, £45 return).

#116 London–St-Malo (1 daily, 13hr, £47 return).

#112 London–Roscoff (1 daily, 15hr, £54 return). Also direct from **Birmingham** (£51 return) or **Bristol** (£44 return).

Full schedules, with connecting services to destinations throughout France, and details of combined **coach and rail** services via Paris, from *International Express* (address overleaf).

FERRY DETAILS

Routes and Prices

	Operator	Crossing time	Frequency	One-way Fares Car, 2 adults, 2 kids	Foot passenger
BRITTANY					
Portsmouth–St-Malo	*Brittany Ferries*	9hr	Feb–Dec 1–2 daily	£96–146	£28–32
Plymouth–Roscoff	*Brittany Ferries*	6hr	8–11 weekly	£93–143	£28–32
NORMANDY					
Portsmouth–Cherbourg	*Sealink*	4hr 45min	6–12 weekly	£82–148	£25
Portsmouth–Cherbourg	*P&O*	4hr 45min	March–Dec 1–3 daily	£79–139	£25
Poole–Cherbourg	*Brittany Ferries*	4hr 15min	May–Sept 3–4 daily	£81–126	£22–26
Weymouth–Cherbourg	*Sealink*	4hr	April–Sept 1–2 daily	£82–148	£25
Portsmouth–Caen	*Brittany Ferries*	5hr 45min	9–19 weekly	£84–134	£22–26
Portsmouth–Le Havre	*P&O*	5hr 45min	3 daily all year	£79–139	£25
Newhaven–Dieppe	*Dieppe Ferries*	4hr	3–4 daily	£88–138	£23
FURTHER EAST					
Folkestone–Boulogne	*Sealink*	1hr 50min	48 weekly all year	£67–116	£19
Dover–Boulogne	*P&O*	1hr 40min	6 daily all year	£55–117	£19
Dover–Calais	*Sealink*	1hr 30min	12–18 daily	£66–121	£19
Dover–Calais	*P&O*	1hr 15min	13–15 daily	£55–117	£19
Dover–Boulogne/Calais	*Hoverspeed*	35–40min	6–29 daily	£73–127	£21
Ramsgate–Dunkerque	*Sally Line*	2hr 30min	5 daily all year	£56–104	£16
FROM IRELAND					
Cork–Roscoff	*Brittany Ferries*	13–17hr	1–2 weekly	£IR200–320	£IR40–60
Cork–Le Havre	*Irish Ferries*	21hr	June–Aug 1 weekly	£IR210–290	£IR50–80
Rosslare–Cherbourg	*Irish Ferries*	18hr	1–3 weekly	£IR210–290	£IR50–80
Rosslare–Le Havre	*Irish Ferries*	22hr	2–3 weekly	£IR210–290	£IR50–80

Special Offers

Brittany Ferries – 5 & 10-day returns, 60-hour returns for foot passengers, and discounts for regular users. *Sealink, Dieppe Ferries, Sally Line* and *P&O* – 60-hour returns for single-fare price, also 5-day returns.

Addresses in England

Brittany Ferries Wharf Rd, Portsmouth PO2 8RU (☎0705/827701); Millbay Docks, Plymouth PL1 3EW (☎0752/221321); Poole (☎0202/666466).

Sealink/Dieppe Ferries Reservations: Charter House, Park St, Ashford, Kent TN24 8EX (☎0233/647047); 24-hour information service for French crossings ☎0233/610340; also at Victoria Station, London SW1 (☎01/834 8122), Dover (☎0304/210755), Newhaven (☎0273/516699), Portsmouth (☎0705/833333) and Weymouth (☎0305/770308).

P&O Channel House, Channel View Rd, Dover CT17 9TJ (☎0304/203388); Continental Ferry Port, Mile End, Portsmouth PO2 8QW (☎0705/827677); also London (☎01/575 8555).

Sally Line Argyle Centre, York St, Ramsgate, Kent CT11 9DS (☎0843/595522); also at 81 Piccadilly, London W1V 9HF (☎01/464 1123).

Hoverspeed Maybrook House, Queen's Gardens, Dover CT17 9UQ (☎0304/240241); also London (☎01/554 7061).

Addresses in Ireland

Irish Ferries 2–4 Merrion Row, Dublin 2 (☎0001/610511); also Cork (☎021/504333) and Rosslare (☎053/33158).

Brittany Ferries 42 Grand Parade, Cork (☎021/277801).

FLIGHTS

There are flights from **London** to four Breton and four Norman airports. While they remain more expensive than the train/ferry or coach/ferry deals – and of course than charter flights to the Med – for speed and convenience they make an attractive option for short breaks.

The **routes** are:

London (Gatwick)–Brest (Guipavas). 1hr 30min flight. 1–2 daily, all year. £187 return, £99 weekend. *Brit Air.*

London (Gatwick)–Caen. 45min (direct), or 1hr 30min via Le Havre. Daily, all year. £151 return, £80 weekend. *Brit Air.*

London (Gatwick)–Deauville. 45min. Daily, July–Aug; 2 weekly, rest of the year. £90 single fare only. *Lucas Aigle-Azur.*

London (Gatwick)–Le Havre. 45min. Daily, Mon–Fri only, all year. £151 return, £80 weekend. *Brit Air.*

London (Heathrow)–Nantes. 1hr. Daily, all year. £161 single; discount returns, booked in advance, range from £90–128. *Air France.*

London (Gatwick)–Nantes (via Rouen). 2hr. Daily, April–Oct; Mon–Fri only rest of the year. £146 single, youth standby £57 single, discount returns £130–152. *Air Vendée.* Also summer service (marketed by *Nouvelles Frontières*: see box) on *Corse Air.* Friday only, £99 return.

London (Gatwick)–Quimper (via Brest). 2–3hr. Daily in summer, 3 flights weekly in winter. £187 return, £99 weekend. *Brit Air.*

London (Gatwick)–Rennes. 1hr 45min (indirect). 1–3 daily, March–Oct, 3 flights weekly in winter. £187 return, £99 weekend. *Brit Air.*

London (Gatwick)–Rouen. 45min. Daily, April–Oct. £108 single, discount returns also £108. *Air Vendée.*

Tickets and details for all of the above can be obtained from *Air France* in London, from *Brit Air* or *Air Vendée* in Brittany, or from major travel agents (all addresses opposite).

Cheaper flights are always available to Paris – an alternative point to fly to en route to Brittany or Normandy – and you might well want to consider the combined **air and rail** deals detailed in the box below.

Flying **from other parts of Britain**, several regional airports, including Glasgow, Manchester and Belfast, offer direct scheduled (and expensive) flights to Nantes. There are also **flights to Cherbourg** from **Bournemouth**, **Bristol** and **Exeter**, operated by *Air Camelot*: again contact the London *Air France* office for schedules.

If you don't mind stopping off in Jersey, you can also fly on *Jersey European Airways* to Dinard/St-Malo from **Bournemouth**, **Birmingham** or **Exeter**.

AIR AND RAIL

Air France, in conjunction with *SNCF*, the French state railway, offer very good value deals whereby you can **fly direct to Paris** from any one of sixteen UK or Irish airports and then take a **train** on. You can buy a return ticket to any specific destination, or get a *France Vacances* pass which entitles you either to four days unlimited train travel within a fifteen-day period, or nine days within one month.

All the prices below include return flights to Paris; the table shows the cost of travel to selected French cities, and of *France Vacances* passes, from various UK and Irish airports. All prices are in sterling, and are for second class rail travel. For further details contact any *Air France* or *SNCF* office.

	London	Belfast	Birmingham	Bristol	Dublin	Edinburgh	Manchester
Brest	£105	£161	£133	£122	£155	£161	£144
Cherbourg	£93	£149	£121	£110	£143	£149	£132
Granville	£91	£147	£119	£108	£141	£147	£130
Lisieux	£83	£139	£111	£100	£133	£139	£122
Nantes	£93	£149	£121	£110	£143	£149	£132
Quimper	£105	£161	£133	£122	£155	£161	£144
Rennes	£93	£149	£121	£110	£143	£149	£132
Rouen	£81	£137	£109	£98	£131	£137	£120
4-day pass	£131	£187	£159	£148	£181	£187	£170
9-day pass	£175	£231	£203	£192	£225	£231	£214

FROM IRELAND

FERRIES

The four ferry links from Ireland to Brittany and Normandy are detailed in the box on p.5. At 14–21hr journey time they're long crossings – but still a great deal more convenient than travelling via the British ports. In addition to these, *Brittany Ferries* offer all-inclusive deals on crossings from **Cork (Landbridge)** to **Swansea** (daily service; 6hr) and then **on to France** on any of their Channel routes.

All **prices** once again fluctuate considerably from season to season, weekday to weekend, and on size of car, number of people, etc. It can again be economic to investigate **package deals**, offered at especially favourable rates (and with unusual flexibility) by both ferry companies.

In high season, **motorists** are strongly recommended to book in advance.

Travelling **by train**, anyone under 26 can buy *BIGE* tickets through *USIT* (see address below) at a discount on standard prices. *InterRail* passes (see p.3) are also an option.

USEFUL ADDRESSES

Air

Air France 158 New Bond St, London W1 (☎01/499 9511).

Air Travel Advisory Service ☎01/636 5000 and ☎061/832 2000; independent advice on flights.

Air Vendée Aéroport Rene Couzinet, La Roche-sur-Yon, Brittany, France 85000 (☎51.62.31.65).

Brit Air BP 156, Morlaix, Brittany, France 29204; ☎98.62.10.22, or in England ☎0293/502044.

British Airways 75 Regent St, London W1 (☎01/897 4000).

Nouvelles Frontières 1–2 Hanover St, London W1 (☎01/629 7772). French agency.

Rail and Coach

British Rail Victoria Station (European Rail Enquiries: ☎01/834 2345).

Eurotrain/Campus Travel 52 Grosvenor Gardens SW1 (☎01/730 8111); and regional *Campus Travel* offices.

International Express (coaches): 23 Crawley Rd, Luton LU1 1HX (☎0582/404511).

SNCF 179 Piccadilly, London W1 (☎01/493 9731).

Thomas Cook 45 Berkeley St, London SW1 (☎01/499 4000); and regional offices.

Wasteels 121 Wilton Rd, London SW1 (☎01/834 7066).

General Agencies and Youth Specialists

Campus Travel 52 Grosvenor Gardens, London SW1 (☎01/730 3402), and throughout Britain.

Euro-Express 227 Shepherd's Bush Rd, London W6 7AS (☎01/748 2607).

Quo Vadis 243 Euston Rd, London NW1 (☎01/387 6122).

STA Travel 86 Old Brompton Rd, London SW7 and 117 Euston Rd, London NW1 (☎01/937 9921). Plus branches throughout Britain.

Worldwide 38 Store Street, London WC1 (☎01/580 7733).

Ireland

Aer Lingus 59 Dawson St, Dublin (☎0001/795030).

Budget Travel 134 Lower Baggot St, Dublin 2 (☎0001/61322).

USIT 7 Anglesea St, Dublin 2 (☎0001/778117).

Australia and New Zealand

STA Travel 1a Lee St, Sydney 2000 (☎212 1255).

STA Travel 220 Faraday St, Carlton, Victoria 3053 (☎03/347 6911).

STA Travel Courtenay Chambers, 15 Courtenay Place, Wellington (☎850 561).

STA Travel 10 O'Connel St, Auckland (☎399 191).

UTA 33 Bligh St, Kinderfley House, Sydney NSW 2000 (☎221 3911).

UTA 57 Fort St, Auckland (☎649/31229, 33521).

PACKAGES

Any travel agent will be able to provide details of **package holidays** in Brittany and/or Normandy. Some are straightforward travel-plus-beach-hotel affairs, which with a fixed base can be frustrating. Others, though, like the French Tourist Board *Gîtes de France* scheme (still the best for renting a cottage; see p.18), offer more flexibility, allowing you a **combination of bases**. As they include ferry crossings, or occasionally flights, in the accommodation package, these can work out very good value. Big savings can come in particular from the special discounts available for travel from where you live to the "start of your journey" – usually London.

In addition to this (necessarily abbreviated) listing of some of the main operators, bear in mind that most of the ferry companies (see p.5 for addresses) also offer their own accommodation deals. More complete lists are available from the **French Government Tourist Office**, 178 Piccadilly, London W1V OAL (☎071/491 7622).

Brittany Direct Holidays (362 Sutton Common Rd, Sutton, Surrey SM3 9PL; ☎01/641 6060). Offer short-break *chambre d'hôte* and hotel packages as well as self-catering accommodation; also specialist golfing holidays. Extra details include travel by air if you prefer, and a babysitting service. Golf holidays, £182–398 per adult for a summer week; *chambre d'hôte* £189–209 per adult for two weeks; self-catering accommodation mostly in large houses, £150–200 each for two weeks in a group of four adults.

Normandy Country Holidays (113 Sutton Road, Walsall, West Midlands WS5 3AG; ☎0922/20278). Self-catering accommodation in any of 130 rural Norman *gîtes*; up to £334 per adult for two weeks in high season. Children free.

Vacances en Campagne (Bignor, nr Pulborough, West Sussex RH20 1QD; ☎07987/433). A wide variety of properties for rent, up to and including positively luxurious (and expensive) châteaux. Two weeks for two in high season, with travel, £210 and upwards per person.

Vacances France (14 Bowthorpe Rd, Wisbech, Cambs PE13 2DX; ☎0945/587830). A fairly small selection of large houses along the Atlantic coast; prices quoted for total rental of house, from £140 per week in low season up to £917 in summer.

Vacances Franco-Brittaniques (VFB Holidays Ltd, 1 St Margaret's Terrace, Cheltenham, Glos GL50 4DT; ☎0242/526338). Cottages all over Brittany and Normandy, especially southern Finistère. Prices, including ferry travel, for a two-week holiday sharing between two people range from £136–200 per person in the low season up to £210–280 per person in summer.

Velo Vacances (ar Dy Feic, Blwch Post 6, Aberteifi, Dyfed SA43 1LN; ☎0766/770167). Very enthusiastically-organised **cycle tours** in West Brittany, including off-road mountain-bike tours in the Monts d'Arée. Prices vary from £185 for one week to a maximum of £395 for two, and as well as travel include half-board accommodation in either one-star hotels or *gîtes d'etape*, courier service, and a van to carry your baggage.

Other companies worth a try include:

Air France Holidays (☎01/568 6981).
Allez France (☎09066/5033).
Angel Travel (☎0732/361115).
Bretagne Holidays (☎0225/335761).
Brittany Villas (☎0892/36616).
France Directe (☎0926/497989).
French Leave (☎01/583 8383).
French Travel Service (☎081/568 8442).
French Villa Centre (☎01/651 1231).
France Voyages (☎01/494 3155).
Just France (☎0225/446 328).
Propriétaires de l'Ouest/Brittany Ferries (☎0705/755715).

Rendezvous France (☎0582/400100).
Starvillas (☎0223/311990).
Sunscene Holidays (☎0533/620644).
Sunvista Holidays (☎0985/217373).
Susi Madron's Holidays (*Cycling for Softies*) (☎061/834 6800).
Travelscene (☎0274/392911).

and for **camping holidays**:

Eurocamp (☎0565/5044).
Canvas Holidays (☎0992/59933).
Sunsites (☎0306/885000).

FLIGHTS FROM IRELAND

There are two – summer only – direct flights between Ireland and Brittany:

Cork–Morlaix 2hr 15min flight. Weekly, June–Sept (Sat or Sun). IR£230 return. *Brit Air*.

Cork–Nantes (via Morlaix). 3hr 30min. Weekly, June–Sept (Sat or Sun). IR£260 return. *Brit Air*.

Details from *Brit Air* agents in Cork (☎021/961277) or Morlaix (☎98.62.10.22).

If you're a student or under 26, *USIT* have special Dublin–Paris rates for most of the year. Alternatively, you might consider flying from Dublin to Paris and making your own way on from there; see the "Air and Rail" box on p.6 for one current offer.

FROM AUSTRALIA & NEW ZEALAND

You're unlikely to find any special deals from Australia or New Zealand direct to France; it makes more sense to fly to London and then make your own arrangements. *STA Travel*, who have offices throughout Australia and New Zealand, are usually a good bet for discount (and youth/student) flights, and they can arrange connections on to France if you want.
See p.7 for *STA* addresses.

RED TAPE AND VISAS

Citizens of EC countries do not need visas to enter France, and can stay for up to ninety days. The British Visitor's Passport and the Excursion Pass, obtainable at post offices, can be used as well as ordinary passports.
If you **stay longer than three months** you are supposed to apply for a *Carte de Séjour*, showing proof of income at least equal to the minimum wage. However EC passports are rarely stamped, so there is no evidence of how long you've been in the country. If your passport *is* stamped, it's possible just to cross the border, and re-enter for another ninety days legitimately.

At present, following "temporary" legislation in 1986, **all other passport holders** (including Australians, Canadians and Americans) must obtain a visa before arrival in France; this cannot be obtained at your destination. Obtaining a visa from your nearest French consulate is fairly automatic, but check their hours before turning up, and leave plenty of time, since there are often queues (particularly in London in the summer).

Three types of **visas** are currently issued: a transit visa, mostly intended for train passengers and valid for three days; a short-stay (*court séjour*) visa, valid for ninety days after date of issue, good for multiple entries; and the most popular multiple-stay *visa de circulation*, allowing multiple stays of ninety days over three years (maximum of 180 days in any one-year period).

See p.29 for the specific problems faced by **black** travellers trying to enter France, and p.31 for a summary of **customs** allowances.

FRENCH CONSULATES

Australia 303 Angas, Adelaide; 492 St Kilda Road, Melbourne; 10 Eagle, Brisbane.

Britain French Consulate (Visas Section), 29/31 Wright's Lane, London W8 (☎01/937 1202). Also: 7/11 Randolph Crescent, Edinburgh (☎031/225 7954); 523/535 Cunard Building, Pier Head, Liverpool (☎051/236 8685).

Eire 36 Ailesbury Road, Dublin 4 (☎0001/694 777).

Netherlands Vyzelgr. 2, Amsterdam.

New Zealand corner Princes St/Eden Crescent, Auckland; c/o Teachers College, Christchurch; c/o University of Otago, Dunedin.

COSTS, MONEY AND BANKS

Brittany and Normandy are not, on the whole, expensive places to visit. Distances (and transport costs) are relatively small; the price of food and accommodation consistently lower than in Britain and much of Northern Europe; and access, at least just across the Channel, straightforward.

On a **shoestring level**, camping and eating at least one picnic meal a day, taking buses or cycling, you could get by easily enough on 120F (£12) a day. Moving slightly **more upmarket**, staying in modest hotels, spending a bit on restaurants and driving, reckon on around 250F (£25) a day and up.

Accommodation is likely to represent the bulk of your expenditure. Hotels average around 120F for a double room, in the simpler places. If you're sharing, that works out at little more per person than the 40F charged by hostels. Camping, of course, can cut costs dramatically, so long as you avoid the plusher private sites; the local *Camping Municipal* rarely asks for more than 15F a head.

Eating out is the real bargain. You should always be able to find a good three-course meal for 50–70F, or a takeaway for a lot less (though *crêperies* seldom work out as cheap as they might appear). Fresh food from shops and markets is surprisingly dear in relation to low restaurant prices, although it's always possible to save money with a basic picnic of bread, cheese and fruit (maybe enhanced by a bottle of wine – cheapest in supermarkets). More sophisticated meals – **takeaway** salads and ready-to-(re)heat dishes – can be put together for reasonable

prices if you shop at *charcuteries* (delis) and the equivalent counters of many supermarkets. As everywhere, **drinks** in cafés and bars are what really make a hole in your pocket – you have to accept that you're paying for somewhere to sit.

Transport costs obviously depend entirely on how (and how much) you travel. Bikes cost nothing if you bring them and around 45F a day if you hire from the network of bikeshops and *SNCF* station outlets (see p.15). Trains and buses normally operate on a fixed tariff of 50 centimes (half a franc) per kilometre. If you're driving, petrol is just under 5F a litre and most motorways have tolls, which mount up at about 17 centimes per kilometre.

As for **sites and museums**, you may find that regular charges make you quite selective about what you visit – even with an *ISIC* student card to soften the blow. But this is no special hardship: the region's attractions lie as much in its towns and landscapes as anything fenced-off or put in a showcase.

MONEY

French currency is the *franc* (abbreviated as F or sometimes FF), divided into 100 centimes. Francs come in notes of 500, 100, 50, and 20F, and there are coins of 10, 5, 2, and 1F, and 50, 20, and 10 centimes. Exchange rates fluctuate regularly and considerably. At the time of writing, they work out at 9.5F to the pound.

Standard **banking hours** are 9am–noon and 2–4pm; closed Sunday and either Monday or, less usually, Saturday. **Rates of exchange** and **commissions** vary from bank to bank; the *Banque National de Paris* usually offers the best rates and takes the least commission.

There are **money-exchange counters** at the railway stations of all big cities, and usually one or two in the town centre as well. However, it would be a sensible precaution to buy some French francs before leaving.

The best way to **carry money** depends on your bank, and what facilities it offers. **Travellers' cheques**, generally considered the safest option, are available from almost any major bank (whether you have an account there or not), usually for a service charge of one percent on the amount purchased. Some banks may take 1.25

percent or even 1.5 percent, and your own bank may offer cheques free of charge provided you meet certain conditions – ask first, as you may easily save £10 to £15. **Eurocheques**, now offered by most British banks, can be better value with just 1 percent commission on each cheque (French banks do occasionally – and wrongly – charge you to cash Eurocheques). You have to pay an annual fee for the service, and to apply for the card some time in advance. However, on the positive side, you can specify the exact amount you want and use them at shops, restaurants, etc, as well as in certain cash-dispensing machines, and it takes up to six weeks for the money to be deducted from your account. A similar delay in debiting usually comes with **credit cards**, too, and these also charge a lower overall commis-

sion. They are certainly worth taking, if you have them, for use in paying hotel and (some) restaurant bills. Getting cash advances at banks, the Visa/Barclaycard – known as the *Carte Bleue* in France – is almost universally accepted; Access (*Mastercard/Eurocard* in France) comes a very poor second – only the *Crédit Agricole* and *Crédit Mutuel* banks provide the facility.

Finally, if you don't have a bank account, or if you're looking for a simple, cheap alternative, there are **International Giro Cheques**, which can be bought and cashed at any main post office. Post offices are open for longer hours and charge a very low commission, and these cheques help you to avoid queues at busy resort banks; but they have yet to catch on in any significant way.

HEALTH AND INSURANCE

The French health service is efficient and reliable, but expensive unless you are covered either by travel insurance or by reciprocal agreements (which entitle all EC citizens to state refunds of 80 percent on hospital fees and 75 percent of all other charges).

In an **emergency** you will always be admitted to the local hospital – and if you call an ambulance (☎17) will be taken there. Although you will have to pay (see below), this follows after whatever treatment is necessary. The hospital will usually be a *Centre Hospitalier*; if you turn up and know what's wrong, ignore the admissions and go straight to the relevant department to avoid bureaucratic delays.

To visit a **doctor** call at any *pharmacie* (chemist) and ask for an address. You will have to pay a consultation fee, generally around 75–85F, and will receive in return a *Feuille de Soins*, a signed statement of treatment that you should keep. Take any **prescription** to the *pharmacie*, where the medicines you buy have little stickers (*vignettes*) attached to them, which you must remove and stick to your *Feuille de Soins*, together with the prescription form. All *pharmacies* are also equipped – and obliged – to give first aid on request; they too will charge, in line with doctors' fees. However, on **minor illnesses**, *pharmaciens* will dispense free advice and can issue you with quite a wide range of medicines (some normally on prescription in Britain or the US).

In order to qualify for **EC refunds**, you need correct documentation. For British citizens this is form **E111**; in theory you should apply for this on form SA30 by post, one month in advance to any DSS office, but it's possible to get one over the counter. The DSS instruction to send this form off to the *Caisse Primaire d'Assurance-Maladie* (sickness-insurance office) is neither helpful nor essential. Far better to keep it with you to show to any doctor or hospital you might need to visit. If you are hospitalised, the refunds will be sorted out for you and you will simply be billed for twenty percent of the costs – at some time in the future. Doctors' visits and prescription costs are a little more complicated: you have to pay the full amount and then send your form and *Feuille de*

Soins to the local *Caisse Primaire* (the doctor or chemist will provide an address). This is best done at the end of your holiday as parting with your E111 makes it impossible to visit a doctor again under the insurance scheme.

INSURANCE

Taking out **travel insurance** is a good idea, even for EC nationals. Most insurance schemes allow 100 percent reimbursement, minus the first £10 or so of any claim. In a serious accident this is invaluable, as charges will include all drugs, nursing, meals and ambulance charges as well as the cost of treatment or operations. In addition, such insurance also covers loss or theft of luggage, tickets and (some) money, and often compensation for delays.

In Britain, **insurance policies** can be taken out on the spot at just about any bank or travel agent. **Non-EC members** should make sure that they aren't already covered by existing policies before taking out **travel insurance**; Canadians, for example, are usually covered for medical expenses by their provincial health plans. North American travel policies do not insure against theft, except in the case of items in possession of a responsible third party.

INFORMATION AND MAPS

is sometimes called – in practically every town and many villages (addresses are given in the guide). From these you can get detailed local information, including full listings of accommodation, bike hire, launderettes, etc., and often car and walking itineraries for the area. They can be useful, too, for informal local advice.

MAPS

The SI handouts include **townplans** – always worth asking for. Very rarely, however, do they contain usable regional maps. To supplement them – and this guide – you will probably want a reasonable **road map**. For most purposes, certainly for driving, the **Michelin** 1:200,000 area maps of Brittany (230) and Normandy (231) are more than adequate. Virtually every road they show is passable by any car, and those that are tinged in green are usually reliable as "scenic routes". A useful free map for car-drivers, obtainable from filling stations and traffic information kiosks in France, is the **Bison Futé**, showing alternative back routes to avoid the congested

The French Government Tourist Offices in various major cities of the world can provide large quantities of glossily produced maps and pamphlets – a good selection of them on Brittany and Normandy.

Once in France, you'll find a **Syndicat d'Initiative (SI)** – or **Office du Tourisme** as it

FRENCH GOVERNMENT TOURIST OFFICES	
UK 178 Piccadilly, London, W1, (☎ 01/491 7622) **Ireland** 35 Lower Abbey St., Dublin 1 (☎0001/30 07 77) **Australia** BWP House, 12 Castlereigh St., Sydney NSW 2000 (☎612/213 5244) **Netherlands** Prinsengr. 670, 1017 KX Amsterdam (☎20/24 75 34)	**Norway** Handelskammer 0152, Oslo 1, Dronningensgate, 8B (☎2 20 37 29) **Denmark** CK 1459 Kobenhavn K, Frederiksberggad **Sweden** S11146 Stockholm, Normalmstorg 1 Av. (☎8/10 53 32)

main roads. If you're planning to **walk or cycle,** check the *IGN* maps – their green (1:100,000 and 1:50,000) and purple (1:25,000) series. The *IGN* 1:100,000 is the smallest scale available with contours marked, though the bizarre colour scheme makes it hard to read. *Michelin* maps have little arrows to indicate steep slopes, which is all the information most cyclists will need. For walkers, the **Topoguides** (produced in transla-

tion by *McCarta*, see below) cover the long-distance GR trails (see p.16) in exhaustive detail.

All the above maps are generally available (by mail or in person) from *Stanfords*, 12 Long Acre, London WC2; *McCarta*, 122 King's Cross Rd, London WC1; *Roger Lascelles*, 47 York Rd, Brentford, Middlesex; *Map Shop*, 15 High St, Upton-on-Severn, Worcs; and *Heffers*, Green St, Cambridge.

GETTING AROUND

The best way to travel around Brittany and Normandy is with a car or a bike. Public transport is not very impressive. *SNCF* trains are efficient, as ever in France, and the new *Atlantique TGV* has reduced the Paris–Rennes journey to a mere two hours. However, the network here circles the coast and, especially in Brittany, barely serves the inland areas. Where the train stops, an *SNCF* bus may continue the route, and local buses can eventually get you anywhere, so long as you're prepared to fit in with timetables geared principally to market, school or working hours. Approximate journey times and frequencies can be found in the "Travel Details" at the end of each chapter and local peculiarities are also pointed out in the text of the guide.

If you come without your own transport, the ideal solution is to make longer journeys by train or bus, then to **hire a bike** (never a problem) to explore a particular locality.

DRIVING

Taking a car has its disadvantages: costs most obviously, but also the strong likelihood of reducing your contact with people. However, you do

gain freedom of movement and, especially if you're camping, can be a lot more self-sufficient. **Car hire** – at upwards of £150 per week – is unlikely to be an economic alternative to bringing a car across the channel.

British, EC and US drivers' licences are valid, though an *International Driver's Licence* could make life easier if you get a policeman unwilling to peruse a document in English. The vehicle registration document and the insurance papers must be carried. You should have your headlight dip adjusted to the right before you go – it's a legal requirement – and as a courtesy change the lights to yellow, or stick on black glare deflectors. All the major car manufacturers have garage/service stations in France – get their lists of addresses before you go. If you have an accident or break-in, you should make a report to the local police (and keep a copy) in order to make an insurance claim (see p.29).

The main **rule of the road** to remember when driving in France is that, unless there are signs to the contrary, you must always give way to traffic coming from your right, even when it is coming from a minor road. This is the law of *priorité à droite* Because it is one of the main causes of accidents, attempts are being made to phase it out – many roundabouts no longer operate *priorité à droite*. As it is, you have to be vigilant, although other than in town centres, there nearly always **are** "signs to the contrary". The main one is the yellow diamond roadsign, which tells drivers on main roads "you have right of way". More crucial, a yellow diamond crossed out means you do not have right of way. Signs saying *STOP* or *CEDEZ LE PASSAGE* also require you to give way.

Fines for driving violations are exacted on the spot, and only cash or a French bank account cheque are accepted. The minimum for speeding is 1300F and for exceeding the drink/driving level 2500–5000F. Speed limits are: 130km/hr (80mph) on the tolled *autoroutes*; 110km/hr (69mph) on two-lane highways; 90km/hr (56mph) on other roads; 60km/hr (37mph) in towns.

Autoroute driving, though fast, is very boring when it's not hair-raising, and the tolls are expensive. (It's also rather irrelevant to the purposes of this book, since if you stay on the autoroute for any length of time you won't be in Brittany and Normandy any more.) For information on road conditions call *Inter Service Route* on ☎1.48.58.33.33 (24hr). Use the *Bison Futé* map, free from petrol stations, especially to avoid the endless traffic jams that build up over the weekends between July 15 and August 15. For full French driving regulations, see the "AA Traveller's Guide to Europe" (AA Publications, £6.95), while on p.239 of this book you'll find a basic French motroing vocabulary.

TRAINS

SNCF **trains** are by and large clean, fast, and frequent and their staff both courteous and helpful. All but the smallest stations have an information desk and *consignes automatiques* – coin-operated lockers big enough to take a rucksack. Many (indicated in the text of the guide) also hire out bicycles. **Fares** are reasonable, at an average – off-peak – of about 50 centimes per kilometre. The ultra-fast *TGV*s (*Trains à Grande Vitesse*) require a supplement at peak times and compulsory reservation costing around 20F. The slowest trains are those marked *Autotrain* in the timetable, stopping at all stations.

While *InterRail*, *EurRail* and *France Vacances* passes (see p.3) are valid on all trains, and are very much worth investigating before you leave home, *SNCF* itself offers a whole range of **discount fares** on *Période Bleue* (blue period) days – in effect, most of the year. A leaflet showing the blue, white (smaller discount) and red (peak) periods is given out at **gares SNCF** (railway stations). Under-26s can buy a *Carte Jeune* for 160F, allowing travel at half-fare on blue period days between June and September, including a free couchette on one journey. The *Carré Jeune* (same price) gives fifty percent (blue) and twenty percent (white) discounts on four journeys made during the year. Married couples can have a free *Carte Couple*, entitling one of them to a half-

fare if they travel together off-peak. If you're over 65, there's a *Carte Vermeille*, for 199F, which gives you one year's half-price blue period travel. Families with several children can use a *Carte Kiwi* for which one child is the holder and pays full fare while the parents, brothers and sisters go half-fare. The card costs 350F and the rest of the family have to buy complimentary cards costing 50F each. And any passenger buying a return ticket for a total distance of over 1000km and willing to start *en periode bleue*, can have a 25 percent discount (*Billet Séjour*).

All tickets – but not passes – must be date-stamped in those orange machines that obstruct the entrance to station platforms. "*Compostez votre billet*", they say, in French only and it is an offence not to. Rail journeys may be broken any time, anywhere, but after a break of 24 hours you must "compost" your ticket again when you resume your journey. On night trains an extra 80F or so will buy you a **couchette** – well worth it if you're making a long haul and don't want to waste a day recovering from a sleepless night.

Regional **rail maps** and complete **timetables** are on sale at tobacconist shops. Leaflet timetables for a particular line are available free at stations. *Autocar* at the top of a column means it's an *SNCF* bus service, on which rail tickets and passes are valid.

For details on taking your bicycle by train – or hiring one at an *SNCF* station – see below.

BUSES

Buses cover far more Breton and Norman routes than the trains – and, even when two towns do have a rail link, they're often quicker, cheaper and more direct. They are almost always short distance, however, so you'll need to change if you're going further than from one town to the next. And, as stressed, **timetables** tend to be constructed to suit working, market, and school hours – all often dauntingly early.

Larger towns usually have a central *gare routière* (bus station), most often found next to the *gare SNCF*. However, the private bus companies (who provide most of the Breton services) don't always work together and you'll frequently find them leaving from an array of different points. The most convenient lines are those run as an extension of rail links by *SNCF*; these always run to/from the *SNCF* station (assuming there is one).

CYCLING

Bikes have good status in France. All the car ferries will carry them for nothing; *SNCF* make minimal charges; and the French respect cyclists – both as traffic and, when you stop off at a restaurant or hotel, as customers. French drivers normally go out of their way to make room for you – it's the British caravanners you have to watch out for.

Most importantly, however, **distances** in Brittany and Normandy are not great, the hills sporadic and not too steep, and the scenery nearly always a delight. Even if you're quite unused to it, cycling forty miles per day soon becomes very easy – and it's a good way of keeping yourself fit enough to enjoy the rich regional food.

Restaurants and hotels along the way are nearly always obliging about looking after your bike, even to the point of allowing it into your room. Most large towns have well-stocked retail and **repair shops**, where parts are normally cheaper than in Britain. However, if you're using a British-made bike it's a good idea to carry spare tyres, as French sizes are different; neither is it easy to find parts for low-gear machines, the French enthusiasm being directed towards racers instead. Inner tubes are not a problem, as they adapt to either size, though you should always be sure that you get the right valves. The best places to find British parts are in *Raleigh* stockists – at Rouen, Rennes and scattered around both provinces.

The **railways** run various schemes for cyclists, all of them covered by the free leaflet *Train et Vélo*, available from any station. *Autotrains* (when marked with a bicycle in the timetable) are usually the only ones on which you can travel with a bike as free accompanied luggage. Otherwise you have to send your bike as registered luggage, for around 35F. Though it may well arrive in less time, *SNCF* won't guarantee delivery in under five days; and you do hear stories of bicycles disappearing altogether.

You can normally load your bike straight on to the train at the **ferry** port, such as on the boat train at Dieppe, but remember that you must first go to the ticket office of the station to register it – there is time. Don't just try to climb on the train with it, as both you and your bike will end up left behind.

At most *SNCF* stations bikes are also available for **hire**. At a cost of around 45F per day, you get the use of what is normally a very good condition Peugeot, and this you can return to any other station (so long as you specify the place when hiring). *SNCF* do ask for a deposit, but will accept a credit or cheque card number. You can also hire bikes from some **SI**s (tourist offices), a fair amount of **bike shops** (which are much more likely to offer you a mountain bike) and, on islands like Belle-Ile and Ouessant, from numerous seasonal **stalls**.

These days more and more cyclists use **mountain bikes**, which the French call *VTT*s (*Vélos*

A CYCLING VOCABULARY

to adjust	ajuster	to deflate	degonfler	rack	le porte-bagages
axle	l'axe	dérailleur	dérailleur		
ball-bearing	le roulement à balles	frame	le cadré	to raise	rélever
		gears	les vitesses	to repair	réparer
battery	la pile	grease	la graisse	saddle	la selle
bent	tordu	handlebars	le guidon	to screw	risser
bicycle	le vélo	to inflate	gonfler	spanner	le clef (mécanique)
bottom bracket	le logement du pédalier	inner tube	la chambre à air		
		loose	dévissé	spoke	le rayon
brake cable	le cable	to lower	basser	to straighten	rédresser
brakes	les freins	mudguard	le garde-boué	stuck	grippé
broken	cassé	pannier	le pannier	tight	serré
bulb	l'ampoule	pedal	le pédale	toe clips	les cale-pieds
chain	la chaîne	pump	la pompe	tyre	le pneu
cotter pin	la clavette	puncture	la crevisse	wheel	la roue

Touts Terrains), for touring holidays, although if you've ever made a direct comparison you'll know it's much less effort, and much quicker, to cycle long distances and carry luggage on a traditional touring or racing bike. (It would be interesting to hear from any mountain-bikers who disagree.) Whichever you prefer, do use cycle panniers; a backpack in the sun is unbearable. One word of warning: most cyclists have a habit of lifting their bicycles by gripping the saddle. If you keep on doing that when you're using panniers, even just to get over kerbs, the entire saddle will eventually snap off when you least expect it, to leave you to ride off in search of a bike shop, sitting on a long sharp spike.

See the "Maps" section on p.12 for advice on which maps to take. The *Cycle Touring Club* (Cotterell House, 68 Meadrow, Godalming GU7 3HS) will suggest routes and supply advice for a small charge, and run a particularly good insurance scheme. *Cycle Touring in France* by Robin Neillands (Oxford Illustrated Press, £7.95) is a useful handbook for general advice on cycling holidays but extremely sketchy when it comes to actual routes. The *Youth Hostels Association* also sells combined bike-hire and hostel packages; details from 14 Southampton St, London WC2 (☎01/836 8541). And *Velo Vacances*, who run cycling tours of Brittany, are included in the box on p.8.

HITCHING

Hitching is generally easiest on the smaller roads – the ones with the least regular traffic. So long as your luck holds, you can make short hops around the countryside without great problems. Longer journeys are a lot more difficult to come by, and you may find them easiest to arrange by asking around campsites rather than standing by the roadside. Worst of all – and not advised unless you're supremely optimistic – is hitching out of any of the channel ports. If you're really short of money, try to fix a lift somewhere (anywhere!) while you're still on the ferry.

For major **long-distance** rides, and for a greater sense of safety, you might also consider using the "hitching" organisation, *Allostop*. You pay to register with them (130F per year or 60F for long trips, 35F for short trips, plus 16 centimes per kilometre) and they find a driver who's going to your destination. *Allostop* seems like a desperate measure and lacks spontaneity, but in some circumstances may well be worth considering. There are offices in Rennes (☎99.30.98.87) and Nantes; and a similar, free, service is based at Le Havre (☎35.22.63.02).

Sexual harassment is on a level with rural areas in Britain.

WALKING

Neither Brittany nor Normandy is serious hiking country. There are no mountains – or extensive areas of wilderness – and casual rambling along the clifftops and along the waterways is the limit of most people's aims. However, if you're into **long-distance walking**, 21 of the French **GR trails** – the *sentiers de grande randonnée* – run through the area. The GRs are fully signposted and equipped with campsites and rest huts along the way. Each is described in an individual *Topoguide* (available in Britain from *McCarta*, see p.13). The most interesting are the *GR 2 (Sentier de la Seine)* which runs from Le Havre to Les Andelys, the *GR 341 (Sentier de Bretagne)* along the Granît-Rose coast between Lannion and St-Brieuc, and the *GR 347 (Val d'Oust au pays Gallo)* between Josselin and Redon.

INLAND WATERWAYS

Boat trips are available on many of Brittany and Normandy's rivers – and are detailed in the text. More excitingly, you can **hire your own canoe**, **boat** or even **houseboat** along sections of the **Nantes–Brest canal**. The route along the canal is the core of Chapter Six, *Inland Brittany*, and the various towns and companies where you can hire transport are detailed on pages 136 and 190.

SLEEPING

Most of the year, accommodation is plentiful in both Brittany and Normandy, and you can just turn up at a town and find a room or a place in a campsite. Booking a couple of nights in advance can, however, be reassuring; it saves the effort of trudging round and ensures that you know what you'll be paying.

Phone numbers as well as addresses are given in the guide, and the "Language" section at the back should help you make the call, though many hoteliers and campsite managers, and almost all youth hostel managers, will speak some English.

Problems arise mainly **between July 15 and August 15**, when the French take their own vacations en masse. The first weekend of August is the busiest time of all. During this period, hotel and hostel accommodation can be hard to come by – particularly in the coastal resorts – and you may find yourself falling back on local SIs for help and ideas. With campsites, you can be more relaxed, unless you're touring with a caravan or camper van.

HOTELS

Hotel **recommendations** are given in the guide for almost every town or village mentioned. Mostly they are in the 90–140F (£9–15) price range (for a double room), though some a little more upmarket have been included when they seem particularly attractive or good value. Full **accommodation lists** are available from any French Government Tourist Office (see p.12) or local SIs. Travelling in peak season, especially, it

is worth getting hold of these, together with a handbook for the *Logis et Auberges de France*. The latter are independent hotels, promoted together for their consistently good food and reasonably priced rooms; they're recognisable on the spot by green and yellow flags.

All French hotels are **graded** with from zero to three stars. The price more or less corresponds to the number of stars, though the system is a little haphazard, having more to do with ratios of bathrooms per guest than genuine quality; ungraded and single star hotels are often very good. At the cheapest level, what makes a difference in **cost** is whether a room contains a shower: if it does, you can add around 30F to a typical 90F double room. **Breakfast**, too, can add 25F per person to a bill – though there is no obligation to take it and you will nearly always do better at a café. The cost of eating **dinner** in a hotel's restaurant can be a more important factor to bear in mind when picking a place to stay. Officially hotels are not supposed to insist that you take meals, but they often do, and in busy resorts you may not find a room unless you agree. If you are unsure, ask to see the menu before checking in; cheap rooms aren't so cheap if you have to eat a hundred-franc meal. **Single rooms** are only marginally cheaper than doubles – and not very common. On the other hand most hotels willingly equip rooms with extra **beds**, for three or more people, at good discount.

In country areas, in addition to standard hotels, you will come across ***chambres d'hôte***, bed-and-breakfast accommodation in someone's house or farm. These vary in standard but are rarely an especially cheap option – usually costing the equivalent of a two-star hotel. However, if you strike lucky, they may be good sources of traditional home cooking. Brown leaflets available in SIs list most of them.

HOSTELS, *FOYERS* AND *GITES D'ETAPE*

At around 45F per night for a dormitory bed, ***Auberges des Jeunesses*** – youth hostels – are invaluable for single budget travellers. For couples, however, and certainly for groups of three or more people (see above), they'll not necessarily save money on the cheaper hotels – particularly if you've had to pay a bus fare out to the edge of town to reach them. However, many of the hostels in Normandy and Brittany are beautifully sited, and they do allow you to cut costs by preparing your own food in their kitchens, or eating in cheap canteens. To stay at any of the *auberges*, you need to be a member of the *Youth Hostel Association* (*YHA*). You can join before leaving (the main British office is at 14 Southampton Street, London WC2; ☎01/240 3158), or on the spot at most French hostels. A confusion is that there are two rival French youth hostel associations: the *Fédération Unie des Auberges de Jeunesse* (6 rue Mesnil, 75116 Paris), which has its hostels detailed in the International Handbook, and the *Ligue Française pour les Auberges de Jeunesse* (83 rue de Rennes, 75006 Paris). *YHA* membership covers both organisations – and you'll find all their hostels detailed in the text.

A few large towns, such as Caen, provide a more luxurious standard of hostel accommodation in **Foyers des Jeunes Travailleurs/euses**. These are residential hostels for young workers and students, in which for around 35F you can usually get an individual room. They normally have a good cafeteria canteen.

A third hostel-type alternative exists in the countryside, especially in hiking or cycling areas, in the **gîtes d'étape**. These are less formal than the youth hostels, often run by the local village or municipality (whose mayor will probably hold the key), and providing basic hospital-style beds and simple kitchen facilities. They are marked on the large-scale *IGN* walkers' maps and listed in the individual GR *Topoguides*. A complete list of all French *gîtes*, *refuges* and hostels is included in the publication *Gîtes et Refuges en France* (65F plus postage from Editions Créer, rue Jean Amariton, Nonette, 63340 Saint-Germain Lembron); selections are also included in the French National Tourist Office booklet, *Accueil à la Campagne* (available from most SIs for around 40F, or £4).

RENTED ACCOMMODATION: GITES DE FRANCE

If you are planning to stay a week or more in any one place it might be worth considering **renting a house**.

You can do this by checking adverts from the innumerable **private and foreign landlords** in British Sunday newspapers (*The Observer* and *The Sunday Times*, mainly), or trying one of the numerous holiday firms that market accommodation/ travel packages (see p.8 for a brief selection of these). Easiest and most reliable, however, is to use the official French Government service, the **Gîtes de France**. Their base in Britain is at 178 Piccadilly, London W1 (☎01/493 3480). Membership (£3) gets you a copy of their handbook, which contains properties all over France, listed by *département*. The houses vary in size and comfort, but all are basically proven holiday homes. There is a photograph and description of each one and the computerised booking service means that you can instantly reserve the one you want, for any number of full weeks. The cost varies with the season from around £70–140 per week – and may include concessionary ferry rates.

CAMPING

Practically every village and town in the country has at least one **campsite**, to cater for the thousands of French people who spend their holiday under canvas.

The cheapest – at around 10–15F per person per night – is usually the **Camping Municipal**, run by the local municipality. In season or when they are officially open, they are always clean with plenty of hot water, and often situated in the prime local position. Out of season, many of them don't even bother to have someone around to collect the overnight charge.

On the coast especially, there are **superior categories** of campsite, where you'll pay prices similar to those of a hotel for the facilities – bars, restaurants, sometimes swimming pools. These have a rather less transitory population than the *Camping Municipals*, with people often spending a whole holiday in the one base. If you plan to do the same, and particularly if you've a caravan or camper van, or a substantial tent, it's wise to book ahead.

Inland, **camping à la ferme** – on somebody's farm – is another (generally facility-less) possibility. Lists of sites are detailed in the Tourist Board's *Accueil à la Campagne* booklet.

Lastly, a **word of caution**: never camp rough (*camping sauvage*, as the French call it) on anyone's land without first asking permission. If the dogs don't get you, the guns might – farmers have been known to shoot before asking any questions. In many parts of France *camping sauvage* on public land is not tolerated – Brittany is the notable exception. With beaches it's best to camp out where there are other people doing so.

EATING AND DRINKING

The superb range of eating available in Brittany and Normandy has to be one of the principal reasons for visiting the area covered in this book; if anything especially so in Normandy. Restaurant quality is consistently high, prices well below British counterparts, and to be honest there are towns and villages where just about the only excitement is the gastronomic output.

Given the long coastlines of the two provinces, the emphasis is on fresh **seafood**, shellfish above all – mussels, oysters, clams, scallops. In **Normandy**, these – and substantial meat dishes – are characteristically cooked in very rich cream and butter sauces, often with the addition of cider or calvados. In **Brittany** food is generally simpler; *crêpes* are a speciality, not just as snacks (as elsewhere in France) but, with a succession of different fillings, as a whole meal.

With no wine production in Normandy (and only the *Muscadet*-style whites coming from the southeast of Brittany), the most interesting local **alcohol** is that derived from the region's orchards. **Cider** is made everywhere, along with its pear equivalent, *poiré*, and there is of course Norman **Calvados** (apple brandy), as well as numerous local firewaters.

SNACKS

A *croissant*, sandwich or pastry in a bar, with hot chocolate or coffee, is generally the best way to eat **breakfast** – at a fraction of the cost charged by most hotels. (The days when hotels gave you mounds of *croissants* or *brioches* for breakfast

seem to be long gone; now it's virtually always bread, jam, and a jug of coffee or tea for about 25F.) *Croissants* and possibly hard-boiled eggs are laid out on bar counters until around 9.30 or 10am. If you stand – cheaper than sitting down – you just help yourself to these with your coffee; the waiter will keep an eye on how many you've eaten and bill you accordingly.

For **midday meals and light snacks**, most bars and cafés – there's no real difference – advertise *les snacks*, or *un casse-croûte* (a bite), with pictures of omelettes, fried eggs, hot dogs, or various sandwiches. Even when they don't, they'll usually make you a half or third of a *baguette* (French bread stick), buttered (*tartine*) and filled. Likely ingredients include *jambon* (ham), *fromage* (cheese), *thon* (tuna), *saucisson* (sausage) or *poulet* (chicken). Toasted sandwiches – most commonly *croques-monsieur* (cheese and ham) or *croques-madame* (cheese and bacon or sausage) – are also invariably on offer. Especially in rural areas, small bars may serve a moderate-priced *plat du jour* (chef's daily special) or *formule* (a limited or no-choice menu).

Many people also recommend **crêpes** for lunch. These filled pancakes are extremely popular in Brittany, where *crêperies* serve the savoury buckwheat variety as a main course and the sweet white-flour ones for dessert. They may taste nice enough, but unless you buy from a market stall *crêpes* are extraordinarily poor value compared to a restaurant meal; you need to eat at least three, normally at over twenty francs each, to feel even slightly full. That they seem to excite children – presumably because they can drench them in chocolate syrup – shouldn't fool parents into thinking of a *crêperie* as a cheap alternative.

For **picnic and takeaway food**, there's nothing to beat the *charcuteries* (delicatessens), which you'll find everywhere – even in small villages. These sell cooked meats, prepared snacks such as *bouchées de la reine* (seafood vol-au-vents), ready-made dishes and assorted salads. You can buy by weight or ask for *une tranche* (a slice), *une barquette* (a carton) or *une part* (a portion). The cheapest, in towns, are the supermarkets' *charcuterie* counters.

Salons de thé, which open from mid-morning to late evening, serve brunches, salads, quiches, etc, as well as cake and ice cream and a wide selection of teas. They tend to be a good deal pricier than cafés or brasseries – you're paying for the ritzy surroundings.

Patisseries, of course, have impressive arrays of cakes and pastries, often using local cream to excess. In addition to standard French pastries, the Bretons specialise in heavy, pudding-like affairs, dripping with butter, such as *kouïgn-anann*, and in *gaufres*, cream-drenched waffles.

FULL-SCALE MEALS

There is no shortage of **restaurants** in Brittany or Normandy, and in the towns the choice is added to by numbers of **brasseries**. There's no distinction between the two in terms of quality or price range, though brasseries, which resemble cafés, serve quicker meals at most hours of the day; restaurants tend to stick to the traditional meal times of noon–2pm and 7–9.30pm. After 9pm or so, restaurants often serve only *à la carte* meals – invariably more expensive than eating the set *menu fixe*. For the more upmarket places it's wise to make reservations – easily done on the same day. In small towns it may be impossible to get anything other than a bar sandwich after 10pm; in major cities, town centre brasseries will serve until 11pm or midnight and one or two may stay open all night. When hunting, avoid places that are half-empty at peak time, and treat the business of sizing up different menus as an enjoyable appetiser in itself. Don't forget that hotel restaurants are open to non-residents – often very good value. On the road look out for the red and blue sign of the *Relais Routiers* – always reasonably priced and gastronomically sound.

Prices and what you get for them are posted outside. Normally there is a choice between one or more *menus fixes*, where the number of courses has already been determined and choice is limited, and the *carte*, the full menu. At the bottom price-range, say below 50F, **menus fixes** revolve around standard dishes, such as steak and chips (*steack frites*), chicken and chips (*poulet frites*), or various offal concoctions, though it's always worth looking out for the *plat du jour*, which may be more appealing. For 50–100F, virtually any of the restaurants recommended in this guide will serve you a good three-course meal, while four-course blow-outs, including a starter as well as separate meat and fish courses, cost from 90–140F. Most expensive of the lot are the special seafood menus, offering giant platters of assorted crustaceans; away from the big centres such as Cancale and St-Malo, quite apart from the price you should be wary of these, as the stuff may have been waiting around for several days for someone foolhardy enough to order it.

Going *á la carte* offers greater flexibility and, in the better restaurants, access to the chef's specialities – though you can expect to pay heavily for the privilege. A simple and perfectly legitimate ploy is to have just one course instead of the expected three or four. You can share dishes or just have several starters – a useful strategy for vegetarians. There's no minimum charge.

In the French sequence of courses, any salad (sometimes vegetables, too) comes separate from the main dish, and cheese precedes a dessert. You will be offered coffee, which is always extra, to finish off the meal.

Service compris (*s.c.*) means the **service charge** is included; *service non compris* (*s.n.c.*), or *service en sus*, means that it isn't, and you need to calculate an additional fifteen percent. **Wine** (*vin*) or a **drink** (*boisson*) is unlikely to be included, although occasionally thrown in with cheaper menus. When ordering wine, ask for *un quart* (quarter-litre), *un demi-litre* (half) or *une carafe* (a litre). You'll normally be given the house wine unless you specify otherwise; if you're worried about the cost ask for *vin ordinaire*.

The French are much better disposed towards **children** in restaurants than the British, not simply by offering reduced-price children's menus

---

VEGETARIANS

On the whole, **vegetarians** can expect a somewhat lean time in Brittany and Normandy. A few towns have specifically vegetarian restaurants (detailed in the text), but elsewhere you'll have to hope you find a sympathetic restaurant (*crêperies* can be good standbys). Sometimes they're willing to replace a meat dish on the *menu fixe* with an omelette; other times you'll have to pick your way through the *carte*. Remember the phrase *je suis végétarien(ne); il y a quelques plats sans viande?* (I'm a vegetarian; are there any non-meat dishes?).

Many vegetarians swallow a few principles and start eating fish and shellfish on holiday; that of course is a matter for your conscience. Vegans, however, should probably forget all about eating in French restaurants; cook your own food, or just stay at home.

but in creating an atmosphere, even in otherwise fairly snooty establishments, that positively welcomes kids. It is regarded as self-evident that large family groups should be able to eat out together. A rather murkier area is that of **dogs** in the dining room; it can be quite a shock in a provincial hotel to realise that the majority of your fellow diners are attempting to keep dogs concealed beneath their tables.

Comprehensive French/English food listings are given in the next few pages. To be extremely selective for a moment, you'll rarely go wrong with *moules marinières* (mussels) or *hors d'oeuvre variés* (a mixed plate) as a starter; the words *pays d'auge* indicate a thick creamy Norman sauce for your main course; and *je voudrai le mousse au chocolat* will stand you in good stead for the pudding.

WINE AND DRINKS

Where you can eat you can invariably **drink**, and vice versa. Drinking is done at a leisurely pace, whether as a prelude to food (*apéritif*), a sequel (*digestif*) or the accompaniment, and **cafés** are the standard venue. Every bar or café has to display its full **price list** (usually without the fifteen percent service added) with progressively increasing prices for drinks at the bar (*au comptoir*), sitting down (*la salle*), and on the terrace (*la terrasse*).

Wine (*vin*) is the regular drink. Red is *rouge*, white *blanc*, or there's *rosé*. *Vin de table* – plonk – is generally drinkable and always cheap; it may be disguised (and priced up) as the house wine, or *cuvée*. Restaurant mark-ups for quality wines can be outrageous, in a country where wine is so cheap in the shops. In bars, you normally buy by the glass, and just ask for *un rouge* or *un blanc*; *un pichet* gets you a quarter-litre jug. The only Breton wines are produced south of the Loire, *Muscadet* and *Gros-Plant*, and are both dry whites. You'll find a brief account of how to visit some of the vineyards where they are made on p.189.

Cider (*cidre*) is extremely popular. In Brittany it's the standard accompaniment to a meal of *crêpes* and it may be offered on restaurant *menus fixes*. Normans more often consume it in bars. There are dozens of local varieties, most of them very dry and very wonderful. *Poiré*, pear cider, is also produced but on a small scale and is not commercially distributed.

The familiar Belgian and German brands account for most of the **beer** you'll find. Draught (*à la pression*, usually *Kronenbourg*) is the cheapest drink you can have next to coffee and wine – ask for *un demi* (defined as 25cl). Bottled beer is exceptionally cheap in supermarkets.

British-style ales and stouts are becoming increasingly popular, with quite a few special beer-drinking establishments appearing in such cities as Rennes and Quimper. There's even now a home-grown Breton real ale, **Coreff** – see p.143 for details.

Strong alcohols are drunk from 5am as pre-work fortifiers, right through the day; Bretons have a reputation for commitment to this. Brandies and dozens of *eaux de vie* (spirits) and liqueurs are always available. The most famous of these in Normandy are **Calvados**, brandy distilled from apples and left to mature for anything upwards of ten years, and **Benedictine**, distilled at Fécamp from an obscure mix of ingredients. Measures are generous, but they don't come cheap, especially in restaurants (where Calvados is traditionally drunk as a *trou*, or hole, between courses). The same applies to imported spirits like whisky (*Scotch*).

On the **soft drink** front, you can now buy cartons of unsweetened fruit juice in supermarkets, although in cafés the bottled nectars such as apricot (*jus d'abricot*) and blackcurrant (*cassis*) still hold sway. Some cafés serve tiny glasses of fresh orange and lemon juice (*orange/citron pressé*); otherwise it's the standard fizzy cans. Bottles of **mineral water** (*eau minérale*) and spring water (*eau de source*) – either sparkling (*pétillante*) or still (*eau plate*) – abound, from the best-seller *Perrier* to the obscurest spa product. But there's not much wrong with the tap water (*l'eau du robinet*).

Coffee in Normandy is invariably expresso and very strong; in Brittany, particularly in villages, it is sometimes made in jugs, very weakly. *Un café* or *un express* is black, *un crème* is white, *un café au lait* (served at breakfast) is expresso in a large cup or bowl filled up with hot milk. Most bars will also serve *un déca*, decaffeinated. Ordinary **tea** (*thé*) is Lipton's nine times out of ten; to have milk with it, ask for *un peu de lait frais*. After overeating, **herb teas** (*infusions*), served in every café, can be soothing. The more common ones are *verveine* (verbena), *tilleul* (lime blossom) and *tisane* (camomile). **Chocolat chaud** – hot chocolate – unlike tea, lives up to the high standards of French food and drink, and can be had in any café.

A LIST OF FOODS AND DISHES

Basics

Pain	Bread	*Poivre*	Pepper	*Verre*	Glass
Beurre	Butter	*Sel*	Salt	*Fourchette*	Fork
Oeufs	Eggs	*Sucre*	Sugar	*Couteau*	Knife
Lait	Milk	*Vinaigre*	Vinegar	*Cuillère*	Spoon
Huile	Oil	*Bouteille*	Bottle	*Table*	Table

Snacks

Crêpe	Pancake (sweet)
au sucre	with sugar
au citron	with lemon
au miel	with honey
à la confiture	with jam
aux oeufs	with eggs
à la crème de marrons	with chestnut purée
Galette	Buckwheat (savoury) pancake
Un sandwich/ une baguette . . .	A sandwich
jambon	with ham
fromage	with cheese
saucisson	with sausage
à l'ail	with garlic
au poivre	with pepper
pâté (de campagne)	with pâté (country-style)
croque-monsieur	Grilled cheese and ham sandwich
croque-madame	Grilled cheese and bacon, sausage, chicken or an egg
Oeufs	Eggs
au plat	Fried eggs
à la coque	Boiled eggs
durs	Hard-boiled eggs
brouillés	Scrambled eggs

Omelette . . .	Omelette . . .
nature	plain
aux fines herbes	with herbs
au fromage	with cheese
Salade de . . .	Salad of . . .
tomates	tomatoes
betteraves	beetroot
concombres	cucumber
carottes rapées	grated carrots

Other fillings/salads:

Anchois	Anchovy
Andouillette	Tripe sausage
Boudin	Black pudding
Coeurs de palmiers	Palm hearts
Fonds d'artichauts	Artichoke hearts
Hareng	Herring
Langue	Tongue
Poulet	Chicken
Thon	Tuna fish

And some terms:

Chauffé	Heated
Cuit	Cooked
Cru	Raw
Emballé	Wrapped
A emporter	Takeaway
Fumé	Smoked
Salé	Salted/spicy
Sucré	Sweet

Soups (*Soupes*) and Starters (*Hors d'Oeuvres*)

Bisque	Shellfish soup
Bouillabaisse	Marseillais fish soup
Bouillon	Broth or stock
Bourride	Thick fish soup
Consommé	Clear soup
Pistou	Parmesan, basil and garlic paste added to soup
Potage	Thick vegetable soup
Rouille	Red pepper, garlic and saffron mayonnaise served with fish soup

Velouté	Thick soup, usually fish or poultry

Starters

Assiette anglaise	Plate of cold meats
Crudités	Raw vegetables with dressings
Hors d'oeuvres variés	Combination of the above plus smoked or marinated fish

Fish *(Poisson)*, Seafood *(Fruits de mer)* and Shellfish *(Crustaces* or *Coquillages)*

Anchois	Anchovies	*Daurade*	Sea bream	*Louvine,*	Similar to sea
Anguilles	Eels	*Eperlan*	Smelt or	*loubine*	bass
Barbue	Brill		whitebait	*Maquereau*	Mackerel
Bigourneau	Periwinkle	*Escargots*	Snails	*Merlan*	Whiting
Brème	Bream	*Flétan*	Halibut	*Moules*	Mussels (with
Cabillaud	Cod	*Friture*	Assorted fried fish	*(marinière)*	shallots in white
Calmar	Squid	*Gambas*	King prawns		wine sauce)
Carrelet	Plaice	*Hareng*	Herring	*Oursin*	Sea urchin
Claire	Type of oyster	*Homard*	Lobster	*Palourdes*	Clams
Colin	Hake	*Huîtres*	Oysters	*Praires*	Small clams
Congre	Conger eel	*Langouste*	Spiny lobster	*Raie*	Skate
Coques	Cockles	*Langoustines*	Saltwater crayfish	*Rouget*	Red mullet
Coquilles St-	Scallops		(scampi)	*Saumon*	Salmon
Jacques		*Limande*	Lemon sole	*Sole*	Sole
Crabe	Crab	*Lotte*	Burbot	*Thon*	Tuna
Crevettes grises	Shrimp	*Lotte de mer*	Monkfish	*Truite*	Trout
Crevettes roses	Prawns	*Loup de mer*	Sea bass	*Turbot*	Turbot

Terms: (Fish)

Aïoli	Garlic mayonnaise served with salt cod and other fish	*Fumé*	Smoked
		Fumet	Fish stock
Béarnaise	Sauce made with egg yolks, white wine, shallots and vinegar	*Gigot de Mer*	Large fish baked whole
		Grillé	Grilled
		Hollandaise	Butter and vinegar sauce
Beignets	Fritters	*A la meunière*	In a butter, lemon and parsley
Darne	Fillet or steak		sauce
La douzaine	A dozen		
Frit	Fried	*Mousse/*	Mousse
Friture	Deep fried small fish	*mousseline*	
		Quenelles	Light dumplings

Meat *(Viande)* and Poultry *(Volaille)*

Agneau (de pré-salé)	Lamb (grazed on salt marshes)	*Langue*	Tongue
		Lapin, lapereau	Rabbit, young rabbit
Andouille, andouillette	Tripe sausage	*Lard, lardons*	Bacon, diced bacon
		Lièvre	Hare
Boeuf	Beef	*Merguez*	Spicy, red sausage
Bifteck	Steak	*Mouton*	Mutton
Boudin blanc	Sausage of white meats	*Museau de veau*	Calf's muzzle
Boudin noir	Black pudding	*Oie*	Goose
Caille	Quail	*Os*	Bone
Canard	Duck	*Porc*	Pork
Caneton	Duckling	*Poulet*	Chicken
Contrefilet	Sirloin roast	*Poussin*	Baby chicken
Coquelet	Cockerel	*Ris*	Sweetbreads
Dinde, dindon	Turkey	*Rognons*	Kidneys
Entrecôte	Ribsteak	*Rognons blancs*	Testicles
Faux filet	Sirloin steak	*Sanglier*	Wild boar
Foie	Liver	*Steack*	Steak
Foie gras	Fattened (duck/ goose) liver	*Tête de veau*	Calf's head (in jelly)
Gigot (d'agneau)	Leg (of lamb)	*Tournedos*	Thick slices of fillet
Grillade	Grilled meat	*Tripes*	Tripe
Hâchis	Chopped meat or mince hamburger	*Veau*	Veal
		Venaison	Venison

Meat and Poultry – Dishes and Terms

Boeuf bourguignon	Beef stew with burgundy, onions and mushrooms
Canard à l'orange	Roast duck with an orange-and-wine sauce
Cassoulet	A casserole of beans and meat
Coq au vin	Chicken cooked until it falls off the bone with wine, onions, and mushrooms
Steak au poivre (vert/rouge)	Steak in a black (green/red) peppercorn sauce
Steak tartare	Raw chopped beef, topped with a raw egg yolk

Terms:

Blanquette, daube, estouffade, hochepôt, navarin and ragoût	All are types of stews
Aile	Wing
Carré	Best end of neck, chop or cutlet
Civit	Game stew
Confit	Meat preserve
Côte	Chop, cutlet or rib
Cou	Neck
Cuisse	Thigh or leg
Epaule	Shoulder
Médaillon	Round piece
Pavé	Thick slice
En croûte	In pastry
Farci	Stuffed
Au feu de bois	Cooked over wood fire

Au four	Baked
Garni	With vegetables
Gésier	Gizzard
Grillé	Grilled
Magret de canard	Duck breast
Marmite	Casserole
Mijoté	Stewed
Museau	Muzzle
Rôti	Roast
Sauté	Lightly cooked in butter

For steaks:

Bleu	Almost raw
Saignant	Rare
A point	Medium
Bien cuit	Well done
Très bien cuit	Very well cooked
Brochette	Kebab

Garnishes and sauces:

Beurre blanc	Sauce of white wine and shallots, with butter
Chasseur	White wine, mushrooms and shallots
Diable	Strong mustard seasoning
Forestière	With bacon and mushroom
Fricassée	Rich, creamy sauce
Mornay	Cheese sauce
Pays d'Auge	Cream and cider
Piquante	Gherkins or capers, vinegar and shallots
Provençale	Tomatoes, garlic, olive oil and herbs

Vegetables *(légumes)*, herbs *(herbes)* and spices *(epices)*, etc.

Ail	Garlic	*Endive*	Chicory	*Piment*	Pimento
Algue	Seaweed	*Epinards*	Spinach	*Pois chiche*	Chick peas
Anis	Aniseed	*Estragon*	Tarragon	*Pois mange-tout*	Snow peas
Artichaut	Artichoke	*Fenouil*	Fennel		
Asperges	Asparagus	*Flageolet*	White beans	*Pignons*	Pine nuts
Avocat	Avocado	*Gingembre*	Ginger	*Poireau*	Leek
Basilic	Basil	*Haricots*	Beans	*Poivron*	Sweet pepper
Betterave	Beetroot	*Verts*	String (French)	*(vert, rouge)*	(green, red)
Carotte	Carrot	*Rouges*	Kidney	*Pommes (de*	Potatoes
Céleri	Celery	*Beurres*	Butter	*terre)*	
Champignons, cèpes, chanterelles	Mushrooms of various kinds	*Laurier*	Bay leaf	*Primeurs*	Spring vegetables
		Lentilles	Lentils		
		Maïs	Corn	*Radis*	Radishes
Chou (rouge)	(Red) cabbage	*Menthe*	Mint	*Riz*	Rice
Choufleur	Cauliflower	*Moutarde*	Mustard	*Safran*	Saffron
Ciboulettes	Chives	*Oignon*	Onion	*Salade verte*	Green salad
Concombre	Cucumber	*Pâte*	Pasta or pastry	*Sarrasin*	Buckwheat
Cornichon	Gherkin	*Persil*	Parsley	*Tomate*	Tomato
Echalotes	Shallots	*Petits pois*	Peas	*Truffes*	Truffles

Vegetables – Dishes and Terms

Beignet	Fritter	*Parmentier*	With potatoes
Farci	Stuffed	*Sauté*	Lightly fried in butter
Gratiné	Browned with cheese or butter	*A la vapeur*	Steamed
Jardinière	With mixed diced vegetables	*Je suis végétarien*	I'm a vegetarian. Are
A la parisienne	Sautéed in butter (potatoes); with	*(ne). Il y a quelques*	there any non-meat
	white wine sauce, and shallots	*plats sans viande?*	dishes?

Fruits (*Fruits*) and nuts (*noix*)

Abricot	Apricot	*Framboises*	Raspberries	*Pistache*	Pistachio
Amandes	Almonds	*Fruit de la*	Passion fruit	*Poire*	Pear
Ananas	Pineapple	*passion*		*Pomme*	Apple
Banane	Banana	*Groseilles*	Redcurrants and	*Prune*	Plum
Brugnon,	Nectarine		gooseberries	*Pruneau*	Prune
nectarine		*Mangue*	Mango	*Raisins*	Grapes
Cacahouète	Peanut	*Marrons*	Chestnuts		
Cassis	Blackcurrants	*Melon*	Melon	**Terms**:	
Cérises	Cherries	*Myrtilles*	Bilberries	*Beignets*	Fritter
Citron	Lemon	*Noisette*	Hazelnut	*Compôte de . . .*	Stewed . . .
Citron vert	Lime	*Noix*	Nuts	*Coulis*	Sauce
Figues	Figs	*Orange*	Orange	*Flambé*	Set aflame in
Fraises (de	Strawberries	*Pamplemousse*	Grapefruit		alcohol
bois)	(wild)	*Pêche (blanche)*	(White) peach	*Frappé*	Iced

Desserts (*Desserts* or *Entremets*) and Pastries (*Pâtisserie*)

Bombe	A moulded ice cream dessert	*Parfait*	Frozen mousse, some-
Brioche	Sweet, high yeast breakfast roll		times ice cream
Charlotte	Custard and fruit in lining of	*Petit Suisse*	A smooth mixture of
	almond fingers		cream and curds
Crème Chantilly	Vanilla-flavoured and sweet-	*Petits fours*	Bite-sized cakes/pastries
	ened whipped cream	*Poires Belle Hélène*	Pears and ice cream in
Crème fraîche	Sour cream		chocolate sauce
Crème pâtissière	Thick eggy pastry-filling	*Yaourt, yogourt*	Yoghurt
Crêpes suzettes	Thin pancakes with orange		
	juice and liqueur	**Terms:**	
Fromage blanc	Cream cheese	*Barquette*	Small boat-shaped flan
Glace	Ice cream	*Bavarois*	Refers to the mould, could
Ile flottante/	Soft meringues floating on		be a mousse or custard
oeufs à la neige	custard	*Coupe*	A serving of ice cream
Macarons	Macaroons	*Crêpes*	Pancakes
Madeleine	Small sponge cake	*Galettes*	Buckwheat pancakes
Marrons Mont	Chestnut purée and cream on a	*Gênoise*	Rich sponge cake
Blanc	rum-soaked sponge cake	*Sablé*	Shortbread biscuit
Mousse au	Chocolate mousse	*Savarin*	A filled, ring-shaped cake
chocolat		*Tarte*	Tart
Palmiers	Caramelised puff pastries	*Tartelette*	Small tart

Cheese (*Fromage*)

There are over 400 types of French cheese, most of them named after their place of origin. *Chèvre* is goat's cheese. Le *plateau de fromages* is the cheeseboard, and bread, but not butter, is served with it. The best-known cheeses from the area covered by this book all come from the Pays d'Auge region of Normandy, *Pont l'Evêque, Livarot*, and, most famous of all, *Camembert*.

And one final note: always call the waiter or waitress *Monsieur* or *Madame* (*Mademoiselle* if a young woman), never *garçon*, no matter what you've been taught in school.

COMMUNICATIONS: POST, PHONES AND MEDIA

French post offices – *postes* or *PTT*s – are generally open 9am–noon and 2–5pm (Mon–Fri), 9am–noon only on Saturday. However, don't depend on these hours: in the larger towns you'll find a main office open through the day, while in Breton and Norman villages, lunch hours and closing times can vary enormously.

POSTE RESTANTE, LETTERS AND PHONE CALLS

You can have letters sent to you *poste restante* at any post office in the country. If you're travelling around, it's simplest to choose towns of some size, though always specify the main post office (*Poste Centrale*) to avoid possible confusion. The addresses of the two largest, in Rouen and Nantes, are:

Poste Restante, Poste Centrale, 76000 ROUEN.

Poste Restante, Poste Centrale, 44000 NANTES.

To collect mail you'll need a passport, and should expect to pay a charge of a couple of francs. If you're expecting mail, it's worth asking the clerk to check under your surname and all possible Christian names as well – filing systems tend to be erratic.

Sending letters, the quickest international service is by *aérogramme*, sold at all post offices. Ordinary **stamps** (*timbres*) you can get at any *tabac* (tobacconist). If you're sending **parcels** abroad, try to check prices in the various leaflets available: small *postes* don't often send foreign

mail and may need reminding of, for example, the huge reductions for printed papers and books.

You can make domestic and international phone calls from any box (or *cabine*) and can receive calls where there's a blue logo of a ringing bell. A 50F **phone card**, obtainable from post offices and *PTT* boutiques can be convenient if you're likely to make a lot of calls. Otherwise, you put your money in (50 centime, 1F, 5F, 10F pieces) after lifting the receiver and before dialling, although you can keep adding more once you're connected. For international calls, dial ☎19, wait for a tone, and then dial the country code (44 for Britain) and the number minus its initial 0. International calls often fail because the main overseas lines are engaged, so keep trying. For calls within France – local or long distance – dial all eight digits of the number (which includes the former area code – displayed in every *cabine*).

An alternative to dialling internationally from *cabines*, and wrestling with piles of loose change, is to use the numbered **booths at main post offices**. You apply at the counter to be assigned a number and then dial as above. The disadvantage – odd, given the French obsession with technology – is that you can't tell how much you're spending. It's worth counting your units and checking calculations – mistakes are made.

To speak to the **operator** dial ☎10; the **international operator**, ☎19.33.11; the **police**, ☎17; **medical emergencies**, ☎15.

NEWSPAPERS, MAGAZINES AND RADIO

British newspapers and the *International Herald Tribune* are intermittently available in Brittany and Normandy. In the larger resorts and in cities like Nantes and Rouen, you should find reasonable selections. Elsewhere, it's mostly *The Sun* or *The Times* – not an inspiring choice.

As for the **French press**, the widest circulations are enjoyed by the **regional dailies**. Throughout Normandy and Brittany, the most important and influential paper is *Ouest-France*. This is based in Rennes but has numerous local editions – worth picking up for their local listings supplements, if nothing else. Of the **national dailies**, *Le Monde* is the most intellectual and respected, with no such demeaning concessions to entertainment as pictures, but a correctly-styled French that is probably the easiest to understand. *Libération* (*Libé* for short), is moderately left-wing, independent and colloquial with good, if choosy, coverage; *L'Humanité* is the Communist party newspaper, now in tabloid form; *Le Matin*, liberal-right and establishment. All the other nationals are firmly right-wing.

Weeklies, on the *Time/Newsweek* model, include the wide-ranging left-leaning *Le Nouvel Observateur*, and its rightist counterweight, *L'Express*. The best, and funniest, investigative journalism is in the satirical *Le Canard Enchaîné*,

unfortunately almost incomprehensible to non-native speakers. There are also the **comics**, occupying a far more prestigious status in the bookshops and newsstands than they do in Britain. *Charlie-Hebdo* is one with political targets, *À Suivre* is a showpiece for amazing graphic talents.

On the **radio**, you can pick up the **BBC World Service** on 463m MW, or between 21m and 31m shortwave; **BBC Radio 4**, too, is usually quite clear, on 1500m long wave. **France Inter**, on 1829m (long wave), has English-language news bulletins at 9am and 4pm, Monday to Saturday, in summer.

BUSINESS HOURS AND PUBLIC HOLIDAYS

Basic hours of business are 8am–noon and 2–6pm: almost everything in France – shops, museums, tourist offices, most banks – closes for a couple of hours at midday. Food shops often don't reopen till halfway through the afternoon, closing just before suppertime between 7.30 and 8pm. So if you're looking to buy a picnic lunch, you'll need to get into the habit of buying it before you're ready to think about eating.

The standard **closing days** are Sunday and Monday, and in smaller towns you'll find everything except the odd *boulangerie* (bakery) shut on both days. This includes **banks**. It's all too easy to find yourself dependent on hotels for money-changing – an alternative that invariably means low rates and high commission.

Museums are not very generous with their opening times, tending to open around 10am, close for lunch at noon until 2pm (sometimes 3) and then run through until only 5 or 6pm. Summer times may differ from winter times; if they do, both are indicated in the listings. Summer hours usually extend from mid-May or early June to mid-September, but sometimes they apply only during July and August, occasionally even from Palm Sunday to All Saints' Day. For museums, the closing days are usually Tuesday or Monday, sometimes both. Admission charges can be very off-putting, though most state-owned museums have one or two days of the week when they're free, and you can get a big reduction at most places by showing a student card (or passport if you're

under 18/over 60). Churches and cathedrals are almost always open all day, with charges only for the crypt, treasuries, or cloister and little fuss about how you're dressed. Where they are closed you may have to go during Mass to take a look, on Sunday morning or at other times which you'll see posted up on the door. In small towns and villages, however, getting the key is not difficult – ask anyone nearby or hunt out the priest, whose house is known as the *presbytère*.

PUBLIC HOLIDAYS

There are thirteen national holidays (*jours fériés*), when most shops and businesses, though not museums or restaurants, are closed.

They are:

January 1

Easter Sunday

Easter Monday

Ascension Day (forty days after Easter)

Pentecost (seventh Sunday after Easter, plus the Monday)

May 1

May 8 (VE Day)

July 14 (Bastille Day)

August 15 (Assumption of the Virgin Mary)

November 1 (All Saints' Day)

November 11 (1918 Armistice Day)

Christmas Day

FESTIVALS AND EVENTS

The most interesting Breton events are without doubt the cultural festivals. At the largest of these, the *Lorient Festival Inter-Celtique* (August), music, performance, food and drink of all seven Celtic nations are featured in a completely authentic gathering that pulls in cultural nationalists (and ethnic music fans) from Ireland to Spain. If you can't get to Lorient, there are two – smaller and more particularly Breton – alternatives in the Nantes *Quinzaine Celtique* (June/July) and Quimper's *Festival Cornouaille* (July).

Look out also for local **club events** put on by individual Celtic folklore groups – the *Cercles* or *Bagadou*. These are most prolific in Nantes, though wherever you are in the province, listings pages of the *Ouest-France* can be worth scrutiny.

The religious **pardons**, sometimes promoted as tourist attractions in Brittany, are rather different affairs. These are essentially church processions, organised by a particular community on the local saint's day. Generally small-scale, some, like that at Sainte-Anne d'Auray, have over the centuries taken on more region-wide status as pilgrimages. These are not, however, carnivals or fêtes but primarily very serious occasions, centred on lengthy and rather gloomy church services. If you're not interested by the religious aspects, only the food and drink stalls, and low-key accompaniments, hold any great appeal.

Normandy lacks any specific cultural traditions to celebrate, doing its best to make up with celebrations of related **historic events** – births and deaths of William the Conqueror, Sainte-Thérèse, etc. The **D-Day** (June 6) landings along the Invasion Beaches are always marked in some way – usually more tasteful than the 40th celebrations when Thatcher and Reagan came along. Avoid, both in Normandy and Brittany, the **Spectacles**, camp and overpriced outdoor shows on some mythical theme or other, held most regularly (and most tackily) at Bagnoles and Elven.

CALENDAR OF EVENTS

Whitsun – **Honfleur** Seamen's Festival

Third Sunday in May – **Treguier** *St Yves Pardon*

June 6 – D-DAY Ceremonies on Invasion Beaches

End June/start July – **Nantes** Celtic events

Early July – **Lamballe** Golden Broom Folk Festival

First ten days of July – **Rennes** *Tombées de la Nuit* theatre and music festival

Second Sun in July – **Locronan** *Troménie Pardon*

July 16 – **La Haye du Routot** *Fête de Ste-Claire*

July 26 – **Ste Anne d'Auray** *Pardon*

July – **St-Brieuc** Festival of Breton Music

Last week of July – **Quimper** *Festival Cornouaille*

Late July – **Huelgoat** Aquatic 2 CVs race

First full week in Aug – **Lorient** *Festival InterCeltique*

Mid August – **Le Roche-Jagu** Jazz Festival

Mid August – **Guingamp** *Saint Loup* Breton Dance Festival

First Sun in Sept – **Le Pin** Horse Show

First Sun in Sept – **Le Folgoet** *Pardon*

Early Sept – **Douarnenez** Film Festival of International Minorities

Second weekend of Sept – **Lessay** Holy Cross cattle & animal fair

Mid-Sept – **Deauville** American Film Festival

Sun nearest 29 Sept – **Mont St-Michel** Archangel Michael Festival

End of October – **St-Brieuc** Art Rock festival

Second week in December – **Rennes** *Les Transmusicales* international rock festival

On the more mainstream **cultural side**, the larger cities – Rouen, Rennes and Nantes – have active theatre, opera and classical music seasons, though little happens during the summer. **Cinema** is most interesting in these cities, too, and the region is host to one of the more accessible French film festivals – Deauville's American Film Festival (September). Almost all foreign films will be dubbed into French; *v.o.* in the listings signifies original language.

Both **Rennes** and **Rouen**, have laid recent claim to be "the capital of French **rock**"; Rennes is increasingly the one to watch, with its December *Transmusicales* attracting international stars to share the stage with local groups. St-Brieuc's rival Art Rock festival caters to more specialist tastes. A few large rock concerts also take place during the holiday season, at places such as Brest and Concarneau, with the usual bland multinational billing of fading "rock giants".

TROUBLE

Relative to Paris or the South of France, Brittany and Normandy have a low-key crime problem. However, you still need to take normal precautions against petty theft, especially in tourist areas.

Drivers face greater problems, most notoriously break-ins. Vehicles are rarely stolen, but tape decks as well as luggage left in cars make tempting targets and foreign number plates are easy to spot. Good insurance is the only answer, but even so try not to leave valuables in sight. If you need to report a theft, go along to the local *gendarmerie*, police station, and do your best to persuade them to give you the requisite piece of paper for a claim; the first thing they'll ask for is your passport. If you have an accident while driving, you have officially to fill in and sign a *constat à l'aimable* (jointly agreed statement); car insurers are supposed to give you this with a policy, though in practice few seem to have heard of it.

For non-criminal **driving violations** such as speeding, the police can impose an on-the-spot fine. Should you be arrested on any charge, you have the right to contact your consulate (see "Directory" on p.31). Although the police are not always as cooperative as they might be, it *is* their duty to assist you – likewise in the case of losing your passport or all your money.

As for offences of your own making, treatment by the **police** is little different from anywhere else in Europe. **Camping** outside authorised sites can bring you into contact with the authorities, though it's more likely to be the landowner who tells you to move off. **Topless sunbathing** is universally acceptable, but **nudity** limited to a few specifically naturist beaches.

People caught smuggling or possessing **drugs**, even a few grammes of marijuana, are liable to find themselves in jail, and consulates will not be sympathetic. This is not to say that hard-drug consumption isn't a visible activity: there are scores of kids dealing in *poudre* (heroin) in the big French cities and the authorities are unable to do much about it. As a rule, people are no more nor less paranoid about marijuana busts than they are in the UK.

Officially, you're supposed to carry **identification documents** at all times in France, and the police are entitled to stop you in the street and demand it. In practice this doesn't happen much to tourists, at least to whites. If you're black, of whatever ethnic origin, it can be a different matter. **French racism** is at its worst in the police force and ordinary people often aren't much better: hotels claiming to be booked up and abusive treatment in the street are horribly commonplace. In addition, being black can make entering the country difficult and immigration officers can be obstructive and malicious to black holidaymakers.

Sexual harassment is generally no worse or more vicious than in the UK, but it can be a problem making judgements without the familiar linguistic and cultural signs. A "*Bonsoir*" or "*Bonjour*" on the street is the standard pick-up opening, and if you so much as return the greeting you've let yourself in for a stream of tenacious chat, and hard shaking-off work. On the other hand, topless bathing doesn't usually invite bother and it's quite common, if you're on your own, to be offered a drink in a bar and not to be pestered even if you accept. **Hitching** is a risk, as it is anywhere, and few French women do it. If you need help, don't necessarily go to the police – who may well worsen your ordeal. In large cities, there may be Women's Organisations (*Femmes Batues, Femmes en Détresse* or *SOS Femmes*) whom you can contact through the Hôtel de Ville; if you can reach one, though, a consulate is likely to be of most immediate assistance.

WORK AND STUDY

Temporary work in Brittany or Normandy is hard to come by. The region has just one wine harvest (around Nantes), almost wholly automated, and there is small chance of picking up any other kind of casual employment. If you arrange things in advance, however, there are work possibilities for outsiders in au-pairing, teaching English as a foreign language, or in the holiday industry. And if you're just looking for an interesting way to fill the summer, a number of archaeological schemes, mostly on Brittany's megalithic sites, sometimes have space for foreign volunteers.

Whatever you are looking for, it's important to plan well in advance. The best **general sources** for all jobs in France are the publications *Emplois d'Eté en France* (£4.95; available in Britain from Vacation Work, 9 Park End St, Oxford; ☎0865/241978) and *1000 Pistes de Jobs* (80F; available from *L'Etudiant*, 27 rue du Chemin Vert, 75011, Paris). *Working Holidays* (£4.80; published by Central Bureau, Seymour Mews House, Seymour Mews, London W1H 9PE) is also useful.

Au Pair work is usually arranged through one of a dozen or so agencies, all of which are listed in *Working Holidays*. As initial numbers to ring, try Euroyouth (☎0702/341434), Scattergoods (☎0483 63640) or Students Abroad (☎01/428 5823); any of them will fill you in on general terms and conditions, and the state of the market.

Teaching English in France, you'll normally need a TEFL certificate. Vacancies are advertised fairly regularly in the *Guardian* and the *Times*

Educational Supplement. Salaries should usually include an allowance for travel costs. The best places to live and to teach would probably be St-Malo, Quimper, Rennes or Rouen.

Temporary jobs in the **travel industry** revolve mainly around courier work – supervising and working on summer campsites. The work may take in putting up tents at the beginning of the season, taking them down at the end, and general cleaning and problem-solving work in the months between. Three companies worth approaching, for work in Brittany and Normandy (and also in the South of France), are: *Canvas Holidays* (☎0992/59933), *Eurocamp* (☎0565/50444) and *Sunsites* (☎0306/887733). Alternatively, go along to a travel agent and pick up holiday company brochures – then just phone any of them you fancy.

Volunteer work on **archaeological sites** varies from year to year, according to available grants and priorities. Recently, there have been opportunities to work on a number of Breton Gallo-Roman and megalithic sites – including Locmariaquer – and on neolithic sites in Normandy. Food and campsite or student hall accommodation is generally provided, though there may be a small weekly charge; travel costs are not normally paid. It's best to write a number of letters to potential authorities asking for details of any projects. Excavations are regularly organised by the following:

Laboratoire d'Anthropologie Préhistorique: write c/o Dr Jean Laurent Monnier, Charge de Recherche au CNRS, Université de Rennes I, Campus de Beaulieu, 35042 Rennes.

Ministère de la Culture Circonscription des Antiquités Historiques et Préhistoriques de Bretagne, 6 rue du Chapitre, BP 927, 35011 Rennes Cedex.

Musée d'Histoire Naturelle: write c/o Jean Pierre Watte, Archaeologue Municipal, place du Vieux Marché, 76600 Le Havre.

CLAIMING BENEFIT

If you're an EC citizen – and you do the paperwork in advance – you can sign on for **unemployment benefit**. To do so, you must collect form E303 before leaving home, available in Britain from any DSS office. The procedure is first to get registered at an *ANPE* office (Agence Nationale pour l'Emploi), then take the form to your local *ASSEDIC* (benefits office) and give them an address, which can be a hostel or a hotel, for the money to be sent. You sign once a month at the *ANPE* and receive dole a month in arrears – theoretically, at least, payments can be delayed in small towns for up to three months. After three months, you must anyway either leave the country or get a *carte de séjour*.

STUDYING IN FRANCE

It's relatively easy to be a student in France. Foreigners pay no more than French nationals (around 400F) to **enrol** for a course, and the only problem then is to support yourself. Your *carte de séjour* and – if you are an EC citizen – social security will be assured, and you'll be eligible for subsidised lodgings, meals and all the student reductions. In general French universities are much less formal than British ones. For full **details and prospectuses** contact the Cultural Service of any French Embassy – in London at 22 Wilton Crescent, London SW1.

Language schools all along the coast provide intensive French courses for foreigners. The most popular are those organised each summer at St-Malo by the University of Rennes.

DIRECTORY

BEACHES are public property up to 5m above the high tide mark; you can walk past the private villas, and arrive on islands. Another law however forbids you to camp.

BUYING PROPERTY If you're looking to buy a home in Brittany or Normandy, the best source for information and advice is *Buying Residential Property in France*, available for £5 from *Chambre de Commerce Française de Grande Bretagne*, Knightsbridge House, 197 Knightsbridge, London SW1 (☎01/225 5250).

CHILDREN AND BABIES are generally made welcome everywhere, and in particular in all bars and restaurants. **Hotels** charge by the room, with a small supplement for an additional bed or cot, and family-run places will usually babysit while you go out. Especially in seaside towns, most **restaurants** have children's menus or will cook simpler food on request. You'll have no difficulty finding disposable nappies (*couches à jeter*), baby foods and milk powders. *SNCF* charge nothing on **trains and buses** for under-4s, and half-fare for 4–12s. With a *Carte Kiwi* (see p.14), one adult pays full fare, and the other, and any children, half. Most local **tourist offices** have details of specific activities for children – in particular, many resorts supervise "clubs" for children on the beach.

CONSULATES There are **British Consulates** at Cherbourg (c/o *P&O*, Gare Maritime), and Nantes (6 rue La Fayette). These will handle urgent business for Irish, Australian and New Zealand nationals. **The Netherlands** have a consulate in Brest, at 6 cours d'Ajot (☎98.80.32.70). Nearest consulates otherwise are in Paris: **USA** (2 av Gabriel, 8° ☎42.96.12.02); **Eire** (12 av Foch, 16°; ☎45.00.20.87); **New Zealand** (7 rue Léonard-de-Vinci, 16°; ☎45.00.24.11).

CONTRACEPTIVES Condoms (*préservatifs*) have always been available at *pharmacies*, though contraception was technically only legalised in 1967. You can also get spermicidal cream and jelly (*dose contraceptive*), plus suppositories (*ovules, suppositoires*) and (with a prescription) the pill (*la pillule*), a diaphragm or IUD (*le sterilet*).

CUSTOMS If you bring in more than 5000F worth of foreign cash, you need to sign a declaration at customs. There are also restrictions on taking francs out of the country, but the amounts are beyond the concern of most people. Tobacco and alcohol import limits are 400 cigarettes and two litres respectively.

DISABLED TRAVELLERS France has no exceptional record for ease of access and facilities, but at least information is available. The tourist offices in most big towns provide a free booklet, *Touristes Quand Même*, covering accommodation, transport and accessibility of public places as well as aids such as buzzer signals on pedestrian crossings. An extensive English-language survey of facilities in Brittany, the *Access Guide to Brittany*, is still available from the *Pauline Hephaistos Survey Project* (39 Bradley Gardens, London W13). The research for the guide was carried out in 1977 and so for the most part is no longer relevant, although accounts of the ease of movement around individual towns remain valid. A more general guide, *Europe for the Handicapped Traveller: Vol 3, France*, can be obtained from *Mobility International* (2 Colombo St, London SE1), while *RADAR* at 25 Mortimer Street, London W1 (☎01/637 5400) is an invaluable source of advice and assistance. *P&O* Channel ferries allow registered disabled to take cars free of charge.

ELECTRICITY is almost always 220V, using plugs with two round pins.

FISHING You get fishing rights by becoming a member of an authorised fishing club – tourist offices have details. The main areas for river fishing are in Brittany, in the Aulne around Châteaulin and in the Morbihan.

GAY/LESBIAN France is more liberal on homosexuality than most European countries. The legal age of consent is 15 and gay communities thrive especially in Paris and many southern towns, though Lesbian life is rather less upfront. Brittany and Normandy however have very little conspicuous gay life; the best source for clubs and meeting places is the *Gai Pied Guide*, widely available in France and at specialist bookshops in Britain.

LAUNDRY Launderettes are not all that common in French towns, although some are listed in the guide. The alternative *blanchisserie* or *pressing* services are likely to be expensive, and hotels in particular charge very high rates. Your best bet is to wash your own using a travel-soap such as Dylon *Travel-Wash*; if you're staying in hotels, keep quantities small as most officially forbid doing any laundry in your room.

LEFT LUGGAGE Lockers of various sizes are available at all *SNCF* stations, as well as *consigne* for longer periods or larger items.

SWIMMING POOLS (*piscines*) are well signposted in most French towns, and reasonably priced. SIs have addresses.

TAMPONS are available from all *pharmacies*, but they are much cheaper in supermarkets.

TIME France is one hour ahead of Britain throughout the year, except for the month of October, when it's the same.

TOILETS are usually to be found downstairs in bars, along with the phone, but they're often hole-in-the-ground squats and paper is rare.

VACCINATIONS are not required, or necessary.

WATER The tap-water is always safe to drink; bottled mineral water, always available, may taste better.

PART TWO

NORMANDY

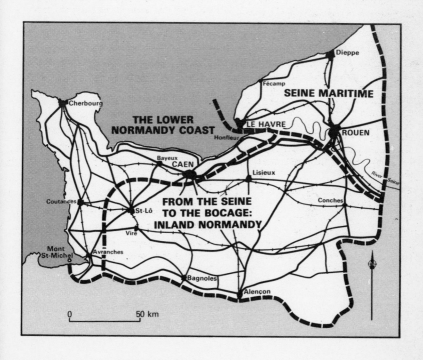

THE LOWER
NORMANDY COAST

SEINE MARITIME

FROM THE SEINE
TO THE BOCAGE:
INLAND NORMANDY

Dieppe

Fécamp

Cherbourg

LE HAVRE

ROUEN

Honfleur

Bayeux

CAEN

Lisieux

River Seine

Conches

Coutances

St-Lô

Vire

Mont
St-Michel

Avranches

Bagnoles

Alençon

0   50 km

CHAPTER ONE

SEINE MARITIME

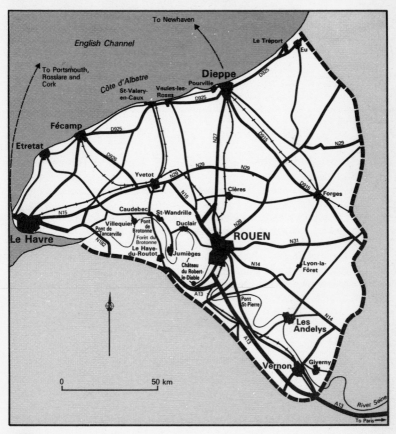

Seine **Maritime** is an untypical introduction to Normandy. Though the *département* is scattered with the characteristic Norman half-timbered houses and small farms, the countryside itself is stark along the coastline and often dull in the flatlands of the chalk Caux plateau behind. Only along the sheltered ribbon of the **Seine valley** do you find the province's usual greenery and profusion of flowers and fruit.

Which is not to say this is all territory to pass through or ignore. Arriving at **Dieppe** you can take advantage of the low-key resorts along the **Côte d'Albâtre**, and there are occasional surprises, too, behind their windswept and tide-chased walks. At **Fécamp** is an absurd Hammer-House-of-Horror Benedictine distillery; at **Etretat** spectacular stacks and arches of rock; at **Varengeville**, architect Edwin Lutyens' wonderful **Bois des Moutiers**. On the Seine estuary, **Le Havre** is less conventionally enticing – but worth attention all the same, for its art collections and, as France's second port after Marseilles, for its liveliness.

It is, however, the extravagant meandering of the **Seine** that is likely to determine most people's travels in this region. **Rouen**, the nexus, is one of the major provincial capitals of France, with its heavily but effectively restored medieval centre making it by far the most interesting Norman city. Along the valley and riverbanks there is plenty to delay your progress: the abbeys of **St-Wandrille** and **Jumièges**; the English frontier-stronghold of **Château Gaillard**; and, an unmissable last stop before Paris, **Monet's garden** and waterlilies at **Giverny**.

NORTH OF THE SEINE

There is no confusing the northern ports of Normandy, **Dieppe** and **Le Havre**, with their rivals to the east. Each has a distinct and individual identity in a way that Calais and Boulogne, with ten times the number of passengers, no longer do; you shouldn't feel you have to rush on out as soon as you arrive, or dice with time to coincide to the minute with the ferries back.

From either port there is an obvious choice of **routes**: inland towards Rouen or along the coast. From Dieppe, with your own transport, the **coast road** is the one to take; there is nothing of interest on the plains inland. **Etretat** and **Fécamp** are within easy reach of Le Havre, though, as stressed above, it's the route along the Seine, covered in the sections following p.44, that has most to inspire and enjoy.

Dieppe

Crowded between high cliff headlands, **DIEPPE** is an enjoyably small-scale port at which to arrive. It is always busy: half the bananas of the Antilles and forty percent of all shellfish eaten in France are unloaded at its commercial docks. The markets sell fish straight off the boats, displayed with all the usual mouthwatering French flair, and it's likely to be the sole, scallops and turbots available in profusion that encourage you to stay – or the restaurants that have enticed you over for a day trip. Even if you are heading south immediately by train, the railway tracks run along the *quais* of the fishing port, so you can get a whiff of what you're missing.

The **town** was once more of a resort than it is today, as a place where Parisians used to take the air before fast cars enabled them to go further afield. In the nineteenth century, the French would promenade along the front, whilst the English colony indulged in the peculiar pastime of bathing. Hence the extravagant space allotted to the seafront and "salt water therapy centre", now hemmed in with car parks. In the centre the streets are run-

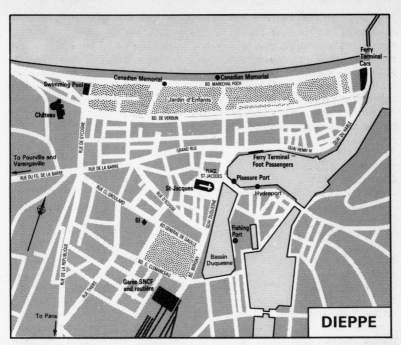

down, and left in continual shadow – little advertisement for the eighteenth-century town planning to which they are supposed to be a monument. More energetic, particularly during its **market** on Saturday, is the pedestrianised **Grande Rue**, which caters efficiently for day trippers doing last-minute shopping before the ferry. As well as clothes and food outlets, numerous antique shops are scattered up the side streets. For large-scale hypermarkets, you need to head away from the sea out on the main road towards Paris.

The obvious and most conspicuous sight is the medieval **castle** overlooking the seafront from the west. This is the home of the **Musée de Dieppe**, which in addition to its exhibition on local history – Dieppe's maritime past means this stretches to include pre-Columbian pottery from Peru – houses two showpiece collections. The first is a group of **Dieppe carved ivories** – virtuoso specimens of sawing, filing and chipping of the plundered riches of Africa. The ivory was shipped back to the town by early Dieppe "explorers", and in the seventeenth century over three hundred craftsmen-carvers lived here. The other permanent exhibition is made up of a hundred or so prints by the co-originator of cubism, **Georges Braque**, who went to school in Le Havre, spent his summers in Dieppe, and is buried just west of the town at Varangeville-sur-Mer (see below). Only a small number of prints are displayed at any one time, but in theory you can see the rest if you ask. (10am–noon & 2–6pm, closed Tues out of season.)

A flight of steps leads down from the castle to the **square du Canada**, originally a commemoration of the role played by sailors from Dieppe in that country's colonisation. After the last war, however, it acquired an additional significance, for it was at Dieppe in August 1942 that the Allied commando raid, Operation Jubilee, took place. The first large-scale assault on the continent after Dunkerque, the operation claimed over a thousand Canadian casualties in a near-suicidal series of landings and attacks up sheer and well-fortified cliff faces. The German defenders are reputed not to have bothered with firing their weapons – simply dropping projectiles over the edge. The Allied Command later justified the carnage as having taught valuable lessons for the 1944 invasion.

Practical details
If you're looking for a **room** in Dieppe – it's by no means packed with hotels – make for *Les Arcades* (1 quai de la Bourse, on the curve of the port towards the ferry terminal; ☎35.84.14.12), *Select* (1 rue Toustain; ☎35.84.14.66) or *La Providence* (157 av de la Republique, in the suburb of Neuville to the west of the ports). The *Arcades* has a good **restaurant**, and there are several others along the *quais*. The **youth hostel** (☎35.84.85.73) is two kilometres to the south, on rue Louis Fromager; take the *Janval* bus from the gare routière and get off at *Ecole Jules Ferry*. The nearest **campsite**, *Pré St-Nicolas* (☎35.84.11.39), is three kilometres down the coastal road towards Pourville. The **gares SNCF** and **routière** are about 150m south of the ferry terminal; the **SI**, in the modern Hôtel de Ville on bd Général de Gaulle, west of the port, can supply maps and plans for the region.

Around Dieppe

The D75, which heads off towards the coast from rue Faubourg de la Barre, leads in two kilometres to a **Musée de la Guerre**. Devoted to the Canadian raid, it is located in some of the German bunkers that were its target. A kilometre or so beyond is the resort of **POURVILLE**, an extremely tranquil last or first night stop for ferry passengers. Among numerous modestly-priced **hotels** is the *Produits de la Mer* (☎35.84.38.34).

Varengeville
VARENGEVILLE, eight kilometres from Dieppe (25 minutes on bus #311 or #312; afternoon only), is just to the west. In its cliff-top **church** are stained glass windows by Georges Braque – and outside is his grave, with a somewhat monstrous tombstone. But the views along the cliffs are wonderful, and in any case the real point of coming out here is to visit the **Bois des Moutiers**, one of the architect Edwin Lutyens' first commissions. Quite un-French in almost every respect, this stands back along the road from Varengeville to the church; you can visit its gardens from March 15 to November 15 (9am–noon & 2–7pm; closed Sat morning), and the house in July and August (closed Sun morning, and Tues). Admission is expensive but you'll be guided with genuine enthusiasm around the quirks and games of the house and garden, the latter featuring some highly innovative engineering. The colours of the Burne Jones tapestry hanging in the stairwell were copied from Renaissance cloth in the studio of William Morris. The rhodo-

dendrons were chosen from similar samples. Paths lead through vistas based on paintings by Poussin, Lorrain, and other eighteenth-century artists, and no modern roses are allowed to update the colours.

Le Tréport

Thirty kilometres east of Dieppe, the town of **LE TREPORT** has been a port since the Romans were in Gaul. It owes its modern popularity to being the nearest seaside resort to Paris – a fact which dominates its character. The seafront may look a bit drab, but it's an enjoyable and active sort of place. The **quai François 1er** is full of restaurants and cafés, and in the streets behind are several cheap **hotels**, such as the *Petit Trianon* (44 bd du Calvaire; ☎35.86.27.01), and the **pension** *Chez Marcel* (61 rue Suzanne; ☎35.86.16.80). There's also a **youth hostel**, at 25 av des Canadiens (☎35.86.23.47).

The Forest of Eu

Queen Victoria twice visited Le Tréport with Albert. She didn't come to the resort for the seaside, though, but to stay at the château at nearby **EU**, and in so doing to become the first English monarch to visit France since Henry VIII arrived for the Field of the Cloth of Gold. The **château**, much restored, is now a rather routine museum (guided tours April–Oct, 10am–noon & 2–6pm; closed Tues). If you're passing through, time would be better spent in the **forest of Eu**, a mysterious and ancient tangled woodland, with a lost Roman city supposedly hidden in its depths. A good way to explore it, though you'll need your own transport, is to follow the river Bresle upstream, along the border between Normandy and Picardy.

The Côte d'Albâtre

From Dieppe to Le Havre the coast is eroding at a ferocious rate, and it's conceivable that the small resorts here, tucked in among the cliffs at the mouths of a succession of valleys, may not last more than another century or so. For the moment, however, they are quietly prospering, with casinos, sports centres and yacht marinas ensuring a modest but steady summer trade.

West from Dieppe

The coastal road immediately beyond Varengeville is not very interesting. **QUIBERVILLE**, the main name on the map, makes a popular target for windsurfers, but in itself is little more than an overgrown caravan park; at Veules, you pass a couple of ludicrous folk-sculptures, including a seashell snowman; **ANGIENS** is a pretty village but with nothing much to linger over.

St-Valery-en-Caux

The first town of any size is **ST-VALERY-EN-CAUX**, almost completely rebuilt after the last war and perhaps the clearest reminder of the fighting – and massive destruction – along the Channel shore during the Allied retreat of 1940. There's a monument on the western cliffs to the French cavalry division who faced Rommel's tanks on horseback, brandishing their sabres with hopeless heroism. Beside the ruins of a German artillery emplacement on the opposite cliffs is another monument, this time to a Scottish division, who were rounded up while fighting their way back to Le Havre and the boats home.

Fécamp

FECAMP, like Dieppe, is a serious fishing port, although one with a more frivolous sideline as holiday resort. It is a striking town, so much surrounded by high cliffs that, approaching from inland, you don't see the sea until you're right upon it. It has kept the railway link which runs right into the small harbour, where fishing boats, pleasure yachts and *vedettes* jostle for position. In the absence of any major attraction out to sea, the *vedettes* offer cruises to watch the sun set.

The town's long promenade runs next to a uniform steep beach of shingle, framed by crumbling and overhanging cliffs. As ever along this coast, windsurfing is more appealing than bathing. The seafront is not particularly plush, and the **hotels** tend to be set back in odd side streets and corners. It's a popular place; book to be sure of a room in the *Hôtel de L'Univers* (5 place St-Etienne; ☎35.28.05.88) or the *Angleterre* (93 rue de la Plage; ☎35.28.01.60; watch out for the hideous pug). The **youth hostel** (July–Sept 15, ☎35.29.75.79; reservations ☎35.29.36.35) is east of the port, along the Route du Commandant Roquigny, on the Côte de la Vierge. A superb **campsite**, the *Camping de Renneville* (☎35.28.20.97) is a short walk away on the western cliffs. The **SI** is just behind the seafront where it meets the yacht harbour; the **gares SNCF** and **routière** between the port and the town centre on av Gambetta.

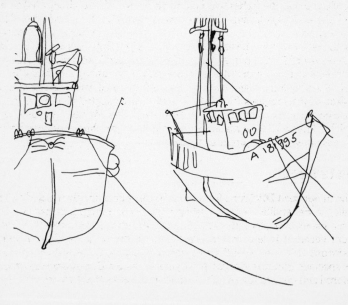

The Benedictine Distillery

Fécamp owes much of its popularity to an utterly bizarre tourist attraction – the **Benedictine Distillery** in rue Alexandre le Grand (amid the narrow strip of streets running parallel to the port towards the town centre). This mock-Gothic monstrosity may look like a decaying haunted mansion that has survived nightmarish aeons, but it was in fact built at the end of the last century for the manufacture of the sweet Benedictine liqueur. You have to go round the building in a rather dismal guided tour, the first part of which comprises a hurried trek through a museum of local antiquities and oddments. Although many visitors are frantic to get to the alcohol at the end, this does have its moments. There are headless bishops, serpentine musical instruments, carved wood and ivory, and – a real kitsch treat – a stained-glass window in which Alexandre le Grand, former owner of the Benedictine company, is being treated to a bottle of his liqueur by an obliging passing angel.

Eventually you pass on to the distillery section (although commercial operations have moved to a new factory outside town), where boxes of exotic herbs are thrown into great copper vats and alembics. There is then a massive surge drinkwards, for the (disappointingly modest) *dégustation* across the road; and it must be said it's nice stuff, especially the *B&B*, served either neat or on *crêpes*. **Tours**, which last about 45 minutes, go from 9.30 to 11.30am and 2 to 5.30pm. Make sure you hang on to your admission ticket to get the free drink.

Eglise de la Trinité

If your aesthetic sensibilities need soothing after the distillery, head away from the sea to the **Eglise de la Trinité**. This medieval abbey church is light and almost frail with age, its bare nave echoing to the sound of birds flying free beneath the high roof. The wooden carvings are tremendous, in particular the dusty wooden bas-relief *Dormition of the Virgin*. Just opposite that is a statue covered with youthful biro scrawls, prayerful petitions for such earthly blessings as exam success or a "*petite amie*". The abbey also has a fine selection of saintly fingers and sacred hips, authenticated with wax seals, and even a drop of the Precious Blood itself, said to have floated all the way here in a fig tree despatched by Joseph of Arimathea. Edward the Confessor is more reliably known to have made extensive gifts to the abbey and may have lived here at some point before his coronation.

On to Etretat

The minor road **D28** runs from Fécamp through a thickly wooded and idyllic valley to Benarville – a good cycling route, even though it manages to lose its river somewhere along the way. The **D150** (covered by buses #261 and #311 from Fécamp) is less pastoral, but leads to the remains of the **Abbaye de Valmont** (10am–noon & 2–6pm; closed Wed and, Oct–April, Sun as well). In its spacious grounds you can feast your eyes on a Renaissance chapel, grass-floored and open to the sky above, and an intact Gothic lady chapel.

Etretat

The cliff formations of **ETRETAT** are the most dramatic sight of the Alabaster Coast, and are consequently splashed across the front of most of the *département*'s tourist brochures. Without the prior publicity, these could be quite thrilling as you first catch sight of the arches and needles from the beach or clifftop. You'll need transport though – Etretat is not on bus or train routes – and to explore the rocks you've only got the three hours either side of low tide.

The standard high vantage point for the rocks is just to the east of the town. It's easy to spot, for set into the turf alongside a sharp futurist arch is a lifesize aeroplane in concrete relief. This semi-abstract and unusual monument is dedicated to the French aviators Nungesser and Coli, and their "Oiseau Blanc", the plane in which they set off from Paris in May 1927, attempting the first transatlantic flight to New York. It was last seen disappearing over Etretat. A small museum dedicated to the two World War I flying aces stands nearby.

Well sheltered from the elements, the town is a pleasant enough little resort. It has one mild idiosyncrasy – **beached boats** converted with thatch roofs into sheds, or these days, bars. If you want to stay, there's not all that much **accommodation** available. Try along the av George V – either the *Windsor* (☎35.27.07.27) at number 9, or *de La Poste* (☎35.27.01.34) at no. 6; or make for the municipal **campsite** (☎35.27.07.67), one kilometre out on the rue Guy de Maupassant (named after the writer, who lived in Etretat). There is an **SI** on the central place de la Mairie.

Le Havre

Most ferry passengers move straight out from the port of **LE HAVRE** and most guidebooks dismiss the city as dismal, disastrous, and gargantuan. But while it's admittedly not the most picturesque or the most tranquil place in Normandy, neither is it the soulless urban sprawl such warnings suggest. Conclusively destroyed during the last war, it was rebuilt along new lines from the plans of a single architect, Auguste Perret, between 1944 and 1964. As such, it is a rather rare entity – and one that stands up well alongside the new towns built over the last decades around Paris. There is exciting use of public space, sensitive integration of the few surviving churches and monuments, and little in the way of tower blocks. On top of which, the city has had a Communist mayor for decades; responsible, most obviously to visitors, for keeping museum charges nominal, and for the inspired choice as twin towns of Leningrad and Southampton.

The city was built on the orders of François I in 1517. Its name, originally Francispolis, soon changed to Le Havre – "the Harbour" – for its function was to replace the ancient ports of Harfleur and Honfleur, then silting up. It became the principal trading port of France's northern coast, and still is, in spite of being the most badly damaged port in Europe at the end of World War II. The docks today extend way beyond the town, occupying the whole northern shore of the Seine estuary, and for once show few signs of decline.

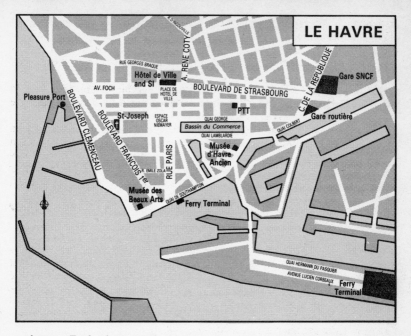

Avenue Foch, the central street, runs east to west, looking on to the sea between the beach and the yacht harbour at one end, and at the other the **SI**, Hôtel de Ville, and a kiosk where you can get a bus map. The **gares SNCF** and **routière** are a kilometre further west along rue Lecesne, and the transport system includes a funicular and giant escalator to get up north. If you're looking for **accommodation**, try *Jeanne D'Arc* (72 rue Honegger; ☎35.21.67.27), *Séjour Fleuri* (71 rue Emile Zola; ☎35.41.33.81), *des Vikings* (overlooking the port at 25 quai Southampton; ☎35.42.51.67; closed Dec), or the municipal **hostel** at 27 rue de la Mailleraye (contact via the SI, ☎33.21.22.88). The **campsite** is in the Forêt du Montgeon (bus #12 from Hôtel de Ville, direction Rouelles, stop *Hallates*, and a bit of a walk through the woods).

Ferry passengers looking to stock up before the journey home do best to head to the *Auchan* **hypermarket**, at the Mont Gaillard Centre Commercial, though this is a fair drive from the port – certainly way beyond walking distance. Otherwise, there's a **market** in the Cours de la Republique on Tuesday, Thursday and Saturday.

The finest buildings in Le Havre surround the **Bassin du Commerce**, with tinted glass at the eastern end, a slender white footbridge and, at the other end, the equally gleaming truncated cooling tower of the **Espace Oscar Niemayer**. Framed by the bridge spire and St-Joseph's lighthouse-like belfry in the distance, the tower holds a theatre and cinema, and expresses an ever-hopeful socialist sentiment by the fountain at its base. A plaza for busking, strolling and idling slopes down to bars and shops, as well as exhibition and concert space (what's on details from SI). **St-Joseph** itself should not be missed, either, for its astonishing stained glass as well as Perret's overall design.

The Beaux Arts

On bd J.F.Kennedy, overlooking the port entrance, is the **Beaux Arts**, one of the best designed art galleries in the country and with one of the loveliest collections of French nineteenth- and twentieth-century paintings – fifty canvases by Eugène Boudin, and works by Corot, Courbet, Pissarro, Sisley, Gauguin, Léger, Braque and Lurcat. Raoul Dufy, a native of Le Havre (1877–1953), has a whole room for his drawings and paintings, in which the windows at the base of the walls show waterlilies in a shallow moat outside. Waterlilies in oil appear along with Westminster and a snowscape sunrise by Monet. Even if you're determined to rush off straight afterwards, allow yourself to be delayed just long enough to visit; it's open 10am to noon and 2 to 6pm, closed on Tuesday.

With more time to spare, you might like to see what the **old Havre** looked like in the prewar days when Sartre wrote _La Nausée_ here. He taught philosophy for five years during the 1930s in a local school, and his almost transcendent disgust with the place cannot obscure the fascination he felt in exploring the seedy dockside quarter of St-François, in those spare moments when he wasn't visiting Simone de Beauvoir in Rouen. Little survives of the city Sartre knew, but there are pictures and bits gathered from the rubble in one of the very few buildings that escaped, the **Musée de l'Ancien Havre** at 1 rue Jérome Bellarmato, just south of the Bassin du Commerce (Wed–Sun, 10am–noon & 2–6pm).

THE SEINE VALLEY

Even in the Bronze Age, the **Seine** was in use as the "Tin Road" linking Cornwall to Paris. Fortresses and monasteries lined its banks from the time of the Romans onwards. Now, with the threat of its tidal bore and treacherous sandbanks all but over, heavy ships make their serene way up its sinuous course to the provincial capital of **Rouen**.

An enormous new bridge across the mouth of the Seine is currently under construction, which will make access between the coasts of Upper and Lower Normandy very much more direct (see p.57). At present, the first place you can cross the river is at the immense **Tancarville** suspension bridge, offering a choice of banks and routes. The best scenically is along the **north (right) bank** – fortunately the route taken by Le Havre–Rouen buses (#191, #192) and incorporating most of the sights, such as the riverside towns of **Villequier** and **Caudebec**, and the abbey of **Jumièges**. If you choose the **south bank** instead, you'll need your own transport in order to stray out and away from the motorway to Paris.

From Tancarville to Rouen, there are just two **bridges** – both with quite hefty tolls. However, there are also intermittent _bacs_ (ferries) along the way; cheaper, these tend to leave on the hour (and to have very long lunch breaks).

Towards Rouen

Le Havre and Rouen are such vast industrial conglomerates that the country-side in between them might not seem to have any obvious promise. The refineries and cement works of Le Havre in particular feel as if they go on forever. However, just beyond them is the **Parc Naturel Régional de Brotonne**, an area that is surprisingly beautiful even if not entirely rural. The park shelters a wide range of conservation projects, and traditional industry initiatives, run by local people, as well as its more obvious abbey and château sites. Details on all its aspects can be obtained from the very helpful *Maison de Parc* at 2 Rond Point Marbec, Le Trait.

If you have your own transport, it's worth taking time to cross over at the **Pont de Brotonne** and to explore the less frequented **southern side** – the edges of the Vernier marshes where Camargue horses and Scottish highland cattle graze, and the deep thick woods of the **Forêt de Brotonne**. As for **accommodation** on this side of the river, there's a *gîte d'étape* at **ROUTOT** (c/o M. Verhaeghe, ☎32.57.31.09), and a few rooms available at the *Maison des Métiers* in **BOURNEVILLE**, which is also a beautifully presented museum of traditional farming and building techniques (2–7pm, April–Dec, closed Mon). **LA MAILLERAYE** has a good municipal **campsite**.

Villequier

The first of the resort towns you come to on the **D81 along the north bank** is quite undeservedly one of the least known – **VILLEQUIER**. As a stop on the way to or from Le Havre it's ideal, having two exceptional **hotels**. The *Grand Sapin* (☎35.56.78.73) is a gorgeous rambling old building, the rooms equipped with eccentric brass and enamel period-piece fittings, and rickety balconies overlooking the river. It's cheap, and magical on a misty morning – all that stops it getting the highest possible recommendation is that virtually next door the *Hôtel de France* (☎35.56.78.70) is just about as appealing, and has always had a better restaurant. It's currently for sale, so it must be hoped that new owners not only keep it open but keep the prices which made it good value unparalleled in Normandy.

There's no entertainment whatsoever in Villequier, and the only possible "sight" is a mournful statue of Victor Hugo, peering out into the Seine, across a helpfully marked concrete arrow, to the spot where his daughter and her husband were drowned six months after their marriage in 1843. The riverside promenade, however, is well laid-out, with shaky wooden quays where the estuary and river pilots for the Seine swap over their responsibilities.

Caudebec and Around

It is only a few kilometres to the bigger and more popular **CAUDEBEC-EN-CAUX**, an old town but with few traces of its past following firestorm devastation in the last war. The damage – and previous local history – is recorded in the museum at the thirteenth-century **Maison des Templiers**, one of the few buildings spared. You can take a look there, too, at pictures of the Seine's regular tidal swell, which still threatens at this narrow point to swamp unwary promenaders. The town has one cheap **hotel**, the *Cheval Blanc* (☎35.96.21.66), with pricey food, and a **campsite**, *Barre Y Va* (☎35.96.11.12). You can hire bicycles from M. Jaubert in rue de la Vicomte. A **market** has been held every Saturday since 1390 in the main square.

Just outside Caudebec, a **stone aeroplane** propels itself out of the cliff-face across the water – a memorial to another curious episode of aviation history, contemporary to that commemorated at Etretat. In 1928, a plane was being prepared here for an attempt at what would have been the first transatlantic flight. But shortly before it was due to set off, the Norwegian polar explorer Amundsen issued a worldwide appeal for help to rescue some Italian sailors who had been shipwrecked off Spitzbergen in the Arctic. The French government offered the plane, and its four crewmen left with Amundsen. Two days later they were lost.

Upstream, the magnificent span of the **Pont de Brotonne**, the world's highest and steepest humpback bridge (charging a toll for motorists), climbs out above the Seine. It has an unexpectedly appealing colour scheme – the suspension cables are custard yellow, the rails pastel green, the walkway maroon, and the vast concrete columns left bare. If you don't lose both heart and hat to the sickening drop and the seaborne winds, walking across it is one of the big treats of Normandy. From a distance, its stays refract into strange optical effects, while far below small capitalist tugs flounder in the mighty wash of communist cargo carriers.

Abbaye de St-Wandrille

The medieval **ABBAYE DE ST-WANDRILLE** is just beyond the bridge, on the north bank. It was founded, so legend has it, by a seventh-century count, who together with his wife renounced all earthly pleasures on the day of their wedding. The buildings form a striking, if mixed, ensemble: part ruin, part restoration and, in the case of the main buildings, part transplant – a fifteenth-century barn brought in here just a few years back from another Normandy village miles away. Monks are on hand to show you around every afternoon at 3 and 4 (also at 11.30am on Sunday).

Abbaye de Jumièges

In the next loop of the Seine, twelve kilometres upstream, squats the more famous **ABBAYE DE JUMIEGES**. A haunting ruin, it was destroyed – as a deliberate act of policy – during the Revolution. Its main outline, as far as that can still be made out, dates from the eleventh century; William the Conqueror himself attended its consecration in 1067. The towers, over 170ft high, are still standing. So too is one arch of the roofless nave, whilst a one-sided yew tree stands in the centre of what were once the cloisters. How evocative you find these bleached stone ruins will depend on your mood. Visits, an unescorted ramble through the lawns and scramble over the walls, are from 9am to noon and 2 to 6pm in summer, 10am to noon and 2 to 4pm in winter.

La Haye du Routot

On the opposite, south, side of the river near **HAUVILLE** you can look round a **windmill**, one of six owned by the monks of Jumièges, who farmed and forested all this area in the Middle Ages. Its outline – based on contemporary castle towers – looks like a kid's drawing. Restored by the *parc*, it is open at weekends from 2.30 until 7pm. If you've time, move on from here to the neighbouring village of **LA HAYE DU ROUTOT**. The churchyard is a novelty, featuring a pair of millennium-old yew trees that have been shaped into a chapel and a grotto. The feature for which the village is best known (at least in Normandy) is its annual **Fête de Ste-Claire**, held on her feast day, July 16. The centrepiece of this is a towering, conical bonfire, topped by a cross which must survive to ensure a good year. The smouldering logs are taken home to serve as protection against lightning. Should you miss the big day, a video recording of the goings on is shown in a reconstructed *boulangerie* (July & Aug, daily except Tues, 2.30–6.30pm; April–June and Sept & Oct weekends only).

If you want to **cycle** beside the river for any distance, the D982 tends to be constantly climbing and descending, and in any event a bit busy. However, the stretch from Le Mesnil (just beyond Jumièges) as far as Duclair is long and flat, quiet, and has a wonderful view of the lush riverside. **DUCLAIR** itself has a couple of cheap **hotels**, the *Hôtel de la Poste* (286 quai de la Libération; ☎35.37.50.04) and *Le Tartarin* (125 place du Général de Gaulle; ☎35.37.50.38). As you continue from here towards Rouen, you get a first panoramic prospect from beside the church at Canteleu, of the docks, the island, and the city. The road onwards coasts endlessly down into the maelstrom.

(Don't attempt to cycle *out* of Rouen in this direction – the gradient, and the fumes, are unbearable.)

Rouen

You could spend a day wandering around **ROUEN** without realising that the Seine ran through the city. The war destroyed all the bridges, the area between the cathedral and the *quais*, and much of the left bank industrial quarter. The immediate riverside area has never been adequately restored, with the result that what you might expect to be the most beautiful part of this ancient city is in fact an abomination.

Instead, enormous sums were devoted to an upmarket restoration job on the streets a few hundred metres north of the river, which turned the centre into the closest approximation to a medieval city that modern imaginations could come up with. (Historians consulted on the project suggested that the houses would have been painted in bright, clashing colours – but this idea was not deemed appropriate by the city authorities.) So far as it goes, the whole of this inner centre can be very seductive, and its churches are extremely impressive by any standards.

Outside the renovated quarters, things are rather different. The city spreads deep into the loop of the Seine to the south, and increasingly into the hills to the north, whilst the riverbank itself is lined with a fume-filled, multi-laned motorway. Rouen's docks and industries stretch endlessly away to the south (as the nearest point that large container ships can get to Paris, the

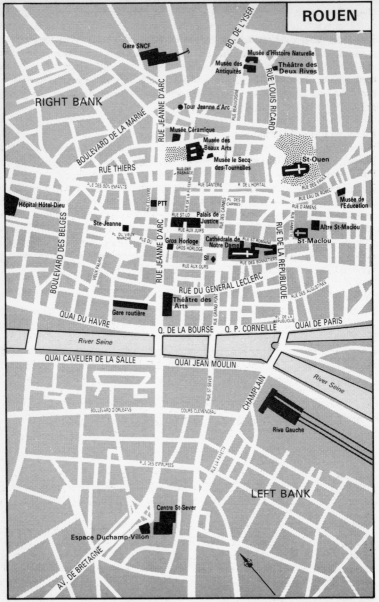

ROUEN

Gare SNCF

BD. DE L'YSER

Musée d'Histoire Naturelle

Musée des
Antiquités

Théâtre des
Deux Rives

RIGHT BANK

RUE JEANNE D'ARC

BOULEVARD DE LA MARNE

Tour Jeanne d'Arc

RUE LOUIS RICARD

RUE BEAUVOISINE

Musée Céramique

Musée des
Beaux Arts

St-Ouen

RUE THIERS

Musée le Secq-
des-Tournelles

RUE DES
BASNAGE

RUE GANTERIE

R. DE L'HÔPITAL

RUE DES 30% ENFANTS

RUE DES EAUX

RUE EAU DE ROBEC

Hôpital Hôtel-Dieu

RUE ECUYÈRE

PTT

RUE DES CARMES

PL. DES
CARMES

RUE D'AMIENS

Musée de
l'Éducation

BOULEVARD DES BELGES

Ste-Jeanne

RUE ST-LO

Palais de
Justice

Altre St-Maclou

PL. DU VIEUX
MARCHÉ

RUE DU

RUE AUX JUIFS

RUE DAMIETTE

St-Maclou

RUE DE LA RÉPUBLIQUE

Gros Horloge

GROS HORLOGE

RUE JEANNE D'ARC

Cathédrale de
Notre Dame

RUE ST-ROMAINE

VIEUX PALAIS

SI

RUE AUX OURS

RUE DES BONNETIERS

RUE DU GENERAL LECLERC

RUE DES AUGUSTINES

Théâtre des
Arts

RUE GRAND PONT

Gare routière

QUAI DU HAVRE

PL. DE LA
RÉPUBLIQUE

Q. DE LA BOURSE

Q. P. CORNEILLE

QUAI DE PARIS

River Seine

QUAI CAVELIER DE LA SALLE

QUAI JEAN MOULIN

River Seine

RUE ST-SEVER

CHAMPLAIN

BOULEVARD D'ORLEANS

COURS CLEMENCEAU

Rive Gauche

RUE DES EMPLPEES

RUE LA FAYETTE

LEFT BANK

Centre St-Sever

Espace Duchamp-Villon

AV. DE BRETAGNE

port remains the country's fourth largest – albeit in decline). Many workers
live outside the municipal boundaries, which might explain why the Left is
never elected to the town hall.

The Town

Rouen spends a higher proportion of its budget on **monuments** than any other provincial town, which maddens many a Rouennais. As a tourist, you will presumably not object. Certainly the great sights are there – the **Cathédrale de Notre-Dame**, the **Gros Horloge**, the **Aître St-Maclou**, all the delightful twisting streets of timbered houses – and the history too, most notably the links with **Joan of Arc**.

Place du Vieux-Marché

One obvious place to start exploring the city is the **place du Vieux-Marché**, in which a small plaque and a huge cross mark the site where Joan was burned to death on May 30 1431. A very new memorial church to the saint has been built in the square – a wacky, spiky-looking thing designed to accommodate some sixteenth-century stained glass rescued from the destroyed church of St-Vincent. It's an architectural triumph, part of an ensemble of buildings that manages to incorporate in similar style a covered food market (more for show than practical shopping). On the south side of the *place* is the privately owned **Musée Jeanne d'Arc**, which draws large crowds to its collection of tawdry waxworks and facsimile manuscripts.

Gros Horloge

From the Vieux-Marché, rue du Gros Horloge leads east towards the Cathedral. Just across the rue Jeanne d'Arc you come to the **Gros Horloge** itself (April–Sept only, 10am–12.15pm & 2.30–5.30pm, closed Tues). A colourful one-handed clock, it used to be on the adjacent Gothic belfry until it was moved down by popular demand in 1529, so that people could see it better. You can climb up rather too many steps to see its workings and, if the sponginess of the lead roofing agrees with your nerves, totter around the top for a marvellous view of the old city. The bell up there, cast in 1260, still rings what's known as the "Conqueror's Curfew" at nine each night. A block to the north are the Renaissance splendours of the former **Palais de Justice**.

Cathédrale de Notre-Dame

The **Cathédrale de Notre-Dame** somehow remains at heart the Gothic masterpiece that was built in the twelfth and thirteenth centuries, although all sorts of different towers and spires have since been added. The most recent of these, in the nineteenth century, was the iron spire of the central lantern tower, which made it at 151 metres the highest in France. The west facade, which is intricately sculpted like the rest of the exterior, was Monet's subject for a series of studies of changing light, which now hang in the Musée d'Orsay in Paris. Inside, the carvings of the misericords in the choir depict fifteenth-century life, in secular scenes of work and habits as well as the usual mythical beasts. Unfortunately, the ambulatory and the crypt, which hold the assorted tombs of various recumbent royalty, among them Richard the Lionheart and the husband of Diane de Poitiers, are only accessible on guided tours.

Aître St-Maclou

A bit further on is the church of St-Maclou, and nearby, with its entrance a little hard to find in between 184 and 186 rue Martainville, the **Aître St-Maclou**. This was built between 1526 and 1533, in an era of mass plague deaths, as a cemetery and charnel house. The ground floor was used as an open cloister, and in the rooms above, the bare bones of countless victims were exposed to view. At first sight it looks very picturesque – just a court-yard of half-timbered houses – but look closely at the carvings on the beams and you see traces of a macabre **Dance of Death**, whilst in the case to the right of the entrance is a mummified cat. The buildings are still in use, and still stimulating morbid imaginations, not as a morgue but as Rouen's Fine Arts school. In the square outside are several good antique bookshops, and a few art shops.

The last of Rouen's great churches is **St-Ouen**, next to the Town Hall in a large open square to the north. It's larger than the Cathedral and has far less decoration, with the result that its Gothic proportions have that instant hard hit with which nothing built since the Middle Ages can compete.

The Museums

Then come the **museums**. Of these, the most interesting and unusual is the ironmongery museum, the **Musée Le Secq Des Tournelles**. Housed in the old and barely altered church of St-Laurent on rue Jacques Villon, it is a brilliant collection of wrought-iron objects of all dates and descriptions – locks and keys, tools of every trade, and numerous spiral staircases that now lead to nowhere. The museum is just behind the **Beaux Arts**, and admission is by the same ticket, which also includes the Gros Horloge belfry. The Beaux Arts itself is not very enthralling but it does include works by the Rouennais Géricault, Sisley and Monet in the Impressionist section, Dadaist pictures by Marcel Duchamp, and a collection of portraits by Jacques Emile Blanche (1861–1942) of his contemporaries – Cocteau, Stravinsky, Gide, Valéry, Mallarmé and others. Both museums are open from 10am to noon and 2 to 6pm, and closed all day Tuesday and on Wednesday morning.

You can pick up a full list of museum times and addresses from the **SI**, 25 place de la Cathédrale. Others include **Antiquités**, a long way north on the rue Beauvoisine, which is particularly good on tapestries, and **Ceramiques**, a speciality of Rouen, very near the Beaux Arts. On the corner of rue Eau de Robec and rue Ruissel there is, too, one of the new breed of intellectually self-conscious French museums – the **Musée de l'Education** (Tues–Sat, 1–6pm), which covers the upbringing, education, and general influences on children. If you're interested in establishment French ideology, it's illuminating. If not, **rue Eau de Robec** is itself a good example of Rouen restoration: a pure, shallow stream makes aesthetic appearances between paved cross-

---

To understand Flaubert himself, and for an insight into the Rouen that he knew, the place to look is not the *Pavillon Flaubert*, which like the other two literary museums in town – the two homes of Pierre Corneille – only proves the pointlessness of the genre. It is, rather, the **Musée Flaubert et de l'Histoire de la Médecine**, at the Hôtel Dieu Hospital. This stands on the corner of rue de Lecat and rue du Contrat Social, in walkable distance (or bus #2a) from the centre, and it's infinitely more relevant to Flaubert's writings than the manuscript copies and personal mementoes in the Pavillon museum. Flaubert's father was chief surgeon and director of the medical school, living with his family in this house within the hospital. Even during the cholera epidemic when Gustave was 11, he and his sister were not stopped from running around the wards or climbing along the garden wall to look into the autopsy lab. Some of the medical exhibits would certainly have been familiar objects to him – a phrenology model, a childbirth demonstrator like a giant ragdoll, and the sets of encyclopaedias. There's also one of his stuffed parrots, as featured in Julian Barnes' *"Flaubert's Parrot"*. Hours are 10am–noon & 2–6pm (closed Mon); ring the doorbell several times.

---

ings to the front doors of neatly quaint houses, now inhabited by successful antique dealers. In an earlier age these were described by one of Flaubert's characters as a "degraded little Venice".

Accommodation and Other Practicalities

Cheap and central **hotel accommodation** is no problem: try the *Cardinal* (1 place de la Cathédrale; ☎35.70.24.42), *des Flandres* (5 rue des Bons Enfants; ☎35.71.56.88), *Saint Ouen* (43 rue des Faulx; ☎35.71.46.44) or *des Arcades* (52 rue des Carmes; ☎35.70.10.30). If you want quiet, stay somewhere in the pedestrian areas around the Cathedral or the Vieux-Marché, as the main roads, especially along the riverside, are unbearably noisy and busy all day and night: the *Hôtel de la Cathédrale* (12 rue St-Romain; ☎35.71.57.95) makes an excellent retreat. The **youth hostel**, away south of the river at 17 rue Diderot (☎35.72.06.45), is ten minutes from the Théâtre des Arts on the bus lines to Grand Quevilly: stop *Diderot* on #5 or *Barcelone* on #6. The **campsites** are all out of town, the two closest being *L'Aubette* (☎35.56.78.70) at 23 rue du Vert Buisson, Leger du Bourg Denis (bus #180 from gare routière, stop *Carville*); and *Le Cheval Rouge* (☎35.60.31.31) at Isneauville (buses #15, #150 or #151 from gare routière, stop *Cheval Rouge*).

Eating and Drinking

Rouen has a good reputation for **food**, with its most famous dish being *caneton*, duckling. This is supposed to be at its best in the *Mapotel*, which is the restaurant of the *Hôtel Dieppe* opposite the SNCF station; the *Pascaline* at 5 rue de la Poterne is a lot less expensive and run to similar standards by the same management. But both are pretty upmarket. If you're looking for a good basic meal, the south side of the place Vieux-Marché and the north side of St-Maclou church are both lined with competing good-quality restaurants. Among specific recommendations, you might try: the Caribbean restaurant on rue des Fosses Louis VIII; the traditional _Vieux Carné_ at 34 rue Ganterie; _Le Green Park_, 9 rue Grand Pont, for a good cheap midday meal; for functional and unpoisonous eating, the _Matussiére_ at 97 rue Ecuyère; or, the best value in town, _Cave Royale_ (just around the corner to the north of St-Maclou at 48 rue Damiette) which serves up mountains of couscous and paella.

There are, too, sumptuous **patisserie** shops everywhere – a stall selling superb cream-laden _gaufres_ does business between the post office and the Beaux Arts on the rue Jeanne d'Arc. The most enjoyable **bars** are in the tangle of streets between the rue Thiers and the place du Vieux-Marché. This used to be the part of Rouen incoming sailors headed for – the small bars are still there even if the sailors aren't.

Entertainment

As well as several **cinemas**, on the main roads north of the river and in the St-Sever complex in the south, Rouen has three **theatres**, which mainly work to winter seasons. The most highbrow and big-spectacle is the _Théâtre des Arts_, but perhaps more promising are the adventurous repertory company of the _Théâtre des Deux Rives_ which has recently moved into permanent premises opposite the Antiquities museum at 48 rue Louis Ricard, and the _Espace Duchamp Villon_ in St-Sever. This latter is the venue for (fairly) **alternative events** – theatre, cinema, dance and jazz. To see exhibitions of modern **visual arts**, try the _Centre d'Arts Contemporains_ at 11 place du Général de Gaulle.

For what it's worth Rouen is also said to be the capital of French **rock**. The place to check out bands is _Exo 7_ (note the militaristic pun) in the place Chartreux, which is a long way south of the river, well off most maps but on bus routes #5, #120, and #170. No. 44 is the venue for live gigs, and there's a disco on Friday and Saturday nights at no. 13. If you're planning to stay for more than a week or so, the annual handbook sold in all the newsagents, _Le P'tit Normand_, is very helpful with addresses.

Shopping

Most of the classier **shops** in Rouen are in the pedestrian streets near to, and slightly north of, the Cathedral. But if you're looking for hypermarkets, cheap clothes, or just a laugh on a rainy day, go south of the river to the modern multi-storey **Saint-Sever** complex. Even if your pockets are empty, the long rides on the travelators are free. There's an open-air **antiques and bric-a-brac market** nearby in the place des Emmurées. Back to the north of the river, the _Dépôt Vente du Rouen_ on rue des Augustins is a **junk shop** where you might find something good. _Maurice_ on the rue Moliére sells and repairs _Raleigh_ **cycles**, and as such is one of the few places cyclists can get (expensive) English-size tyres. There are two shops with large stocks of English-language **books** – _l'Armitiére_ at 5 rue des Basnage, and _FNAC_ on the rue Ecuyère.

Transport

The main **Rive-Droite SNCF** station is high up above the river at the top of the rue Jeanne D'Arc, not immediately conspicuous on maps as the actual train lines go under the ground. From there, buses #12, #15 and #20 take five minutes to get down to the town centre, it making little difference whether you get off at the third, fourth or fifth stop. The last of these is the *Théâtre des Arts*, with the **gare routière** one block to the east, again not very obvious as it is tucked away behind the riverfront buildings. From there, out-of-town buses include #191 and #192 to Le Havre along the river via Jumièges and Caudebec, #163 to Dieppe via Totes and Bacqueville, #150 to Dieppe and Le Treport, and #261 to St Valery.

Outskirts: a Château, a Forest and a Zoo

A long and very badly signposted haul southwest from central Rouen, past the docks and refineries of Petit and Grand Quévilly (where there are at least a few cycle lanes), suddenly climbs from Moulineaux up to the ruined **Château du Robert-le-Diable**. Robert the Devil is a legendary figure who may or may not have been William the Conqueror's father, but certainly didn't build this early Norman castle. It's now privately run, with a crazy golf course, a slightly clumsy reconstruction of a Viking *drakkar*, and tacky waxworks of the Battle of Hastings and other such scenes. But its strengths are the very damp and spooky passages underground, and then the magnificent view from the top of the tower down to the Seine, the port of Rouen, and the châteaux on the other side. The only drawback is that it's pressed right against an extremely busy motorway.

Just across the motorway is the **Forêt de la Londe**. Although dissected by a number of busy railway lines, it survives in the gaps – and is used by local cyclists to race the fumes of Rouen out of their systems.

In the other direction from the city, and reachable on bus #161, **CLERES** has a large and popular **zoo**. The château there was devastated by a fire, which the animals survived. Colette made the impenetrable but presumably complimentary remark that "At Clères, in the zoo park, it is easy to lose the melancholy feeling of inevitability."

Upstream: Les Andelys and Giverny

Leaving Rouen, the Seine becomes enticing again as it is joined by the Andelle river at **PONT ST-PIERRE**, where any surplus money you may have could be enjoyably spent on a stay at the *Hostellerie la Bonne Marmite* (250F and upwards per night, ☎32.49.70.24; closed last week of July and first two weeks in August). At this crossing you are confronted with the spectacularly sharp **Côte des Deux Amants**. This is a sheer escarpment leading to a plateau high above the Seine. It takes name from a twelfth-century legend, in which a cruel king stipulated that the man who would marry his daughter must first run with her in his arms to the top of this hill. Noble Raoul sprinted up carrying the fair Caliste, but then dropped dead, and, out of sympathy, so did she. That story provides precious little incentive for anyone else to make the climb – but rumour has it that the view from the top does.

Les Andelys

The next town of any size is **LES ANDELYS**, which is in fact two towns. Petit Andely lies along the riverfront, with a couple of quite pricey hotels, including the eighteenth-century *Chaîne d'Or* (27 rue Grande; ☎32.54.00.31; closed Jan). Grand Andely is at the end of a mile-long boulevard stretching inland, and is the centre for shops, bars, and a **market** on Saturday. The *Soleil Levant* at 2 rue Général de Gaulle (☎32.54.23.55) is the best value for food (restaurant closed on Sunday) and a room, but it's a bit too far to walk back to the river for an evening stroll.

Château Gaillard

High above Les Andelys, and looking especially awesome and magical by night, are the ruins of the **Château Gaillard**. This was constructed in the space of a single year, 1196–97, under the auspices of Richard the Lionheart and the Duke of Normandy, who had to bribe the Pope for permission to do so. Their object was to bar the King of France's access to Rouen through total control of traffic along the Seine by road and river. That was successful until after Richard's death, when Philippe-Auguste managed to storm the castle in 1204. It would probably have survived intact into this century, though, had Henry IV not ordered its destruction in 1603. Even then, it would have taken more recent devices to reduce Château Gaillard to rubble: the substantial outline remains and, for once, there's free access at all times.

On foot, you can climb up to the castle from the path off rue Richard Coeur-de-Lion in Petit Andely. By car you have to follow a long-winded one-way system from opposite the church in Grand Andely. You can then scramble about over green and chalky knolls, and across the ruined moat, to explore Richard's one-year wonder.

Forêt de Lyons

Les Andelys also makes a good base for trips into the oak and beech **Forêt de Lyons**, where there is virtually nowhere to stay. In such agreeable countryside so close to the capital, where large country estates abound and whole villages have turned into weekend colonies of Paris, it's assumed that any visitor has if not a residence then at least a car.

Monet's Gardens at Giverny

At **GIVERNY**, twenty kilometres on from Les Andelys, Claude Monet lived from 1883 until his death in 1926 and laid out the **gardens** which many of his friends considered his masterpiece. Each month is reflected in a dominant colour, as is each room in the house – hung as he left them with his collection of Japanese prints. None of Monet's own paintings is at Giverny; there are just shoddy reproductions on sale. If you want to see the originals, the best collections are in Paris, at the Marmottan, Musée d'Orsay, and Orangerie.

At the bottom of the garden, reached by a passage under the road, is the famous **waterlily pond**. May and June, when the rhododendrons flower around the pond, and the wisteria that winds over the Japanese bridge is in bloom, are the best of all times to visit. But any month, from spring to autumn, is overwhelming in the beauty of this arrangement of living shades and shapes.

The gardens are not large, and you'll have to contend with crowds of camera-happy visitors snapping up images of the famous waterlilies. If you've brought a picnic, it's forbidden to eat in the grounds, and the surrounding countryside is not particularly pleasant. But for all that, there's no place like it, and this has to be one of the most pleasurable visits anywhere in Normandy. The gardens are open from 10am until 6pm, the house 10am to noon and 2 to 6pm, closed Monday; both are closed from November to March.

Access

Neither Giverny nor the Château Gaillard is easily accessible by public transport. For Les Andelys there's an infrequent bus from Rouen, or, a bit more expensive but very scenic, a tourist boat from next to the **Poses Dam** (bus #130 from Rouen); the boat goes to Les Andelys and Vernon, contact Rouen SI for details. For Giverny, your best bet is the train to Vernon, and then, if you're lucky with its erratic schedule, a ten-minute ride on the *Gisor* bus from the station.

Vernon

VERNON straddles the Seine just before it leaves Normandy altogether. There are walks laid out along either bank, a couple of very snooty and expensive hotels, and a hard-to-find **youth hostel** – at 28 av Ile de France (☎32.21.20.51). Elvis Presley's dad was called Vernon.

travel details

Trains

Through trains to Paris connect with all ferries.

From Dieppe 5 daily to Rouen (45min); 5 daily to Paris-St-Lazare (2hr 15min).

From Le Havre at least hourly to Rouen (45min) and Paris (2hr).

From Rouen 8 daily to Caen (2hr 15min); at least hourly to Fécamp (1hr) and to Paris-St-Lazare (1hr 15min).

From Fécamp 6 daily to Rouen (45min) via Breauté.

From St-Valery 4 daily to Rouen (30min) via Motteville.

Buses

From Dieppe 5 daily to Paris (2hr 15min); 1 daily to Fécamp (1hr 30min), #311 or #312 via St Valery.

From Rouen hourly to Le Havre (2hr 45min), #191 or #192 via Jumièges and Caudebec; 2 daily to Dieppe (1hr 45min) #163, and #150 on to Le Tréport, Fécamp (2hr 30min) and Lisieux (2hr 30min). Also to Clères, #161, to Le Neubourg, #337, and to Elbeuf.

Ferries

For details of ferries from Dieppe and Le Havre, see p.5.

CHAPTER TWO

THE LOWER NORMANDY COAST

The **coast of Lower Normandy** takes on very different characters as you move from east to west. Along the **Côte Fleurie**, from Honfleur to Cabourg, it is moneyed and elegant, a would-be northern counterpart to the Côte d'Azur. Then, through the **Côte de Nacre** and into the area known as the **Bessin**, around Caen and Bayeux, it drifts into anonymity: wide stretches of sand, backed by scrubland and still dominated by the memories of 1944 when they served as the landing beaches for the Allied forces. West again, separated from the bulk of the mainland by a series of marshes, is the **Cotentin peninsula**, with low-key harbour villages along its east front, cliffs across the north, and vast dunes and wild beaches to the west. And finally there is the **bay of Mont St-Michel**, where the island abbey is swept by treacherous tides.

The most enjoyment along the **Côte Fleurie** is to be had from **Honfleur** – a real gem of a harbour town, familiarised by Eugène Boudin, Monet and other Impressionists. Elsewhere, only the Proust connections soften the air of wealthy sterility. **Trouville**, **Deauville** and **Cabourg** preoccupy themselves with such events as Rolls Royce rallies, forever harking back to a nineteenth-century past of leisured aristocrats – though with futuristic prices.

The **Côte de Nacre** and the **Bessin**, despite the prominence of their war past, are much more likeable; small-scale traditional resorts where, if the sea's a little overexposed, you can at least eat well and wander without crowds. The history of the D-Day landings – and the numerous cemeteries and memorials – draws its own kind of tourists, still with many veterans among them. A tour can be instructive and moving. For sites actually to enjoy, however, **Bayeux** must be the pre-eminent destination. It holds, of course, the famous **tapestry**, its drama remaining as vivid as its colours, and is a stylish and interesting town in its own right. Considerably more so, in fact, than war-ravaged **Caen**, Normandy's newest ferry destination since the opening of the harbour at **Ouistreham**.

Cherbourg is even less of a ferry port to linger over. But if you arrive here, the **Cotentin peninsula** has beaches, dunes and amazing windsurfing along its west coast, between Carteret and Coutainville. They are enough at least to delay progress towards the **Mont St-Michel**, France's most visited and most distinctive monument (after Versailles), which from **Granville** onwards is visible across the bay. Beaches hereabouts, however, are no temptation –

dangerous for the most part and flanked by generally tacky resorts. Having come this far, better to head straight on to the delights of the Breton **Côte d'Emeraude** (see *Chapter Four*).

Honfleur

HONFLEUR, the best preserved of the old ports of Normandy, is a perfect seaside town in all but its lack of a beach. It used to have one, but with the accumulation of silt from the Seine the sea has steadily withdrawn, leaving the eighteenth-century waterfront houses of the bd Charles V stranded and a little surreal. The ancient port, however, still functions – the channel to the beautiful **Vieux Bassin** is kept open by regular dredging – and though only pleasure craft now use the moorings in the harbour basin, fishing boats tie up alongside the quay nearby. There is usually fish for sale either directly from the boats or from stalls on the quay, still by right run by fishermen's wives. It's all highly picturesque, a little too upmarket perhaps, but not altogether different to the town that held such appeal for artists in the second half of the nineteenth century. With the construction of a vast new bridge across the mouth of the Seine, which is due for completion in 1993 and will make Honfleur a few minutes' drive from giant Le Havre, this may change. The population is divided as to whether connecting roads should be built to encourage new trade, or bypasses to keep the traffic as far away as possible.

Though the town has modern suburbs and developments, it's the old centre, around the *bassin*, to which you'll inevitably gravitate. At the bassin, slate-fronted houses, each of them one or two storeys higher than seems possible, harmonise despite their tottering and ill-matched forms, into a backdrop which is only excelled by the **Lieutenance** at the harbour entrance. This latter was the dwelling of the King's Lieutenant, and has been the gateway to the inner town from the time that Samuel Champlain sailed from Honfleur to found Quebec in 1608. The church of **St-Stephen** nearby is now a **Musée Maritime**, which with its accompanying ethnographic collection is open for rather formal guided tours in high season (2.30–5.30pm daily, 10.30am–noon as well Sun & holidays). Just behind it are two seventeenth-century salt stores where temporary art exhibitions are staged in summer.

Honfleur's artistic past – and its present concentration of galleries and painters – owes most to the Impressionist Eugène Boudin. He was born and worked in the town, trained the fifteen-year-old Monet, and was joined for various periods by Pissarro, Renoir and Cézanne. There's a fair selec-

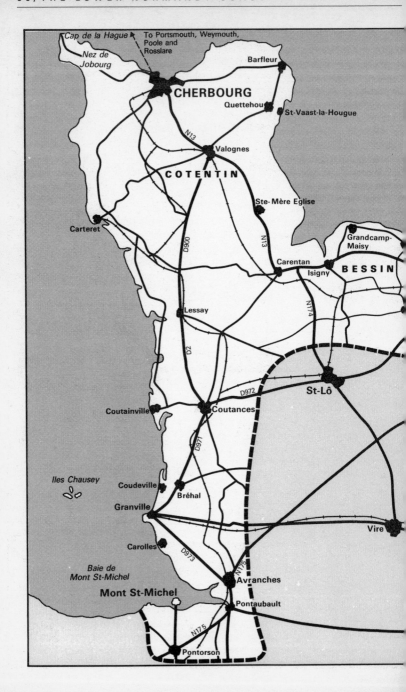

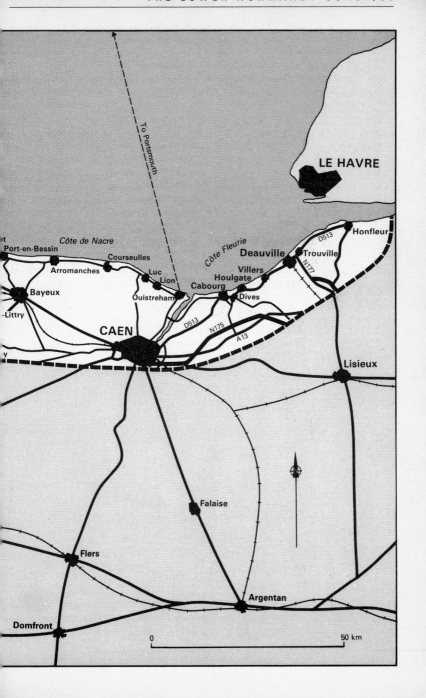

tion of his works at the **Musée Eugène Boudin** and they've a definite appeal here in context, particularly the crayon landscapes. However, it's the Dufys, Marquets, Frieszs, and above all the Monets, alongside, that most impress. The collection is open daily except Tuesday: in summer from 10am until noon and 2 to 6pm, winter from 2.30 to 5pm (& 10am–noon at weekends); closed January to mid-February.

The church of **Ste-Catherine**, with its distinctive detached belfry (one of Monet's favourite subjects), is the town's most remarkable building. It is built almost entirely of wood, supposedly due to economic restraints during the Hundred Years' War. The changing patterns on its tiles, both along the main body and the belfry, delineate religious symbols. Inside, the church is unusually divided into twin equal naves, with one balcony running around both. Nearby, along the rue de l'Homme de Bois are incongruous views which combine the stately backs of what were once shipbuilders' houses with the huge industrial desert of Le Havre's docks in the distance.

A couple of blocks below, past the public gardens by the place Augustin Normand, you can follow the **shipping channel** out towards the mouth of the Seine and the sea. A rusty old pipeline runs alongside, inside which you

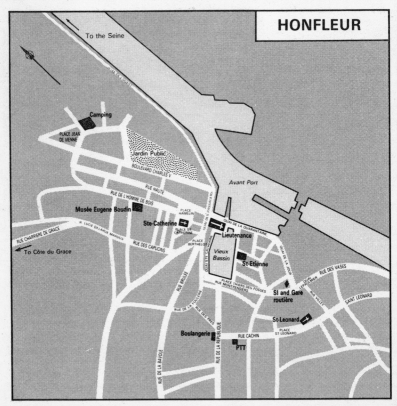

HONFLEUR

To the Seine

Camping
PLACE JEAN DE VIENNE
Jardin Public
BOULEVARD CHARLES V
RUE HAUTE
Avant Port
RUE DE L'HOMME DE BOIS
Musée Eugène Boudin
PLACE HAMELIN
QUAI DE LA QUARANTAINE
Ste-Catherine
PLACE STE CATHERINE
Lieutenance
R. LUCIE DELARUE MARDRUS
RUE DES CAPUCINS
PLACE BERTHELOT
RUE CHARRIÈRE DE GRACE
QUAI STE CATHERINE
QUAI DE LA PLANCHETTE
QUAI DE LA JOUR
RUE DES VASES
To Côte du Grace
Vieux Bassin
St-Étienne
RUE BRÛLÉE
RUE HAUT DES FOSSES
RUE MONTPENSIER
RUE DE L'HOMME DE BOIS
RUE WALTER
SAINT LEONARD
RUE DE LA CHAUSSÉE
RUE DES PRÉS
SI and Gare routière
RUE DE LA VILLE
RUE DE LA RÉPUBLIQUE
St-Leonard
PLACE ST LEONARD
RUE DE LA BAVOLE
Boulangerie
RUE CACHIN
PTT

can hear rats and mice scampering to and from the sea. However, it would not occur even to the most hard-nosed mud-caked sewer rat to swim in the sea once it got there – the shore is a slimy grey wasteland, the water foul and sluggish. Nonetheless, it is possible to slip and squirm your way on to the shingle and then walk along the sea coast, with the beautiful wooded hills of the Côte du Grâce tantalisingly above you. Inland, the grand old houses of ancient aesthetes, and the **Chapelle Notre-Dame de Grâce**, beloved of the Impressionists, nestle dry-footed in the forests.

Practical Details

The best **restaurants**, and liveliest **bar**, are on the rue Haute, between the Boudin museum and the gardens. The bar, *des Amis*, is at no. 35; the restaurants, *Le Crystal* and *Au P'tit Marayeur*, at nos. 3 and 4; a speciality (mainly in October/November) is *crevettes gris*, tiny shrimps eaten with an unsalted Spanish-style bread, *pain brié*. The composer Erik Satie (born in Honfleur) lived on the same street at no. 88.

None of the **hotels** in Honfleur is very affordable. *Des Cascades* (19 cours des Fossés; ☎31.89.05.83) and *Le Moderne* (20 quai Le Paulmier; ☎31.89.44.11) are the cheapest, although the two-star *logis*, *Hostellerie du Belvédère* (36 rue Emile Renouf; ☎31.89.08.13) is not much more expensive. There's a **campsite** at the west end of bd Charles V on place Jean de Vienne. If you need help, the **SI** is just outside the **gare routière** at 33 cours des Fosses. The town is on the direct **bus** route #20 from Caen to Le Havre, with eight buses per day in each direction; the nearest train station is at **Pont l'Evêque**, connected by bus #50 (which also runs to Lisieux).

Lastly, a few incidentals. An excellent *boulangerie*, selling granary and wholemeal breads, is on the corner of the rue des Prés and av de la République; there's a **launderette** at 17 rue Cachin near the St-Leonard church; and the *Salles des Ventes* at 7 rue Nicole auctions off all kinds of unlikely stuff – most actively on summer Sundays.

Along the Côte Fleurie

For the fifteen kilometres **west along the corniche** from Honfleur to Trouville, green fields and fruit trees line the land's edge, and cliffs rise from sandy beaches. The resorts, Villerville most conspicuously, aren't cheap, but they're relatively undeveloped, and if you want to stop by the seaside this is the place to do it. The next section, from Trouville to Cabourg, is the **Norman Riviera**, with Trouville playing at Nice to Deauville's Cannes.

Trouville and Deauville

TROUVILLE retains some semblance of a real town, with a constant population, industries other than tourism and a history that includes Henry V landing on his way to Agincourt. But it is primarily a resort, and has been ever since Napoleon III – whose Empress, Eugénie, fled France from here in 1870 in the yacht of an English admirer – started bringing his court here for the summer in the 1860s. Spectacular villas line the beach, patterned with complex brickwork, and topped by ornate turrets.

One of the Emperor's dukes, looking across the river, saw not marshlands but money, and lots of it, in the form of a racecourse. His vision materialised, and villas appeared between the racecourse and the sea to become **DEAUVILLE**. Now you can lose money on the horses and then cross five streets to lose more in the Casino (where Winston Churchill spent the summer of 1906 gambling every night until five in the morning) and finally lose yourself in the 200 metres of sports and "cure" facilities and private bathing huts that intervene before the *planches*. Beyond this half-kilometre of duckwalk, rows of primary coloured parasols obscure the view of the sea. French exclusiveness and self-esteem oozes from every suntanned pore and a visit to the **SI** on place de la Mairie in Deauville – or by the casino in Trouville – is repaid with some spectacularly revolting brochures (in English). As you might expect, **hotels** are upmarket and overpriced. If desperate, try *Le Lutrin* (48 rue Gambetta; ☎31.88.32.38) in Deauville, *La Paix* (4 place F Moureaux; ☎31.88.35.15) and *Les Charmettes* (22 rue de la Chapelle, ☎31.88.11.67; rooms without showers start at 120F) in Trouville, or one of the three **campsites** (two in Trouville, one in Deauville). One reasonable value **place to eat** in Trouville is the bistro *Les Vapeurs*, opposite the fish market in the harbour.

The **gares SNCF** and **routière** are between the two towns just south of the marina. A possible excuse for staying could be the **American Film Festival** held in Deauville in the first week of September – a festival that's the antithesis of Cannes, with public admission to a wide selection of previews.

Towards Cabourg

The smaller resorts on **towards Cabourg** are equally crowded and equally short of inexpensive hotels. But they're less snobbish, and there are plenty of campsites: *les Falaises* (☎31.91.09.66) at Gonneville-sur-mer; *Camping Simar* (☎31.87.52.41) and *Bellevue* (☎31.87.05.21) straddling the Greenwich Meridian at **VILLERS**. With an eye on the tides, you can also escape the never-ending villas along the promenades, and walk beneath the **Vaches Noires** cliffs from Villers to Houlgate; though with industrial Le Havre so visible across the water it's not an especially picturesque stroll.

Cabourg

At **CABOURG**, you are confronted by little more than an exercise in style – a pure creation for a certain aged class. The town centre fans out in perfect symmetry fronted by the straightest promenade in France. The resort, contemporary with Deauville, seems to have become stuck entirely in the nineteenth century, as typified by the **Grand Hôtel** – one of an outrageous ensemble of buildings around the **Jardins du Casino**. Notices request that you "avoid noise on the beach", and picnics are forbidden. There's an **SI** here with full details on rooms – try the **hotels** *L'Oie qui Fume* (a *logis*, on av de la Brèche-Buhot; ☎31.91.27.79) or *Le Rally* (5 av du Général Leclerc;

☎31.91.27.35). Arriving by **bus** you'll be dropped off at the gardens on av Pasteur; walk through them and turn right down av de la Mer to reach the Jardins du Casino.

PROUST IN CABOURG

As both child and adult, between 1881 and 1914, Marcel Proust stayed repeatedly at the *Grand Hôtel* in Cabourg. The town is the "Balbec" of *Du Côté de Chez Swann,* and the hotel itself now thrives on its Proustian connection. All guests are served with a *madeleine* for breakfast, and Proust's own room is available at a cost of 910F per night (not the most expensive in the hotel by any means). The main dining room, which has a superb sea view, is now called "Le Balbec". For the ambivalent Proust it was "the aquarium"; each night locals would press their faces to its window in wonder at the luxurious life within, "as extraordinary to the poor as the life of strange fishes or molluscs".

Dives

Just across the river from Cabourg is the more interesting – and much older – town of **DIVES**, the port from which William the Conqueror sailed for Hastings. This has nothing in common with the aristocratic resort, other than its significance for Proust, whose dream vision "land's end church of Balbec" is the town's **Notre Dame** church.

Trains run to the joint Dives-Cabourg gare SNCF on Sundays, holidays, and throughout July and August. Breaking a journey here, there's a reasonable **hotel**, the *de la Gare* (☎31.91.24.52), or a **campsite** in between Cabourg and Dives (and a couple of others off the Cabourg–Lisieux road). The town has a lively **Saturday market** around the ancient timbered *halles*; in early August it hosts a **puppet festival**.

Continuing along the coast towards Caen, in **FRANCEVILLE** the main road passes another *logis*, the half-timbered *Hôtel de la Gare* (☎31.24.23.37), with adequate rooms and good food, and the bizarre *Le Light's*, a disco concealed in a German bunker. A little further on, you can turn right, across Pegasus Bridge (see p.67), for direct access to Ouistreham and the Landing Beaches.

Caen

CAEN, capital and largest city of Basse-Normandie, is not a place you're likely to spend much time over. In the protracted months of fighting before its capture in 1944, it was devastated. The central feature is a ring of ramparts that no longer has a castle to protect, and, though there are the scattered spires and buttresses of two abbeys and eight old churches, the wide spaces in between are taken up by roundabouts and junctions. Approaches are along thunderous roads through industrial suburbs – once an economic success story, currently hammered by unemployment.

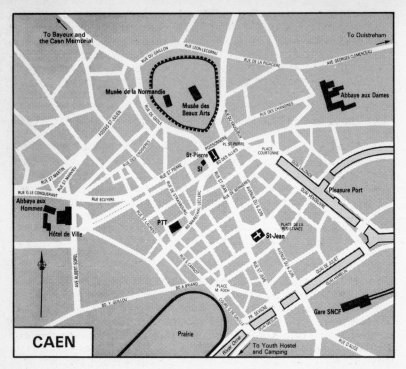

To Bayeux and
the Caen Memorial

To Ouistreham

RUE DU GAILLON
RUE LEON-LECORNU
RUE DE LA PIGACIERE
AVE. GEORGES CLEMENCEAU

Musée de la Normandie

Musée des
Beaux Arts

RUE DES CHANOINES

Abbaye aux Dames

FOSSES ST JULIEN
RUE ST JULIEN
RUE DE GEOLE

POISSONNERIE
RUE D'AUGE

PL. ST PIERRE
PLACE
COURTONNE

RUE DES CROISIERS

St-Pierre
Si

QUAI LONGE

RUE ST PIERRE
RUE ST MARTIN
RUE ST MANVIEU
RUE G.LE CONQUERANT

BD DES ALLIÉS
RUE ST JEAN
RUE DE BERNIÈRES
AVENUE DU 6 JUIN

QUAI VENDEUVRE

Pleasure Port

RUE DE STRASBOURG
RUE ECUYERE

Abbaye aux
Hommes

Hôtel de Ville

RUE ST LAURENT
BD MARECHAL LECLERC

PTT

PLACE DE LA
RESISTANCE

St-Jean

AVE. ALBERT SOREL

RUE E CARNOT

RUE ST JEAN
AVENUE DU 6 JUIN

QUAI DE JUILET
QUAI HAMEL

BD A BRIAND
BD Y GUILLOU

PLACE
M. FOCH

PR. SEVIGNE
COURS C DE CAILLE

Gare SNCF

RUE D'AUGE

Prairie

QUAI MESLIN

River Orne

To Youth Hostel
and Camping

CAEN

Nonetheless, Caen, favoured residence of William the Conqueror, is in parts still impressive. Around the **château ramparts**, a virtue has been made of the necessity of clearing the rubble of the medieval houses which formerly pressed up against the walls. The resulting open green space means that those walls are now fully visible for the first time in centuries. Within are two **museums** (10am–noon & 2–6pm; closed Tues), devoted to Norman history and Fine Arts. The former is unmemorable but the **Beaux Arts** is something of a treat. Amidst comprehensive displays – from fifteenth-century Italian and Flemish primitives to contemporary French artists – it includes masterpieces by Poussin, Géricault, Monet and Bonnard, as well as an exceptional collection of engravings by Dürer and Rembrandt. A walk around the castle walls also gives a fine view of the reconstructed fourteenth-century facade of the church of **St-Pierre**. On the ground, take a look at the church's east end where some magnificent Renaissance stonework has survived intact.

Just to the north of the château lies the complex of **University** buildings, founded in 1432 by Henry VI of England. Their latest acquisition is the largest nuclear particle accelerator in Europe. An expensive toy built with EC money, it has done little for the city's economy.

Over to the west is the **Abbaye aux Hommes**, founded by William the Conqueror and designed to hold his tomb. His burial here, in 1087, was hopelessly undignified. The funeral procession first caught fire and was then held to ransom, as various factions squabbled over his rotting corpse for any spoils they could grab hold of. A man then interrupted the service to object that the grave had been constructed without compensation on the site of his family house, and the assembled nobles had to pay him off before William could finally be laid to rest. During the Revolution the tomb was again ransacked and it now holds at most a solitary thigh-bone rescued from the river. Still, the building itself is a wonderful Romanesque monument, although not enhanced by the latest desecration – "multi-lingual, computer-ized audio-visual visits". Look out for the huge wooden clock to the left of the altar.

The Town Hall alongside, which almost obscures the Abbaye, is housed in what used to be its convent buildings; which would explain why the two blend together with such surprising harmony.

William's queen, Mathilda, lies across the town in the **Abbaye aux Dames**. She had commissioned the building of the abbey church, La Trinité, long before the Conquest. It's starkly impressive, with a gloomy pillared crypt, wonderful stained glass behind the altar, and odd sculptural details like the fish curled up in the holy water.

Practical Details

Most of the centre of Caen is taken up with busy new shopping developments and pedestrian precincts, where the cafés are distinguished by such names as *Fast Food Glamour Vault*. The **shops** are good, possibly the best in Normandy or Brittany if Parisian style is what you're after. There are branches of all the big department stores – *Nouvelles Galeries, Printemps, Bon Marché* – and a fair selection of specialists. Rue Ecuyère has a fine assort-ment of shops full of unusual and cheap oddments; antiques, stuff for collec-tors, and jokes. For books and records, there's a branch of *FNAC* in the Centre Paul Doumer, on the corner of Rue Doumer and Rue Bras, and *L'Arcane University Bookshop* at 6 rue Léon Lecornu also has a large selection of English books. In the Cours des Halles, *Hediard* must be one of the most inspired *épiceries* in the country. The main city **market** takes place on Friday, spreading along both sides of Fosse St-Julien, and there's also a Sunday market in place Courtonne.

The port is also the area where most of the **hotels** are situated, including a number of good, inexpensive ones like the *Univers* (12 quai Vendeuvre; ☎31.85.46.14), the *Weekend* (14 quai Vendeuvre; ☎31.86.39.95), and the *Bernières* (50 rue de Bernières; ☎31.86.01.26). The **youth hostel** (☎31.52.19.96) is a bit further out, southwest of the railway station in the *Foyer Robert-Remé* at 68 bis rue E-Restout. Close by the hostel is the town **campsite** – set beside the river Orne on route de Louvigny (bus #13, stop *Camping*). There's a **launderette**, the *Lavomagic*, at 8 rue Strasbourg.

The prime area for **restaurants** these days is the pedestrianised rue du Vaugueux, which at last count had three serving couscous, two pizzerias, one Chinese eatery and one Madagascan, a fondue place and even a traditional French restaurant. In the rue de Geôle, which runs alongside the western ramparts to place St-Pierre, are some useful Vietnamese and Chinese ones, and another good area to try is around the Abbaye aux Hommes: for a large traditional meal here, go to *Le Boeuf Ferré* at 10 rue des Croisiers, or for lighter nouvelle cuisine, *La Mandarine* at 18 rue Froide.

As to other practicalities, the **SI** is on the central place St-Pierre, and from here regular buses leave for the **gare SNCF** on the south side of the river. The **gare routière** is a few blocks west of the SNCF on rue des Bras. The main services are operated by *Bus Verts*, which run throughout Calvados. Buses to **Ouistreham**, the *Brittany Ferries* terminal port, leave from (and arrive at) the gare SNCF and are timed to coincide with crossings.

The Caen Memorial – A Museum for Peace

North of Caen, at the end of av Marshal-Montgomery, is a brand-new museum, the **Caen Memorial**. It stands on a plateau named after General Eisenhower, which ends on a clifftop beneath which the Germans had their HQ in June and July 1944. Funds and material for it have come from the US, Britain, Canada, East and West Germany, Poland, Czechoslovakia, the USSR and France. It is a war museum with a big and very welcome difference, in that it proclaims itself to be a "Museum for Peace", and for the most part succeeds admirably in that intention.

All visitors have to follow a prescribed route through the ultra-modern building, which with a slightly heavy-handed literalism leads you on a downwards spiral from World War I and the Treaty of Versailles towards the maelstrom of World War II. From the start you hear the voice of Hitler booming in the distance; his image recurs with increasing size and frequency on screens beside you as the events of the 1920s and 1930s are recounted.

The war itself is superbly documented, with a greater emphasis on the minutiae of everyday life in occupied France than on military technology. Nothing is glossed over in the attempt to provide a fully rounded picture of the nation under occupation and at war, and the analysis is always even-handed. The collaborationist Vichy government is set in its context without being excused, with such statements as Pierre Laval's "I wish for the victory of Germany, because without it Bolshevism will spread everywhere" on prominent display alongside a book of the "99 most touching answers of French schoolchildren to the question 'Why do you love Maréchal Petain?'". Secret Nazi reports show how Resistance activity in Normandy grew as the war continued, and what reprisals were taken.

Each visit culminates with three films, each one in a separate auditorium. The first is a harrowing account of D-Day itself; the second traces the course of the rest of the war; and the third makes a forceful moral case for the need to establish lasting peace in the world. This last is very moving without being all that convincing, in that the words of Martin Luther King, uttered in a different cause and at a different time are perhaps not sufficiently relevant to what has come before – particularly in view of his tragic assassination.

Nevertheless, this museum creates something new in a genre which, particularly in Normandy, can all too often seem morally suspect, and the display cannot be recommended too highly for anyone with a serious interest in the war and its lasting legacy. Allow at least two hours for a visit, as the films alone occupy a whole hour. It is open June to August from 9.30am until 10pm, last entry 8.30pm; winter 9.30am to 7.30pm, last entry 6pm. Admission is steep though there are reductions for students, the young and the over-65s, and it's free for World War II veterans. Bus #12 during the week or #14 at the weekend (from the *Tour le Roi* stop in the centre of town) go direct to the museum (about 20min). By car the route is well signposted – if you get lost ask for La Folie Couvrechef, the name of the area.

Ouistreham

OUISTREHAM, connected with Portsmouth since 1986 by ever more frequent ferries, is a major and growing resort. Although the boats are good and convenient, Ouistreham itself is not especially appealing, and most arriving passengers press straight on out. This is one of the channel's simpler ports to leave, as you dock just a few hundred metres from the central square, **place Courbonne***. The main road to Caen, served by regular buses, runs due south from here, and passes close by **Pegasus Bridge**, where a museum and memorial mark the landing site of Allied gliders during the night before D-Day.

If you do stay in Ouistreham, place Courbonne is filled with cafés, **restaurants** and **hotels**, all relishing their new-found opportunity to separate tourists from their leftover francs. *Le Chanel* (79 av Michel-Cabieu; ☎31.96.51.69) is the best value for both food and accommodation (rooms are in a separate building across the street), closely followed by *Le Phare* (place de Gaulle; ☎31.97.13.13). Further down av Michel-Cabieu, towards the church, there's a striking half-timbered cinema, *Le Cabieu*, which might be useful for filling in time before a ferry crossing.

Slightly cheaper **accommodation** options may be found by wandering along the seafront to the main drag of the **beach**, which is edged by clusters of paint-peeling bathing huts, a large casino and a War Museum (recording the local Sword Beach landings). The hotels here can be a bit too run-down, verging on the squalid, but the *Bellevue* (place A-Thomas; ☎31.97.17.43) and the *St-Georges* (51 av Andry; ☎31.97.18.79) are good enough. Continuing along the coast, it's only a short – even walkable – distance to a succession of very pleasant quiet resorts, such as **Luc** and **Lion**, covered on p.72.

Bayeux

BAYEUX, with its perfectly preserved medieval ensemble, magnificent Cathedral, and world-famous Tapestry, is only fifteen minutes by train from Caen. It's a smaller and much more intimate city, and a far more enjoyable place to visit despite the large crowds of summer tourists.

It was the first French city to be liberated in 1944, somehow managing to escape any serious damage despite being only ten kilometres from the invasion beaches. A monument stands where an emotional General de Gaulle made his first speech upon returning to French soil.

---

* Drivers catching a ferry back to England in high season should leave good time to negotiate the clogged-up traffic of Ouistreham town centre.

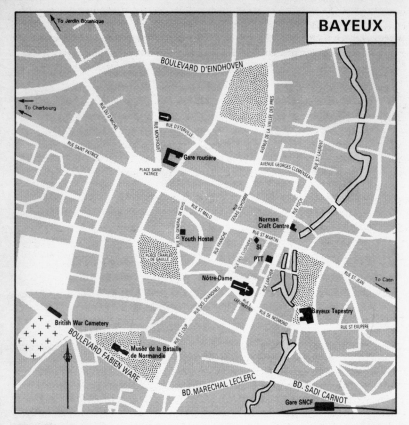

The Tapestry

Centre Guillaume le Conquérant, rue de Nesmond. Open every day (mid-May to mid-Sept 9am–7pm; mid-March to mid-May & mid-Sept to mid-Oct, Mon–Sat 9am–12.30pm & 2–6.30pm, Sun 9am–7pm; rest of the year, 9.30am–12.30pm & 2–6pm).

The **Bayeux Tapestry**, now housed in its own specially-designed museum, is a seventy-metre strip of linen which recounts the story of the Norman Conquest of England. Although embroidered nine centuries ago, the brilliance of its coloured wools has barely faded, and the tale is enlivened throughout with scenes of medieval life, popular fables and mythical beasts. The quality of the draughtsmanship, and the sheer vigour and detail, are stunning. The work is thought to have been done by nuns in England, working under commission from Bishop Oddo, William's half-brother, for the inauguration of Bayeux Cathedral in 1077.

The tapestry looks – and reads – like a modern comic strip. It's thought to be historically accurate, albeit presented inevitably from a Norman perspective. The villain of the piece is King Harold, with his dastardly little moustache and shifty eyes; he swears an oath to accept William as King of England, and then takes the throne for himself (with a particularly smug expression on his face). William, the noble hero, crosses the Channel and defeats the English armies at Hastings. It's such a bullish and effective piece of propaganda that Napoleon exhibited it in Paris, to show that it was possible to invade England.

Visits are well planned, if slightly tortuous. You can't actually touch, or linger over, the tapestry itself, which is in any case kept for its preservation under very dim light. However, the display is excellent. First of all, there is a slide show, projected on to billowing sheets of canvas hung as sails; you then pass along a photographic replica of the tapestry, with enlargements and detailed commentaries, before coming to a plush cinema for a general introductory film (French and English-language versions alternate). By the time you come to the real thing, you can do without the taped headsets (and their synthesized "medieval" music), and follow the story at your own pace.

The Town

Admission tickets for the tapestry are also valid for the **Musée Baron-Gérard**, a rather dull jumble of porcelain and lace, next to the Cathedral. The huge Liberty Tree in the courtyard, planted in 1797, is more exciting – though it is comprehensively dwarfed by the main Romanesque facade of the **Cathédrale Notre-Dame**. This is a beautifully constructed church – Bishop Oddo's Romanesque plan for the most part sensitively merged with Gothic additions. The crypt, entirely original, is particularly wonderful with its frescoes of angels playing trumpets and bagpipes, looking exhausted by their eternal performance. Along the nave is some tremendous twelfth-century sculpture.

Set behind massive guns, next to the ring road on the western side of Bayeux, the **Musée de la Bataille de Normandie** is an old-style war museum which with any luck will be driven out of business by the new one in Caen. Privately owned and highly subjective, it combines grossly offensive interpretations with showroom mannequins posturing in Nazi uniforms, the emphasis firmly on hardware rather than humans. By way of example, unattributed pages summarising the war's death toll, on display near the exit, refer to Italian Resistance claims of 150,000 dead as "typical Communist propaganda flavoured with Italian peasant exaggeration". Very much in keeping with this tone – an unintended irony presumably – are the Nazi leaflets distributed to the advancing US forces, predicting World War III against the Russians. It all makes a very sorry contrast with the understated and touching **British War Cemetery** immediately across the road (see box on p.73).

If you need to escape somewhere more peaceful, there's a **Jardin Botanique** to the north of the town, and in the centre, astride the river Aure, a **watermill**.

Practical Details

None of Bayeux's **hotels** is especially cheap. *Notre Dame* (44 rue des Cuisiniers; ☎31.92.87.24) and *de la Gare* (26 place de la Gare; ☎31.92.10.70) are the best value; the *Argouges* (21 rue St-Patrice; ☎31.92.88.86) is pricier but old and very stylish. Something which calls itself the *Family Home* at 39 rue Général-du-Dais (☎31.92.15.22), a little north of the cathedral, doubles up as the **youth hostel**; its prices are above usual odds and it's a bit self-consciously jolly. Final options are the two **municipal accommodation centres**, or *Foyers des Jeunes Travailleurs*, run by the **SI** (whom you'll find at 1 rue des Cuisiniers, ☎31.92.16.26); ring for details.

As for food, most of the **restaurants** are in the pedestrianised rue Saint-Jean – *La Rapière* at no. 53 is the most popular though they all tend to be very full. Try the *Angevin* (open on Sunday evening) in rue Genas Duhomme if the others are too busy. **Buses** leave from the central place St-Patrice; the **gare SNCF** is on the other side of town. There's a **launderette** next to the Norman Craft Centre (whose activities centre around teaching tourists How to Make Tapestries) in place aux Pommes.

Southwest from Bayeux

Heading **southwest from Bayeux**, towards St-Lô, you pass close to two remarkable buildings: the Abbaye de Cerisy-la-Forêt and Château de Balleroy. Neither is easy to get to without transport, but with a bike or car they shouldn't be missed.

Cerisy

CERISY-LA-FORÊT is most pleasurably reached via Le Molay-Littry, which has a **mining museum** and *Raleigh* cycle shop. An eleventh-century Romanesque abbey, its triple tiers of windows and arches, lapping light into its cream stone, make you sigh in wonder at the skills of medieval Norman masons. It is open (for free) from 9am until 6pm daily.

Balleroy

At **BALLEROY**, eight and a half kilometres south of Cerisy across the D572, you switch to an era when architects ruled over craftsmen. The main street of the village leads straight to the **château**, masterpiece of the celebrated seventeenth-century architect François Mansard. It stands like a faultlessly reasoned and dogmatic argument for the power of its owners and their class and, suitably enough, the present owner is the American press magnate Malcolm S. Forbes, pal of presidents Nixon, Ford and Reagan. You can tour the house to see its eclectic furnishings, pieces of modern sculpture, and an original *salon* – with superb royal portraits by Mignard.

The focus, however, is on Forbes himself. An acquisitor untrammelled by financial restraint – he owns the world's largest collection of Fabergé jewelled eggs (which were almost scrambled by a fire early in 1990) and has a palace in Tangier, containing 100,000 lead soldiers, scene of a notoriously extravagant seventieth birthday party – he has created at Balleroy a museum to his principal passion, **ballooning**. It's all a bit absurd, beginning with some interesting history, but degenerating into egomania: photos of Malcolm S. Forbes in various Forbes balloons winning various Forbes prizes (as seen, of course, in his own *Forbes Magazine*). Admission is expensive and seems a poor substitute for indulging in the real thing, which despite all impressions is more than a hobby for self-publicising millionaires. The château is open every day except Wednesday (9am–noon & 2–6pm), as is the museum (April–Oct only).

The Landing Beaches

It is hard now to picture the scene at dawn on **D-Day**, June 6 1944, when Allied troops landed along the Norman coast from the mouth of the Orne to Les Dunes de Varneville on the Cotentin peninsula*. For the most part, these are innocuous beaches backed by gentle dunes, and yet this foothold in Europe was won at the cost of 100,000 lives. That the invasion happened here, and not nearer to Germany, was partly due to the failure of the Canadian raid on Dieppe (see p.38) in 1942.

The **beaches** are still often referred to by their wartime codenames. The British and Commonwealth forces landed on **Sword, Juno**, and **Gold** beaches between Ouistreham and Arromanches; the Americans further west on **Omaha** and **Utah** beaches. Physical traces of the fighting are rare, though at Arromanches the remains are visible of one of the prefabricated Mulberry harbours that made such large-scale landings possible, and at Pointe du Hoc, the cliff heights are still deeply pitted with German bunkers and shell-holes. Elsewhere, the reminders are **cemeteries** – British and Commonwealth, American and German, each highly distinct in character – and **war museums**, examples of which you'll find in almost every coastal town.

The D-Day events provide a focus for most foreign visitors to this part of the coast; travelling through, you are bound to come across veterans, and their descendants, paying their respects. Taken simply as holiday territory, however, some of the villages and towns can offer rewards. They are traditional seaside resorts, without the inflated prices or flashiness of the Deauville area – old-fashioned, seafront villages, with rows of boarding houses and little wooden bathing huts that must have been kept in storage somewhere during the war. And increasingly there is **windsurfing** on offer – better suited to these resorts than chilly (north-facing) bathing.

In theory **Bus Verts** run all along this coast. **From Bayeux**, bus #74 goes to Arromanches and Corseulles, bus #70 to Port-en-Bessin and Vierville, bus #7 to Isigny. **From Caen**, bus #30 runs directly inland to Isigny via Bayeux, bus #1 to Ouistreham and on to Luc. None of these services, however, except for those linking Caen with the Ouistreham ferries, is all that reliable; you're better off cycling, or at least trying to hitch while you wait for the bus.

* The "D" in "D-Day" stands simply for "day"; hence it is known as "*J-Jour*" in France.

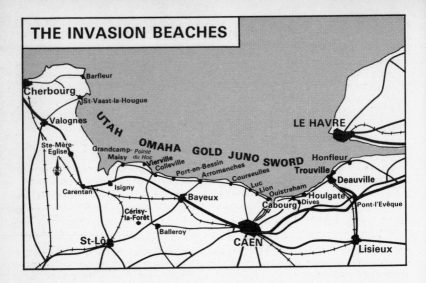

THE INVASION BEACHES

Ouistreham to Arromanches: Sword and Juno beaches

The coast along Sword and Juno beaches is generally featureless – but the towns themselves are welcoming. A long promenade curves by the sea all the way from Ouistreham to Lion – it's built-up, though always in a low-key way.

COLLEVILLE-MONTGOMERY, the first village after the port, is one of the few "Montgomeries" in the area really to be named after the British general rather than his Norman ancestors. It's not otherwise distinguished. **COURSEULLES** is a bit more of a town, with an enjoyable Friday market in an old square set back from the sea, and, allegedly, the best oysters in Normandy. Its main activity, though, is as a yachting port, and apart from an excellent crêperie, *du Moulin*, on the outskirts, there's not much of a choice of hotels and restaurants.

Attractive individual seaside hotels are scattered all along this coast, meaning that ferry passengers have a choice of several *logis* for a first- or last-night stop. *L'Océanide* (58 rue de Gal-Leclerc; ☎31.96.32.50) in **LANGRUNE** is definitely one of the best, while the *Hotel de la Breche* (rue du Dr Turgis; ☎31.97.20.40) in **HERMANVILLE**, which has been weathered virtually to the point of extinction, seems to offer a quite spectacularly soporific time.

If you're looking for atmosphere – albeit sedate – **LUC-SUR-MER**, eleven kilometres from Ouistreham, is probably the best place to stop along here; a gentle resort with a small wooden pier, neon-lit crêpe-stands, and tearooms along the promenade. The **hotel** *Beau Rivage* (1 rue du Dr-Charcot; ☎31.96.49.51) is reasonable, and there's a Senegalese restaurant, *Timiss*, which was opened by the holidaying president of Senegal. At 1 place de l'Etoile, on the main (inland) road, the *Crepuscule* **restaurant** specialises in paella and couscous.

THE WAR CEMETERIES

The war cemeteries of the Norman countryside are filled with foreigners; most of the French war dead are buried in the churchyards of their home towns. After the war, some people felt that the soldiers should remain buried in their original make-shift graves. One farmer, for instance, himself buried a Canadian and a German in his farmyard where they fell, and vowed to keep them there forever. Instead, commissions went about gathering the remains into purpose-built cemeteries devoted to the separate warring nations. It is both a moving and a salutary experience to visit these cemeteries, and to consider their contrasting styles.

The **British** and **Commonwealth** cemeteries are magnificently maintained, and open in every sense. They tend not to be screened off with hedges or walls, or to be forbidding expanses of manicured lawn, but instead intimate, punctuated with bright flowers. The family of each soldier was invited to suggest an inscription for his tomb, making each grave very personal, and yet part of a common attempt to bring some meaning to the carnage. Some epitaphs are questioning – "One day we will under-stand"; some are accepting – "Our lad at rest"; some matter of fact, simply giving the home address; some patriotic, quoting the "corner of a foreign field that is forever England". And interspersed among them all, the chilling refrain of the anonymous "A soldier . . . known unto God". Thus the cemetery at **Ryes**, where so many of the graves bear the date of D-Day, and so many of the victims are under twenty, remains immediate and accessible – each grave clearly contains a unique individual. Even the monumental sculpture is subdued, a very British sort of fumbling for the decent thing to say. The understatement of the memorial at **Bayeux**, with its painfully contrived Latin epigram commemorating the return as liberators of "those whom William conquered", conveys an entirely appropriate humility and deep sadness.

An even more eloquent testimony to the futility of war is afforded by the **German** cemeteries, filled with soldiers who served a cause so despicable as to render any talk of "nobility" or "sacrifice" simply obscene. What such cemeteries might have been like had the Nazis won doesn't bear contemplation. As it is, they are sombre places, inconspicuous to minimise the bitterness they must still arouse. At **Orglandes** ten thousand are buried, three to each of the plain headstones set in the long flat lawn, almost hidden behind an anonymous wall. There are no noble slogans and the plain entrance is without a dedicatory monument. At the superb site of **Mont d'Huisnes** near Mont St-Michel, the circular mausoleum holds another ten thousand, filed away in cold concrete tiers. There is no attempt to defend the indefensible, and yet one feels an overpowering sense of sorrow – that there is nothing to be said in such a place bitterly underlines the sheer waste and stupidity.

The largest **American** cemetery is at **St-Laurent-sur-mer** near the Pointe du Hoc. Here by contrast the atmosphere is one of certainty. The rows of crosses are so neat, so clinical, as to give the appearance of graph paper. At one end, a muscular giant dominates a huge array of battlefield plans and diagrams, covered with surging arrows and pincer movements. Endless rows of impersonal graves stretch away into the distance; there are no individual epitaphs, just gold lettering for a few exceptional warriors. The place is like a balance sheet or corporate report; the implication is that it is all "worth it". This seems something more than a mere difference of emphasis, explicable in terms of national style. The monuments insist so loudly on their own objectivity; your response to the tragedy is so specifically prescribed. The American cemetery is the only one which has placards telling you where to walk, what to wear, and how to behave. It attempts to preclude an individual, emotional response. What is so alarming is that for all its lip-service to "humility" it seems to prefer the ancient myths of martial glory; and above all that it leaves you with the feeling that the Americans are the only ones who really wouldn't mind having another war.

Arromanches

At **ARROMANCHES** an artificial **Mulberry harbour**, "Port Winston", protected the landings of two and a half million men and half a million vehicles during the invasion. Its bulky remains are a strange intrusion on the beach and shallow sea bed. There are war memorials everywhere, with Jesus and Mary high up on the cliffs above the invasion site and helicopter trips available to overlook the area. In spite of which, it somehow manages to be quite a cheerful place to stay, with a lively pedestrian street of bars and brasseries, and a long expanse of sand where you can hire windsurf boards. Among **hotels**, *La Marine* (mid-Feb to Nov only, quai Canada; ☎31.22.34.19) is a little expensive but has an excellent restaurant overlooking the sea; the *Normandie* (also mid-Feb to Nov, 5 place du 6 Juin; ☎31.22.34.32) may look better value but you'll have to put up with rude staff.

West to Cotentin: Omaha and Utah beaches

PORT-EN-BESSIN, the nearest beach resort to Bayeux (on the #70 bus route), has a thriving fishing industry and – rare on this coast – a sheltered, enclosed site. The fish, caught off Devon and Cornwall, are auctioned three times a week. It's an attractive, unaffected place and a promising stop – try the **hotel** *de la Marine* (Feb–Nov, ☎31.21.70.08) on quai Letourner.

At **ST-LAURENT** is the larger of the two **American war cemeteries**; unlike the British and Commonwealth forces, the Americans repatriated most of their dead. It's a disturbing place, described in detail on the previous page. Just beyond St-Laurent, at **VIERVILLE**, the twin to Arromanches' Mulberry harbour was sited. It lasted only thirteen days before breaking up in a storm. There's a **youth hostel** in the Stade Municipal, open June to September (☎31.22.00.33).

Further round the coast, more dramatic American landings took place along the cliff heights of the **POINTE DU HOC**, still today deeply pitted with German bunkers and shell-holes. Standing amidst the scarred earth and rusty barbed wire, looking down to the rocks at the base of the cliff, it seems inconceivable that the first US sergeant was at the top five minutes after landing, and the whole complex taken within another quarter of an hour.

Grandcamp-Maisy

GRANDCAMP-MAISY, centred on its fishing harbour and market, has a good **campsite**, the *Camping du Juncal* (☎31.22.61.44), and the **hotels** *du Guesclin* (4 quai Crampon; ☎31.22.64.22) and *Grandcopaise* (84 rue A-Briand; ☎31.22.63.44). **ISIGNY** nearby is renowned for its dairy products, butter in particular; though of no great beauty or interest, it does have a cheap **hotel**, *du Commerce* (5 rue E-Demagny; ☎31.22.01.44), if you're stuck.

Moving on to the **Cotentin peninsula**, the D913 continues around Utah Beach. Inland on the N13 is the market town of **STE-MERE EGLISE**, whose church featured in the film *The Longest Day* – with an unfortunate US paratrooper dangling from its steeple during the heavy fighting. The film was based on fact and the man in question used to return occasionally to re-enact and commemorate his ordeal.

Cherbourg and Around

If the murky metropolis of **CHERBOURG** is your port of arrival, best to head straight out and on. The **gares SNCF** and **routière** are on either side of av Millet – five minutes' walk from the ferry terminal behind the inner dock. The town itself is almost devoid of interest. Napoleon inaugurated the transformation of what had been a rather poor, but perfectly situated, natural harbour into a major transatlantic port, by means of massive artificial breakwaters. An equestrian statue commemorates his boast that in Cherbourg he would "recreate the wonders of Egypt". But there are no pyramids, and if you're waiting for a boat the best way of filling time is to settle into a **restau-**

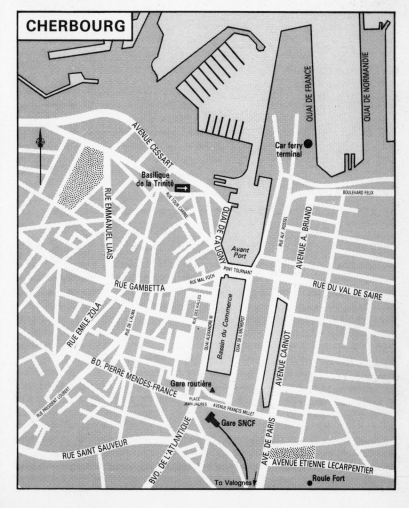

CHERBOURG

rant. Along the quai de Caligny there are some excellent places; *Le Brigueville* at no.16 is a new restaurant with a good 69F menu; while the *Café de Paris* is ideal for an expensive last-night blow-out, with its 1930s decor and very fresh fish. Don't, however, leave your food shopping for the town. Unless you hit the Thursday **market**, held around rue des Halles, there are few delights to be had. The *Le Continent* hypermarket, a real monster opposite the ferry quay, is the standard fallback.

For walking off a lunch, the only area that really encourages a ramble is over by the **Basilique de la Trinité** and the town **beach** – an unexpected pleasure, even if you wouldn't dream of swimming from it. Over to the south, back behind the stations, you could alternatively climb up to **Roule Fort** for a view of the whole port; the fort itself contains a museum of the war and liberation.

If you need to stay, there are enough **hotels** to feel reasonably sure of finding a room, if not perhaps a cheap one. The *Croix de Malte* (5 rue des Halles; ☎33.43.19.16) and *de la Gare* (10 place Jean-Jaurès; ☎33.43.06.81) are possibilities; *Divette* (rue Louis-XVI; ☎33.43.21.04) perhaps the most pleasant choice.

East from Cherbourg

East from Cherbourg, the **D901** switchbacks through a series of valleys, past Tourlaville and Gringor, to the sea at Barfleur. If you're cycling, you'd do best to go by way of Valognes, inland.

Barfleur

BARFLEUR, now a pleasant little harbour village, was once, seven centuries ago, the biggest port in Normandy. The population has since dwindled from nine thousand to six hundred, and fortunes have diminished alongside – most recently through the advent of a strain of plankton which poisoned the mussel harvest. The more modestky priced **hotels** include the *du Phare* (March–Oct only, ☎33.54.02.07) and *Le Moderne* (closed Feb to mid-Mar, 1 place du Gal-de-Gaulle; ☎33.23.12.44). Near the town, half an hour or so's walk, is the **Gatteville lighthouse**, the tallest in France, guarding the rocks on which William, the son and heir of Henry I of England, was drowned, together with 300 nobles, in 1120.

St-Vaast

ST-VAAST-LA-HOUGUE, eleven kilometres south, is more of a resort, with lots of tiny Channel-crossing yachts moored in the bay where Edward III landed on his way to Crecy. The **hotel** *de France et des Fuchsias* (18 rue Foch; ☎33.54.42.26) is a good stopover for the ferry. On the narrow spit of sand called **La Hougue** there are various sporting facilities, such as tennis courts and a diving club, although the tip itself is a sealed-off military installation; the fortifications are graceful, courtesy (as ever) of Vauban. The whole area is at its best at high tide; low tide reveals, especially on the sheltered inland side, bleak muddy flats dotted with (some of the country's best-reputed) oyster beds.

Valognes

VALOGNES, through the woods from St-Vaast, is somewhat ludicrously passed off in tourist handouts as "the Versailles of Normandy". That may have been a fair description before the war, when the region was full of aristocratic mansions. Now, only a scattering of fine old houses remains, and all Valognes has to show for itself is a cider museum, a little public garden, and a big empty square – activated only for the Friday **market**. But it's again a quiet, convenient alternative to waiting about in Cherbourg, and the country lanes around are enjoyable. The rambling ivy-coated *logis*, the *Hôtel du Agriculture* (16 rue L-Delisle; ☎33.40.00.21) is the best of several inexpensive **hotels**, and serves top-quality food.

La Hague and the West Coast

The D901 **west from Cherbourg** leads to **LA HAGUE**, the northern tip of the Cotentin. The cape is approached by wild and isolated countryside, where you can lean against the wind, watch waves smashing against the rocks, or sunbathe in a spring profusion of wild flowers. The **Cap Hague** nuclear re-processing plant should, however, keep you well away from the water. Like its sister installation at Sellafield, it is designed to treat spent nuclear fuel, including the "hotter" thermal oxide fuel used by Advanced Gas-Cooled Reactors (AGRs), and it discharges "low-level" radioactive waste into the sea. Originally its re-processing was supposed to include waste from such countries as West Germany, Sweden and Holland, but the plant has recently come under pressure to abandon plans for a further extension in view of the fact that it has been consistently unable to meet its commercial contracts. In February 1980 the Greenpeace ship *Rainbow Warrior* chased a ship bringing spent Japanese fuel into Cherbourg harbour. The *Rainbow Warrior*'s crew were arrested, but all charges were dropped when 3000 Cherbourg dockers threatened to strike in their support.

From the cape, bracken-covered hills and narrow valleys run west to the cliffs of the **Nez de Jobourg**. Local optimism claims these as the highest in Europe; they are at least dramatic. On the other side, facing north, **PORT RACINE** proclaims itself more plausibly the smallest port in France. **Accommodation** is distinctly lacking in these half tumbled down villages. There are **campsites** at Omonville-la-Rogue, Vauville, and further afield at **URVILLE-NACQUERVILLE**, which also has the **hotel** *Beaurivage* (☎33.03.52.40).

South of La Hague a great curve of sand – some of it military training ground – takes the land's edge to **FLAMANVILLE** and another nuclear installation. But the next two sweeps of beach down to **CARTERET**, with sand dunes like miniature mountain ranges, are among the best **beaches** in Normandy if you have transport and want solitude. There are no resorts, no hotels, and just two **campsites**, at Le Rozel and Surtainville.

The road around the headland joins the main **D900** at **LESSAY**, which has an important Romanesque monastery. Until the war it was one of the few early Norman churches still intact. When it had to be restored afterwards, the job was done using not only the original stone but also the original tools and methods. The square central tower is similar to that which collapsed centuries ago on Mont St-Michel.

If you have time, it's worth straying east of the main roads **towards Coutances**, and spending a while on the **D57**, enjoying the magnificent countryside. The village square of **FEUGERES** is completely taken up by an amazing tangle of warped wood, once some sort of cider press and mill. From there on to **LE MESNILBUS**, which has a **hotel** in the *Auberge des Bonnes Gens*, the undulating meadows are filled with rich flowers and sleek animals placidly waiting to be eaten.

Coutances

COUTANCES is a lovely old hill-town – confined by its site to just one main street. Its **Cathédrale de Notre-Dame** dominates the countryside in every direction, Gothic essentially yet very Norman in its unconventional blending of architectural traditions. The light stone is seen to advantage in the *Sons et Lumières* – unusually tasteful – held on Sunday evenings and throughout the summer. Also illuminated (and left open) on summer sights are the **Jardins Publiques**, highly formal gardens with smooth rolling lawns, a well of flowers, a fountain of obelisks and an odd ziggurat of hedges. They enclose a small museum with a rather dull collection of paintings but a nice line in pretentious art exhibitions.

If you stay, the **SI** in the modern *Les Unelles* cultural centre will be happy to find you a room. The best place is the **hotel** *Relais du Viaduc* (☎33.45.02.68) at the junction of the D7 and the D971 to the south of the town, which has the unusual distinction of being both a *logis de France* and a *Routiers*, and the food to deserve both and more.

COUTAINVILLE, the nearest resort to Coutances, is a large beach sprawl, crammed with bronzed and glamorous posers and their turbo-charged status symbols. **MONTMARTIN** and **HAUTEVILLE** are a bit more manageable and down-to-earth.

Granville to Avranches

GRANVILLE guards the Norman approaches to the bay of Mont St-Michel, facing across to Cancale in Brittany. It is the most vibrant and energetic place in the region and a popular resort, with its citadel, the rather severe **Haut Ville**, and ferries out to the Channel Islands and offshore Iles Chausey. It had an unexpected brush with destiny on March 9 1945, when it was overrun for an hour and a half by German commandoes from Jersey. Most of the shops and hotels are in the new town towards the **SNCF station**, and in view of the numbers of visitors Granville attracts it's well worth booking a **hotel** room in advance, at for example the *Terminus* (5 place de la Gare; ☎33.50.02.05) or

Clemenceau (1 rue G-Clemenceau; ☎33.50.00.05). For a good simple meal, grilled over an open fire, try *L'Echanguette* at 24 rue St-Jean.

The **Iles Chausey** are now an uninviting and virtually uninhabited wasteland, though at one time their quarries provided the granite that built the Mont. They may once have been part of the ancient Forest of Scissy, which was otherwise submerged below the sea twelve centuries ago.

If you prefer to be out of town, the coastal countryside is best to the **north**, although the villages tend to be non-events. As well as the ubiquitous windsurfers, the huge flat sands attract hordes of sand-yachters. Among **accommodation** possibilities, **BREVILLE** has the small *Auberge des Quatre Routes* (☎33.50.20.10); **COUDEVILLE** two good campsites on its long beach, the *Phare-Ouest* (☎33.61.67.08) and the *Dunes* (☎33.51.76.07), and a large (and highly unrecommended) hotel in a converted sanatorium, the *Relais des Iles*.

To the **south**, **JULLOUVILLE** is younger, more upbeat and very tacky, with an endless drag of amusements, fast-food joints and soda bars. **CAROLLES** has a good beach, but little more; its one hotel is uninviting. At **ST-JEAN-LE-THOMAS**, a single street leading up to a beach, the bay becomes so narrow that at low tide it is possible to walk across to Mont St-Michel. However, as the notices advise, "It's dangerous to risk you in the bay during the rising tide. This can surprise you at each time". They have a special telephone line with details of the times of the tides, on ☎33.50.02.67.

Avranches

AVRANCHES is the nearest large town to Mont St-Michel and it has always had close connections with the abbey. The Mont's original church was in fact founded by a bishop of Avranches, spurred by Saint Michael who reputedly became so impatient with the lack of progress that he prodded a hole in the bishop's skull (it is displayed in Avranches' St-Gervais basilica). Robert of Torigny, a subsequent abbot of Mont St-Michel, played host in the town on several occasions to Henry II of England, the most memorable being when Henry was obliged, barefooted and bare-headed, to do public penance for the murder of Thomas-à-Becket. The arena for this act of contrition was Avranches Cathedral, designed by Robert himself, though without expertise; it swiftly "crumbled and fell for want of proper support" and all that marks the site is a fenced-off platform. A more vivid evocation of the area's medieval splendours comes from the illuminated manuscripts, mostly from the Mont, on display in the town **museum** (Easter–Sept, 9am–noon & 2–6pm; closed Tues).

Avranches is a bit relentlessly cheery, with piped disco music in the streets in summer. Still, it does have decidedly good views across to the Mont from its hillside position, a lively Thursday **market** and some reasonable **hotels**, such as *Le Central* (2–4 rue du Jardin des Plantes; ☎33.58.16.59) and *Bellevue* (2 place du Général Patton; ☎33.58.01.10). The **gare SNCF** is a long way below the town centre.

If you're **camping**, a better base for the Mont than Avranches would be the *La Selune* site (☎33.58.41.30) at **PONTAUBAULT**, to the south.

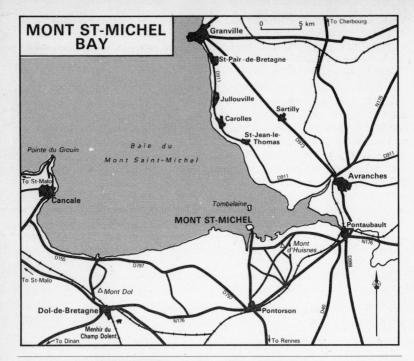

MONT ST-MICHEL

The island of **MONT ST-MICHEL** was once known as "the Mount in Peril from the Sea". The Archangel Michael was its vigorous protector, the most militant spirit of the Church Militant, a warrior against the threat of paganism who was in the habit of leaping from rock to rock in titanic struggles with evil.

The Mont is barely an island any more – the causeway that now leads to it is never submerged, and is silting up to either side. But for at least a hundred years of its history the abbey was literally under siege. It was never captured, not even when the English had a permanent fort on nearby Tombelaine, and it took the Revolution to close it down. Although it was a large community – a fortress town – there were never more than forty monks. The Benedictines were allowed to return on the Abbey's 1000th anniversary in 1966; today, three nuns and three monks maintain a presence.

The Abbey church, long known as the *Merveille*, is visible from all around the bay, and it becomes if anything more awe-inspiring the closer you approach. In Maupassant's words :

> *I reached the huge pile of rocks which bears the little city dominated by the great church. Climbing the steep narrow street, I entered the most wonderful Gothic building ever made for God on this earth, a building as vast as a town, full of low*

rooms under oppressive ceilings and lofty galleries supported by frail pillars. I entered that gigantic granite jewel, which is as delicate as a piece of lacework, thronged with towers and slender belfries which thrust into the blue sky of day and the black sky of night their strange heads bristling with chimeras, devils, fantastic beasts and monstrous flowers, and which are linked together by carved arches of intricate design.

The Mont's rock comes to a sharp point just below what is now the transept of **the church**. The Chausey granite used in its construction was sculpted to match the exact contours of the hill. Space was always limited, and yet the building has grown through the centuries, with an architectural ingenuity that constantly surprises in its geometry – witness the shock of emerging into the light of the cloisters from the sombre Great Hall. The building of the monastery was not, however, a smooth progression; the original church, choir, nave and tower all had to be replaced after collapsing. The style of decoration has varied, too, along with the architecture. That you now walk through halls of plain grey stones is a reflection of modern taste, specifically that of the director of the French Department of Antiquities. In the Middle Ages, the walls would have been festooned with tapestries and frescoes.

To visit the abbey it's obligatory to join a **tour**. These run from 9.30am to 5.30pm in summer, 10am to noon and 1.30 to 4pm in winter; a timetable at the entrance lists those in English. The visit lasts for about an hour, and the guides are informative and expert. There is a church service at 12.15pm every day, with a crèche provided below for under-8s.

The base of Mont St-Michel rests on a primeval slime of sand and mud. Just above that, but just as unpleasantly slimy, is a jumble of over-priced postcard and souvenir shops, maintaining the ancient tradition of separating pilgrims from their money. An absurd **Musée d'Histoire** here contains such edifying specimens as a wax model of a woman drowning in a sea of mud.

More interest is to be had from the **North Tower**, from which you can watch the tide sweep in across the bay. Especially for the high tides of the equinoxes (September and March), large crowds gather to watch the waters rush in – like a foaming galloping horse, as the hype would have it. Seagulls wheel away in alarm, and those foolish enough to be wandering too late on the sands toward Tombelaine have to sprint to safety.

Practical Details

The island's **hotels** and **restaurants** can be predictably expensive; the most famous, the hotel *La Mère Poulard* (☎33.60.14.02), uses the time-honoured legend of its fluffy omelettes to justify extortionate charges – possibly worth the test if you're feeling rich. Higher up the one twisting street, though, prices fall to surprisingly realistic levels. The *Hôtel Croix Blanche* (☎33.60.14.04) has very inexpensive rooms – at a premium in summer (like all on the Mont) – and an exceptional restaurant.

If you're visiting by car, it's best to **park** on the mainland well short of the Mont, in order both to enjoy the walk across the causeway and to avoid hefty parking fees.

Pontorson

Most visitors to Mont St-Michel find themselves lodging either at Avranches or **PONTORSON**, six kilometres distant. The latter has the nearest **SNCF station** – connected to the Mont by an overpriced bus service (but as ever hiring cycles, too). Nothing much about Pontorson itself is worth staying for, although the café attached to the station isn't bad. The **hotels** are ordinary, but the *Montgomery* (13 rue du Cuesnon; ☎33.60.00.09) has a very distinguished restaurant – worth saving money on a room to try. The best budget hotel is the *de France* (2 rue Rennes; ☎33.60.29.17), next to the level crossing; it has a late, youthful bar, with a pool table and a good jukebox.

The most direct **route from Pontorson to the Mont** runs alongside the river Couesnon, which marks the Normandy-Brittany border. The sands at the mouth of the Couesnon are those from which Harold can be seen rescuing two floundering soldiers in the Bayeux Tapestry, in the days when he and William were still getting on with each other. The sheep that graze on the scrubby grass at the sea's edge provide meat for the morbidly-named local delicacy *mouton pré-salé* – the pastures ensure that they are conveniently "pre-salted".

A more roundabout road to the abbey can take you to the **German war cemetery** at **MONT D'HUISNES**, a grim and unforgettable concrete mausoleum on a tiny hill (see p.73).

travel details

Trains

From Cherbourg frequently to Caen (1hr 15min) and Paris (3hr 15min).

From Trouville-Deauville to Lisieux (30min) and Paris (2hr); about 6 daily out of season and much more frequently in summer; service extends to **Villers**, **Houlgate** and **Dives-Cabourg** (40min from Trouville) on Sundays and holidays throughout the year, and daily in July & Aug .

From Caen frequently to Tours (3hr) and Rouen (2hr); 4 daily to Pontorson (2hr 15min) via Bayeux and Coutances.

From Granville frequently to Paris (3hr 30min).

From Coutances 2 daily to Cherbourg (1hr).

Buses

From Caen to Le Havre (3hr); either #20 via Cabourg (40min), Deauville (1hr) and Honfleur (1hr 30min), or #38 via Pont L'Evêque (1hr 30min); to Ouistreham (35min), Lion, Courseulles, and Arromanches; to Bayeux (40min) and Carentan; to Fécamp (1hr 30min); to Vire (connections for Brittany); to Flers; to Falaise; to Lisieux.

From Bayeux to Balleroy (30min) and St-Lô (50min).

Ferries

From Ouistreham *Brittany Ferries* to Portsmouth (6hr). See details on p.5.

From Cherbourg *Sealink* to Portsmouth (4hr 45min) and Weymouth (4hr 30min), ☎33.20.43.38; *Truckline Ferries* to Poole (4hr 30min); *P&O* to Portsmouth (3 daily, 4hr 45min), ☎33.44.20.13; *Irish Continental* to Rosslare (17hr), ☎33.44.28.96. Further details on all these services can be found on p.5.

From Granville to Jersey, Guernsey, and Chausey Islands. *Vedettes Armoricaines*, 12 rue Clémenceau, ☎33.50.77.45. *Vedettes Blanches*, 1 rue Le Campion, ☎33.50.16.36. *Jolie France*, gare maritime, ☎33.50.31.81.

From Carteret to Jersey. *Vedettes Armoricaines*, gare maritime, ☎33.04.60.60. *Vedettes Blanches*, gare maritime, ☎33.53.81.17.

Air

From Cherbourg *Aurigny-Air-Service* to Jersey, Guernsey and Aurigny; *Air Camelot* to Bournemouth, Bristol and Exeter. Both from Maupertus Airport, ☎33.22.91.32.

CHAPTER THREE

FROM THE SEINE TO THE BOCAGE: INLAND NORMANDY

I t is hard to pin down specific highlights in **inland Normandy**. The pleasures lie not so much in sights, or the individual towns, as in the feel of particular landscapes – the lush meadows, orchards and forests of the Norman countryside. And, of course, in the **food**, a major motivation in these rich dairy regions.

To the French, the regions of **Pays d'Auge**, **Calvados** and **Suisse Normande** are synonymous with cheeses, creams, apple and pear brandies and ciders. A guide to these parts has to focus more than usually on the **restaurants**, of which personal favourites – and they are no more than a scratch selection – would direct travels to Vire, Pont d'Ouilly and Conches.

All of which said, the territory is not exactly devoid of other sensory pursuits. There are spas, forests, rivers and lakes for lazing or stretching the muscles in, and, everywhere, classic half-timbered houses and farm buildings. If you are staying on the Norman coast, trips inland – even just a dozen or two kilometres – will show rewards. If you arrive at a Norman port, but with Brittany as your principal destination, you may find yourself tempted to linger, or at least to take a circuitous route.

From **east to west**, there are five main regions. **South of the Seine**, a natural target from Le Havre, Dieppe or Rouen, are the **river valleys** of the **Eure**, **Risle** and **Charentonne**. These have their industrial side, especially the Charentonne, but for the most part they are lush and rural, with the occasional château, castle ruin or abbey to provide a focus – most memorably at **Bec-Hellouin**, near Brionne, and at the lovely country town of **Conches**. Moving west, and directly inland from Honfleur or Cabourg, you find yourself in the classic cheese and cider country of the **Pays d'Auge**, all rolling pastoral hills, grazing meadows and orchards, with **Livarot** the great cheese centre and **Lisieux**, birthplace of Sainte-Thérèse, one of the biggest French pilgrimage towns. To the **south** of the Pays d'Auge extend the forests of the **Parc Naturel Régional de Normandie-Maine**, with the sedate and famous spa at **Bagnoles** and the national stud at **Le Pin**.

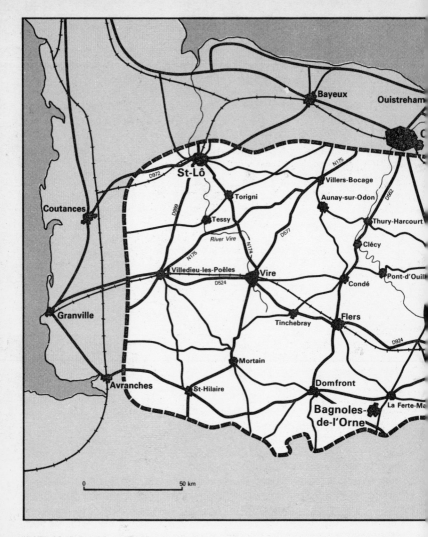

Further west, on the routes inland from Caen/Ouistreham or from Cherbourg and the Cotentin, there is something of a shift. Around Thury-Harcourt and stretching south to Pont D'Ouilly and Putanges is the area dubbed the **Suisse Normande**, for its "alpine" valleys and thick woods; fine walking country if not genuinely mountainous. To its west is the **Bocage**, which begins with the grim memories of war around **St-Lô** – this was the main 1944 invasion route – but subsides into pastoral once more, as you hit the gastronomic centres of the **Vire**.

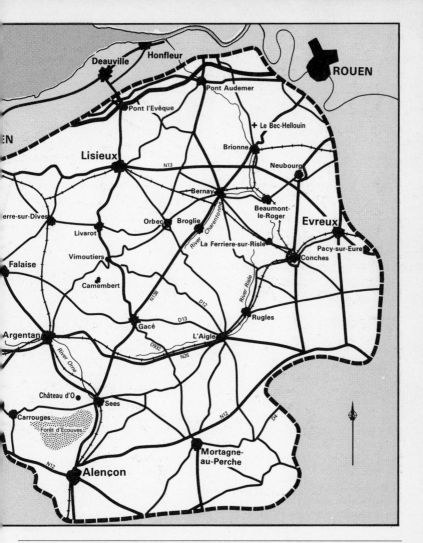

South of the Seine: Evreux and Conches

South across the Seine from Rouen is the long and featureless **Neubourg plain** – intensive agricultural land where the crumbling barns, Tudor-style houses and occasional grazing horses look oddly out of place. The only town of any size is **LE NEUBOURG**, which blows any possibility of being charming by festooning its streets with deafening loudspeakers. Its one feature is a shop that sells roadsigns – including some bizarre "Men-At-Work" motifs.

Twenty kilometres further south is **EVREUX**, capital of the Eure *département*, although it's not on the river itself. Again it's almost disconcertingly lifeless, but an afternoon's wander in the vicinity of the cathedral – a minor classic with its flamboyant exterior decoration and original fourteenth-century windows – and along the ramparts by the Iton river bank is pleasant enough. Most of the cheaper hotels in the town tend to shut during August and in any case there is no great reason to stay. Of an evening, you'd be much better off at Conches or, if you want to see the Eure, at **PACY-SUR-EURE**, where the *Hôtel de l'Etape* (☎32.36.12.77) nestles at the water's edge.

Conches-en-Ouche

Everybody you meet in Normandy seems to recommend **CONCHES-EN-OUCHE** – both for the town and for the forest around. The town stands above the Rouloir river on a spur so narrow and abrupt that the railway line is forced to tunnel right beneath its centre. Arriving, you're barely aware that the place exists at all; all you see is the cutting, deep into the hill.

On the highest point of the spur, in the middle of a row of medieval houses, is the church of **St-Foy**, its windows a sequence of Renaissance stained glass. Opposite is an interesting ironmongery shop, full of old-style metal jewellery. Behind, in the gardens of the **Hôtel de Ville**, a robust, if anatomically odd, stone boar gazes proudly out over a spectacular view, raising its eyes to the horizon far beyond the sewage works. Next to that, you can scramble up the slippery steps of the ruined twelfth-century **castle**, one of the many haunts of the ubiquitous Bertrand du Guesclin. From these sights the town takes its character but it is given a more contemporary flavour, too, by the pieces of modern sculpture that you come upon round seemingly every corner.

Across the main street from the castle is a long **park**, subtly formal with parallel avenues of trees, a large ornamental lake and fountain, and the **hotel** *Grand'Mare* (☎32.30.23.30). This has cheap rooms and very pricey gastronomic dinners; the lovely old building of the *Cygne* (☎32.30.20.60), at the north end of town, is more affordable; or there's a **municipal campsite** (☎32.30.22.49). On Thursday the whole town is taken up by a **market**.

The Forêt de Conches

The **Forêt de Conches** is a wild and open woodland. If you feel the need for a direction in your wanderings, head for the village of **LA FERRIERE-SUR-RISLE**, where there's an especially beautiful church, with a garish altar but some fine wooden statues, and an old covered market hall. Paddocks and meadows lead down to the river and there are two small and inviting **hotels**, the *Croissant* (☎32.30.70.13) and the *Vieux Marché* (☎32.30.70.69).

Moving **on from Conches**, by far the best route is the one taken by the railway – **northwest** to Beaumont-le-Roger and then on down the Risle and Charentonne rivers. **South**, the towns of Rugles and L'Aigle are both industrial and uninteresting; although the latter was the scene in September 1986 of an astonishing airborne drugs raid, in which the police used dogs to round up petty offenders who were then whisked away in waiting aeroplanes.

The Charentonne and the Risle

The **Risle** is joined by the **Charentonne** near Serquigny. En route, upstream at **BEAUMONT-LE-ROGER**, the ruins of a thirteenth-century priory church are gradually crumbling to the ground, the slow restoration of one or two arches unable to keep pace. Little happens in the village beyond the hourly hammering of the church bell – next door to the abbey – by a nodding musketeer; and with each passing hour, the ruins crumble a little more.

Just across the Risle from here, on the D25 near Le Val-St-Martin, huge stables are spread across an absurdly sylvan setting, and horses are available for hire. At **SERQUIGNY**, where the rail lines and roads converge, in addition to the two rivers, the banks become industrial, clogged with factories and fumes. Best to move on fast, either to Bernay or Brionne.

BERNAY, to the west, has a few humpback footbridges interspersed between the more serious traffic routes, and one of those churches typical of the region with a spire that looks like a stack of inverted octagonal ice-cream cones. Work has been in progress to restore the ancient **abbey church** for years – it should look good when it is finished. The town has few other claims to renown, though one of its bakers has found fame for *running* each stage of the Tour de France during the night before the cyclists race over it.

Upstream from Bernay, the Charentonne loses its industry, sprawling lazily between its banks on a wide flood plain. It is classic inland Normandy, uneventful and totally scenic; the one flaw in the whole thing is the unseemly preponderance of porcelain donkeys in people's front gardens. At **ST-**

QUENTIN-DES-ISLES, halfway along the valley, old houses are over-shadowed by a derelict sawmill, which looms like a primordial swamp monster from among the riverside willows, in a dripping bulk of red ivy.

Broglie and Brionne

The last town of any size along the Charentonne is **BROGLIE**, on the brow of whose hill stands an awesomely impressive **château**. This is the ancestral home of the de Broglie family, whose last but one owner, Prince Louis, won the Nobel Physics Prize for demonstrating that matter, like light, has wave-like properties. His work – to "seek the last hiding places of reality", as he put it – formed the foundation of the whole discipline of Quantum Mechanics. Originally a medieval historian, Louis was supposed to have been attracted to his great theory "purely on the grounds of intellectual beauty".

North, the first stop from Serquigny on the rail line to Rouen, is **BRIONNE**, a small town with large regional **markets** on Thursday and Sunday. The fish hall is on the left bank, the rest by the church on the right bank. Above them both, with panoramic views, is a **donjon**. If you decide to **stay**, the *Auberge du Vieux Donjon* (☎32.44.80.62) on the marketplace is good, though very pricey; the *Routiers*, next door, more manageable.

The Abbaye de Bec-Hellouin

Following the **Risle** on towards Honfleur and the sea, the **D39** is lined with perfect timbered farmhouses. Four kilometres from Brionne, you come to the **ABBAYE DE BEC-HELLOUIN** whose size and tranquil setting give a monastic feel to the whole valley. Bells echo between the hills and white-robed monks go soberly about their business. From the eleventh century onwards, the abbey was one of the most important centres of intellectual learning in the Christian world; the philosopher Anselm was abbot here before becoming Archbishop of Canterbury in 1093.

Most of the monastery buildings are recent – monks didn't return here after the Revolution until 1948 – but there are some survivals and appealing clusters of stone ruins; and the present Archbishop of Canterbury has maintained tradition by coming here on retreat. (Tours at 10am, 11am, 3pm, 3.45pm, 4.30pm, 5.15pm; Sun & hols at 9.30am, noon, 2.45pm, 3.30pm, 4.15pm & 6pm; closed Tues). In the rather twee adjacent town of **Bec-Hellouin** is a **vintage car museum** and a distincly un-ascetic **restaurant**, the wonderful *Auberge de l'Abbaye*.

Continuing north, the last major crossing point over the Risle is at **PONT-AUDEMER**, where medieval houses lean out at alarming angles over the criss-crossing roads, rivers, and canals. From there you have the choice of making for the sea at Honfleur (see p.57), passing some tottering Giacometti-style barns on the way to St-Georges along the thickly-wooded valleys of the D38, or going on towards the Seine. If you are cycling across the Forêt de Brotonne (see p.45) towards Caudebec, be warned that, to discourage motorists from spoiling the nicest part of the forest, the roadsigns direct you the long way round via La Mailleraye.

Lisieux

LISIEUX is the main town of the Pays d'Auge, and an effective introduction to the wonders of its cuisine. It's an historic place, still boasting the Norman Gothic cathedral where Henry II married Eleanor of Aquitaine, but these days its identity is thoroughly wrapped up in the life and death of **Sainte-Thérèse** – France's most influential spiritual figure of the last hundred years.

The town certainly has its pilgrims, and even a casual visitor will find the Thérèse cult inescapable. A white, flag-bedecked, funfair train runs around the holiest sites, chuntering through the open, wide streets and squares, and past the flower-filled park. This latter, raised above street level behind the Cathédrale St-Pierre, is a delight.

The colossal **Basilique de Ste-Thérèse**, on a slope to the southwest of the town centre, was modelled on the Sacré-Coeur in Paris. Completed in 1954, it was the last major religious building in France to be erected solely by public subscription. Thérèse is in fact buried in the chapel of the Carmelite convent, though her presence in the basilica is ensured by bones from her right arm (in a reliquary given by Pius XI) and by ubiquitous photographs. Huge mosaics of her face decorate the nave and every night at 9.30pm, as part of a stunningly tasteless (and expensive) laser show, her face is simultaneously projected on every column in the church.

Practical Details

The quantity of pilgrims means that Lisieux is full of good-value places to stay. Try the **hotels** *de la Terrasse* (25 av Ste-Thérèse; ☎31.62.17.65), *Condorcet* (26 rue Condorcet; ☎31.62.00.02) or *de l'Avenue* (4 av Ste-Thérèse; ☎31.62.08.37). There is also a large **campsite**, but campers would probably be better off somewhere more rural nearby, such as Livarot or Orbec. If Thérèse isn't your prime motivation, Wednesday and Saturday are the best days to visit, for the large **street market** – stacked with Pays d'Auge cheeses.

SAINT THERESE

Born at Alençon in 1873, **Thérèse Martin** lived for the last nine years of her life in the Carmelite convent in Lisieux, until she died of TB at 24. She had felt the call to join when only nine, but it took a pilgrimage to Rome to receive a special dispensation from the Pope before she was allowed into the convent at the age of fifteen. The prioress said then that "a soul of such quality should not be treated as a child".

Thérèse owes her fame to her book *Story of a Soul*, in which she describes the approach to life she called her "Little Way" – a belief that all personal suffering, all thankless work and quiet faith, is made holy, and made worthwhile, as an offering to God. What to modern sensibilities might appear a meekness and lack of worldliness verging on the selfish proved astonishingly popular after her death, particularly in trying to make sense of the vast suffering of World War I. Thérèse was rapidly beatified and by 1945 was declared France's second patron saint. The recent success of Alain Cavalier's film *Thérèse*, and a visit by Pope John Paul II, suggest that she is still felt to have contemporary relevance.

Into the Pays d'Auge

South of Lisieux, the rolling hills and green twisting valleys of the **Pays d'Auge** are scattered with magnificent half-timbered manor houses. The sprawling farms often consist of a succession of such "Tudor" (in fact the Norman tradition predates the English) treasures, each family house as it becomes too dilapidated to live in being converted for use as a barn, and a new one built alongside. The pastures here are the lushest in the province, producing the world-famous cheeses of Camembert, Livarot, and Pont L'Evêque. And beside them are acres of orchards, yielding the best of Norman ciders, both apple and pear (*poiré*), as well as Calvados apple brandy. For really good solid Norman cooking, however, this is the perfect area to look out for **Fermes Auberges,** working farms which welcome (paying) visitors to share their meals.

Cheese and Cider

The tourist authorities promote two main Pays d'Auge itineraries, the **Route de Fromage** and the **Route du Cidre**. It's not difficult to join either of these well-signposted routes, each of which serves as a welcome opportunity to get off the main highways. For the former, the best starting points are at St-Pierre-sur-Dives and Livarot; for the latter, head for Cambremer, just north of the N13 between Caen and Lisieux. In any event, it doesn't matter much if you stray off the routes; much of the appeal of this area lies in the scope just to wander, rather than to look for any specific sights, and to fill the days sampling the different ciders and cheeses. That said, the manor houses of **Beuvron-en-Auge** on the Cider route, and **Montpinçon** and **Lisores** on the Cheese route, are well worth the finding, and at Lisores there's also the *Ferme-musée Fernand Léger* (10am–noon & 2–7pm, closed Wed), with its unlikely mosaics. **Cambremer** has a special crafts market on Sunday morning in July and August. Lists of the **farms** which welcome visitors are available from local SIs and from *Calvados Tourisme* (place du Canada, Caen; ☎31.86.53.30). The cider farms are signposted with the words "*Cru de Cambremer*" in green on white.

There was little left after the war of the old **PONT L'EVEQUE**, the northernmost Pays d'Auge town. Since then it has become such a turmoil of major roads as to be no place to stay. **CORMEILLES**, on the other hand, is a tiny (Friday) market centre, with several half-timbered restaurants to its credit.

Orbec and Livarot

ORBEC lies just a few miles along a valley from the source of its river, the Orbiquet. It consists of little more than its main road, with the huge tower of Notre Dame church at one end and a good but slightly expensive **hotel**, *de France* (☎31.32.74.02), at the other. Along the street are several houses in which the gaps between the timbers are filled with the region's characteristic patterns of coloured tiles and bricks. You can visit a museum in the oldest, **Le Vieux Manoir**, a tanner's house built in 1568, but it's more fun just to walk down behind the church to the river, and its watermill and paddocks.

The centre of the cheese country is the old town of **LIVAROT**, with the (not particularly good) **hotel** and restaurant *du Vivier* (☎31.63.50.29), and the enjoyable *Café de la Paix*, in its centre. The main attraction is the **Conservatoire du Fromage**, a small-scale working cheese factory. For a few francs, you can see Camembert, Pont L'Evêque and Livarot cheeses at every stage of their production. There's a good view of the valley from the thirteenth-century church of St-Michel de Livet, just above the town; to visit you contact a M. Jean Fromage.

At **ST-PIERRE-SUR-DIVES**, the medieval market hall has been converted into a slightly academic annex to the Livarot cheese museum (10am–6pm, closed Tues). It's an impressive building, though, almost rivalling the Gothic-Romanesque church (whose windows depict the history of the town). A large **market** still takes place every Monday in the adjacent square.

West of Livarot, just off the D47 towards Orbec, you'll find some of the Pays d'Auge's rare budget **accommodation** – the unlikely-sounding *Happy's Holiday Homes*. These large luxury chalets are available at a cheap weekly rent from former racing cyclist Wally Happy – who also, naturally enough, hires out cycles. Contact him in advance in England (2 Regent Close, Fleet, Hampshire; ☎02514 21164), or in France on ☎31.32.35.96.

Heading **south from Livarot** towards Vimoutiers, the D579 passes through the village of **STE-FOY DE MONTGOMMERY**, where, outside the *Café La Gosselinais* on the night of July 17 1944, Field-Marshal Rommel was seriously injured when RAF Typhoons attacked his *Mercedes*. Rommel never returned to the battlefield, and committed suicide three months later. That his nemesis should overtake him in a place called "Holy Faith of Montgommery" became part of the legend surrounding the British field-marshal.

Vimoutiers and Camembert

VIMOUTIERS contains another **cheese museum**, featuring a glorious collection not to be missed by tyrosemiophiles – cheese-label collectors (they do exist) – who will find Camembert stickers ranging from remote Chilean dairies to *Marks & Spencers*. Most of the cheese on display however turns out to be polystyrene.

A statue in the main square honours Marie Harel, who, at the nearby village of **CAMEMBERT**, developed the original cheese early in the nineteenth century, promoting it with a skilful campaign that included sending free samples to Napoleon. There's a photo in the museum of the statue with its head blown off after a US air raid in June 1944; its replacement was donated by the cheese-makers of Ohio. The **hotels** *Soleil d'Or* (16 place Mackau; ☎33.39.07.15) and *Couronne* (9 rue du 8 Mai; ☎33.39.03.04) are good, economic places to stay, and there is also a campsite. Nearby is the **Escale du Vitou**, a lake, beautifully sited, with everything you need for windsurfing, swimming, and horseriding.

The **D26** runs along the **valley of the Vie** south of Vimoutiers – a route that takes in many of the best features of Normandy, lined along the way with ramshackle old barns, outhouses and farm buildings. Faded orange clay crumbles out from between the weathered wooden beams of these flower-covered beauties. At the crossroads with the D13 is the **hotel-restaurant** *Relais St-Pierre*. For any sensible kid this should be a principal holiday target – mini 125cc motorbikes and three-wheelers are for hire to hurtle around a course of bales of hay. There's additional lodging available at a farm a little further north, and several further **hotels** at **GACE**.

Four kilometres north of Gace on the D979, *La Chasterie* (☎33.35.73.42) is a farm which has been converted into a hotel, with its own restaurant in an outbuilding standing in its orchard.

Argentan and Le Pin

ARGENTAN centres on a **castle ruin** – the site where Henry II of England stayed on New Year's Day 1171 and received the news that his knights had taken him at his word and murdered Thomas-à-Becket. The ruin, and the adjoining market square (active on Tuesday) make an enjoyable enough halt, and there are boat trips on the river Orne. But there is not much to see – the church of **St-Germain** which dominates all approaches to the town has been closed for years for restoration – and it is in any case not monuments but horses that draw visitors to Argentan. Outside the town are numerous equestrian centres, with riding schools, stables, racetracks and studs.

Le Pin-au-Haras

At **LE PIN-AU-HARAS**, fifteen kilometres east of Argentan on the N26, is the most essential stop for horse lovers – the **National Stud** (*Haras National*). The plan for the Stud was originally conceived by Louis XIV's minister, Colbert, and the ground subsequently laid out by Le Nôtre from 1715 to 1730. It can be approached via a number of woodland avenues, but the most impressive is the D304, which climbs slowly from the hippodrome and is lined with jumps and hedges. The buildings are magnificent, but not as sumptuous as the residents – 79 all in – incalculable investments that number among them champions of Epsom and Longchamps, as well as prize specimens of the indigenous Norman *percheron*.

Tours of the stud leave every half hour (9am–noon & 2–6pm) from the main entrance; admission is free. You are escorted by a groom through stables full of stomping, snorting, glistening stallions, rooms of polished harnesses and fine carriages, and great doorways labelled in stone, until eventually you come out to a pastoral vision of the horses grazing in endless sequences of gardens and paddocks. Each tour lasts for half an hour; if you find it hard to follow the rapid French-only commentary, you can amuse yourself by watching the way everybody scrupulously affects not to notice the rampant sexuality – which of course is the place's *raison d'être*.

Displays of horsemanship are held at 3 o'clock every Thursday through the summer, with special events on the first Sunday in September, the second Sunday in October, and a few other summer weekends. Between February 15 and July 15, most of the horses are away; and the château itself is never open.

The Château d'O

Just outside Mortrée, six and a half kilometres northwest of Sees on the N158, is the **Château d'O**. This turreted château – one of the prettiest anywhere – is in perfect condition, with a full moat that widens out into a lake. The house dates from the end of the fifteenth century and, unusually, was designed purely as a domestic residence, with no military pretensions. The grounds, with a pitch and putt golf course on the lawns, are open all day from July to September, though you may have to attract the attention of the custodians by means of a very Heath Robinson-ish bell pull. A sign at the entrance proclaims this to be "the Worldwide Place Where The International Cultural Passport And The Raised Relief Stamp Created For It Were First Circulated On July 30 1985". Once again, you can't go into the house itself. If you're making a day of it, the expensive restaurant and tearooms in the adjoining *Ferme d'O* have quite a gastronomic reputation.

Sées

SEES, midway between Argentan and Alençon, has long had an air of being lost in its own history. A succession of dusty and derelict squares, all with medieval buildings intact, surround the great Gothic, white-ceilinged **Cathedral**, which is the fifth to stand on the site. One of its predecessors was burnt down by its own bishop, attempting to smoke out a gang of thieves – much to the scorn of the Pope.

Sées has, however, recently experienced something of a revitalisation, under the influence of the Australian Brian Kirby, who bought the *Normandy Garden Hotel* (rue des Ardrillers; ☎33.27.98.27) in 1988. A man who knows his own mind, he's adopted what he likes about the French way of doing things, but been ready to reject what he doesn't, taking what had been a dismal and run-down hotel and transforming it into a comfortable and exceptionally welcoming place to stay. The major sign of his presence however is his *Boomerang* restaurant, directly opposite the main door of the Cathedral, with a huge neon sign outside and a bright and busy atmosphere within – enlivened by the unexpected Australian bonhomie of its host. It's a cheap and enjoyable brasserie that deliberately doesn't compete with Sées' two long-established (and also good) hotel/restaurants, the *Cheval Blanc* (☎33.27.80.48) and the *Dauphin* (☎33.27.80.07). The Cathedral itself is now magnificently illuminated every night during the summer.

The *Hotel de la Poste* (27 pl de Gaulle; ☎33.27.60.13) in **LE-MELE-SUR-SARTHE** is a *logis* worth stopping at if you're heading on south from here.

Alençon and Around

ALENCON, a fair-sized and busy town, is known for its traditional – and now pretty much defunct – lace-making industry. The **Musée des Beaux Arts et de la Dentelle**, housed in a former Jesuit school, has all the best trappings of a modern museum; but the highly informative history of lace-making, with examples of numerous different techniques, can be rather deadly for anyone not already fascinated by the subject. The temptation to leave without a visit to the "Minor Lace Exhibition Room" is almost overwhelming; but the room beyond it holds a collection of gruesome Cambodian artefacts, spears and lances, tiger skulls and elephants' feet, gathered by a "militant socialist" French governor at the turn of the century. The paintings in the adjoining *Beaux Arts* section are fairly nondescript, except for a touching *Nativity* by the Norman artist, Latouche, and a few works by Courbet and Géricault. Further wanders around the town might take you to Ste-Thérèse's birthplace on rue St-Blaise, just in front of the gare routière – if, that is, you haven't had a surfeit of the saint at Lisieux. The **Château des Ducs**, the old town castle, looks impressive but doesn't encourage visitors – it's a prison. People in Alençon have nightmare memories of its use during the war by the Gestapo.

Practical Details

If you want to stay, Alencon has good shops and cafés in a few well-pedestrianised streets at the heart of its abysmal one-way traffic system. The main concentration of **hotels** is around the **SNCF** station on the north side of the centre. The two *logis*, *L'Industrie* (20 pl de Gaulle; ☎33.29.06.51) and the *Grand Hôtel de la Gare* (50 av Wilson; ☎33.29.03.93) are good, with menus starting at around 50F. There's a **youth hostel** out on the D204 towards Colombiers, at 1 rue de la Paix, Damigni (☎33.29.00.48). For a few days **horseriding** – trekking along the Orne – contact the *Association Département-ale de Tourisme Equestre et d'Equitation de Loisirs de l'Orne* at 60 Grand Rue.

The Forêt d'Ecouves and Carrouges

The **Forêt d'Ecouves**, reached (under your own steam) from either Alençon or Sées, is the centrepiece of the *Parc Régional Normandie-Maine*, an amorphous area stretching from Mortain in the west to within a few kilometres of Montagne-au-Perche in the east. A dense mixture of spruce, pine, oak and beech, the Ecouves forest is unfortunately a favoured spot of the military – and in autumn of deerhunters, too. To avoid risking life and limb, check with the park's offices (see below). You can usually ramble along the cool paths, happening on wild mushrooms and even the odd wild boar. The *gîte d'étape*, on the D26 near Les Ragotières on the edge nearest Alençon, is an ideal spot from which to explore the forest (contact the local *gîte* office at 60 rue St-Blaise in Alençon, ☎33.32.09.00).

Alternatively, at the western end of the woods, you could base yourself in **CARROUGES**, at the *Hôtel du Nord* (☎33.27.20.14) or *Saint-Pierre* (☎33.27.20.14). Carrouges' **château** (10.30am–noon & 2–6.30pm), a proper castle, contains the offices of the *Parc Régional Normandie-Maine* (☎33.27.21.15), which is attempting to re-vitalise the region, encouraging small-scale agricultural producers – rabbit and bee farmers, cider-makers and the like. They also direct tourism in the region and can provide original information on footpaths and birdwatching trails. In the **Maison de Métiers**, the former castle chapel, they have installed local craftsmen, whose products are for sale.

Heading onwards on the D908 towards Bagnoles, you come after a few kilometres to the delightful village of **JOUE-DU-BOIS**, with a diminutive château, lake and a cheap restaurant, the *Pomme d'Or*.

Bagnoles

The spa-town of **BAGNOLES DE L'ORNE** lies at the centre of a long, narrow wood, the **Forêt des Andaines**. Broad avenues radiate into the forest from the centre of the town. As you approach, you begin to encounter pale figures shuffling slowly outwards, blinking as if unused to the light of day, as though silently fleeing some nameless evil. In fact, the forbidding nineteenth-century building from which they emerge contains nothing more fearsome than **thermal baths**. Bagnoles is a mecca for the sick and the invalid from all over France; its springs are such big business that they maintain a booking office next to the Pompidou Centre in Paris.

Although life in the town is conducted at a phenomenally slow pace, it is all surprisingly jolly – redolent with aged flirtations. The lakeside gardens are the big scene, with pedalos, horse drawn calèches and an enormous Casino. And with so many visitors to keep entertained, and spending money, there are innumerable cultural **events**, concerts and stage shows, throughout the summer; the ostensible high spot, the annual *Spectacle* in July, is one of the less enthralling.

Whether you'd actually want to spend time in Bagnoles, though, depends on your disposable income as well as your health. The numerous **hotels** are expensive and sedate places, in which it's possible to be too late for dinner at 7 o'clock and locked out altogether at 9, and the **campsite** is rather forlorn. You may do better at Bagnoles' less exclusive sister town of **TESSE-MADELAINE**. **Restaurants**, in both towns, are better value; the *de la*

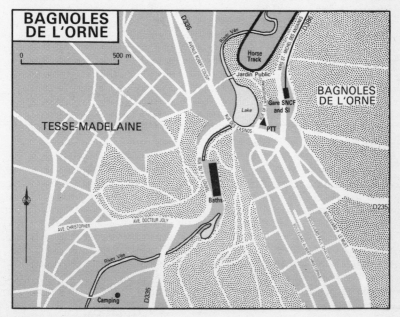

Terrasse in Bagnoles is well-tried and popular. If you go in for the traditional activities of **taking the waters**, a "complete cure" of 21 sessions costs around 1400F, with individual baths and showers as little as 30F.

Away from its main roads, the **Forêt des Andaines** is pleasant, with scattered and unspoilt villages, such as Juvigny and St-Michel, and the secluded, private **Château de Couterne**, a visual delight even from the gates, with its lake and long grass-floored avenue approach.

Domfront and onwards

The road **through the forest** from Bagnoles, the D335 and then the D908, climbs above the lush woodlands and progressively narrows to a hog's back before entering **DOMFRONT**. Less happens here than at Bagnoles, but it has the edge on countryside. A public park, near the **gare SNCF**, leads up to **castle ruins** on an isolated rock. Eleanor of Aquitaine was born in the castle in October 1162, and Thomas-à-Becket came to stay for Christmas 1166, saying mass in the nearby Notre-Dame-sur-l'Eau. The views from the gardens surrounding the mangled keep are spectacular, including a very graphic panorama of the ascent you've made to get up. Domfront is a useful stopover, with several **hotels** around the railway station; beware though that the **campsite** is limited to ten pitches.

The best excursions from Domfront, more focussed than exploring the Forêt des Andaines, are to the northwest, at the edge of the **Forêt de Lande-Pourrie**. **LONLAY L'ABBAYE**, nine kilometres out on the D22 towards Tinchebray, has a biscuit factory along with various vestiges of its eleventh-century Benedictine past. West from here you can cut across country to the **Fosse d'Arthur**, one of the many claimants to King Arthur's death scene. A couple of waterfalls disappear into deep limestone caverns, but there's really very little to see. At nearby **BARENTON**, *Le Relais du Parc* is a good cheap restaurant, and the **Maison de la Pomme et de la Poire** a mildly diverting cider museum.

Falaise

William the Conqueror is more familiarly known to Normans as "William the Bastard" – and it was in the castle at **FALAISE** in 1027 that he was so born. His mother, Arlette, was a laundress, who was spotted by his father, Duke Robert of Normandy, at the washing-place below the château. She was a shrewd woman, scorning secrecy in her eventual assignation by riding publicly through the main entrance to meet him. During her pregnancy, she is said to have dreamed of bearing a mighty tree that cast its shade over Normandy and England.

The keep of the **castle**, and the **Fontaine d'Arlette** on the riverside beneath it, still exist, though so heavily restored as to be scarcely worth the ten-minute tour. The town itself was devastated in the war. The struggle to close the "Falaise Gap" in August 1944 was the climax of the Battle of Normandy, as the Allied armies sought to encircle the Germans and cut off their retreat. By the time the Canadians entered the town on August 17, they could no longer tell where the roads had been and had to bulldoze a new 12ft strip straight through the middle. Set in almost derelict wilderness right next to the town centre is an isolated survivor, the **Château de la Fresnaye**, housing a rather earnest local museum during the summer. Opposite, on rue Georges Clémenceau, the main Caen–Argentan road, is the **SI**, which hires out bicycles. The few **hotels** are mostly situated along this road, too – all very noisy. The **campsite**, *Camping du Château* (☎31.90.16.55), next to Arlette's fountain and the municipal swimming pool, is much better positioned.

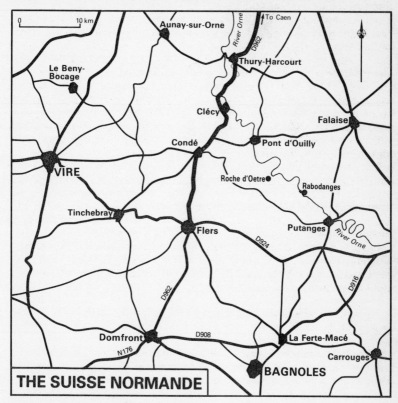

The Suisse Normande

The area known as the **"Suisse Normande"** lies along the gorge of the river Orne, between Thury-Harcourt and Putanges. It is not exactly Swiss – there are certainly no mountains – but its deep and numerous valleys do create a vaguely alpine feel. It is essentially outdoors activities country. The energetic race along the Orne in canoes and kayaks, their lazier counterparts contenting themselves with pedalos or a bizarre species of inflatable rubber tractor, while high above them climbers dangle from thin ropes and claw desperately at the sheer rockface. For mere walkers the Orne can be frustrating: footpaths along the river are few and far between, whatever maps may say, and often entirely overgrown with brambles. At least one road sign in the area warns of unexploded mines, so tread carefully.

The Suisse Normande is most usually approached from Caen or Falaise, and contrasts dramatically with the prairie-like expanse of wheatfields en route. Cycling, the least stressful approach to follow from Caen is along the D212, cruising across the flatlands to Thury-Harcourt, although swooping down the D23 from Bretteville, with thick woods to either side of you, is pretty exhilarating. By train, there are occasional summer special excursions from Caen, or *Bus Verts* #34 will take you to Thury-Harcourt or Clécy on its way to Flers.

Thury-Harcourt

At **THURY-HARCOURT**, the **SI** in place St-Sauveur can suggest walks, rides and *gîtes d'étape* throughout the Suisse Normande; *SIVOM* at 15 rue de Condé hire out canoes. Thury-Harcourt is really two separate towns; a little village around a bridge across the Orne, and a larger market town on the hill which overlooks it. The **hotels** are all quite expensive, though the restaurants down by the river are good, and there are a couple of three-star **campsites** – *Vallée du Traspy* (☎31.79.61.80) and *Camping du Bord de l'Orne* (☎31.79.70.78; June–Sept only). From July to September, the grounds of the local manor house are open (for an 18F fee) from 2.30–6.30pm every day, giving access to the immediate riverside.

Clécy

CLECY is a slightly better bet for finding a room, although its visitors outnumber residents in high season. The *logis* in town, *Au Site*, isn't as good value as the *Alpes Normands* (☎31.69.45.39), a short way along the road which faces the church. For advice on accommodation and the wide variety of holiday activities available in Clécy, the **SI** is tucked in behind the church. The village centre is about a kilometre above the actual river at Pont du Vey. On the way down, in the Parc des Loisirs, is a **Musée du Chemin de Fer Miniature** (June to mid-Sept 10am–noon & 2–7pm), featuring a model railway which may appeal to children. At the bridge is a restored watermill, run as a restaurant and hotel. The riverbank continues in a brief splurge of restaurants, takeaways and snackbars as far as the 100-pitch **campsite**.

Pont d'Ouilly

If you're planning on walking, or cycling, a good central spot to base yourself could be **PONT D'OUILLY**, at the point where the main road from Vire to Falaise crosses the river. It's a small town, with a few basic shops, an old covered market hall and a promenade (with bar) slightly upstream alongside the weir; you can walk along the riverside down to Le Mesnil Villement. As well as the **campsite** overlooking the river, there's an attractive **hotel**, the *du Commerce* (☎31.69.80.16), with cheap rooms and wonderful food, in a dining room appropriately filled with stuffed animals. About a kilometre north, the much more upmarket *Auberge St-Christophe* (☎31.69.81.23) stands in a beautiful setting on the right bank of the Orne, covered with ivy and geraniums and opposite a roofless and now overgrown Art Deco factory. A *Grand Pardon du Sainte-Roche* takes place along the river on the third Sunday in August.

The Roche d'Oëtre

A short distance south of Pont D'Ouilly is the **Roche d'Oëtre**, a high rock affording a tremendous view, not over the Orne but into the deep and totally wooded gorge of the Rouvre. The rock itself is private property, though you're under no obligation to visit the café there. The river widens soon afterwards into the **Lac du Rabodanges**, formed by the many-arched Rabodanges Dam. It's a popular spot, with a multi-facility **campsite**, *Les Retours*, perfectly situated between the dam and the bridge on the D121. There's a play area for kids, and grassy picnic slopes lead down to the water's edge where the occasional bather risks a swim among the waterskiers, speedboats, windsurfers, canoes, and kayaks. The imposing Rabodanges château, higher up the hillside, is now a stud farm.

Further climbing roads bring you to **PUTANGES**, another possible place to stay, with a small **campsite**. The town lies a bit beyond the main attractions of the region, but nevertheless it's a pleasant stop – a few bars out on its pavements and, just upstream from the bridge, the weirs over which the Orne appears from its source just to the south.

The Bocage

The fields of the **Bocage Normande** are cut by tight hedgerows rooted into four-foot-high walls of earth. An effective form of smallhold farming, at least in pre-industrial days, it is also, by chance, a perfect system of anti-tank barricades. When the Allied troops tried to advance through the region in 1944 it proved almost impenetrable – certainly bearing no resemblance to the East Anglian plains where they had trained. The war here was hand-to-hand, inch-by-inch slaughter; the destruction of villages often wholesale.

St-Lô

The city of **ST-LO** is still known as the "Capital of the Ruins". Black and white postcards of the wartime devastation are on sale everywhere and you keep coming on memorial sites as you wander about. In the main square, the gate of the old prison commemorates Resistance members executed by the Nazis, people deported east to the Concentration camps and soldiers killed in action; when the bombardment of St-Lô was at its height, the Germans refused to take any measures to protect the prisoners – and the gate was all that survived. In similar vein, behind the cathedral, a monument to the dead of the First World War is pitted with shrapnel from the Second. Less depressingly, at the foot of the rock under the castle, you can see the entrance to caves where the citizens sheltered from the onslaught, whilst somewhere far below are great vaults used by the German command. In Studs Terkel's book, *The Good War*, a GI reminisces about the huge party thrown there after the Americans found vast stockpiles of champagne; Thomas Pynchon's *Gravity's Rainbow* has a crazed drinking scene based on the tale.

The newness of so much in St-Lô is also revealing of the scale of the fighting. Between the SNCF station and the castle rock, for example, a walk leads along the canalised channel of the Vire – an attractive course but unmistakably an attempt to patch over the ravages. All the trees in the city are the same height, too, all planted to replace the battle's mutilated stumps. But the most visible – and brilliant – reconstruction is the **Cathédrale de Notre Dame**. The main body of this, with its strange southward veering nave, has been conventionally repaired and rebuilt. Between the shattered west front and base of the collapsed north tower, however, a startling sheer wall of icy green stone makes no attempt to mask the destruction.

By way of contrast to such memories, a lighthouse-like 1950s folly spirals to nowhere on the main square; should you feel the urge to climb its stairway, ask at the Mairie opposite. More compelling, round behind the Mairie, is a **Musée des Beaux Arts**. This is full of treasures: a Boudin sunset; a Lurcat tapestry of his dog Nadir and the Pirates; works by Corot, van Loo, Moreau; a Léger watercolour; a fine series of unfaded sixteenth-century Flemish tapestries on the lives of two peasants; and sad bombardment relics of the town. The museum is free, and open from 10.30am until noon, and 2.30 to 6pm (5pm in winter), closed all day Tuesday and Sunday morning.

St-Lô Practicalities

St-Lô makes an interesting pause but it's virtually abandoned at night. Most of the hotels, restaurants and bars are by the river and **gare SNCF**. The *Terminus* (3 av Briovère; ☎33.05.08.60), one of a row of modern, slightly expensive riverside hotels, has a good 50F menu. Better value for rooms, if you get through the owners' eccentric vetting, is the *des Remparts* (3 rue des Prés; ☎33.57.08.06). A cycle shop, *Boulot*, on rue Torteron by the bridge, is helpful and efficient. The **gare routière** is on the rue du 80e & 136e, which leads south from the **SI** on the main square.

The Vire Valley

Once St-Lô was taken in the Battle of Normandy, the armies moved speedily on for their next confrontation. The **Vire Valley**, trailing south from St-Lô, saw little action – and indeed its towns and villages have rarely been touched by any historic or cultural mainstream. The motivation in coming to this landscape of rolling hills and occasional gorges is essentially to consume the region's cider, Calvados and fruit pastries.

Although the countryside is filled with orchards of apples and pears, the land is less fertile than elsewhere in Normandy – and has suffered heavily from the recent depression in the fruit market. A booming trade, however, has grown up around illicit Calvados, bolstering the faltering economy of many Vire farmers. Bootleggers smuggle hundreds of thousands of litres throughout France, using the hydraulic suspension of their *Citröen* cars to obscure the heavy loads they are carrying from the eyes of watching taxmen. One much-arrested smuggler has such James Bond accessories as automatically rotating licence-plates, smoke screens and even oil jets for use against pursuing motorcycles.

The best section of the Vire is the valley that comes down from St-Lô through the Roches de Ham to Tessy-sur-Vire. The **Roches de Ham** are a pair of sheer rocky promontories high above the river. They are promoted as a "viewing table", though the pleasure lies as much in the walk up, through lanes lined with blackberries, hazelnuts and rich orchards. Just downstream from the Roches, and a good place to stop over for a night, is **LA CHAPELLE-SUR-VIRE**. Its church, towering majestically above the river, has been an object of pilgrimage since the twelfth century. There's a weir nearby and a scattering of grassy islands. Next to the bridge on the lower road is the *Auberge de la Chapelle* (☎33.56.32.83), a good but rather expensive restaurant that has a few cheap **rooms**.

An alternative base for the Roches, over to the east, is **TORIGNI-SUR-VIRE**, which was the base of the Grimaldi family before they attained royalty in Monaco. A spacious country town, it boasts a few grand buildings and an attractive **campsite**, *Camping du Lac* (☎33.56.91.74). At **TESSY-SUR-VIRE** there's little to see other than the river itself, banked by rolling meadows, though the town again has a luxurious **campsite**, along with a couple of **hotels** and a Wednesday **market**.

Vire

The pride and joy of the people of **VIRE** are their *andouilles*, the blood sausages known in English as chitterlings. If you can avoid these hideous parcels of pigs' intestines, and the assortment of abattoirs that produce them, it's possible to have good time; in fact Vire is a town worth visiting specifically for the food. The biggest treats are to be found at the *Hôtel des Voyageurs* (☎31.68.01.16), at the bottom of av de la Gare, by the station. For around 50F you can have a sublime and endless meal, of salmon trout fresh from the river washed down with local *poiré*, in opulent surroundings. Good **restaurants** are to be found, too, at the more central *Hôtel de France* (4 rue Aignaux; ☎31.68.00.35) and *Hôtel du Cheval Blanc* (2 place du 6-Juin-1944; ☎31.68.00.21).

The only problem is what to do when you're not eating. You can look at the collection of minerals and fossils in the belfry that stands alone in the town

centre. You can visit the museum of How to Restore Old Norman Farmhouses. Or you can wander by the little scrap of **canal**, equipped with twee floating houses for the ducks, that lies just below the one stark finger that survives of the castle. The only action is at the Friday **market**, again obsessively dedicated to food.

For some exercise, head six kilometres south along the D76 to **Lac de la Dathée**. Set in open country, the lake is circled by footpaths or can be crossed by hired sailing boat or wind-surfer (contact the *Maison des Jeunes et de la Culture*, 1 rue des Halles, Vire; ☎31.68.08.04).

West and South from Vire

West from Vire, the road to Villedieu passes through **SAINT-SEVER**, not in itself much to write home about but backed by a dark and magical **forest** in which there's a dolmen, an abbey and a scattering of pukka picnic spots marked by signs showing a champagne bottle in a hamper.

VILLEDIEU-LES-POELES – literally "City of God the Frying Pans" – is a lively though touristified place. Copper souvenirs and kitchen utensils gleam from its rows of shops and the **SI** (on place des Costils) has lists of dozens of local *ateliers* for more direct purchases and details of the copperwork museum. All of which seems a bit over-enthusiastic and phoney, though there is more authentic interest at the **Fonderie Cornille Havard** at 13 rue du Pont Chignon, one of the twelve remaining bell foundries in Europe. Work here is only part-time due to limited demand but it's always open to visits during the week and you may find the forge lit. If you're charmed into staying, there's a **campsite** by the river and excellent basic food and accommodation at the *Hôtel de Paris* (☎33.61.00.66) on Route de Paris.

South from Vire, if you are heading for Fougères or Domfront, you pass through the **Forêt de Mortain** and its continuation, the **Forêt de Lande-Pourrie**. The forests' most interesting sites – the Fosse d'Arthur and the abbey at Lonlay – are easiest approached from Domfront (see p.96). At the town of **MORTAIN** there are **waterfalls** and a tiny chapel on a high rock from which the neighbouring province of Maine spreads before you. On a clear day you can even see Mont-St-Michel.

South again, at **ST-SYMPHORIEN-DES-MONTS**, the park of the now non-existent château is run as a **wildlife sanctuary**. Contented-looking beasts, like yaks and bisons, and threatened domestic animals, graze in semi-liberty in fields and woods around a lake inhabited by swans and flamingos. In order to attract French visitors, there are wolves, too. Admission (mid-March to mid-November only, 9am–8pm daily) is expensive but justifiably so. This is just off the N176, a few kilometres short of the thriving (Wednesday) **market** town of **ST-HILAIRE DE HARCOET**.

travel details

Trains

From St-Lô 4 daily to **Caen** (1hr) via Bayeux (30min); 4 daily to **Rennes** (2hr) via Coutances and Pontorson.

From Vire Regular service to **Paris** via Argentan (1hr) and L'Aigle (1hr 30min); to **Villedieu** (20min) and Granville (1hr).

From Alençon 6 daily to **Caen** (1hr 15min) via Sées, Argentan, and St-Pierre; to **Tours** (2hr) via Le Mans.

From Lisieux 6 daily to **Rouen** (1hr 30min) via Bernay (25min) and Serquigny (30min); regular service to **Paris** (2hr) via Bernay and Evreux (45min); to **Cherbourg** (2hr 40min) via Caen

(30min) and Bayeux (50min); to **Trouville-Deauville** (30min), about 6 daily out of season and more frequently in summer; service extends to **Villers**, **Houlgate** and **Dives-Cabourg** (40min from Trouville) on Sundays and holidays throughout the year, and daily in July & Aug.

From **Evreux** 5 daily to **Conches** (17min) and **Serquigny** (40min).

Buses

*The main inland bus network is the **Bus Verts**, based at STDC, Place du Canada, 14000 CAEN, ☎31.86.55.30*

From **Caen** *Bus Verts* #32 and #33 to **Vire** (1hr 30min) via Villers-Bocage; *Bus Verts* #34 (5 daily, 2 on Sun) to **Flers** (1hr 20min) via Thury-Harcourt (36min) and Clécy (50min); *Bus Verts* #35 to **Falaise** (45min); to **Lisieux** (45min).

From **Lisieux** *Bus Verts* #50 to **Pont l'Evêque** (25min) and on to **Honfleur** (50min) or **Deauville** (45min); *Bus Verts* #52 to **St-Pierre-sur-Dives** (35min); *Bus Verts* #53 to **Vimoutiers** (1hr) via Livarot; *Bus Verts* #56 to **Orbec** (45min).

From **St-Lô** to **Bayeux** (30min); to **Cherbourg** (1hr 30min); to **Coutances** (30min).

From **Vire** *Bus Verts* #81 to **Condé-sur-Noireau** (30min); to **Fougères** (1hr 30min); to **Avranches** (45min).

From **Alençon** to **Bagnoles** (30min); to **Evreux** (2hr) via L'Aigle.

PART THREE

BRITTANY

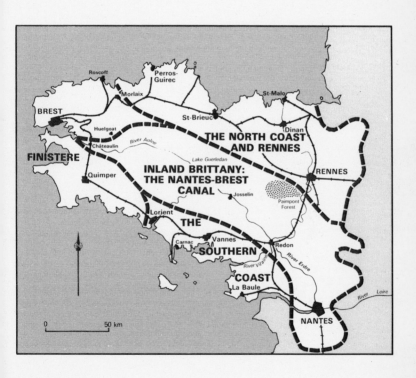

Roscoff

Perros-
Guirec

Morlaix

St-Malo

BREST

St-Brieuc

Dinan

Huelgoat

**THE NORTH COAST
AND RENNES**

Châteaulin

River Aulne

FINISTERE

Lake Guerledan

RENNES

Quimper

**INLAND BRITTANY:
THE NANTES-BREST
CANAL**

Josselin

Paimpont
Forest

Lorient

THE

Carnac

Vannes

Redon

SOUTHERN

River Vilaine

River Erdre

COAST

La Baule

River   Loire

NANTES

0   50 km

CHAPTER FOUR

THE NORTH COAST AND RENNES

Brittany's **northern coast** has its extremes. There are long sections, open to the full force of the Atlantic, that are spectacular but much too dangerous for swimming; others that shelter some of the region's best natural harbours and most peaceful resorts. The old *citadelle* port of **St-Malo** is an attractive point of arrival, from which you are well positioned for exploration, even if your main goals are elsewhere, in the south or in Finistère.

The best of the **resorts** are concentrated along the two strips of coast designated as the Côte d'Emeraude and Côte de Granit Rose. The **Côte d'Emeraude**, as green as its name suggests, remains largely unspoiled, especially the heather-covered wilds of Cap Fréhel. Its best-known resorts are traditionally English-dominated – and perhaps a little too much in the Anglo-Saxon image for their own good. But **Le Val-André** and **Erquy** have superb beaches, and everywhere there are secluded campsites for a night or two's stopover. Further west, beyond the placid **Baie de St-Brieuc** (St-Brieuc itself is for most holiday-makers a nuisance to be avoided) the coastline erupts into an almost garish tangle of pink granite boulders, the famed **Côte de Granit Rose**. This is harsher territory which was once, at **Paimpol** and elsewhere, the home of cod and whaling fleets. It is today more reliant on the tourist business, most resolutely so at the big twin resorts of **Perros-Guirrec** and **Ploumanac'h**. These are attractive nonetheless, and there are plenty of smaller places where you can avoid the crowds, such as **Loguivy** on the mainland, and, just offshore, the **Ile de Bréhat** – perhaps the most beautiful of all northern French islands.

Heading **inland** from St-Malo, the Rance estuary and the road south to Rennes provide most of the interest. On the latter, you are introduced to prehistoric and megalithic sights at **Dol**, and to the characteristic Breton **forests** at **Ville-Cartier** and **Fougères**. Down the Rance, **Dinan**, connected frequently by boat with both St-Malo and Dinard, is the medieval fortress town *par excellence*, the legacy of piratical and trading wealth through the Middle Ages and beyond; **Jugon-les-Lacs**, nearby, is a lakeside retreat. To the **east**, the **citadelles** of **Fougères** and **Vitré** still guard the frontier with Normandy. **Rennes** is less martial but after centuries of rivalry with Nantes is now firmly established as the Breton capital. It is by no means the prettiest

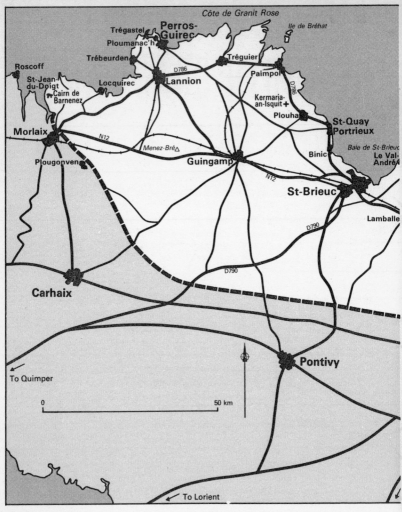

town in the province but is without doubt the liveliest, hosting a very considerable university and most of the Breton political and cultural organisations.

Rennes takes pride of place as far as **festivals** in the region are concerned, playing host in July to the **Tombées de la Nuit**, ten days of theatre and music, and in December to **Les Transmusicales**, which has become one of the major dates in the French rock calendar. Among numerous other annual events, the biggest and most compelling is the **Breton Music** festival, held each July at **St-Brieuc**, where there's also the ominous-sounding **Art Rock** festival at the end of October. The major traditional celebration is the *pardon* of St-Yves in **Tréguier** on the third Sunday in May.

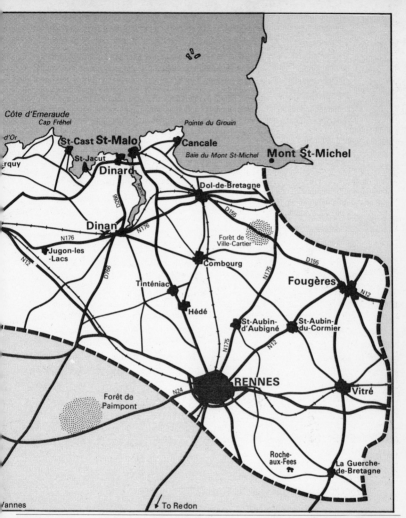

EAST: THE RANCE AND RENNES

Whether you approach across the Channel on the ferry from Portsmouth, or along the coast from Mont St-Michel in Normandy, the wide estuary of the **Rance river** makes a spectacular introduction to Brittany. The twin towns of **St-Malo** and **Dinard** stand to either side of its mouth, with **Dinan** guarding the head of the river itself twenty kilometres upstream. The few crossing places, such as along the top of the **Barrage de la Rance**, the tidal power dam, take in magnificent views of the sheltered banks – rich, fertile, and repeatedly pierced by tributaries.

To the east of the river, spreads **Mont St-Michel bay**, unwelcoming (and unrealistic) for swimming, but with its own drama – the sweeping tides and the pinnacle of the *Mont* (see Normandy, p.80). **Cancale**, the bay's most sheltered point in Brittany, is a good viewpoint from which to appreciate this, filling up meanwhile with the town's famed and acclaimed oysters.

Inland, all roads curl eventually to **Rennes**, or out towards Normandy. The attractions of the medieval fortress towns – **Fougères** and **Vitré** – have already been stressed. Quieter pleasures are to be found in the **Forêt de Ville Cartier**, south of Dol, and along the **Ile et Villaine canal**, around **Hédé** and **Tinténiac**.

Getting around, anywhere away from the coast or off main routes to Rennes, can be a problem. If you don't have your own transport, keep your sights low – even Fougères is served only by a scattering of market buses.

St-Malo

ST-MALO, walled and built with the same grey granite as Mont St-Michel, presents its best face to the sea. If you're not planning to come here by ferry from Portsmouth you may well want to consider the shuttle across the river from Dinard. Approaches by road are somewhat dismal: the signposts seem designed to confuse and all the roads seem to fizzle out into tram-lined docksides. Lost and bewildered cars circle the port like seagulls.

The city was originally a fortified island at the mouth of the Rance, controlling not only the estuary but the open sea beyond. For centuries its piratemariners forced English ships passing up the Channel to pay tribute. They brought wealth from further afield, too. Jacques Cartier who colonised Canada lived in and sailed from St-Malo, and the Argentinian name for the Falklands, *Las Malvinas*, derives from the islands' first French colonists, *Les Malouins*. St-Malo was itself an independent republic for four years in the sixteenth century, under the motto "*Ni Français, Ni Bretons, Malouins Suis*", and the long succession of pirates were never quite under anybody's control but their own.

These days, St-Malo is the most visited place in Brittany – and not just for the use of its ferry terminal. It can at times seem a little claustrophobic in the *intra-muros* streets of the old *citadelle*, which in any case hardly provides the most authentically Breton experience. However, it's a lively place with lots going on and you can drink – and eat – here as well as anywhere. A night spent before or after a ferry crossing is certainly no hardship.

The Citadelle and Suburbs

The old **citadelle** was for many years joined to the mainland only by a long, single causeway, before the original line of the coast was hidden forever by the construction of the harbour basin. It is very much the place to head for. Although the streets can be crowded, and the souvenir shops a little overpowering in their density, away from the more popular thoroughfares random exploration is fun, and you can surface to the light on the ramparts or pass through them to the beaches. The **ramparts** are complete, with wonderful

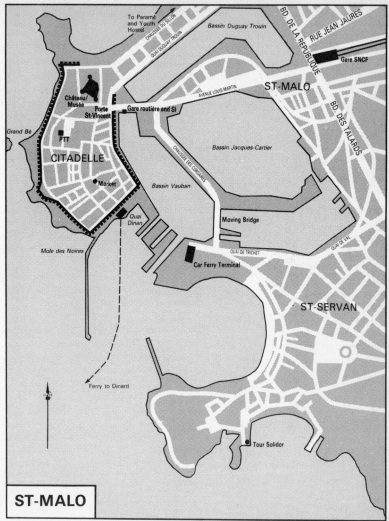

ST-MALO

views all around, especially to the west as the sun sets over the sea. Inside, the houses look much as they must have in the seventeenth century, stern and grim for all the lightness of their stone. This despite the fact that they are almost entirely reconstructed – photographs of the damage suffered in 1944, when General Patton bombarded the city for two weeks before the Germans surrendered, show barely a building left standing.

The main gate of the *citadelle* is the **Porte St-Vincent**, and in the castle to the right is the **town museum** (June–Oct daily 10am–noon & 2–6pm, rest of the year same hours but closed Tues). This is something of a hymn of praise to the "prodigious prosperity" enjoyed by St-Malo during its days of piracy, colonialism, and slave-trading. Climbing up the 169 steps of the castle keep, you pass a fascinating mixture of maps, diagrams and exhibits: chilling hand-bills from the Nazi occupation; accounts of the "infernal machine" used by the English to blow up the port in 1693; the savage four-pronged *chausse-trappes*, thrown by pirates onto the decks of ships being boarded to immobil-ise their crews. At the top a gull's-eye prospect takes in the whole *citadelle*.

It is possible to pass under the ramparts at a couple of points and on to the open shore, where a huge **beach** stretches away beyond the rather feature-less resort-suburb of **Paramé**. When the tide is low, the most popular walk is out to the small island of **Grand-Bé** – sometimes you even need to queue to get on to the short causeway. Solemn warnings are posted of the dangers of attempting to return from the island when the tide has risen too far – if you're caught there, there you have to stay. The island "sight" is the tomb of the nineteenth-century writer Chateaubriand, who was described by Marx as "the most classic incarnation of French *vanité* ... the false profundity, Byzantine exaggeration, emotional coquetry ... a never-before-seen mish-mash of lies". Suitably enough he features heavily on all the tourist brochures, which – with no apparent irony – extol his "modesty" in choosing so "isolated" a burial spot.

If you want more active pursuits, you can hire **bicycles** from *Diazo Vélocation* at 3 bd des Talards near the railway station, or as ever from the station itself. The coast is safer for paddlers than for swimmers, but is very popular for **windsurfing**. Boards are available for hire at *Technic Plongée Comarin* (15 bd de la République; ☎99.56.63.33), as well as several training schools; most surfers make for the beaches further along the coast towards Cancale, the **Plage du Verger** and the larger **Anse du Guesclin**.

A regular passenger **ferry to Dinard** operates from the **quai Dinan**, just outside the westernmost point of the ramparts in front of the port. The trip across the estuary takes an all-too-short ten minutes. There are also trips up the river to Dinan, and excursions along the coast, and from the ferry port itself boats go to Jersey as well as Plymouth.

Market days in St-Malo are Tuesday and Friday, as they are in **St-Servan**, a distinct suburb (within walking distance along the corniche) which curves around several small inlets and beaches to face the Barrage of the Rance. The **Tour Solidor** here, three linked towers built in 1382, is open all the year round for ninety-minute guided visits to its museum of clipper-ships (April–Sept morning and afternoon; winter afternoon only, closed Tues). In **Paramé** there are Wednesday and Saturday markets.

Practicalities

St-Malo's **gare SNCF** is convenient neither for the town nor the ferry: if you're planning a tight connection, beware. Similarly, travelling by car, reckon with the *Chaussée des Corsaires* in mind: this links the old town with the ferry termi-nal and can be closed for long periods while its moveable bridge is opened to let boats out of the *Bassin Jacques Cartier*. The **gare routière** – not a building, just an expanse of concrete – is for once more accessible, right in front of the city walls, and next to the **SI** (Port des Yachts; ☎99.56.64.48).

The city boasts of having a hundred **hotels**, including the traditional seaside boarding houses just off the beach. It's more fun to stay somewhere within the city walls, since that's where any nightlife takes place and it's a fair walk in through the docks from any of the surrounding suburbs. The disadvantage is that the *intra-muros* hotels tend to take advantage of the high summer demand by insisting that you eat in their own restaurants. This isn't strictly legal, but you won't get very far arguing. Preferred places to try for a room in the *citadelle* include the *Auberge Au Gai Bec* (corner of rue des Lauriers and rue Thévenard; ☎99.40.82.16), the *Moderne* (10 rue Corne-du-Cerf; ☎99.40.85.60), and the *Marguerite* (2 rue St-Benoît; ☎99.40.87.03). Otherwise, you have the choice of the rather staid family hotels in Paramé, or the array near the station on bd de la République, such as the *Europe* (no. 44; ☎99.56.13.42), the *Petite-Vitesse* (no. 42; ☎99.56.31.76) and *l'Arrivée* (no. 52; ☎99.56.30.78).

For information on **campsites** ring ☎99.56.41.36, which is a central number for the various municipal campsites, all inevitably quite a way from the town centre. There is a sort of **youth hostel**, one of the busiest in France although not formally part of the national network. It's at 37 av Pére Umbricht (☎99.56.15.32), the main street in Paramé, which runs parallel to the beach a couple of blocks inland.

Eating, the choice is enormous. The best restaurant is commonly acknowledged to be the *Duchesse Anne* (5 & 7 place Guy La Chambre), but since it's virtually double the price of any of the others you'd do well to stroll around just inside the ramparts comparing menus. The prices on the open café terraces can be exorbitant, but with so much competition you'll find any number of mouth-watering **menus** to choose from; the *Etoile de Mer* (5 rue Jacques-Cartier) and the *Auberge Au Gai Bec* (see above) are particularly recommended.

The *citadelle* is, however, not a good place for last-minute **shopping** if you're catching the ferry home. There are a few specialists – *Au Poids du Roy* (place du Poids du Roy) is a superb, if somewhat upmarket, *épicerie* – but for buying in any quantity you'd do better to head for *Le Continent* hypermarket on the southwest outskirts of town.

Across the Rance

The road from St-Malo to Dinard crosses the Rance along the top of the world's first **tidal power dam**, built in 1966 but alas failing to set a non-nuclear example to the rest of the province (where less than a hundred years ago there were 5000 working windmills). You can see how the dam works in a half-hour visit (8am–8pm) from the entrance on the west bank, just downstream from the lock. If you come here on foot or bicycle, try and make your way on the small roads through St-Servan, following the line of the estuary southwards rather than the signposted (circuitous) inland route. Taking the St-Malo to Dinard bus, get off at *Le Richardais* for the dam, and at *Gallic* for the centre of Dinard.

Dinard

DINARD, with casino, spacious shaded villas and a social calendar of regattas and ballet, owes its metamorphosis from a fishing village – like the Côte d'Azur resorts it resembles – to the tastes of the affluent nineteenth-century English. It is an expensive and not especially welcoming place to stay, though pleasant enough – and quite amusing in its uncanny resemblance to an enlarged mini-golf course. If you want to while away the odd hour, there's an enjoyable **coastal path**, the *Promenade du Clair du Lune*, which goes up from the estuary beach, the plage du Prieuré, over the tiny and now-exclusive port, and up to Pointe du Moulinet for views over to St-Malo. You can continue round the point to another **beach**, by the Casino, and on round more rocky outcrops to a more secluded strand at neighbouring St-Enogat.

Dinard is perhaps best seen as a boat excursion from St-Malo, as only a few of its many **hotels** are affordable. Try the *des Sables* (place Calvaire; ☎99.46.18.10), *de l'Arrivée* (5 place de la Gare; ☎99.46.13.05) or *Altair* (18 bd Féart; ☎99.46.13.58). There are two **campsites** just outside the town, the *Camping Municipal de Port-Blanc* (April–Sept; 99.46.10.74), beside the sea and consequently often very full, and *La Ville Mauny* (☎99.46.94.73) in the woods southwest of the centre. A third, *Le Prieuré* (May–Sept; ☎99.46.20.04), is a little way back from the beach on av de la Vicomte, about two kilometres up the Rance from the Pointe du Moulinet.

In Dinard, tickets for the **boat to St-Malo** are sold at 27 av George V. Just as from St-Malo, there are also trips **up the Rance** as far as Dinan.

Dinan

DINAN, like St-Malo, is a place seen to its best advantage when arriving by water. Behind the houses along the left bank quay where the boats arrive, a steep and cobbled street with fields and bramble thickets on either side climbs up to the 600-year-old ramparts, partly hidden by trees. Above that, St-Sauveur church sends the skyline even higher. The city itself is rather wonderful. The citadel has preserved almost intact its three-kilometre encirclement of protective masonry and street upon colourful street of late medieval houses within. For all its slightly unreal perfection, it's not excessively deluged with tourists. There are no very vital museums: the monument is the town, and time is easiest spent wandering from crêperie to café, admiring the overhanging houses along the way.

Unfortunately, there's only one small stretch of the **ramparts** that you can walk along, from the gardens behind St-Sauveur to a point just short of the Tour Sillon. You can however get a good general overview from the **Tour de l'Horloge** (July & Aug only, 10am–noon and 2–6pm, closed Sun) on rue de l'Horloge, or from the top of the keep that protects the town's southern approach. This latter contains a small local history museum, and together with the adjacent **Tour Coëtgen** is known as the Château Duchesse Anne (9am–noon & 2–7pm). On the lowest floor of the Tour Coëtgen lie a group of

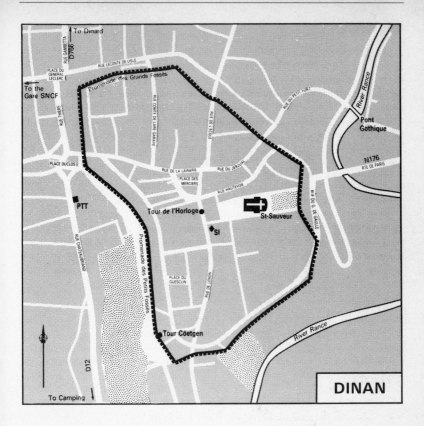

To Dinard
RUE GAMBETTA
D766
RUE LECONTE DE LISLE
PLACE DU
GENERAL
LECLERC
To the
Gare SNCF
Promenade des Grands Fossés
RUE DU PETIT FORT
River Rance
RUE THIERS
RUE COMTE DE LANT GARAYE
RUE DE L'ECOLE
Pont
Gothique
N176
RTE DE PARIS
PLACE DUCLOS
RUE DE LA LAINERIE
RUE DU JERZUAL
PLACE DES
MERCIERS
RUE HALITEVOIR
PTT
Tour de l'Horloge
St-Sauveur
RUE DU G. DE GAULLE
SI
Promenade des Petits Fossés
RUE CHATEAUBRIAND
PLACE DU
GUESCLIN
RUE DE LEHON
Tour Cöetgen
River Rance
D12

DINAN

To Camping

stone fifteenth-century notables – looking like some kind of medieval time
capsule about to de-petrify at any moment. In the valley beyond the château
there's an animal park and playground.

St-Sauveur church, very much the town's focus, is a real mix-up of ages,
with a Romanesque porch and an eighteenth-century steeple. Even its nine
Gothic chapels feature five different patterns of vaulting in no symmetrical
order; the most complex pair, in the centre, would make any spider proud. A
cenotaph contains the heart of Bertrand du Guesclin, the fourteenth-century
Breton warrior who fought and won a single combat with the English knight
Thomas of Canterbury (in what is now the place du Guesclin), to settle the
outcome of the siege of Dinan in 1364. Relics of his life and battles are scattered all over Brittany and Normandy; in death he restricted himself to four
separate burial places for different pieces of his body. North of the church,
the rue du Jerzual leads down to the gate of the same name, and then further
(as rue du Petit Fort) to a majestic old bridge over the Rance, lined with artisans' shops and restaurants. There's a **market** on Thursday.

Practicalities

Modern Dinan does exist, though as a rather gloomy exile from the *enclos*. In it you'll find the **gares SNCF** (with an art deco interior) and **routière**, a short walk away from place Duclos and the Grande Rue entrance to the citadel (left along rue Carnot and right at place G. Leclerc). Two **hotels** near the station are *de France* (7 place du 11 Novembre; ☎96.39.22.56) and *de la Consigne* (40 rue Carnot). Within the walls there's *du Théâtre* (2 rue Ste-Claire; ☎96.39.06.91) and *La Duchesse Anne* (10 place du Guesclin; ☎96.39.09.43). The **SI** is opposite the Tour de l'Horloge in the Hôtel Kératry (☎96.39.75.40).

The closest **campsite** is *La Nourais* (☎96.39.35.38) at 103 rue Chateaubriand which runs parallel to the western ramparts. Dinan's **youth hostel** (all year; ☎96.39.10.83) in the Moulin de Méen at Taden is not on any bus route; if you follow the *quai* seawards from the port on the town side, you'll see a small sign to the left after two kilometres.

The centre of town is better for **restaurants** than the port area, with the bar/grillhouse *Au Prélude* (20 rue Haute-Voie) being an especially enjoyable place to spend an evening. Don't be tempted by the rare "Indian" restaurant near the port, which is French-run and not recommended.

Around Mont St-Michel Bay

The **coastal road** D201 runs east from St-Malo to Cancale, past a succession of coves and beaches, where lines of dunes attempt to hang on against the battering from the sea. Look out for the **sculpted rocks** at Rothéneuf, shaped in the 1870s by the hermit priest Abbé Fouré into the forms of sea monsters. At the Pointe du Grouin, the line of cliffs turns sharply back on itself, at one extremity of the **Baie de Mont St-Michel**. This is a huge flat expanse of mud and sand, over which the tide – as just about every piece of literature on this region will tell you – can race faster than a galloping horse. It is dangerous to wander out too far, quite apart from the risk of quicksands, and, in the Breton part of the bay at least, the beaches have little appeal for bathers.

The course of the river Couesnon, which marks the border between Brittany and Normandy, has shifted much over the centuries. So too has the shoreline of the bay – in which traces of drowned villages can be seen when the tide is out. Bretons like to say that it is just an accident that the river now runs west of Mont St-Michel; be that as it may, the *Mont*, and Pontorson, the nearest town to it, are both in Normandy (see p.80). The pinnacle of *La Merveille*, however, remains clearly visible from every vantage point along the coast. The most spectacular views of all are from the **Pointe du Grouin**, a perilous and windy height which also overlooks the bird sanctuary of the **Iles des Landes**, to the east.

Cancale

CANCALE is not so much a one-horse as a one-mollusc town; the whole place is obsessed with the oyster, and with "*ostréiculture*". Its current population is, at 4600, less than it was a century ago, but the town looks much bigger than that would suggest – and the reason must be the visitors attracted by its edible hinged bivalves.

Oysters may have been a staple cheap working-class food in the past; these days in Cancale they are clasped to the bosoms, and slurped by the lips, of elegant *bourgeois* holiday-makers. In the old church of **St-Méen**, at the top of the hill, a small **Musée des Arts et Traditions Populaires** (July & Aug 10.30am–12.30pm & 3.30–7.30pm daily, closed Mon morning; rest of the year open Mon & Sat afternoon only) documents this obsession with meticulous precision. Cancale oysters have been found in the camps of Julius Caesar; were taken daily to Versailles for Louis XIV; and even accompanied Napoleon on the march to Moscow. The most famous symbol of the town – and its oyster cultivation – is the stark *Rocher du Cancale* just offshore; the museum lists all the *"Rochers du Cancale"* restaurants that have ever existed, including ones in Shanghai, Phnom Penh, and one in Moscow which closed in the 1830s.

From the rue des Parcs, next to the jetty of the port, you can see at low tide the **parcs** where the oysters are grown. At one time there was an annual event, *La Caravanne*, when a huge flotilla of sailing vessels dragged nets along the bottom of the sea for wild oysters; now they are farmed like any other crop. The seabed is divided into countless segments of different sizes, each segment having an individual owner who has the right to sell what it produces. The oysters are cultivated from year-old "spat" bought in from elsewhere. Behind, the rocks of the cliff are streaked and shiny like mother-of-pearl; underfoot the beach is littered with countless generations of empty shells.

The port area is very pretty and very smart, with a long line of upmarket glass-fronted hotels and restaurants. Cancale's **hotels** mostly insist that you eat if you want to stay – no great problem considering that there's nothing much else to do in the town. The *Continentale* (☎99.89.60.16) and the *Emeraude* (☎99.89.61.76) on the quai Thomas are among the more reasonable, both well worth a visit. Restaurants without exception specialise in every kind of seafood. The best **bar** around is the *Rayon Vert*, about four kilometres north of Cancale, just short of Port-Mer, which puts on regular **jazz and rock concerts** (☎99.89.61.61 for details). Cancale has a **market** on Sunday in the streets behind the main church, the rue de la Marine and the rue Cocar.

Dol

All approaches to Dol-de-Bretagne are guarded by the former island of **Mont Dol** – now eight rather marshy kilometres in from the sea. This abrupt granite outcrop, looking mountainous beyond its size on such a flat plain, was the legendary site of a battle between the Archangel Michael and the Devil. Various fancifully-named indentations in the rock, such as *the Devil's Claw*, testify to the savagery of their encounter, which was inevitably won by the saint. The site has been occupied since prehistoric times – flint implements have been unearthed alongside the bones of mammoths, sabre-toothed tigers, and even rhinoceri. Later on, it appears to have been used for worship

by the druids, before becoming, like Mont St-Michel, an island monastery. Traces of the abbey have long vanished, though the mythic battle may recall its foundation, with Christianity driving out the old religion. A plaque proclaims that visiting the small chapel on top earns a Papal Indulgence (presumably on the condition that you don't add to the copious graffiti on its walls). The climb is pleasant, too, a steep footpath winding up among the chestnuts and beeches to a solitary bar.

During the Middle Ages, **DOL-DE-BRETAGNE** was an important bishopric. It no longer has a bishop, though its **Cathedral** endures, with its strange, squat, tiled towers. Nearby is a **Musée d'Histoire et d'Art Populaire** (Easter to the end of September, 9.30am–6pm daily), bloated by the usual array of posed waxworks but with two rooms of astonishing wooden bits and pieces rescued in assorted states of decay from churches, often equally rotting, all over Brittany. These carvings and statues, some still brightly polychromed with their crust of eggy paint, range from the thirteenth to the nineteenth centuries.

There is not a great deal more to Dol, for visitors anyway. The commercial part of town is lively without being too modern; the *Katédral* bar, between the church and museum, is worth some of your time. And there's one very good value **hotel**, the *Bretagne* (pl Chateaubriand, ☎99.48.02.03; closed Oct).

The Menhir du Champ-Dolent

A short way out of town to the south, a small picnic area fenced-off among the fields contains the **Menhir du Champ Dolent**. According to one legend, this 9.6-metre standing stone dropped from the sky to separate two brothers who were on the point of mutual fratricide. Another has it that the menhir is inching its way into the soil, and the world will end when it disappears altogether. It has to be said, this would not be a particularly interesting spot on which to experience the end of the world. The unadorned stone, big though it undoubtedly is in its banal setting, has little of the romance or mystery of the megalithic sites of the Morbihan and elsewhere.

Combourg

The *Circuit Touristique* signposted from Dol continues beyond the menhir and the village of Trans to the **Forêt de Ville-Cartier**. The pines and beech of the forest sweep thickly down to a lake in which it is possible – in fact almost irresistible – to swim. Keeping to the *circuit*, along the D155, would lead eventually to Fougères (see p.122). Head back instead to **COMBOURG** if you want to see the castle that was the childhood home of the writer Chateaubriand, now buried at St-Malo. The *Tour du Chat* of the castle may be haunted, by a ghost taking the form of a cat. Chateaubriand himself claimed it was haunted by the ghost of the **wooden leg** of a former lord – and that the cat was merely an acquaintance of this phantasmal limb.

Beside the Canal: Hédé and Tinteniac

The main road **south to Rennes**, the N137, crosses a particularly pleasant stretch of the **Canal d'Ille-et-Vilaine**, between the two old towns of **HEDE** and **TINTENIAC**. There are excellent places to collapse in the sun between the many locks and lock-keepers' cottages, although the towpath isn't consistent enough to follow for any distance on foot, let alone bike. Hédé, with the *Hostellerie du Vieux Moulin* (☎99.45.45.70), and Tinténiac, with the *Auberge du Halage* (☎99.68.03.64), have excellent *logis*. St-Aubin d'Aubigne and St-Aubin du Cormier (see p.123) are other possible bases. The **Forêt du Paimpont** (see p.179), too, is well within reach and allows you to bypass Rennes.

Rennes

For a city which has been the capital and power centre of Brittany since the 1532 union with France, **RENNES** is, outwardly at least, uncharacteristic of the province. The layout is neo-classical and the buildings pompous. What potential it ever had as a picturesque tourist spot was destroyed on December 22 1720, when a drunken carpenter managed to set light to virtually the whole city. Only the area known as *Les Lices*, at the junction of the two rivers, the Ille and the Vilaine, was undamaged. The remodelling of the rest of the city was handed out to Parisian architects, not in deference to the capital but in an attempt to rival it.

The one central building to escape the fire was symbolically enough the **Palais de Justice**, home of the old Rennes *parlement* – a mixture of high court and council with unelected members. It is possible to see round this building, where the *parlement* fought battles with the French governor from the reign of Louis XIV up until the Revolution, and where the second trial of Dreyfus was held in 1899. Tours are at 9.45am, 10.30am, 11.15am, 2.15pm, 3pm, 4pm and 4.45pm daily in season, except Tuesday, and they start from the far right-hand corner of the courtyard. Each of the seventeenth-century chambers is more opulently gilded and adorned than the one before, culminating in the debating hall hung with Gobelin tapestries depicting scenes from the history of the duchy and the province. Every centimetre of the walls and ceilings is decorated – the Sun King style but on a relatively small scale.

The Vilaine flows through the centre of Rennes, narrowly confined into a steep-sided channel, and even forced underground at one point. At 3 quai Emile Zola, on the south side, the **Musée de Bretagne** gives one of the best possible introductions to the history and culture of Brittany. The prehistoric section is good, and includes the bones of a woolly rhinoceros found at Dol, but the greatest strength of the museum is the audiovisual presentation of the transition from the last century to the present – very much an ongoing process which you'll experience in peculiar jolts travelling around Brittany. In addition, there are charts to explain Brittany's role in current, and past, French history; one, especially enlightening, shows how in every presidential election since 1958 the Left has had a smaller share of the vote than in any other province.

The **Musée des Beaux Arts**, in the same building, owns some Leonardo drawings in addition to more local exhibits. Its specifically Breton room combines paintings of mythical themes – the Ile d'Ys legend (see p.160) by Luminais – and real life – a woman waiting for the fishermen to come back through stormy seas. The two museums are open 10am until noon and 2 to 6pm, closed on Tuesday, with a cheap combined ticket.

Food and Drink

The surviving **medieval quarter**, bordered by the canal to the west and the river to the south, radiates out from the **Porte Mordelaise**, the old ceremonial entrance to the city used by the Dukes of Brittany. This is the liveliest part of town, and it stays up late, particularly in the area around St-Aubin church. The twin market buildings in the **place des Lices** are splendid decaying monstrosities, with most of the city's interesting bars, restaurants and nightlife in general taking place in the streets to the north. Good solid country food is to be found at *Au Marché des Lices* (3 place du Bas-des-Lices, closed Sun) and *Le Grandgousier* (29 rue de Penhoët, closed Sun lunchtime). Round the back of the excellent *crêperie* at 5 place Ste-Anne, through an archway off rue Motte-Fablet, is an extraordinary view of medieval high-rise housing.

The **restaurants** and **bars** of the rue St-Malo, nearby, are the more or less exclusive preserve of students – very alternative by Breton standards, with what is virtually the only visible **gay scene** in the province. As for the rest of the city, there are concentrations of restaurants and cafés around the station, some way out from the centre – though don't use the absurdly priced buffet at the station itself. A little nearer the river is a **vegetarian restaurant**, *Le Thérébinthe*; *L'Opus* (closed Sun), on the place du Bretagne at 24 rue de la Chalotais, serves cheap meals and puts on occasional jazz concerts; *La Bodega* in the place St-Germain on the north bank has a good Spanish menu.

Culture

The presence of so many students – 35,000 all told – means that Rennes also has rather more visible **political and cultural activity** than most places in Brittany. If you're interested in talking to nationalist Breton campaigners the place to go is the *Centre Rennais d'Informations Bretonnes* (30 place des Lices). The co-operative **bookshop** *Breizh* at 17 rue Penhoët has cassettes of Breton and Celtic music along with with books and posters, and the people there are friendly. *L'Arvor* **cinema** at 29 rue d'Antrain shows *v.o.* (original language) films, and there's a large selection of English **books** in the *FNAC* bookshop in the *Colombier* shopping centre south of the river. Apropos of nothing, the Czech Milan Kundera wrote *The Book of Laughter and Regretting* as a lecturer at Rennes university, which is on a huge campus to the east.

Rennes is seen at its best in the first ten days of July, when the **Festival des Tombées de la nuit** takes over the whole city to celebrate Breton culture with music, theatre, film, mime and poetry, in joyful rejection of the influences of both Paris and Hollywood. In the second week of December an annual **rock festival**, *les Transmusicales*, attracts big-name acts from all over France and the world at large, though still with a Breton emphasis, and over the last ten years has made Rennes a rival to Rouen as the capital of French rock.

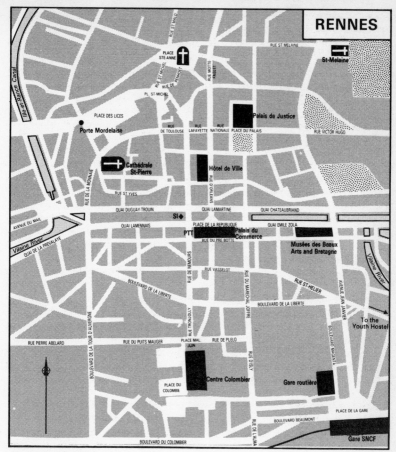

Accommodation

There are few **hotels** (and they are hard to find) in the old part of town and, if you've arrived by train or bus, it's easier to stay near the **gares SNCF** and **routière**. Those in the place de la Gare itself include the *Brest* (no. 15; ☎99.30.35.83) and the *Bretagne* (no. 7; ☎99.31.48.48). Closer in to the centre, the *Angleterre* (19 rue du Maréchal-Joffre; ☎99.79.38.61) is clean and friendly, while once you get there *Au Rocher de Cancale* (no. 10 in the medieval rue St-Michel, by the place des Lices; ☎99.79.20.83) is perfectly situated for Rennes' nightlife. The main **tourist office** for the province, and the **SI** for Rennes, are on the Pont du Nemours, where the Vilaine goes subterranean.

The **youth hostel** (☎99.33.22.33) is three kilometres out at 10–12 Canal St-Martin (on bus routes #20, #21 and #22 towards St-Gregoire: stop *Coëtlogon*). Bus #3 takes you northeast to Gayeulles (direction *St-Laurent*) where there's a bit of a walk down a lane to the city's **campsite** (☎99.36.91.22). Finally, if you're planning long-distance hitching, *Allostop* (see p.16) is on ☎99.30.98.87.

Fougères

FOUGERES has a topography impossible to grasp from a map; streets that look a few metres long turn out to be precipitous plunges down the escarpments of its split-levelled site, lanes collapse into flights of steps. The only way to get around, needless to say, is on foot.

Perhaps the oddest feature of the site is the positioning of the **castle**, built well below the main part of the town, on a low spit of land that separates, and is towered over by, two mighty rock faces. Massive and stunningly strong, it is protected by great curtain-walls and circled by a hacked-out moat full of weirs and waterfalls. In its heyday it also had the additional protection of the river Nançon. None of this, however, prevented its repeated capture by such medieval adventurers as, of course, du Guesclin.

Beyond the square by the castle, a little cluster of medieval houses still stands along the riverbank. From there you can cross the Nançon to the panoramic **Jardin des Arbres**, and the main street of the old fortified town. The castle keep, a romantic setting in *Les Chouans* (see below), is now a shoe museum, the main industry of the modern town below, leading down to the old (and now inactive) gare SNCF.

The two *logis de France*, in old Fougères, are the best value **hotels**. *Du Commerce* (☎99.94.40.40) is in the large market square near the station; the *Moderne* (☎99.99.00.24) at 15 rue du Tribunal, further up towards the town centre, has a good restaurant. A surprising alternative to French cooking is to be found in the excellent **Iranian restaurant** *Persépolis*, at 70 rue de la Pinterie, in front of the main gate of the castle, which serves an unusual but very appetising melange of Greek, Persian and Breton dishes. There is a **youth hostel** at 11 rue Beaumanoir (☎99.99.22.06). The **SI** at 1 place Aristide-Briand provides copious information on all aspects of the town and local countryside.

The **Forêt de Fougères**, a short way out on the D177 towards Vire (see p.101), is one of the most enjoyable in the province. The beech woods are spacious and light, with various megaliths and trails of old stones scattered in among the chestnut and spruce. It's quite a contrast to their normal bleak and windswept haunts to see dolmens sporting themselves in such verdant surroundings. If you have time, walk through the forest as far as **Le Chatellier**, a village set high in thick woods. For a **horseback** tour, contact the *Centre D'Initiation Aux Activités de Plein Air* in Chennedet (☎99.99.18.98).

BALZAC'S FOUGERES

The flavour of eighteenth-century Fougères is evoked in Balzac's *Les Chouans*, a bit of a potboiler with its absurd soap-opera twists but nonetheless an essentially historical account of the events surrounding the *Chouan* rebellion in Brittany, the attempt to restore the monarchy after the Revolution. Balzac makes great play of the town's unusual layout and of the various bloodthirsty survivors of the revolt that he met whilst doing his research: "In 1827, an old man accompanied by his wife was selling cattle at the Fougères market unremarked and unmolested, although he was the killer of more than one hundred persons."

St-Aubin-du-Cormier

Halfway between Fougères and Rennes on the N12, **ST-AUBIN-DU-CORMIER** makes a peaceful overnight stop. A bit too peaceful perhaps, the kind of town where the only entertainment in the only bar open at ten o'clock on a Saturday night is to take it in turns to look at a pet white hamster. But the very cheap *Hôtel du Bretagne* (68 rue de l'Eçu; ☎99.39.10.22) has to be recommended, a wonderful rambling old building, lumpy lino corridors stretching off in random directions upstairs and good food down.

There is, too, a major sight in St-Aubin – the keep of its old **castle**, which was demolished after the great battle here in 1488 in which the forces of Duke Francis were defeated by the French army. Many of the Breton soldiers were dressed in the English colours, of a black cross on white silk, to scare the French into believing that the Duke had extensive English reinforcements. The victorious French were told to spare all prisoners except the English; and so the hapless Bretons were massacred. Just one sheer wall of the castle survives, with a fireplace visible halfway up.

Immediately below the castle, next to a small lake, is the municipal **campsite**. A few kilometres out of town, the **Ville Olivier** on the D102 between St-Ouen and Mezières is a château which organises riding, canoeing and kayaking, and has its own *gîte d'étape*.

Vitré

VITRE runs Dinan close for the title of best-preserved medieval town in Brittany. Its walls are not quite complete, but their effect is enhanced by the fact that what lies outside them has changed so little. To the north are stark wooded slopes, while into the hillside beneath the castle in the west burrow the thickets of stone cottages that must once have been its medieval slums. This little suburb is called **Rachapt**, a corruption of the French for "repurchase", in memory of the time when the defendants of the castle finally paid the English army, that had been besieging it unsuccessfully for several years, to go away. The towers of the **castle** have sharp-pointed slate-grey roofs that make them look like pencils. Inside is a museum of local history. Hours are 10am to 12.15pm and 1.30 to 6pm; closed Tuesday in winter.

Vitré is a market town rather than an industrial centre, with its principal market held on Monday in the square in front of Nôtre-Dame church. The old city is full of twisting streets of half-timbered houses, a welcome proportion of which are bars. The **rue Beaudrairie** in particular has a fine selection. *Le Chaperon Rouge* at 12 bd des Jacobins is a **vegetarian restaurant**. An unusual incidental sight is the **post office**, with its modern stained-glass window behind the counter. Most of the **hotels** are around the station, where the ramparts have disappeared and the town imperceptibly blends into its newer sectors. This is a cheap as well as a pleasant place to stay; the *Petit-Billot* (place du Général-Leclerc; ☎99.75.02.10), and *Chêne-Vert* (place de la Gare; ☎99.75.00.58) are both good value, and the *Hôtel du Château* (5 rue Rallon, ☎99.74.58.59; closed Sun out of season), on a quiet road just below the castle, is a delight.

Around Vitré

There are several interesting smaller towns in the area. **DOMPIERRE** is attractive in its own right and claims a tiny (and disputed) place in history as the town where Roland, Charlemagne's nephew, might have died, were one to accept that the *Chanson de Roland* got the story entirely wrong. **CHAMPEAUX** has – is – a central paved square, surrounded by stone houses, with an ornate well in the centre. **CHATEAUBOURG**, halfway to Rennes, has a wonderful but ludicrously expensive hotel, the *Ar Milin* (☎99.00.30.91), straddling the river Vilaine.

About fifteen kilometres to the south, standing well off the D341 near Retiers, the **ROCHE-AUX-FEES** is the least-visited of the major megalithic monuments of Brittany. The "fairy rock" is a twenty-metre-long covered alleyway of stones, with no apparent funerary purpose or indeed any evidence that it was ever buried.

WEST ALONG THE COAST

To the west of the Rance, beyond Dinard, begins the green of the **Côte d'Emeraude**. Though the main image of this stretch is of developed family resorts, like **St-Jacut** and **Le Val-André**, it also offers wonderful camping, at its best around the heather-surrounded beaches near **Cap Fréhel** – for once unencroached upon by the military.

As you move further west, the coast becomes wilder and harsher; past **St-Brieuc** the seaside towns tend to be crammed into narrow rocky inlets or set well back in river estuaries, and only a few beaches are able to break out from the rocks. Beyond **Paimpol** the shoreline is known as the **Côte de Granit Rose** – no mere figure of speech for this primeval tangle of vast pink granite boulders. They should at least be seen, if only as a quick detour before catching the ferry at Pointe de l'Arcouest (near Paimpol) for **Bréhat**.

The Côte d'Emeraude

The coast immediately to the **west of Dinard** is one of Brittany's most traditional family resort areas, with old-fashioned holiday towns, safe sandy beaches and a plethora of well-organised campsites. **ST-JACUT** has everything young children could want – good sand, rocky pools to clamber about, and woods to scramble in. **ST-CAST** too is pleasant, and convenient for St-Malo.

Cap Fréhel

The only really out-of-the-ordinary place on this stretch, however, is **CAP FREHEL**. This high, warm expanse of heath, cliffs and heather is overvisited, but camping is prohibited for five kilometres around the tip and the headland itself, 400m walk from the road, remains unspoilt with no more than a few ruins of old buildings and a small "tearoom" nearby. Offshore, the heather-covered islands are grand to look at, although too tiny to visit; the view from the cape's lighthouse can extend as far as Jersey and the Ile de Bréhat. The **Fort la Latte**, to the east, is used regularly as a film-set. Its tower (containing a cannonball factory) is accessible only over two draw-bridges. To visit, you have to take guided tours (June–Sept 10am–12.30pm & 2.30–6.30pm; rest of the year Sun and holidays only, 2.30–5.30pm). Nearest places to stay are the ideal, isolated **campsite** at Pléhérel, and a summer-only **youth hostel** at Plévenon (☎96.61.91.87).

Erquy and Le Val-André

Further round, Erquy and Le Val-André both have huge beaches. At **ERQUY**, a perfect crescent dominated in the centre by a sailing school, the tide disappears way beyond the harbour entrance, leaving gentle ripples of paddling sand. The *Hôtel Beauséjour* (☎96.72.30.39) has a good view of the bay, and excellent fish dinners, while there are several campsites on the promontory (dotted with tiny coves) that leads to the Cap d'Erquy north of town.

At **LE VAL-ANDRE** the long pedestrian promenade at the sea-front feels oddly Victorian, consisting solely of huge old houses undisturbed by shops or bars. What amusements there are lurk on rue A. Charner behind. The recently refurbished *Hotel de la Mer* (no. 63; ☎96.72.20.44), compares well with any hotel anywhere; as well as having good cheap rooms, it serves food that is utterly magnificent, transporting *moules marinières* onto a hitherto undreamed-of plane.

A few kilometres to the west, the small lagoon of **DAHOUET** is more secluded, and has its own **campsite**.

Jugon-Les-Lacs and Lamballe

An alternative route west from Dinard and Dinan heads inland to **JUGON-LES-LACS**. This tiny old town lies at one end of its own lake (the *grand étang*), well below the water level but shielded by a massive cobblestone dyke. At the opposite end of town, the main road from Dinan to St-Brieuc crosses high above the valley on a viaduct. Jugon nestles cosily in between the two, with no room to expand even if it wanted to – a subdued place whose few streets are almost deserted in the evenings. If you want to stay, there are two good and moderately priced **hotels**, *La Grande Fontaine* (☎96.31.61.29) and *Le Petit Palace* (☎96.31.65.24).

For most of the way around **the lake**, there's no approach road or footpath, only meadows and trees sweeping down to the water. However, at *Le Bocage* **campsite** (☎96.31.60.16), just out of town along the D52 towards Mégrit, there's a small beach from which you can go swimming. It's very much a family campsite, with a heated swimming pool as well, and the hire of boats and **windsurfers** available with tuition from its *Ecole de Voile*.

The main N176 westwards from Jugon brings you after twenty kilometres to **LAMBALLE**, an old town crammed into a narrow valley beside a broad river, dominated by a church high up on battlement walls. The **hotel-restaurant** *A La Porte St-Martin* (☎96.34.71.61), and the half-timbered *Tête Noire* next door to the SI both have cheap rooms.

The Bay of St-Brieuc

ST-BRIEUC is far too busy being the industrial centre of the north to concern itself with entertaining tourists. It's an odd-looking city, with two very deep wooded valleys, spanned by viaducts, at its core, and it's almost impossible to bypass, however you're travelling. The streets are hectic, with the town centre cut in two by a virtual motorway, unrelieved by any public parks, and not much distinguished either by a mega-shopping complex. Motorists and cyclists, unfortunately, have little choice but to plough straight through rather than attempting to negotiate the backroads and steep hills around.

The most central **hotel** is *A Tournebride* (10 rue Mireille Chrysostome; ☎96.33.09.60), though a preferable base is the **youth hostel**, two kilometres out, at rue Alphonse Daudet, Ty Coat; this has bicycles and canoes for hire. There's a "biological" **restaurant** at 19 rue de Maréchal-Foch, *Le Grain de Sel*, which serves **vegetarian** meals made with the fresh organic produce it also sells both on the spot and at local markets.

Every July, St-Brieuc makes a concession to summer visitors by organising a **Festival of Breton Music**, while at the end of October comes the **Art Rock festival**; if you're interested, the **SI** at 7 rue St-Goueno can supply relevant information on both. Worth looking in on, too, are the **Comité Départmentale de Tourisme** for the Côtes-du-Nord at 1 rue Chateaubriand

(☎96.61.66.70); throughout the summer they organise one-day tours in the area to visit craft workshops of every variety – taxidermists, bakers, farmers, makers of furniture and cider.

Around the Bay

Continuing along the western edge of the V-shaped bay, the countryside becomes especially rich – it's called the *Goëlo* – but few of the resorts are particularly exciting. **BINIC** is probably the place to stay, all on a very small scale with a narrow port, a sandy beach, a tiny promenade around the town and to either side Devon-like meadows that roll down to the sea. The main industry is the sale of mud from the Ic for fertiliser. The *Galion* (☎96.73.61.30) and the *Printania* are good **hotels**, and there are several **campsites**, the best of them *Les Korrigans*.

ST-QUAY, a little to the north, is considerably more upmarket and a bit soulless, though there's certainly a lot of activity going on in its sister town of **PORTRIEUX**, where a new yachting marina seems to be attracting the growth of a slightly seedy waterfront. In St-Quay itself, the *logis Gerbot d'Avoine* (2 Bd de Littoral; ☎96.70.40.09) beside the beach makes an entertaining place to stay; the food is good, and the decor upstairs is quite astonishing. Crimson carpets creeping up the corridor walls make it look hideously like the hotel in *The Shining*, while in the rooms themselves washbasins and even showers are discreetly hidden away in cupboards.

Kermaria-an-Isquit

You may well get your first exposure to spoken Breton (see box below) in smaller villages such as **KERMARIA-AN-ISQUIT**. This is not an easy place to find, especially coming from Lanloup to the north; the best signposted of its approaches is along the D21 from Plouha. It is so much hidden away that rarely more than one or two visitors a day get to see the village's **chapel** and its extraordinary *Dance of Death*, one of the most striking of all French medieval images. Even in the summer, the church is not open regularly – you have to find Mme Hervé Droniou in the house just up the road on the left to let you in.

The **Dance of Death** is no medieval miniature. This huge series of frescoes covers the arcades all round the chapel. Painted in the plague-fearing fifteenth century, they show Ankou, the skeletal death-figure, leading representatives of all social classes in a *Danse Macabre*. Some of the original

At **Plouha**, a short way along the D786 from St-Quay, you cross what was traditionally the boundary between the French-speaking and Breton-speaking areas of Brittany. As a general indication, you can tell which language used to be spoken in a particular area by its place names. Thus from here on west there is a preponderance of names beginning with the Breton "PLOU" (meaning parish), "TREZ" (sand or beach), "KER" (town) or "PENN" (head). See p.236 for a comprehensive glossary of Breton words that you are likely to come across.

colours have faded, as a consequence of having once been whitewashed over, and many of the figures are now just silhouettes, but the fresco has lost little of its power to shock. In yellow, on a red background, the skeleton alternates with such living characters as a King, a Knight, a Bishop and a Peasant. Verses below, now mostly illegible though available in transcription, have each person pleading for life and lamenting death while Ankou insists that all must in the end come to him. Elsewhere in the church is a representation of the classic medieval theme of the encounter between the *Trois Vifs*, three finely-apparelled noblemen out hunting, with the *Trois Morts*, three corpses reflecting in a cemetery on the transience of all things human –

> *Nous avons bien este en chance*
> *Autrefoys, comme estes a present*
> *Mais vous viendrez a nostre dance*
> *Comme nous sommes maintenant*

In other words, we were lucky enough once to be like you, but you'll have to come and join our dance in the end.

The chapel was originally the private property of the lords of the manor of Noë Vert, and there is a tunnel, now flooded, linking it with the manor house five kilometres away. A small display case behind the altar contains the skull of one of the lords, and a couple of grotesque heart-shaped boxes hold the hearts of another and his wife. There is also a unique statue of the infant Jesus refusing milk from the Virgin's preferred breast, symbolising the choice of celestial over terrestrial food. A processional boat, raised on poles, and the ship-like vaulting of the roof, decorated with stylised yellow stars, lends an oddly Egyptian air.

Guingamp

The only town of any size in the centre of this northern peninsula, on the most direct route towards Finistère, **GUINGAMP** is an old weaving centre – its name possibly the source of the striped or checked fabric "gingham". It's a good-looking sort of place, although beyond the main square, with its fountain bedecked in griffins and gargoyles, and the Black Virgin in the basilica, there's not actually much to see. On the road out towards Morlaix is the "mountain" of the **Ménéz Bré**, a spectacular height amid these plains. In the mid-nineteenth century the local rector was often observed to climb to the mountain's peak on stormy nights, accompanied only by a donkey laden with books. For all his exemplary piety, his parishioners suspected him of sorcery and witchcraft; he was in fact doing early research into natural electrical forces.

Paimpol

PAIMPOL is an attractive town that has nonetheless lost something in its transition from working fishing port to pleasure harbour. It was once the centre of a cod and whaling fleet that sailed for the fisheries of Iceland each February, sent off with a ceremony marked by a famous *pardon*. From then until August or September the town would be empty of all young men. Soon after the annual expedition first took place, in 1852, as many as fifty vessels, with twenty-five men in each, set sail. A haunting glimpse of the way Paimpol used to look can be seen in the recently re-released silent film of Pierre Loti's book *Pêcheur d'Islande*, made on location here by Jacques de Baroncelli in 1924. Loti, and the heroine of his book, lived in the **place du Martray** in the centre of the town.

Paimpol is doubtless a very pleasant place to arrive by yacht, threading through the rocks, but from close quarters the tiny harbour looks disappointing, very much rebuilt and quite plain. It is, however, lively and busy in summer. The best value **hotels** are in the ugly new block that lines one side – *le Goëlo* (☎96.20.82.74) and *Duguay Truin*. As for **restaurants**, the menu of the *Restaurant du Port* may be appealing, but it's spoiled by rude service and meagre portions; *La Cotriade* which faces it across the harbour is a much better bet. There's an **alternative bookshop**, *Nouvelle Vague*, near the market place, and a **youth hostel** in the grand old *Château de Kerraoul* (all year; ☎96.20.82.15).

Loguivy-sur-mer

If Paimpol is too crowded for you, it's well worth continuing a few kilometres further across the headland to reach the little fishing hamlet of **LOGUIVY**. All of the long river inlets along this northern coast tend to conceal tiny coves; at Loguivy a working harbour manages to squeeze into one such gap in the rocks. There are no hotels, but *chambres d'hôte* (which don't work out any cheaper) are available at **Kéréveur** (M. Chaboud; ☎96.55.82.76) and **Kerloury** (I. Le Goaster; ☎96.20.85.23). Lenin came here for his summer holidays in July 1902. Both Loguivy and Paimpol are within easy reach of the spectacular **Pointe de l'Arcouest** and Bréhat.

The Ile de Bréhat

The **ILE DE BREHAT** – in reality two islands joined by a slip of a bridge – gives the appearance of spanning great latitudes. On the north side are windswept meadows of hemlock and yarrow, sloping down to chaotic erosions of rock; on the south, you're in the midst of palm trees, mimosa and eucalyptus. All around is a multitude of little islets – some walkable at high tide, others *propriété privée*, most just pink-orange rocks. Connected regularly by **ferry** (8.30am–7pm) from Pointe de l'Arcouest, Bréhat has to be one of the most beautiful places in Brittany, or for that matter France; and made all the better by the absence of cars.

Which isn't to say that it is a discovery. Over half the island houses now have temporary "second-home" residents – inevitably Parisian – and young Bréhatins leave in ever-increasing numbers for want of a place, let alone a job, of their own. In winter the remaining three hundred or so natives have Bréhat to themselves, without even a *gendarme*; the summer sees two officers imported from the mainland, along with upwards of three thousand tourists. As a visitor, you should find the Bréhatins friendly enough – it's the holiday-home owners that they really resent.

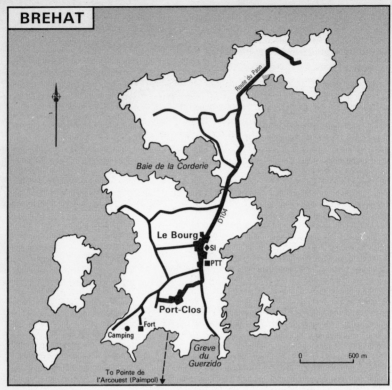

The island's three **hotels** are expensive and in any case booked all summer; in winter only *Aux Pêcheurs* stays open. But for **campers** there's a wonderful site in the woods high above the sea west of the port, and when that's closed you can pitch your tent almost anywhere. From the port, the right-hand track leads past the only **bike hire** outlet* and then turns north towards **Le Bourg** – Bréhat village – where the square is the centre of all activity. An **SI** is in the old Mairie on the right, and most days there's a small market; there are three or four restaurants, none cheap, so picnic fare is the best bet.

The beach to swim from (at low tide) is the eastern **Grève de Guerzido**, facing the mainland. Nearer the town the water is a bit murky, and the east coast generally is less accessible because of private estates. But in the north, even when Le Bourg is blocked up with visitors, you can walk and laze about in near solitude. Bréhat no longer has a castle (blown up twice by the English), but it does have a lighthouse, and a nineteenth-century **fort** in the woods before the campsite – with outer defences and an inner courtyard planted with azaleas, nasturtiums, potatoes and garlic by a dozen squatters protected by the sympathy of the island council from any threat of eviction.

---

* Bréhat is so small it's hardly worth bothering to hire a bike – or to take your own, the additional ferry fare being pretty exorbitant.

The Côte de Granit Rose

The whole of the northernmost stretch of the Breton coast, from Bréhat to Trégastel, has loosely come to be known as the **Côte de Granit Rose**. There are indeed great granite boulders scattered in the sea around the island of Bréhat, and at the various headlands to the west, but the most memorable stretch of coast lies around **Perros-Guirrec** where the pink granite rocks are eroded into fantastic shapes.

Pink granite is an absolutely gorgeous stone, wearing smooth and soft but also glittering sharply; it's hard to tire of it, despite being given every opportunity to do so. Which is just as well, for everything in this area seems to be made of it. The houses are faced with granite blocks, and the streets paved with them; the breakwaters in the sea are granite, and the polished pillars of the banks are granite. The hotels even have overgrown granite mini-golfs with little pink granite megaliths as obstacles; and the markets claim to sell *granit-smith* apples.

Tréguier

The D786 turns west from Paimpol, passing over a green *ria* on the bridge outside Lézardrieux before arriving at **TREGUIER**. This is one of the very few hill-towns in Brittany, set at the junction of the Jaudy and Guindy rivers. It was rebuilt on this fortified elevation in 848 after an earlier monastery was destroyed by Norman raiders. Its central feature is the **Cathédrale de St-Tugdual**, whose geometric Gothic spire, dotted with holes, contrasts sharply with its earlier Romanesque "Hastings" tower. Inside, the masonry blocks are appealingly crude, and dripping with damp that has somehow spared the wooden stalls. The cathedral contains the tomb of St Yves, a native of Tréguier who died in 1303 and – for his incorruptibility – became the patron saint of lawyers. Attempts to bribe him continue to this day; his tomb is surrounded by marble plaques and an inferno of candles invoking his aid, including one special plea from a group of American lawyers. A *pardon* of St Yves is held each year on the third Sunday in May.

The half-timbered houses of the square outside look down on a statue of Ernest Renan, a local writer and philosopher whose work formed part of the great nineteenth-century attempt to reinterpret traditional religious faith in the light of scientific discoveries. Worthy Catholics were so incensed at the erection of this memorial in 1903 that they soon built their own "Calvary of Reparation" on the quayside.

Tréguier has a **market** on Wednesday, with clothes and so on up by the Cathedral and food further down by the port. The assorted cafés and delis of the main square save their best displays for that day.

About ten kilometres inland from Tréguier and Lézardrieux, overlooking the Trieux river just where it starts to widen, is the fifteenth-century **château de la Roche-Jagu**. Its rooms are not especially interesting in themselves, but there are regular temporary exhibitions, and the château is worth visiting for its site alone (daily all year; 10am–noon & 2–7pm).

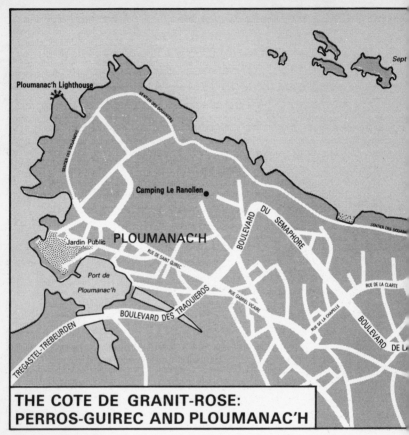

Sept

Ploumanac'h Lighthouse

SENTIER DES DOUANIERS

SENTIER DES DOUANIERS

Camping Le Ranolien

BOULEVARD DU SEMAPHORE

SENTIER DES DOUANIERS

Jardin Public

PLOUMANAC'H

RUE DE SAINT GUIREC

RUE DE LA CLARTE

Port de
Ploumanac'h

RUE GABRIEL VICAIRE

RUE DE LA CHAPELLE

BOULEVARD DES TRAOUIEROS

BOULEVARD DE LA

TREGASTEL-TREBEURDEN

THE COTE DE GRANIT-ROSE:
PERROS-GUIREC AND PLOUMANAC'H

Perros-Guirrec

PERROS-GUIRREC is the most popular resort along this coast, though not perhaps the most exciting. It has a reputation that seems to attract the retired – its tourist brochures list "playing *Scrabble*" as an attraction – and an array of shops intended to match: antiques, bric-a-brac and pottery with a big line in granite guillemots and puffins. And Perros is, too, a lot less city-like than it looks on the maps: most of its network of roads turn out to be tree-lined avenues of suburban villas.

Unless you have your own transport the town is surprisingly hard to reach; what buses there are arrive at and leave from the **Bassin du Lin Kin** in the port – a few hundred metres down from the town centre. If you arrive this way and plan to stay, a good first move is to hire a **bike**; there's a shop near the gendarmerie in the bd Aristide Briand. Preferable to the commercial streets is the walk around the headland to see the magnificent view from the *Table d'Orientation* at the sharp curve of the Boulevard Clémenceau.

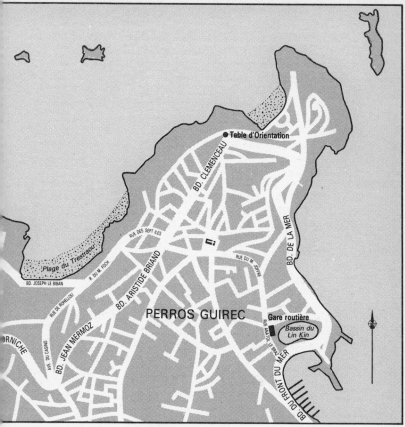

The best beach is the **Plage de Trestraou**, on the opposite side of town to the port, a long curve of sand speckled with bars and restaurants (the *Homard Bleu* and *l'Excelsior* are recommended). From here, boats sail on three-hour round trips to the bird sanctuary of **Sept-Iles**, circling though not actually landing on the seven craggy islands. The trips leave at 2pm every day from June to August, with extra sailings in high season at 9am. The ticket office (closed 11am–1.30pm) is next to the *Centre Nautique*, which offers sailing lessons and courses for both adults and children.

The Sentier des Douaniers

The Trestraou beach is made of ordinary sand; the pink granite coast proper starts just beyond its western end. The long **Sentier des Douaniers** pathway winds round the clifftops to **Ploumanac'h** past an astonishing succession of deformed and water-sculpted rocks. Birds wheel overhead towards the sanctuary, and battered boats shelter in the narrow inlets or bob uncontrollably out on the waves. There are patches and brief causeways of grass, clumps of purple heather and yellow gorse. Occasionally the rocks have crumbled into a sort of granite grit to make up a tiny beach; one boulder is strapped down by bands of ivy that prevent it rolling into the sea.

The rocks, in good French cataloguing fashion, have all been given "names" based on supposed resemblances in their shapes. The more banal ones – such as the great big *Foot* and the *Pancake* – are in a way the best; you can't help wondering, though, what committee it was, and when, that went along labelling the *Torpedo*, the *Armchair*, the *Tortoise* and *Napoleon's Hat*. Still, there's nothing to stop you making up your own, apart from the fear of revealing what may lurk in your imagination. Backing on to the path near a little beach about halfway round, though directly accessible on the other side by road, is an excellent **campsite** – *Le Ranolien* (open all year; ☎96.23.21.13).

Ploumanac'h

PLOUMANAC'H is a more active resort than Perros-Guirrec, though again with a dominant and specific clientele – this time families with youngish children. A pleasantly wild municipal park separates its two halves, the Bourg and the Plage; a tiny château on one of the many little islands frames the horizon above the high tides.

Next to the beach, there's a small lively square of restaurants and snackbars. The *Mao-Snack* is very good value and (like most places in this town) has special cheap menus for children. The emphasis on children does mean that Ploumanac'h goes to bed early; you can find yourself locked out of a slumbering hotel at 9.30pm. But prices at the **hotels** *Roch Hir* (☎96.23.23.24) and *du Parc* (☎96.23.24.88) are at least very reasonable. For a blow-out, go to *Le Relais* restaurant on the hill up to the village of La Clarté.

Trégastel and Trébeurden

Of the smaller villages further round the coast to the west, **TREGASTEL**, with a **campsite**, and **TREBEURDEN**, with a **youth hostel** (*Le Toëno*; ☎96.23.52.22), are functional stopovers. Trébeurden has managed to squeeze in an **aquarium** under a massive pile of boulders, and has a couple of huge lumps of pink granite slap in the middle of its fine beach.

The strangest sight along this coast, however, outdoing anything the erosions can manage, is just south of Trégastel on the **route de Calvaire**, where an old stone saint halfway up a high calvary raises his arm to bless or harangue the gleaming white discs and puffball dome of the **Pleumier-Bodou Telecommunications Centre**. A new pink granite "dolmen" commemorates its opening by De Gaulle in 1962, when it was the first receiving station to pick up signals from the American Telstar satellite. (Guided visits March 26–Oct 15, except Saturdays before June and after Sept.)

The Bay of Lannion

LANNION, set amidst plummeting hills and stairways, has streets of medieval housing, a modestly interesting church and a **youth hostel** conveniently positioned very near the station and the town centre (6 rue du 73e Territorial; ☎96.37.91.28). But it's the nearby bay to which Lannion gives its name that makes the biggest impression. One enormous beach stretches from St-Michel-en-Grève, which is little more than a bend in the road, as far as Locquirec; at low tide you can walk hundreds of metres out on the sands.

Locquirec
LOCQUIREC, across the bay, manages to have beaches on both sides, without ever quite being thin enough to be a real peninsula. Around the main port, smart houses stand in sloping gardens, looking very southern English with their whitewashed stone panels, grey slate roofs and jutting turreted windows. It's all dangerously close to the over-twee and none of the **hotels** is exactly cheap either – although the *Armorique* has so gorgeous a setting that perhaps it doesn't matter. The municipal campsite, a kilometre south along the corniche, is beautifully positioned, too.

On the last Sunday in July, Locquirec holds a combined *pardon de St-Jacques* and Festival of the Sea.

St-Jean-du-Doigt and Ploumilliau
Locquirec is just across the border of the department of Finistère, and by the direct road it is only a few kilometres further to Morlaix (see p.141). Following the coast, however, you come to ST-JEAN-DU-DOIGT, where the parish church contains an object held in veneration as the finger of John the Baptist. This sanctified digit is dipped into the Sacred Fountain to produce holy water. It was brought here in 1437 and is the principal object of the *pardon* on June 23 and 24 each year. A more recent tradition of pilgrimage has made St-Jean the site of massive anti-nuclear demonstrations.

An alternative inland route – or just a detour from Lannion – is to PLOUMILLIAU on the D30. Here the parish church contains a unique wooden representation of Ankou, the skeletal symbol of death. The statue, carrying a scythe to catch the living and a spade to bury them, was once carried in local processions.

The Cairn du Barnenez
At the mouth of the Morlaix estuary, the CAIRN DU BARNENEZ is a megalithic stone cairn to compare with that on the island of Gavrinis in the Morbihan (see p.210). There are actually two distinct pyramids, which were once buried under the same eighty-metre-long mound. Local tradition has it that a tunnel links the two cairns of this "home of the fairies", and continues out deep under the sea. The cairns themselves are now completely exposed to view, but most of the subterranean passages are closed to the public. The site is officially open from March until September, 9.30am until noon and 2 to 6.30pm, and closed on Tuesday and Wednesday, but outside those times virtually all there is to see is visible anyway from beyond the surrounding fence.

travel details

Trains

From Rennes 8 daily to Morlaix (2hr), via Lamballe, St-Brieuc, Guingamp, Plouaret, and continuing to Brest (2hr 45min) or Roscoff (2hr 45min); 8 daily to Paris-Montparnasse (3hr 15min; 2hr by the *Atlantique* high-speed *TGV*); 4 daily to Caen (3hr) via Dol and Pontorson; 4 daily to Vannes (1hr) and Quimper (2hr 30min); 4 daily to Nantes (1hr 30min).

From Lannion connecting service with Plouaret, holidays & June–Sept.

From Paimpol connecting service with Guingamp.

Buses

From St-Malo to Dinan (4 daily, 45min); to Fougères via Pontorson (3 daily, 2hr).

From Rennes to Fougères (7 daily, 1hr); to Dinan (hourly, 1hr 30min); to Dinard, (8 daily, 1hr 45min).

From Fougères to Vitré (4 daily – all early or late in the day, 35min); to Vire (Normandy) (2 daily, 1hr 30min).

From St-Brieuc to Lannion via Guingamp (4 daily, 1hr 40min); to Cap Fréhel via Val André (4 daily, 1hr 40min); to Carhaix (1 daily, 3hr), more frequently to Rostrenen; to Paimpol (7 daily, 1hr 30min); to Dinan (4 daily, 1hr); to Moncontour (4 daily, 1hr).

From Lannion to Trégastel and Perros-Guirrec (6 daily, 1hr).

Ferries

St-Malo to Portsmouth, *Brittany Ferries* (☎99.56.68.40 in St-Malo, ☎0705/827701 in Portsmouth), 9hr crossing (details on p.5); to the Channel Islands, run by *Emeraude Ferries* (☎99.81.61.46) and *Vedettes Blanches* (☎99.56.63.21); *Vedettes Blanches* also operate the regular 10min crossings to Dinard, and cruises on the Rance to Dinan.

Bréhat Island is reached by regular 10min trips from Pointe de l'Arcouest.

Barges

Boats for use on the Rance river and the Canal d'Ille-et-Vilaine can be hired from the following companies:

Chemins Nautiques Bretons, M et Mme Alan Gaze, **La Vicomte-sur-Rance**, 22690 Pleudihen-sur-Rance (☎96.83.28.71).

Diffusion Nautique R.M., M René Michel, **La Vicomte-sur-Rance**, 22690 Pleudihen-sur-Rance (☎96.83.35.40).

Breiz Marine, 5 Quai de la Donac, 35190 **Tinteniac** (☎99.68.10.15).

Argoat Nautic, B.P. 24 Port de Betton, 35830 **Betton** (☎99.55.70.36).

Base Nautique de Pont-Réan, M le Teinturier, Pont-Réan, 35580 **Guichen** (☎99.42.21.91).

Blue-Line, Port de Plaisance, 35480 **Messac** (☎99.34.60.11).

CHAPTER FIVE

FINISTERE

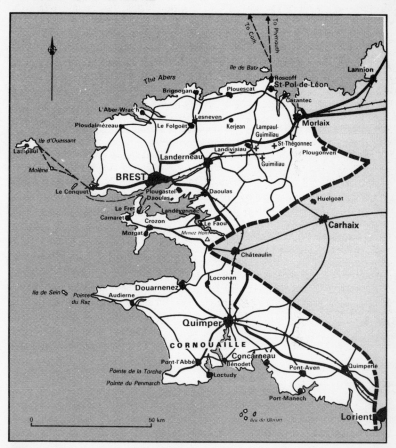

Finistère – "the End of the World" – has always been isolated from the French, even from the Breton, mainstream. It was the last refuge of the Druids from encroaching Christianity, and its forests and elaborate parish closes are testimony to its role as the province's spiritual heartland. Today – even though the port of Roscoff has re-opened the old maritime links with England, and the motorway now makes a complete loop around the end of the peninsula – it remains only sporadically touched by tourism and modern industry. It is here that you'll most often hear the Breton language spoken; here too, especially in the "Bigouden country" in the south, that you will see the traditional costumes worn for other than commercial reasons.

Memories of when Brittany was known as "Petit Bretagne", to distinguish it from "Grand Bretagne" across the water, still linger in the names of Finistère's two main areas. The northern peninsula is **Léon** (once Lyonesse), the southern is **Cornouaille** (the same word as "Cornwall"); both feature prominently in Arthurian legend. **The coast**, as ever, dominates the region's character, with the estuaries of this ragged shoreline, each sheltering its own tiny harbours, being its prime attractions. Rarely are conditions as bleak as you might expect from a land so exposed to the force of the Atlantic; heading west from **Roscoff**, your most likely point of arrival, there are possible stopping places all the way to **Le Conquet** (detailed in the following section). What can be a treacherous stretch of ocean separates that from **Ouessant** and **Molène**; and yet those two islands have the mildest winter climate of all France.

In the south, Cornouaille has two classic resorts in **Loctudy** and **Bénodet**, either side of the Odet estuary, while if you'd rather stay in a genuine lived-in town, **Quimper** is just upriver – the liveliest place here and one of the most pleasant, and least-sung, in France. A short distance east is **Pont-Aven**, which was Gauguin's home before he made off to the South Seas and which still maintains its artistic traditions. There are surprises everywhere – take the amazing **museum of Mechanical Musical Instruments** near Combrit, or the perfectly-preserved medieval village of **Locronan**, used as a film set for Polanski's *Tess*.

All Finistère offers the enticement of growing but not yet full-blown tourist development – facilities without the crowds. Its most popular region for holiday-makers is the **Crozon peninsula**, jutting into the sea beneath the **Ménez-Hom** mountain as a distinct entity between the two ancient realms. **Morgat** and **Camaret** here are both ideal for long and leisurely seaside stays, and all around there are opportunities for secluded camping.

LEON

The sequence of estuaries which score the coast in the north – the wildest and most dramatic in Brittany – are known both as *abers* (as they are in Welsh place names) and as *rias* (as they are in Spanish Galicia). In season, the vast beaches and dunes on the open Atlantic coast, for example around **Porspoder**, can be magnificent, while at any time you can stumble across tiny and deserted coves where the twisting and narrowing estuaries reach inland. One of the choicest spots is at **Trémazan**, the ruins of an ancient castle looking out across a great expanse of sand, while the working fishing village of **Le Conquet** is perhaps best of all. The one coastal place to avoid is the regional capital, and lone big city, of **Brest**, the base of the French Atlantic Fleet.

Inland, the **Parish Closes** lie strung out southwest of **Morlaix**, their churches and associated ensembles still perpetuating a fierce medieval rivalry. Also deserving a detour from the coast are the Renaissance **château of Kerjean** and the **menhir de Kerloas** (the highest still standing).

Roscoff

ROSCOFF has long been a major port – it was here for example that Bonnie Prince Charlie landed when fleeing after his defeat at Culloden – and the opening of its deep-water harbour in 1973 had especial significance in the general revitalisation of the Breton economy. The town itself, however, has remained a small resort. It may not look so on the map, but almost all activity is confined to the **rue Gambetta** and the **old port** – the rest of the roads are residential back streets full of retirement homes and stern institutions. The preservation of its old character is helped by the fact that both the ferry port and the **SNCF station** are some way from the town centre, which has recently been pedestrianised.

To **reach the town from the ferry**, turn right from the terminal, and follow the signs across a narrow promontory and down into the crescent of Roscoff's original natural harbour. Later than 9.15pm it's difficult to find a restaurant still serving; if you're on an evening ferry it's probably best to eat on the boat. **Hotels** are used to late arrivals, but may well be full. Two where it's well worth reserving a room – by phone from England if necessary – are on the main rue Amiral Réveillère: *des Arcades* (☎98.69.70.45) at no. 15, which has an unusually trendy bar and good cheap food in a dining-room with a stunning sea view; and the quieter *Les Chardons Bleus* (no. 4; ☎98.69.72.03), more expensive at around 200F per double. The **SI** in the converted Chapelle Saint-Anne (☎98.69.70.70) can give details on alternatives, including the **youth hostel** on the Ile de Batz (see below) and the municipal **campsite** a couple of kilometres west at **pointe de Perharidy** (Easter–Sept, ☎98.69.70.86). You can **hire bicycles** in Roscoff from *Desbordes* (rue Brizeux, ☎98.69.72.44).

ALEXIS GOURVENNEC AND BRITTANY FERRIES

Few British holiday-makers sailing to France with Brittany Ferries will realise the significance of ideology in the origins of that company. The ferry services from Roscoff to Plymouth and to Cork were started not simply to bring tourists, but also to revive the traditional trading links between the Celtic nations of Brittany, Ireland, and southwest England – links which were suppressed for centuries as an act of French state policy after the union of Brittany with France in 1532.

Until the 1960s there were no direct ferries crossing the Channel to Brittany, and until Brittany Ferries started up all the cross-Channel operators were British-owned. Brittany Ferries is the creation of Alexis Gourvennec, who in 1961, at 24, was the militant leader of a Breton farmers' co-operative. Frustrated at the lack of French government support, the farmers decided to start their own shipping line to find new markets for their produce – the immediate region of Roscoff and Morlaix being particularly noted for its artichokes and cauliflowers.

The financial success of the company has been such that it has expanded to run services from Britain to the Norman ports of Cherbourg and Caen, as well as to Spain; but it has also been an important factor in a resurgence of Breton fortunes that has as much cultural as commercial significance. Meanwhile the latest project of the Breton farmers is to expand Brest airport (at Guipavas) so that it will be able to handle Jumbo-jet loads of artichokes, for same-day sale in New York !

See p.230 for more details.

Most of the other hotels are further on round the headland, their prices in keeping with the rather grand atmosphere of the **Thalassotherapy Institute of Rockroum**, whose seawater cures attract many of their customers. Walk down past this and you'll come to the equally grand **Aquarium** (July 1–Sept 3 9.30am–noon and 2–7pm; Easter–Oct afternoons only; closed in winter). Part of a major Centre of Oceanographic Research, it has a well-displayed and comprehensive collection of the marine fauna of the Channel – interesting, if a little unsensational for anyone expecting the exotic.

The **harbour** is livelier, mixing an economy based on fishing and lobster-farming with relatively low-key pleasure-trips to the Ile de Batz. The *île* in fact looks almost walkable: a narrow pier stretches out three or four hundred metres towards it before abruptly plunging into deep rocky waters.

Until the last couple of centuries, the town made most of its money from piracy – like so many other ports along the Breton coast. There are a few reminders of that wealth in the ornate stone houses and the church with its sculpted ships and protruding stone cannons, all dating from the sixteenth century. One long-lasting relic no longer survives; the fig tree in the **Couvent des Capucines**, which was planted in 1625, and grew to 25 metres wide, producing up to four hundred kilos of fruit per year, was chopped down in 1987 to make room for a new building (two days before a preservation order came into effect).

Ile de Batz

In the summer there are several sailings each day to the **Ile de Batz** (pronounced Ba). The point from which boats leave Roscoff depends on the tide; at low tide it's the end of the pier, otherwise it's the port (from Roscoff, hourly 7.30am–8pm, from Batz 6.30am–8pm; two-hourly in winter). Batz is a somewhat windswept spot but well-endowed with sandy beaches; for campers looking to have a stretch of coastline to themselves, it could be ideal.

The island's first recorded inhabitant was a "laidley-worm", a dragon that infested the place in the sixth century. Such dragons normally symbolise pre-Christian religions, in this case perhaps a Druidic serpent cult. Allegorical or not, when Saint Pol arrived to found a monastery he wrapped a Byzantine stole around the unfortunate creature's neck and cast it into the sea. These days, there are no dragons; there aren't even any trees, just an awful lot of seaweed which is collected and sold for fertiliser.

The **boats** arrive at the quayside of the old island town. Walk uphill from here and you'll come to the **youth hostel** (April–Oct only, reservations essential; ☎98.61.77.69), at the picturesquely named Creac'h ar Bolloc'h, and the **campsite** (☎98.61.77.76). Higher still, on the island's peak, is a lighthouse you can visit. And beyond that, it's just the sands . . .

St-Pol

The main road **south from Roscoff** passes by fields of the famous Breton artichokes before arriving after six kilometres at **ST-POL-DE-LEON**. Pleasantly sited amidst rich gardens, this is not an exciting place but – assuming you've your own transport – has two churches that at least merit a pause.

The **Cathedral**, in the main town square, was rebuilt towards the end of the thirteenth century along the lines of Coutances – a quiet classic of unified Norman architecture. The remains of Saint Pol are inside, alongside a large bell, rung over the heads of pilgrims during his *pardon* on March 12 in the unlikely hope of curing headaches and ear diseases. Just downhill is the **Kreisker Chapel**, notable for its sharp-pointed soaring granite belfry, now coated in yellow moss. It was originally modelled on the Norman spire of St-Pierre at Caen, which was destroyed in the last war, but as an elegant improvement on its Norman counterpart was itself much copied. All over rural Brittany are dotted similar "Kreisker" spires. The dramatic view to be seen if you climb this spire (daily 10–11.30am and 2–6pm), out across the **Bay of Morlaix**, should be enough to persuade you to follow the road along the shore.

Carentec

From St-Pol, take the small foliage-covered lane down to join the D58, just in time to cross the **Pont de la Corde** that takes you to the resort and peninsula of **CARENTEC**. Studded with small coves and secluded beaches – and with the **Ile de Callot** an enticing hour's walk at low tide – this stretch of coast comes alive in summer with a scattering of seasonal **campsites**, among them the excellent *Les Mouettes* (☎98.67.02.46). For rooms, the **hotels** *La Falaise* (☎98.67.00.53) and *Porspol* (☎98.67.00.52) are both exceptional value. The Ile de Callot is the scene of a *pardon* and blessing of the sea on the Sunday after August 15 – a rather dour occasion, as are most of the serious religious festivals around Finistère.

The D78 runs on from Carentec by the sea, the estuary narrowing until at Locquenolé it is just the width of the River Morlaix. From then on it is a beautiful deep valley, with promenades and gardens along the stone-reinforced banks, and views across to isolated villages such as Dourduff on the other side.

Morlaix

Coming from the north, the opening view of **MORLAIX** is of the shiny masts of yachts, paralleling the enormous pink granite pillars of its viaduct. The viaduct was built in the 1860s to carry the Paris–Brest railway, and still looms almost two hundred feet above the central place des Otages despite all the English attempts to bomb it during World War II. The original plan was to have a funicular railway descending from the **SNCF station** to place Thiers, but, that never having been built, the station remains a sheer ascent from the town proper. SNCF have a ticket office down in the square to spare you the climb, which on foot is best made along the Venelle de la Roche, leading from just north of the viaduct. The first level of the viaduct is itself intermittently open to visitors, usually (but not always) from 11am to 7pm each day.

Although these days the port is dominated by pleasure craft, Morlaix has a long history as a trading centre, with tobacco – both legal and illegal – its main cargo. Hints of this past remain in the presence of a large cigar factory and in the estuary the Château de Taureau (now a sailing school), built as protection against English depredations. The most famous event of its history was the arrival in 1548 of Mary Stuart, the future Mary Queen of Scots, who landed here on her way to marry the French Dauphin. She was at the time just five years old, an aspect which may have contributed to local interest in the spectacle. A contemporary account records that the crush to catch a glimpse of the infant was so great that the inner town's "gates were thrown off their hinges and the chains from all the bridges were broken down."

The old centre of town is no longer walled and moated, though it remains in part medieval. There are few actual sights but the pleasure anyway is more in roaming the length of the steep stairways leading up from the **places des Otages and Cornic**, or in walking up to the viaduct from the top of Venelle aux Prêtres, along an almost rural overgrown path lined with brambles. The town **museum**, in the place des Jacobins, has a reasonably entertaining assortment of Roman wine jars, bits that have fallen off medieval churches, cannons and kitchen utensils, and a few modern paintings (9am–noon and 2–6pm, closed Tues). The only drawback is the powerful stench of fish that seeps up from the market held immediately below on the ground floor of this former church.

While it is known that Anne of Brittany stayed in Morlaix – a few years before Mary Stuart's arrival – there is no evidence to connect her with the **Maison de Duchesse** at 33 rue du Mur. However, the house is interesting in its own right, with intricate carvings on the outside, and a Renaissance winding staircase within. On the other side of the rue de Paris, the church of **St-Mathieu** contains a sombre and curious statue of the Madonna and Child – Mary's breast, reputedly, was lopped off by a prudish former priest, leaving the babe suckling at nothing. The whole statue opens down the middle to reveal a separate figure of God the Father, clutching a crucifix.

Practical Details

Getting your bearings in Morlaix is little problem. The old part of town begins just past the Hôtel de Ville. The **SI** is central, on the place des Otages, and the bus station two squares in towards the port on place Cornic. **Hotels** to try in the centre include *des Halles* (23 rue du Mur; ☎98.88.03.86), *Ste-Mélaine* (at the foot of the viaduct, but quiet; 77 rue Ange de Guernisac, ☎98.88.08.79), or *des Arcades* (11 place Cornic; ☎98.88.20.03); and nearer the station, *Calvez* (place Martin; ☎98.88.03.29). The **youth hostel** (Easter–Oct, ☎98.88.13.63) is two kilometres from the centre: take the *Kernégues* bus as far as either rue de Paris or place Traoulen, and it is just off to the left at 3 route de Paris. For the municipal **campsite** (June–Sept, ☎98.88.38.96), take the same bus, but in the opposite direction, as far as *La Vierge Noire*, and then continue north another 250m.

The streets between St-Mélaine church (above the SI) and the place des Jacobins are the best **restaurant** hunting grounds. One positive recommendation is the Spanish *El Marisco* (15 rue Ange de Guernisac, closed Wed), which specialises in seafood dishes from Galicia, and *paellas*; you can also get a good value meal at the *Hôtel des Halles*, as above. There are a few interesting **bars**

COREFF – REAL ALE IN BRITTANY

1985 saw the inauguration of an unlikely new product in Morlaix – the first Breton real ale! Two young Frenchmen, Christian Blanchard and Jean-François Malgorn, set up their own brewery, with the ambition of emulating the beers they had enjoyed on visits to Wales.

You should be able to find the resultant brew, *Coreff*, both locally and throughout Brittany in those bars which take pride in all things Breton. It's also possible to visit the brewery, the *Brasserie des Deux-Rivières*, at 1 place de la Madeleine (groups of ten, Tues–Thurs by arrangement; ☎98.63.41.92).

As for the beer itself, it's a sweet, rich and reasonably authentic brown ale which can make a welcome change to the lagers everywhere on offer.

---

on the adjacent place des Halles, including one on the south side where you can get Guinness. In the evenings, *Le Père Ubu*, close by the youth hostel at 37 rue du Callac, has fortnightly **café-théâtre** and good taped music, along with boisterous darts-playing Bretons; it stays open to 1am during the summer, closed Sunday and Monday. If you've transport, you might also consider driving out the twelve kilometres to **Plougonven**, where the *Club Coâtélan* (☎98.72.50.71) presents regular jazz, rock and blues concerts, with an eclectic and quirky selection of French and foreign performers.

Moving on from Morlaix, you are strategically poised. To the **west** are the **Parish Closes** – described in the following section – and, beyond them, access to the best of the **Finistère coast** around Le Conquet and the Crozon peninsula. **South**, via the sadly ruined **Forêt de Huelgoat** (see p.173) is the direct route to **Quimper**; and **east** you can take in the remarkable **Cairn du Barnenez** (p.135) en route to the **Côte de Granît Rose** (p.131).

The Parish Closes

A few miles west of Morlaix, bounded by the valleys of the Elorn and the Penzé rivers, lies an area remarkable for the wealth and distinction of its church architecture. This is where the best-known examples of what the French call *enclos paroissiaux* are to be found. The phrase translates into English as "parish close", and is used to describe a walled churchyard which incorporates a trinity of further elements – a cemetery, a calvary and an ossuary – in addition to the church itself.

The **ossuaries** – which now tend to contain nothing more alarming than a few rows of postcards – were previously charnel-houses, used to store the exhumed bones of less recent burials. They are in some ways the closes' most striking featurex, making explicit that peculiarly Breton closeness and continuity between the living and the dead. Parishioners would go to pray, with the informality of making a family visit, in the ossuary chapels where the dead bones of their families were on display. The relationship may have originated with the builders of the megalithic passage graves, which by this account served as doorways between our world and the netherworld. The actual cemeteries tend to be small, and in many cases have disappeared altogether.

The **calvaries**, which complete the ensemble, are tenuously based on the hill of Calvary, and thus surmounted by a crucifixion – but the definition is loose enough to take in any cluster of religious statuary, not necessarily even limited to Biblical scenes, standing on a single base.

That there are so many and such fine *enclos* in this region is due to a period of intense inter-village rivalry during the sixteenth and seventeenth centuries, when parishes competed to outdo each other in complexity and ornament. The interest today is partly in sensing this competition; partly in the contrast between the riches on show and the relative lack of prosperity of the present-day villages. An additional, more positive, layer is contributed, however, by the current revival of artesan traditions in the parishes. In several of the towns and villages you find stonemasons once more producing sculptures in granite.

A clearly signposted **route** leading past several of the most famous churches – St-Thégonnec, Guimiliau and Lampaul-Guimiliau – can be joined by leaving the N12 between Morlaix and Landivisiau at St-Thégonnec.

St-Thégonnec.

At the **ST-THEGONNEC** *enclos*, the church **pulpit**, carved by two brothers in 1683, is the acknowledged masterpiece, although it is covered so completely in detail – symbolic saints, sybils and arcane figures – that it is almost too ornate to appreciate. The painted oak **entombment** in the crypt under the ossuary, with a stunning life-size figure of Mary Magdalene, has more immediate effect.

Guimiliau

The showpiece at **GUIMILIAU** is the calvary, an incredible ensemble of over two hundred granite figures, enacting scenes from the life of Christ. A uniquely Breton illustration, just above the Last Supper, depicts the unfortunate Katell Gollet being torn to shreds by demons in punishment for stealing consecrated wafers to give to her lover (who of course turned out to be the Devil). It's not hard to imagine how the moral of this heavy-handed tale was used against women. Inside the church, the gutted shell of the seventeenth century organ, a lovely tangle of mangled wood, provides welcome contrast to all the neatness around; the 750 villagers are collecting for its restoration, but it seems fine as it is.

OTHER BRETON CHAPELS

If you're inspired by the closes to go in search of similar village churches elsewhere in Brittany, other notable closes and chapels include those at **Kermaria-an-Isquit** (p.127), **Ploumilliau** (p.135), **Grouannec** (p.147), **Pleyben** (see p.170), **St-Fiacre** (p.171) and **Guehenno** (p.179).

Lampaul-Guimiliau

The third of the major parish closes, **LAMPAUL-GUIMILIAU**, is a few miles further on. The church features a surprising deep blue ceiling, and an oak carved baptistry.

There are further interesting details in some of the **lesser-known churches** in the vicinity, particularly the representations of the skeletal figure of *Ankou*, symbol of death. At **La Martyre**, the oldest of the *enclos*, built in 1460, he clutches a skull; at **La Roche Maurice** he declares "I kill you all", a remark given extra force by the nearby ruined castle – in which Katell Gollet is supposed to have lived.

Alternative bases: Landivisiau and Landerneau

LANDIVISIAU is an alternative to Morlaix as a base from which to tour the parish closes. There's not much there, but coach tours operate regularly (from its main square) and you've a choice of several cheap **hotels**, best value of them *de l'Avenue* (☎98.68.11.67).

LANDERNEAU, a little more out of the way, is another possibility. Its hotels are slightly more expensive than those of Landivisiau but the town itself is a lot prettier, sited at the mouth of the Elorn estuary.

Kerjean

KERJEAN is little more than fifteen kilometres from Roscoff, and, if not quite the "Versailles of Brittany", as it is promoted, is a surprisingly classic château for this remote corner of France. It's not that easy to find however – you need to be on the D30, running from Plouescat to Landivisiau, and to turn right shortly after St-Vougay. The nearest stop on the Roscoff–Brest bus route is **Lanhouarneau**.

What you're confronted by when you do arrive is a moated Renaissance **château**, set in its own park. It was built in the sixteenth century by the lords of Kerjean, with the express intention of overshadowing the mansion of their former feudal overlord, the Carman of Lanhouarneau. Under some archaic quirk of fealty the Kerjean lords had been obliged each year to take an egg, in a cart, and to cook it for the Carman (whatever a Carman may have been). The château must have made the memory a whole lot easier to bear.

The building, state property these days, is an odd jumble of the authentic, the restored, and the imported. There is one original ceiling, one original floor, and one original door; and the guide on the 45-minute tour has one original joke to match. Nevertheless it's an interesting place, and there's a certain amusement to be derived from the odd placing of objects and the lack of explanations. In the scullery are two thirteenth-century choirstalls from St-Pol cathedral, each seat carved with the head of its occupant; a statue of Saint Sebastian "run through with arrows" has not an arrow in sight; and it is unclear quite what Saint Anthony is doing "with the little pig". More standard Breton furnishings are the cupboard-like panelled box-beds, which people used to climb inside to sleep – shut in tight for the night. **Tours** run from 9 to 11am and 2 until 5pm, daily except Tuesday; the castle gates are shut while each tour is in progress.

Lesneven and Le Folgoët

Continuing inland, whether you are headed for Southern Brittany or for Le Conquet and Ouessant island, Le Folgoët is another stop worth planning for. It is more easily accessible than Kerjean, though by bus you'll probably find yourself dropped a couple of kilometres out at the small town of **LESNEVEN**. This is not itself of great interest, though its ivy-coated café is an attractive place to break your journey. There is an abbey, too, on the main square, and some eccentric houses – slate-roofed and convex-panelled – in the narrow lanes. A visit to the **German war cemetery** a short distance southeast of the centre is a sobering experience (see p.73 for a general piece on war cemeteries).

LE FOLGOET is about half an hour's walk. At first sight no more than a small village, with a well-kept and rather English-looking green, it owes its **Notre-Dame** church – as well as its name, "Fool's Wood" – to a fourteenth-century simpleton called Solomon. After an unappreciated lifetime repeating the four Breton words for "O Lady Virgin Mary", he found fame in death by growing a white lily out of his mouth. The church was erected on the site of his favourite spring, and holds a *pardon* on September 8 or the preceding Sunday. (On the fourth Sunday of July there is also a *pardon* of St Christopher, which involves a blessing of cars that non-motorists may find verging on the blasphemous.) In its quieter moments however it's a lovely church, colourfully garnished with orange moss and clinging verdure (a sign of the penetrating damp inside), and with a bumpy and stubbly approximation of a "Kreisker" spire. It has been restored bit by bit since the damage of the Revolution, and an unusual amount of statuary has been placed on the many niches low down all around the outside. The most recent expenditure has been to put fresh white plaster noses on the apostles guarding its entrance, who in consequence look like hastily rounded-up choirboys. Immediately opposite, a fifteenth-century manor house has arranged in the lush lawns by its front path a selection of decaying sculpture from the church, gargoyles and griffins and an armless Jesus.

The Abers of the Northwest Coast

The coast west from Roscoff is some of the most dramatic in Brittany – a jagged series of *abers*, deep narrow estuaries amidst which are clustered small, isolated resorts. It's a little on the bracing side, especially if you're making use of the numerous campsites, but that is generally seen as part of the appeal. In summer, at least, the temperatures are mild enough, and things get progressively more sheltered as you move round towards Le Conquet and Brest.

Plouescat
PLOUESCAT is the first real resort, coming from Roscoff. It is not quite on the sea itself but there are **campsites** at each of its three adjacent beaches – **Pors-Guen**, **Pors-Meur** (☎98.69.63.16), and **Poul Foën** (☎98.69.80.81). In

the town, you'll find a high-roofed old wooden market hall, excellent for picnic provisions, and a statue of a seahorse with a yin and yang symbol in its tail. At the edge of the bay, about a kilometre out from the centre, the *Auberge Le Kersabiec* serves good food. Of the **hotels**, best value is the *Baie de Kernic* (☎98.69.63.41). The bus from Roscoff to Brest stops at Plouescat before turning inland.

> The council of **Plouescat** attained a certain notoriety in July 1987, when its members decided they could no longer live with the embarrassing presence of an exceptionally phallic rock on one of the local beaches, and dynamited it to smithereens at dead of night. Local artists responded by creating several much more embarrassing substitutes which you might care to look out for.

Brignogan-Plage

BRIGNOGAN-PLAGE, on the next *aber*, has a small natural harbour, once the lair of wreckers, with beaches and weather-beaten rocks to either side, as well as its own menhir. The two high-season **campsites** are the *Keravezan* (☎98.83.41.65) and the *du Phare* (☎98.83.45.06), while the hotel *Castel Regis* (☎98.83.40.2) is expensive but beautifully situated. There are also schools of both sailing and riding. In between Brignogan and Plouescat, the village of **KEREMMA**, inland and set along a green avenue lined with meadows of purple and yellow flowers, also has a small **campsite** (☎98.61.62.79).

Grouannec

Moving west again, along the D10, **PLOUGUERNEAU** has the **hotel/ restaurant** *Les Abériades* (☎98.04.71.01; closed out of season on Sunday evening and Monday) to recommend it. It's also near to an unexpected pleasure, the church of **Notre-Dame de Grouannec**, a small but complete parish close ensemble about four kilometres inland. It has been extensively restored, and looks all the better for it, with its fountain, ossuary, mini-cloister and profusion of gargoyles.

Aber Wrac'h

As a place to stay any length of time, the yachting port of **ABER-WRAC'H** is more promising. An attractive, modest-sized resort, this is in easy reach of a whole range of sandy beaches and a couple of worthwhile excursions. At **LILIA** you can take a boat to visit the 252ft **Vierge lighthouse**, and near the tip of the next headland is the castle of Trémazan.

Trémazan

Once past **PORTSALL**, the coast becomes a glorious succession of dunes and open spaces, with long beaches stretching at low tide way out towards tiny islands. A particularly romantic spot is where the crumbling walls of the **castle** of **TREMAZAN** look down on a magnificent beach. This is where the fleeing Tristan and Iseult are said to have landed in Brittany, and the cracked ivy-covered keep still stands proud, pierced by a large heart-shaped hole.

This "Sleeping Beauty" castle is not formally open to the public; it's totally overgrown, and to reach it you have to scramble your way through the brambles that totally fill its former moat. Once you're there, however, it's a real haven for a summer afternoon.

In the immediate vicinity, the *logis* at **Kersaint Landunvez**, the *Hostelerie du Castel* (☎98.48.63.35) is a good overnight stop. That's a little isolated, though, and you migh⁺ prefer to stay either in Aber Wrac'h or in Porspoder a few kilometres further on – pausing to look at the exquisite wooden seaside **chapel of St Samson** on the way.

Porspoder

PORSPODER is itself a pretty quiet place, but does serve as a centre for the many campers who set themselves up on the dunes of the **Presqu'île St-Laurent** which faces it. Most of the houses around are empty other than in summer – it must be pretty bleak in winter – but in season it's an attractive place to be, open to the ocean. There's a cheap **hotel**, the *Pen Ar Bed* (☎98.89.90.38), as well as **rooms** to let (for example from Mme Gautier, ☎98.89.99.72) along the long seafront Rue de l'Europe.

Le Conquet

LE CONQUET, the southernmost of the *abers* resorts, makes the best holiday base of all. A wonderful place, scarcely developed, it is flanked by a long beach of clean white sand, protected from the winds by the narrow spit of the Kermorvan peninsula, and has ferry access to the islands of Ouessant and Molène. It is very much a working fishing village, the grey stone houses leading down to the stone jetties of a cramped harbour – which occasionally floods, to the intense amusement of the locals, the waves washing over the cars left by tourists making the trip to Ouessant.

The coast around Le Conquet is low-lying, not the rocky confrontation with a savage sea that one might expect, and Kermorvan, across the estuary, seems to glide into the sea – its shallow cliffs topped by a strip of turf that looks as if you could peel it right off. Apart from the lighthouse at the end, the peninsula is just grassland, bare of buildings, and a lovely place to walk in the evening across the footbridge from Le Conquet.

The *Hôtel du Bretagne* (16 Rue Lt-Jourden; ☎98.89.00.02), has cheap **rooms** looking out across this view, and reasonable food. The larger *Pointe Ste Barbe* (☎98.89.00.26), right next to the ferry harbour, is more expensive, with something of a gourmets' reputation, and there are also two well-equipped campsites, *Le Théven* (☎98.89.06.90) and *Les Sablons Blancs* (☎98.89.01.64). **Market** day is Tuesday.

The most exciting trips out from Le Conquet are to the islands – detailed below. As a variation, though, a good walk five kilometres south brings you to the lighthouse at **Pointe St-Mathieu**, looking out to the islands from its site among the ruins of a Benedictine abbey.

The Islands : Ouessant And Molène

The island of **Ouessant**, Ushant in English, lies thirty kilometres northwest of Le Conquet, and its lighthouse at Creac'h (said to be the strongest in the world) is regarded as the entrance to the English Channel. It's at the end of a chain of smaller islands and half-submerged granite rocks. Most are uninhabited, or like Beniguet the preserve only of rabbits, but **Molène**, midway, has a village and can be visited. Not all boats from Le Conquet (or from Brest), however, stop at both islands and it would be hard to visit more than one in a single day.

Ouessant

The ride to **OUESSANT** is generally a tranquil affair – though the ferry has to pick its way from buoy to buoy, through a sea which is liable suddenly to blow up and become too dangerous to navigate. There have been many wrecks among the reefs, most famously the *Drummond Castle* which foundered as the finale to a concert celebrating the end of its voyage in June 1896.

TIMETABLE OF ISLAND FERRIES			
	Ouessant to Molène, Le Conquet and Brest	Brest to Le Conquet, Molène, and Ouessant	Le Conquet to Molène and Ouessant
Monday	5pm	8.30am	9.30am
Tuesday	8.30am		
Wednesday	5pm	8.30am	9.30am
Thursday	8.30am, 5pm	8.30am	9.30am
Friday	5pm*, 7.30pm	8.30am	9.30am, 6.30pm
Saturday	8.30am, 10.30am*, 5pm	8.30am	9.30am, 1.30pm
Sunday	5pm	8.30am	9.30am
	* To Le Conquet **only**		
For all details, including weather conditions (liable to affect sailings): ☎98.80.24.68			

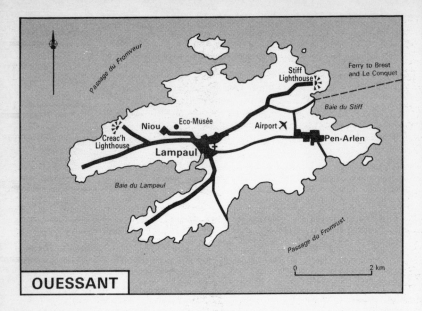

OUESSANT

For all its storms, though, the climate is mild – Ouessant even records the highest mean temperatures in France in January and February.

You arrive on Ouessant at the new **harbour** in the ominous-sounding Baie du Stiff. There are a scattering of houses here, and dotted about the island, but the only town (with the only hotels and restaurants) is four kilometres distant at Lampaul. Everybody from the boat heads there, either by the bus that meets each arriving ferry, on bicycles hired from one of the many waiting entrepreneurs, or in a long walking procession that straggles along the one road. Bicycle hire is a good idea, as the island is really too big to explore on foot.

LAMPAUL, as well as its more mundane facilities, has Ouessant's best beaches sprawled around its bay. There are few specific sights, and the whole place quickly becomes very familiar. But the town cemetery is worth visiting, with its war memorial listing all the ships in which the townsfolk were lost, graves of unknown sailors washed ashore, and chapel of wax _proëlla crosses_ symbolising the many islanders who never returned from the sea. So too is the **Eco-Musée** – a reconstruction of a traditional island house – at nearby **Niou**.

The **Creac'h lighthouse**, though itself closed to the public, is a good point from which to set out along the barren and exposed rocks of the north coast. Particularly in September and other times of migration, this is a remarkable spot for bird-watching; puffins, storm petrels, cormorants and penguins can all be seen. The star-shaped formations of crumbling walls are not extra-terrestrial relics, but built so that the sheep – peculiarly tame here – can shelter from the strong winds.

Practical details

Staying overnight, you could camp almost anywhere on the island, making arrangements with the nearest farmhouse (which may well let out rooms, too). In Lampaul, the **hotels** *Océan* (with the best food; ☎98.48.80.03), *Roch ar Mor* (☎98.48.80.19) and *Fromveur* (☎98.48.81.30) are all reasonably priced, for a fairly minimal standard; the Océan also organises musical evenings. There is, too, a small official campsite, the *Pen ar Bed* (☎98.48.84.65). **Restaurants** are at standard prices. If you just come for a day, though, it's a good idea to buy a picnic before you set out – the Lampaul shops have limited and rather pricey supplies.

Molène

MOLENE is quite well-populated for a sparse strip of sand. The port itself is better protected than that of Ouessant, and so there are more fishermen based here. The island's inhabitants derive their income from seaweed collection and drying – and to an extent from crabbing and crayfish, which they gather on foot, canoe and even tractor at low tide. The tides are more than usually dramatic, halving or doubling the island's territory at a stroke. Hence the origin of the name Molène, which comes from the Breton for "the bald isle".

Few people do more than look around for an afternoon's excursion from Le Conquet, but it's quite possible to stay on Molène, and to enjoy it. There are rooms – very chilly in winter – at *Kastell An Doal* (☎98.84.19.11), one of the old buildings by the port, and it's also possible to arrange to stay in a private house (☎98.84.19.05 for details). As for sights, there is even less of tangible note than on Ouessant. Walking the rocks and the coast is the basic activity. Once again, though, the island cemetery is poignant and interesting, redolent of small community life in its concentration of babies' graves from a typhoid epidemic in the last century; they are marked by silver crosses, repainted each November 1. Equally small-community is the island's main anecdote, told to anyone drinking an evening away, of the time in 1967 when the whole population gathered to watch the oil tanker *Torrey Canyon* floundering offshore in the passage de Fromveur.

Brest

BREST is set in a magnificent natural harbour, the *Rade de Brest*, sheltered doubly from the ocean storms – by the bulk of Léon, and to the south by the Crozon peninsula. It's a site, given utility by an almost two-kilometre-wide deepwater channel, that has for centuries attracted the navy. Richelieu, Vauban and Napoleon all developed the port and it is today the base of the French Atlantic fleet.

From a distance, from across the bay, the city can look appealing. But closer in it takes a real effort of will to decide to stop longer than it takes to change buses or trains. The roads are racetracks; the suburbs remorselessly industrial; and the last war comprehensively destroyed any historic interest that may once have existed. It was necessary for the city to resume normal life as soon as possible, which meant the rebuilding had to be rushed at the expense of restoration. The most rational reason for an outsider to visit would probably be for the bagpipe festival, held here for three days in August.

If you're committed, however, a walk along the **Cours Dajot**, which displays the docklands in all their glory, is the best way of filling the odd hour. There are schools of various naval disciplines; arsenals; the Inscription Maritime (the marine records office); and the largest lifting bridge in Europe, the **Pont de Recouvrance**. The dry dock, with its capacity for ships up to 550,000 tons, is one of the six biggest ship-repairing centres in the world. (Only French citizens may visit the naval base itself.)

The **château** looks impressive on its headland, and offers a superb panorama of the city and the bay, but once inside it's not especially interesting. Three of its towers house the National Marine Museum (9.15am–noon & 2.20–6pm, daily except Tues).

Practical details

Brest's very central **SI** (☎98.44.24.96) is in a new building in the Place du Général-Leclerc. Reasonable **hotels**, for anyone stranded, include the welcoming *Siam* (8 rue de Couédic, ☎98.44.44.94), the *Bellevue* (53 rue Victor-Hugo, ☎98.80.51.78), or the upmarket *des Voyageurs*, 15 av Clemenceau (☎98.80.25.73). The **youth hostel** (☎98.41.90.41) is three kilometres east at *Moulin Blanc* near the mouth of the Elorn, reached by the "Bus Albatros" from the SNCF station. Campers – don't even think about it.

For an evening out, *Chez Buchir* (13 rue Borda, near the Pont de Recouvrance; go for the couscous) and *Le Tire-bouchon* (20 rue de l'Observatoire) are **restaurants** to relish; the liveliest bar (though as ever that's a euphemism for "full of students") is the *Café de la Plage* in the place Guérin.

Around Brest

Exploring Léon from a base in Brest, Le Conquet and Ouessant are very much the places to head for – ideally by boat from the Port du Commerce (see p.149 for timetable). Otherwise, the immediate area around Brest is far from bursting with interest. Take **ST-RENAN** for example. French towns often set up signs along approach roads to advertise their splendours – "son chateau", "sa charme" and so on. St-Rénan can only find "Son Syndicat d'Initiative" to boast about – but for all that it's quite a pleasant small town and there are two noteworthy prehistoric sites in the immediate area.

Lanrivoaré

Five kilometres northwest of St-Rénan is the **church** of **LANRIVOARE**, which has a tiny plot in its graveyard where, alongside eight round stones, the 7777 victims of a fifth-century massacre are supposed to lie buried. Legend records that the stones were transformed from loaves of bread by Saint Hervé – but they're in fact most likely to be "cursing-stones", which exist in several Irish chapels and were used for calling down disease or destruction on an enemy. The person invoking the curse, after a certain number of prayers, turned the stone round seven times.

The Menhir de Kerloas

To find the **Menhir de Kerloas** (also known as Kervéatous or Plouarzel), you need to walk or drive (there's no bus) about five kilometres west of St-Rénan on the *old* Plouarzel road, parallel to the more modern D5. The menhir stands in a small clearing hedged-in by fields, and is the highest point for miles around in these flatlands. Although the tip was knocked off by lightning 200 years ago (and was subsequently used as a cattle-trough), it is at 37ft the tallest menhir still standing in Western Europe. The stone is probably at its best looming out of a damp and ominous Breton mist, producing, in this isolated spot, a powerful effect on the imagination. A further aid to fantasy are the circular protuberances about four feet from the ground on either side, against which newly married couples (who can only have been rather ill-informed) would rub their naked bodies in the hope of begetting children.

Towards the Crozon Peninsula

Heading south from Brest, cyclists and pedestrians can cut straight over to the Crozon peninsula by **ferry**. A regular service will shuttle you across the bay, for a few francs, to Le Fret (see "Travel Details" on p.166). The ferry doesn't, however, carry cars, so **drivers** have a longer and more circuitous route, crossing the Elorn river over the vast spans of the **Pont Albert-Louppe** (42m high and almost a kilometre long) and then skirting the estuaries of the **Plougastel peninsula**.

PLOUGASTEL-DAOULAS, just across the bridge, is a possibly rewarding stop on this latter route. It's sited at the edge of the main Parish Closes region and has a particularly nasty calvary depiction of Katell Gollet (see p.144).

A very different, and earlier, image of religion is provided by the **abbey** at **DAOULAS**, ten kilometres beyond. This has Brittany's only Romanesque cloister – beautiful and isolated at the edge of cool monastery gardens, since its surrounding buildings were destroyed during the Revolution. The abbey is a short walk above the town, and a welcome oasis on a hot summer's day. Since 1984 it has been used as a cultural centre for Finistère, used each summer to stage some major exhibition.

From Daoulas the motorway and railway cut down to Châteaulin (see p.169) and Quimper. For Crozon, you'll need to veer west at **LE FAOU**, a tiny medieval port, still with some of its sixteenth-century gabled houses and set on its own individual estuary. A sheltered corniche follows the river to the sea, where there are sailing and wind-surfing facilities. Accommodation is to be found at the **hotels** *Relais de la Place* (☎98.81.91.19) or *La Vieille Renommée* (☎98.81.90.31; closed Monday other than in July & Aug).

From Le Faou, **Crozon** and the **Menez-Hom**, which overlooks the peninsula's eastern reaches, are visible and easily accessible. You cross the river Aulne – outlet for the Nantes–Brest canal – over the **Pont du Térénez**, and, amid forests, you have arrived.

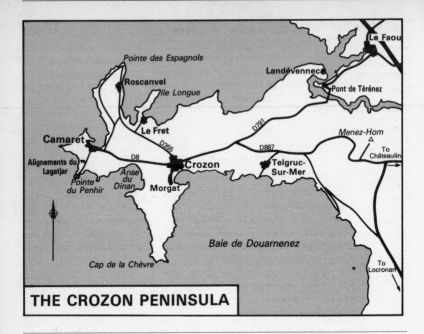

THE CROZON PENINSULA

THE CROZON PENINSULA

The **Crozon peninsula** forms part of the *Parc Régional D'Armorique*, a haphazard area stretching from the forest of Huelgoat to the island of Ouessant that is, in principle at least, a protected natural landscape area. What this means in reality is hard to fathom. Doubtless there are firm French bylaws against disturbing the wild flowers. However, for some reason these don't prevent nuclear submarines from lurking in the bay of Brest, nor low-flying helicopters from sporadically sweeping the skies above.

Nevertheless, military installations (and operations) notwithstanding, Crozon, with its wild beaches and craggy cliffs, is an attractive slice of countryside. A dramatic one too, especially if you make the detour to climb up the **Menez-Hom** for an initial overview.

The Menez-Hom and around

At just 1082ft, the **Menez-Hom** is not really a mountain. But the summit stands sufficiently alone to command tremendous views across Crozon – a chaos of water, with lakes, rivers and bridges wherever you look, and usually a scattering of hang-gliders dangling in the sky. The exposed and windswept viewing table reveals it to be 300 miles from both London and Paris.

A magnificent road sweeps down across the heather on to the Crozon peninsula. At the foot of the hill, to the south, **ST-NIC PENTREZ** has excellent beaches – this is the sandy side of the peninsula – and several **campsites**, largest among them the *Menez Bichen* (☎98.26.50.82). There is another good beach and campsite, *Le Panoramic* (☎98.27.78.41), further round towards Crozon at **TELGRUC-SUR-MER**, and some of the smaller towns inland have **hotels** and **gîtes d'étapes**. Among them are Plomodiern with *La Cremaillère* (☎98.81.50.10), and a *gîte* at the nearby Polébret Plage (c/o M. Kervella, ☎98.26.50.14), Tal Ar Groas with the *de l'Aber* , and lastly a *gîte* at Kerdiles, 1km from Landévennec (c/o M. & Mme.Gall; ☎98.27.31.49).

The Musée de l'Ecole Rurale

Roughly three kilometres north of the Menez-Hom is the village of **TREGARVEN**, with its **Musée de l'Ecole Rurale** in what used to be the local secondary school. This is one of those small, quirky French museums that sound slightly ludicrous on paper but are distinctly fascinating on the spot. The school was closed down due to lack of numbers in 1974, then re-opened a decade later as a re-creation of a Breton classroom circa 1920. Its interest lies in the fact that at this date all the kids would have spoken Breton at home but been forbidden to speak it here. The teacher gave a little wooden cow to the first child to utter a Breton word and they could get rid of the *vache* only by squealing on the next offender. The lesson, to parents and pupils alike, was obvious enough: that Breton was backward and a handicap. A familiar cultural tactic of imperialism, it was highly successful throughout the province. Only recently – and far too late – has a counter-strategy emerged. Breton language primary schools do now exist; a sixth-former was eventually allowed, after battles with Paris, to pass all his *Baccalauréat* papers which he'd written in Breton; and the SNCF had to back down after refusing a cheque made out in Breton. If such matters hold interest, the museum is open from May to September, 2.30 to 7pm; it stands, off the bus routes, at the crossroads of the Argol–Dineault and Trégarven–Menez-Hom roads.

Morgat, Camaret and the beaches

The first town on the peninsula proper, **CROZON** is not much more than a one-way traffic system to distribute tourists among the various resorts – though it does keep a market running most of the week.

Morgat

MORGAT, just down the hill, is a more realistic and enticing base. It has a long crescent beach that ends in a pine slope, and a well-sheltered harbour full of pleasure boats raced down from England and Ireland – and the leathery rich telling each other about their spinnakers. The main plebeian attractions are **boat trips** around the various headlands, such as the Cap de la Chèvre (which is a good clifftop walk if you'd rather make your own way). The most popular is the 45-minute tour of the **Grottes** (May–Sept), multicoloured caves in the cliffs, accessible only by sea but with steep "chimneys" up to the clifftops, where in bygone days saints would lurk to rescue the shipwrecked. Organised by two rival companies on the quay, the trips run every quarter of an hour in high season; they often leave full, however, so it's worth booking a few hours in advance. It's also possible, on Wednesdays and Sundays in July and August, to take a ferry service across to **Douarnenez** (☎98.27.09.54).

Morgat's **hotels** are all quite expensive. The cheapest, *des Grottes* (☎98.27.15.84) is a long (albeit pleasant) walk from what centre there is, and in any case insists on guests paying for *demi-pension*. Better, if you can afford it, is to splash out 150F or so on the *du Kador* (☎98.27.05.68) where you can eat excellent seafood and enjoy the view of the bay. Or alternatively, **camp**. With a total of 865 pitches available, campers are spoilt for choice; best perhaps are the 3-star sites at *Plage de Goulien* (☎98.27.17.10) and *Plage de Trez-Rouz* (☎98.27.93.96). The **SI** for the whole peninsula is at the start of the beach crescent on the bd du France. There are sailing and diving schools in the harbour.

Camaret

CAMARET is another sheltered port, at the very tip of the peninsula. It has two beaches – a small one to the north and another in the rather marshy *Anse de Dinan* – and boasts one moment of historical significance. It was here in 1801 that an American, Robert Fulton, tested the first submarine. This was a stuffy, leaking, oar-powered wooden craft, whose five-man crew spent some time scuttling about beneath the waves in the hope of sinking a British frigate. Fulton was denied his glory, though, by the frigate choosing to sail away, ignorant of the heavy-breathing peril that was so frantically seeking it out.

The town of Camaret is not large, though in season there are all the shops and supplies you could need. A little walk away from the centre, around the port towards its long protective jetty, the quai du Styvel contains a row of excellent **hotels**. The *Vauban* (☎98.27.91.36) is especially hospitable, though the food in *du Styvel* (☎98.27.92.74) is marginally better; both have rooms that look right out across the bay. There are also various **campsites** to fall back on, like the *Lambézen* (☎98.27.91.41) and the *Lannic* (☎98.27.91.31). From mid-June until September, *Vedettes Sirènes* (☎98.27.91.41) run boat trips that tour the offshore bird sanctuary of the Tas de Pois; their office is next to the SI in the port.

The Pointe du Penhir
A couple of worthwhile excursions can be made from the towns of the Crozon peninsula. At the **Pointe du Penhir** are sheer cliffs and a little natural amphitheatre to view the Tas de Pois rocks, scattered out in the sea. A monument to the Breton Resistance stands nearby. To one side of the road on the way out to the point, amid the brilliant purples and yellows of the heathland, are the megalithic **Alignements of Lagatjar**. Perhaps, though, you need to imagine that this heath is still blasted and empty, and that there's no "Dolmens" housing estate next to the stones, to appreciate this forlorn, unsignposted prehistoric ruin. The stones are little more than weatherbeaten stumps and it's hard to discern a pattern on the ground; the experts responsible for their restoration say there are four distinct lines rather than a circle.

The Pointe des Espagnols

The other popular trip is to the **Pointe des Espagnols**, where a viewing point signals the end of the peninsula. Brest is very close and very visible – without being any the more enticing. Around the cape are several forbidden military installations and abandoned war-time bunkers. You're not allowed to leave the road, and should need no extra dissuasion to avoid straying onto the range. Neither are you encouraged to turn the provided telescope towards Robert Fulton's modern counterparts at the nuclear submarine base on the Ile Longue. Nearby **ROSCANVEL** offers a hotel, *Kreis ar Mor* (☎98.27.48.93).

Locronan

LOCRONAN is a short way from the sea on the minor road that leads down to Quimper from the Crozon peninsula. It's a prime example of a Breton town that has remained frozen in its ancient form by more recent economic decline. From 1469 through to the seventeenth century it was a hugely successful centre for woven linen, supplying sails to the French, English and Spanish navies. It was then first rivalled by Vitré and Rennes, before suffering the "agony and ruin" of the nineteenth century so graphically described in its small museum. The consequence of that ruin has been that the rich medieval houses of the town centre have never been superseded or surrounded by modern development. Film directors love its authenticity, even if Roman Polanski, to film *Tess*, deemed it necessary to change all the porches, put new windows on the Renaissance houses, and bury the main square in several feet of mud to make it all look a bit more English.

Locronan is today once more a prosperous town, with its main source of income the tourists who buy wooden statues carved by local artisans, pottery brought up from the Midi, and handbags and leather jackets of less specified provenance. This commercialisation shouldn't, however, put you off making at least a passing visit, for the town itself is genuinely remarkable, centred around the focal **Eglise Saint-Ronan**. The **museum** is worthwhile, and take the time also to walk down the hill of the **rue Moal**, where there's a lovely little stone chapel, with surprising modern stained glass, and a wooden statue of a depressed-looking Jesus, sitting alone cross-legged.

Each year on the second Sunday in July the town hosts a **pardon** at St-Ronan church; the procession, known as the *petit Tromenie*, expands to a week-long festival, the *grand Tromenie*, every sixth year (next, 1995). The processions follow a time-hallowed route said by some to be Saintt Ronan's favourite Sunday walk, by others to be the outline of a long-vanished Benedictine abbey, or even to be a pre-Christian circuit of megalithic sites.

Practical Details

The latest craze in Locronan is to follow the *Tromenie* route on a **mountain bike**, which you can hire from a garage in rue des Charettes (☎98.91.71.71). If you decide you want to stay in the town, it can be an expensive business. One of the artisans suggested to the local authorities that the loft above his studio be converted to a *gîte d'étape* for young visitors, but that was felt not to be in keeping with the town's character – a character affording few opportunities of any kind for the young. As it is, there are two **hotels**, the *Fer à Cheval* (☎98.91.70.67) and the *du Prieure* (☎98.91.70.89), both quite expensive and normally reserved well in advance. In season, and probably out, you'll do a lot better heading on to the bay of Douarnenez.

CORNOUAILLE

Once past Locronan, you enter the ancient kingdom of **Cornouaille**. Its capital, **Quimper**, is a city as enticing as any in France, and along the south coast Bénodet, Loctudy and Pont Aven are thriving resorts. Roads radiate from Quimper in all directions, but the **western tip** of Finistère, if you follow the line of the Bay of Douarnenez, still feels isolated. With a few exceptions – most notably its "land's end" capes – it has kept out of the tourist mainstream. Beaches are few; resorts do not in any real sense exist; and traditions endure.

Douarnenez

DOUARNENEZ is an unpretentious but also rather unexciting port, for which the holiday trade is only a sideline. The beaches around its bay look pretty enough, but they are dangerous for swimming. It is, however, a functional enough place to stay – and to eat.

The part to make for is the **port de Rosmeur**, where the quayside is a line of cafés and restaurants. Sardines and crustaceans are still landed at Douarnenez in huge quantities – in 1923 the eight hundred fishing boats brought in 100 million sardines during the six-month season. You can buy fresh fish at the waterfront, or go on a sea-fishing excursion yourself. Boats also cross the bay to Morgat (see "Travel Details" on p.166).

Although for most purposes the modern commercial harbour on the other side of town, **Port-Rhu**, is best avoided, in the place de l'Enfer there's a **Boat Museum** (May–Sept 10am–noon & 2–6pm, rest of the year by special arrangement only; ☎98.92.65.20). As well as the usual exhibitions and films, this doubles as a working boatyard, where visitors can watch or even join in the construction of seagoing vessels, using techniques from all over the world and from all different periods. The emphasis, unsurprisingly, is on fishing, and the craft on display include a *moliceiro* from Portugal and coracles from Wales and Ireland.

To stay in Douarnenez, try the **hotels** *de la Rade* (31 quai du Grand-Port; ☎98.92.01.81) or *des Halles* (in the old market place; ☎98.92.02.75). Alternatives, close by in the bay, are the *Ville d'Ys* (37 rue Sables Blancs; ☎98.74.00.87), or campsite *Croas Men* (☎98.74.00.18), at Tréboul/les Sables Blancs; and north of town, at the **Plage du Ris**, there's an excellent and fairly secluded hotel and restaurant, *Les Mouettes* (☎98.92.01.67), facing the (again treacherous) beach.

The seaside village of **STE-ANNE-LA-PALUD**, further north of Douarnenez, holds one of the best-known *pardons* in Brittany on the last Sunday in August.

Audierne

It has to be said, even once you get round to the Bay of Audierne, this coast is no area for a classic summer sun-and-sand holiday. Where it's not marshy, it tends to be bleak and rocky, and it is generally unsuitable for swimming.

But there is a beach of sorts near **AUDIERNE** itself, and the town is a wholly pleasant stop – a low-lying harbour long-known for its prawns and crayfish. To try them, the best place is reputed to be the **hotel-restaurant** *Le Goyen* (☎98.70.08.88). *Hôtel des Dunès* (☎98.70.01.19), however, is more affordable, and only a hundred metres from the beach.

Most people take in Audierne only en route to the Pointe du Raz, which is connected directly to Quimper by bus. Midway, signalled by fading graffiti on its walls and hoardings, is the tiny village of **PLOGOFF**, where ecologists, autonomists and above all the local people fought riot police and paratroopers for six weeks in 1980, attempting to stop the opening move in a nuclear power station project. Although they lost the fight, abandonment of the project was part of François Mitterand's manifesto for the 1980 presidential election – and he has kept his promise to do so.

The Pointe du Raz

The **Pointe du Raz** – the Land's End of both Finistère and France – can be a spectacular sight. Not at first view, though; as you arrive the ocean is all but obscured by souvenir shops and breeze-block barracks (it is flanked by another military zone). But once away from the coach park, things are more promising. You can walk out to the plummeting fissures of the *pointe*, filling and draining with a deafening surf-roar, and beyond, high above on precarious paths. (Shoes that can grip are not a bad idea.) The **Baie du Trépassés** (Bay of the Dead) just to the north gets its grim name from the shipwrecked bodies that are washed up there, and is a possible site of sunken Ys (see over page).

Sein

A short way out to sea is the little **ILE DE SEIN**, made famous during World War II when the entire male population answered General de Gaulle's call to join him in exile in England. It was reputed also to have been the very last refuge of the Druids in Brittany, a misty and inaccessible spot where they held out long after the rest of the country was Christianised. Roman sources tell of a shrine served by nine virgin priestesses.

A popular saying has it that "Who sees Sein, sees his death"; but that's more because it happens to rhyme in French (*qui voit Sein, voit sa fin*) than because of any particular evil there. The island is featureless enough to have been completely submerged by the sea on occasion; if you do want to stay, the *Hôtel Armen* (☎98.70.90.77) is open from June until the end of September.

Two companies operate **boats to Sein**, leaving from Audierne-Plage, three kilometers from the town centre. The official service operates all the year round, with three boats making the seventy-minute journey each day in July and August (☎98.70.02.38 for times), and one daily boat at 9.30am every day except Wednesday for the rest of the year. Their commercial rivals compete only in the summer (☎98.70.13.78 for details).

Quimper

QUIMPER, capital of the diocese, the kingdom and later the duchy of Cornouaille, is the oldest Breton city. According to the only source – legend – the original bishop of Quimper, Saint Corentin, came with the first Bretons across the Channel from Cornwall to the place they named Little Britain some time between the fourth and seventh centuries. He lived all his life off the flesh of half a regenerating and immortal fish and was made bishop by one King Gradlon, whose life he later saved when the seabed city of Ys was destroyed (see box below).

Modern Quimper is very relaxed, active enough at night to have the bars – and the atmosphere – to make it worth going out café-crawling. It's a nice-looking place, too, of a very manageable size – it takes at most half an hour to cross it on foot. The word *"kemper"* denotes the junction of the two rivers, the Steir and the Odet, around which are cobbled streets of old granite buildings, with the cathedral nearby. Overlooking it all is Mont Frugy, now denuded following the devastation of its wooded slopes by the hurricane of 1987. The Odet is crossed by numerous low flat bridges, bedecked with geraniums, and though there are one or two ultra-modern new edifices along its banks, they blend in a surprisingly harmonious way with their ancient surroundings. There's no pressure in Quimper to rush around monuments or museums, and the most enjoyable option of the lot is to take a boat and drift down the Odet valley to the sea.

A short walk along the Odet brings you from the **gare SNCF** and main (open-air) **gare routière** to the centre of the city around the enormous **Cathédrale St-Corentin**. A construction problem faced this, back in the fifteenth century, when the nave was being added to the old chancel : the extension would either have hit existing buildings or the swampy edge of the then unchannelled river. The masons eventually hit on a solution, and placed the nave at a slight angle – a peculiarity which, once noticed, makes it hard to concentrate on the other Gothic splendours within. The exterior, however, gives no hint of the deviation, with King Gradlon mounted in perfect symmetry between the spires – though whether he would have advised a riverbed nave is another question. Before the Revolution, each Saint Cecilia's Day a climber would ascend to give the King a drink, and there was a prize of 100

THE DROWNED CITY OF YS

Legend has it that King Gradlon built Ys in the Baie de Douarnenez, protected from the water by gates and locks to which only he and his daughter had keys. She sounds like a pleasant sort, giving pet sea-dragons to all the citizens to do their errands, but Saint Corentin saw decadence and suspected evil. He was proved right: at the urging of the Devil, the princess used her key to open the floodgates, the city was flooded, and Gradlon escaped only by obeying Saint Corentin and throwing his daughter into the sea. Back on dry land, and in need of a new capital, Gradlon founded Quimper. Ys remains on the sea floor – it will rise again when Paris (*"Par-Ys"*, equal to Ys) sinks – and, according to tradition, on feast days sailors can still hear church bells and hymns under the water.

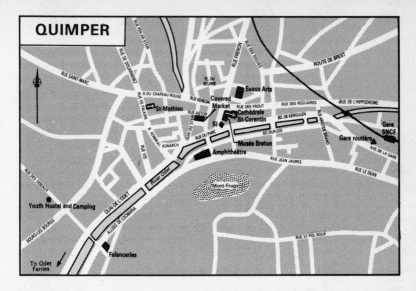

écus for whoever could catch the glass, thrown down afterwards. During the sixteenth century, 1500 refugees died of plague inside the building.

Alongside the cathedral, the **Bishop's Palace** is quirky from the outside, and has a wonderful staircase within, but its Museum of Breton oddments is small and forgettable. Much more compelling is the **Beaux Arts** in the Hôtel de Ville (summer 9.30am–noon & 1.30–7pm, winter 10am–noon & 2–6pm; closed Tues) with its amazing collections of drawings by Cocteau, Gustav Doré and Max Jacob (who was born in Quimper), nineteenth- and twentieth-century paintings of the Pont-Aven school, and Breton scenes by the likes of Eugène Boudin. Only the dull Dutch oils upstairs let the collection down.

If you're interested in seeing pottery made on an industrial scale, and an exhibition of the changing styles since the first Quimper ateliers of the late 1600s, the **Faïenceries de Quimper** is another visit to make. It's on place Berardier, downstream from the centre on the south bank of the Odet (half-hour guided visits, Mon–Fri 9.30–11.30am & 1.30–5pm).

Quimper's latest tourist attraction, three kilometres out on the road to Pont l'Abbé, was not yet open at the time this book went to press. It's a pancake museum – the **Musée des Crêpes Bretonnes** – promising to combine serious history with an element of gluttony (Mon–Sat 10am–6pm, free).

Practical Details

Quimper's old market hall burned down in 1976, but the light and spacious new **covered market** built to replace it is quite a delight, not just for the food, but for the view past the upturned boat rafters through the roof to the cathedral's spires. The **SI** is now housed upstairs in the market building, offering the usual lists of just about anything you might have in mind (July & Aug 8.30am–8pm, otherwise 9am–noon & 2–6pm; ☎98.95.04.69). If you're leaving by **bus** check with them where to make for – departure points for different companies and destinations are spread all over town.

The liveliest corner of Quimper tends to be around the top of **rue Aristide-Briand**, just north of the river and half-way between the stations and the Cathedral. Two enthusiastically **Breton bars** co-exist next door to each other, *Les Deux Cornouailles* at no. 2 and *Ceili* at no. 4, while opposite them at no. 3 is the town's most popular **restaurant**, *L'Astragale*, which specialises in delicious seafood *paellas*. If you're keen for a change from standard French menus you could also try the **Polish** restaurant, *Mamuska*, north of the cathedral at 47 rue E. Fréron. Other areas worth checking out include the **place du Beurre**, with a couple of crêperies and the militant *Keltia-Musique* **record shop**; around the church of **St-Mathieu** can be enjoyable, too, and across the river there are a couple of good bars on **rue St-Catherine** – draught *Guinness* at no. 15.

Best value of the **hotels** are the *Transvaal* (57 rue Jean-Jaurès, ☎98.90.09.91) a *logis* just south of the river with doubles from 114F, or any of the several to be found by the *gares*, such as the *Terminus* (15 Av de la Gare, ☎98.90.00.63). The **campsite** and **youth hostel** (☎98.55.41.67) are downstream at 6 av des Oiseaux in the Bois de Séminaire (Bus 1, direction Penhars; stop *Chaptal*). **Bikes** can be hired at *M. Hénaff* (107 av de Ty Bos), and there's a Peugeot **cycle shop** at 35 Av de la Gare (closed Sun and Mon). **Car hire** is also available in the Av de la Gare, with *Avis* at no. 8 and *Hertz* at no. 19. The *Fédération Bretonne des Clubs de Windsurfers*, (run by M. Carn, route du Bénodet 29000 Quimper) has information on all aspects of **wind-surfing**.

Finally, during the week preceding the last Sunday in July there's the **Festival de Cornouaille**: a jamboree of Breton music, costumes, theatre and dances, with every room in the town taken. They have guest performers from the other Celtic countries and a scattering of other, sometimes highly unusual, ethnic-cultural ensembles. The official programmme does not appear until July, but you can get provisional details at any time from 2 place de la Tour d'Auvergne – BP 77 – 29103 Quimper (☎98.55.53.53).

Bénodet

From April to September, one or more boats a day sail from Quimper down the Odet to the rivermouth town of **BENODET**. This is one of the most popular resorts in Brittany, with a long sheltered beach on the ocean side. The town is a little over-developed but the beach is undeniably good, especially for kids, for whom there's a lot laid on – including horse-riding and wind-surfing; "beach club" crèches, too. **Boat excursions** from Bénodet or Quimper to the rather nondescript **Iles de Glénan** are less exciting than the river trips between the two towns.

There are several very large **campsites** in Bénodet: the 4-star *Letty* (☎98.57.04.69) and the 3-star *La Pointe St Gilles* (☎98.57.05.37) each have 500 pitches. Most of the **hotels** are comparatively expensive – try the *Beau Rivage* (☎98.57.00.22) or *L'Hermitage* (☎98.57.00.37) for cheap rooms, or splash out a bit on *L'Ancre de Marine* (☎98.57.05.29). There are also chalets and caravans to stay in, and **bicycles** to wobble about on, for hire.

The Penmarch peninsula

At one time the **Penmarch peninsula** was one of the richest areas of Brittany. That was before it was plundered by the pirate La Fontenelle, who led three hundred ships in raids on the local peasantry from his base on the island of La Tristan in the Bay of Douarnenez; also before the cod, staple of the fishing industry, stopped coming. Now, in the local tourist literature, the region is known as the *Pays de Bigouden*, after the elaborate lace *coiffes* you see worn in many of the villages. Often as much as a foot high, they are sometimes supported by half-tubes of cardboard, sometimes just very stiffly starched. The white of the coiffes swaying in the wind provide one of the memorable colours of the area, along with the red fields of poppies and verges of purple foxgloves.

Pont l'Abbé

PONT L'ABBE, the principal town of this corner, has a Bigouden museum – though you'd need to be quite inspired by the costumes to find it of great interest. More accessible pleasures, however, lie in a stroll through the woods along the banks of its estuary.

To the west, the world **wind-surfing** championships are often held at **Pointe de la Torche**, and at any time there are likely to be aficionados of the sport twirling effortlessly about on the dangerous water. The coast only becomes swimmable, however, as you round the Pointe de Penmarch towards Loctudy. The first village you come to, **LE GUILVINEC**, is a surpisingly busy fishing port (the boats start to come home around 4pm most afternoons), and its *Hôtel du Port* (53 avenue du Port; ☎98.58.10.10) is thoroughly recommended; especially, of course, for its fish suppers.

Loctudy

LOCTUDY is a good target – an equally well-positioned but much less commercial version of Bénodet, which it faces across the mouth of the Odet. There are several **campsites** along its main beach, including the *Kergall* (☎98.87.45.93) and the *Langoz*, (☎98.87.44.03), and some good-value **hotels**, such as the *des Iles* (☎98.87.40.16) and *de Bretagne* (☎98.58.60.60). There are also **boats** from here up the Odet. These should depart daily during the summer, but you need to make sure they are running on any particular day; the boats are cancelled in bad weather or simply if there aren't enough people around.

The Museum of Mechanical Musical Instruments

If you do find yourself stranded on a rainy and boatless day, don't despair. On the D44 between Pont l'Abbé and Bénodet, just before **COMBRIT**, is a wonderful **Musée des Mechaniques Musiques** – the lifetime obsession of one Monsieur Dussour, a rotund old man who cheerfully admits that he's never had the ear to play a musical instrument himself. The museum is only a small garage behind an antiques warehouse, but each visitor gets a personally guided tour with M. Dussour miming at innumerable automatic keyboards. These range from barrel organs and claviers, through penny-in-the-slot machines and even a musical lemon, to a huge cabinet with two full size accordions topped with cymbals and drums. You hear all sorts of punch-tape polkas and cylinder Carmens, each recording individually made by a musician playing the same tune over and over again. The twin highpoints are the deafening sound of the restored fairground organ, and the full symphonic sweep of the "Aeolian Orchestrelle". From June 15 to September 15, the museum is open from 2pm until 7pm every day; out of season, ring ☎98.56.36.03 to make an appointment.

Along the South Coast

The coast that continues east of Bénodet is rocky and repeatedly cut by deep valleys. It suffered heavily in the hurricane of 1987, but the small resort of **BEG-MEIL** survives, albeit with fewer trees to protect its vast expanse of dunes. These are ideal for **campers**, with several official sites; and right on the seafront there's also the hotel *Thalamot* (☎98.94.97.38).

Around la Fôret-Fouesnant in particular the hills are much too steep for cyclists to climb, and forbidden to heavy vehicles (*poids lourds*) such as caravans. The la Fôret-Fouesnant minor road may look good, but there are few beaches or places to stop. Motorists would do best to take the more direct D44, a few kilometres inland, followed by the D783, which leads close to the major towns along the route.

Concarneau

The first sizeable town you come to heading east is **CONCARNEAU**, a fishing port that does a reasonable job of passing itself off as a holiday resort. Its great asset is its **Ville Clos**, the old walled city situated across a slender causeway on an irregular rocky island in the bay. Its ramparts, like those of the citadelle at Le Palais on Belle-Ile, were completed by Vauban in the seventeenth century. The island itself however had been inhabited for at least 1000 years before that, and is first recorded as the site of a priory founded by King Gradlon of Quimper. Concarneau boasts that it is a *ville fleurie*, and the flowers are most in evidence inside the walls, where roses climb all over the various giftshops, restaurants and crêperies.

The **Musée de la Pèche**, immediately inside the Ville Clos, provides an insight into the traditional life Concarneau shared with so many other Breton ports. The four rooms around the central quadrangle illuminate the history and practice of four specific aspects of fishing. The whaling room contains model boats and a genuine open boat from the Azores; the tuna room shows boats dragging nets the size of central Paris; there's a herring room, and a model of a sardine cannery – which this building once was. And there are oddities collected by fishermen in the past; the swords of swordfish and the saws of sawfish; a Japanese giant crab; photos of old lifeboatmen with fading beards, cases full of sardine and tuna cans, and a live aquarium where the lobsters little realise they are in no immediate danger of being eaten. In addition, you can buy diagrams and models of ships, and even order a diorama of the stuffed fish of your choice. The museum is open every day (July & Aug 9.30am–8.30pm, otherwise 10am–12.30 pm & 2.30–7pm).

The one thing the Ville Clos lacks completely is **hotels**. Those that there are in Concarneau lurk in the backstreets on the mainland, and tend to be full most of the time. The *Bonne Auberge* (Le Cabellou, ☎98.97.04.30) and the *Crêpe d'Or* (3 rue du Lin, ☎98.97.08.61) are worth trying, but the best bet in Concarneau is probably the **youth hostel** (☎98.97.03.47), for once very near the city centre. It's just around the tip of the headland on the place de la Croix, with a good crêperie opposite and a **wind-surfing shop** a little further along. The town's main **market** is held in front of the Ville Clos on Friday, with a smaller one on Monday. For a cheap **meal** in the centre, *Ty Mad* near the place du Guesclin features on its menu a Breton rarity – affordable scallops. *Chez Armand* (15 avenue du Dr-Nicholas; closed Wed) is a bit more expensive, but still very good value.

Pont-Aven

PONT-AVEN, at the tip of the Aven estuary, is a small port packed with tourists and art galleries. This was where Gauguin came to paint in the 1880s, before he left for Tahiti in search of a South Seas idyll. By all accounts Gauguin was a rude and arrogant man who lorded it over the local population (who were already well used to posing in "peasant attire" for visiting artists). As a painter and print-maker, however, he produced some of his finest work in Pont-Aven, and his influence was such that the **Pont-Aven School** of fellow artists developed here. He spent some years working closely with these – the best-known of whom was Emile Bernard – and they in turn helped to revitalise his own approach. For all the local hype however the town has no permanent collection of Gauguin's work. The so-called **Musée Gauguin** (Easter–Sept, 10am–12.30pm & 2–7pm) in the Mairie goes so far as holding annual exhibitions of the numerous members of the school, but you can't count on paintings by the man himself.

Still, Gauguin aside, the town is pleasant in its own right and the countless galleries can easily while away an afternoon. There is a small and neat port, with a watermill and the odd leaping salmon, and occasional cruises run down to the sea at Port-Manech. Upstream, a walk can take you into the **Bois d'Amour**, wooded gardens which have long provided inspiration to visiting painters – and a fair tally, too, of poets and musicians.

If you need to stay, be warned that the three **hotels** are expensive, and the nearest **campsite** (May–Sept; ☎98.06.03.13) is four kilometres away in the park at Roz Pin, on the road to Nevez.

Quimperlé

The final town of any size in Finistère, **QUIMPERLE** straddles a hill and two rivers, the Isole and the Elle, cut by a sequence of bridges. It's an atmospheric place, particularly in the medieval muddle of streets around **Ste-Croix** church. This was copied in plan from schema brought back by crusaders of the Holy Sepulchre church in Jerusalem and is notable for its original

Romanesque apse. There are some good bars nearby and, on Friday, a market on the square higher up on the hill. The **hotels** *L'Europe* (☎98.96.00.02) and *Auberge de Toulfoen* (☎98.96.00.29) both have good value rooms.

travel details

Trains

From Brest to Paris-Montparnasse (10 daily, 6hr), via Landerneau (15min), Landivisiau (30min), Morlaix (45min), and Rennes. (The *Atlantique* high-speed *TGV* reduces the Brest–Paris journey time to less than 4 hours, if you're prepared to pay extra.) From Brest also to Quimper (6 daily, 1hr 30min), with connecting SNCF buses at **Châteaulin** for Crozon, and inland to Carhaix.
From Roscoff to Morlaix (8 daily, 30min).
From Quimper to Redon (8 daily, 2hr, continue to Rennes or Nantes, and on to Bordeaux or Toulouse) via Quimperlé (30min), Lorient (45min) and Vannes (1hr 30min).

Buses

From Brest to Roscoff (5 daily, 1hr 30min), via Plouescat, Lanhouarneau, Lesneven, and Gouesnou; to Le Conquet (4 daily, 30min); to Quimper (6 daily, 1hr 30min).
From Morlaix to Roscoff (2 daily, at 3.50pm and 8.30pm, 35min); Carantec (4; 20min); Plougasnou and St Jean-le-Doigt (5; 30min); Lannion (2, not Sun; 1hr); Huelgoat (45min) and Carhaix (1hr 30min); Quimper (1; 2hr).
From Châteaulin to Crozon and Camaret (5 daily, 30min/50min); less often to Carhaix.
From Landévennec 3 daily to Camaret via Roscanvel and Crozon.
From Quimper 5 daily to Locronan (25min), Telgruc (1hr), Crozon (1hr 20min) and Camaret (1hr 30min); 3 daily to Audierne (1hr) and Pointe du Raz (1hr 15min); 6 daily to Concarneau (30min) and Quimperlé (1hr 30min); 6 daily to Fouesnant (1hr) and Beg-Meil (1hr 10min); 9 daily to the airport at Plugaffan; 8 daily to Bénodet (45min); also to Douarnenez (5; 40min), Lorient (2hr) and Vannes (3hr).

Ferries

From Roscoff to Plymouth (6hr) and Cork (13–17hr). Both services *Brittany Ferries*, (Roscoff ☎98.69.76.22, Plymouth ☎0752/21321, Cork ☎215/07666). See p.5 for more details.
From Roscoff to Ile de Batz (very frequently, 15min), contact ☎98.61.79.66; and in July and August tours of the **Bay of Morlaix**.
From Le Conquet and **Brest** to **Ouessant** and **Molène** (2 daily high season, 1 low season); ☎98.80.24.68. Journey from Le Conquet to Ouessant takes 1hr, from Brest up to 3hr. See timetable on p.149.
From Brest to **Le Fret** on the Crozon peninsula, 3 daily April–Sept, 45 minutes (☎98.44.44.04). Foot passengers and cyclists only, each trip is met by a minibus for **Crozon** and **Camaret**. Trips also run from Brest around the **Rade de Brest**.
From Morgat, trips to caves and headlands. ☎98.27.07.54.
From Douarnenez to **Morgat**, 4hr 30min return trips in July & Aug – which you can also use as a one-way ferry service (☎98.27.09.54); also trips around **Bay of Douarnenez**.
From Audierne to **Sein** island, 1hr 10min, ☎98.70.02.38 all year (except Weds out of season), or ☎98.70.21.15 summer only.
From Quimper down the Odet to **Bénodet**, and vice versa (May–Sept, ☎98.57.00.58).
Also **tour the Odet**, daily from **Loctudy** (☎98.57.00.58), daily from **Concarneau** (June 15 –Sept 15; ☎98.97.10.31), and thrice weekly from **Port-la-Forêt** and **Beg-Meil** (☎98.94.97.94). All the Odet companies also do trips (average 1hr) to the **Glénan** islands.

Air

From Brest airport (Guipavas), 2 daily flights to **Ouessant**, subject to good weather; (☎98.84 .64.87). Every two days, March–Oct, to **London** (**Brit Air**; in Morlaix ☎98.62.10.22 and in London ☎01/499 9511).
From **Quimper** airport (Plugaffan), 2 daily flights to **Paris** (☎98.94.01.28). Also connecting flights to **Brest** for London flights, as above.

CHAPTER SIX

INLAND BRITTANY: THE NANTES–BREST CANAL

The **Nantes–Brest canal** is a meandering chain of waterways, linking existing rivers with purpose-built stretches of canal, right the way from Finistère down to the Loire. En route it passes through an assortment of medieval riverside towns, like **Josselin** and **Malestroit**, that long pre-date its construction; commercial ports and junctions – **Pontivy**, most notably – developed along its path during the nineteenth century; the old port of **Redon**, a checkerboard of water, where the canal crosses the river Vilaine; and a sequence of scenic splendours, including the string of lakes around the **Barrage de Guerlédan** near Mur-de-Bretagne.

As a focus for exploring **inland Brittany**, perhaps cutting in to the towpaths along the more easily accessible stretches, and then detouring out

THE CANAL

The idea of joining together the inland waterways of Brittany dates back to 1627 – though as ever nothing was done to implement the scheme until it was seen as a military necessity. That point came during the Napoleonic wars, when the English fleets began to threaten shipping circumnavigating the Breton coast. To relieve the virtual blockade of Brest in 1810, Napoleon authorised the construction of a canal network to link it with both Nantes and Lorient.

In the event, economic disasters held up its completion, but by 1836 a navigable path was cut and the canal officially opened. It was not an immediate success. Having cost 60m francs to construct, the first years of operation, up to 1850, raised a mere 70,000 francs in tariffs. It survived, however, helped by a navy experiment of transporting coal cross-country to its ports. By the turn of the century the canal's business was booming. In the years between 1890 and the outbreak of the First World War, an annual average of 35,000 tons of cargo were carried. Alongside coal, the cargoes were mainly slate, from the quarries near Châteaulin, and fertiliser, which helped to develop agricultural production inland.

After the War, motor transport and more effective roads brought swift decline. The canal had always been used primarily for short journeys at either end – from Brest to Carhaix and Pontivy to Nantes – and in 1928 the building of a dam at Lac Guerlédan cut it forever into two sections, with the stretch from Carhaix to Pontivy becoming navigable only by canoe. Plans for the dam were approved on the basis that either a hydraulic lift, or a side channel, would enable barges to bypass it – but neither was ever built. In 1945 the last barge arrived at Châteaulin. These days, the only industry that has much use for the canal is tourism.

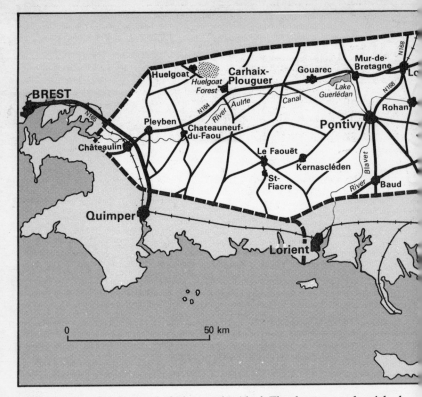

to the towns and sights around, the canal is ideal. The detours can be picked almost at will – the **sculpture park** at Kerguéhennec, near Josselin, is one of the least known and most enjoyable.

All of inland Brittany is supposed – in myth if not in literal fact – to have been covered by one vast forest, the *Argoat*. Vestiges of ancient woodland remain in several areas, and it's well worth making the effort to seek them out. Sadly, however, the **forest of Huelgoat,** which with its boulder-strewn waterfalls, bubbling streams and grottoes was the most dramatic natural landscape in Brittany, was utterly devastated by the hurricane of 1987. At least **Paimpont** survives – the legendary forest of Brocéliande which concealed the Holy Grail.

You cannot make the whole journey described in this chapter alongside the canal. For much of the way there is no adjacent road and whilst the **towpath** is normally clear enough for walking it's not really practicable to cycle along for any great distance. However, it is certainly worth following the canal in short sections, which you can do quite easily by car, better by bike, or best of all by hiring a **boat**, **barge** or even a **houseboat** along one or more of the navigable stretches. Full listings of **hire** outlets are given in the "Travel Details" at the end of this chapter.

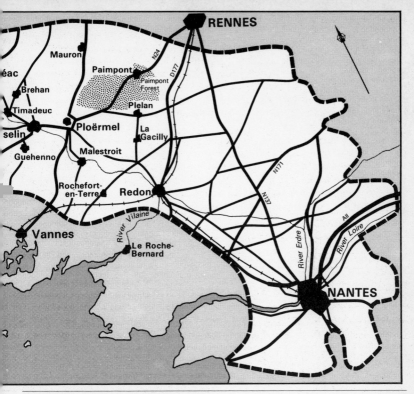

The Finistère Stretch

As late as the 1920s, there were steamers making their way across the Rade de Brest and down the Aulne river to Châteaulin. The contemporary *Black's Guide* reckoned the six-hour journey "tedious (in a) boat often overcrowded with cattle"; a judgement that seems a little churlish now that such pleasures are no longer available.

Châteaulin

CHATEAULIN is the first real town on the canal route, though in actuality no more than a brief, picturesque strip along the waterside. It's a quiet place, where the main reason to stay is the river Aulne itself. Enticingly rural, it is renowned for some of the best salmon and trout fishing in the region; if you're interested, most bars (as well as angling shops some of which hire tackle) sell permits. The only other factor that might draw you is cycling: regional championships are held each September on a circuit that races through the centre and on occasion it's used for the French professional championship, too. But, these times aside, you should have little difficulty finding a room at the two modest **hotels**. Both are good and inexpensive, with *Le Chrismas* (☎98.86.01.24) just having the edge; it's on rue des Ecoles, which climbs from the town centre towards Pleyben. If you're camping, the nearest site is at Pont Coblant (see below).

Along **the riverbank**, there's a statue to Jean Moulin, the Resistance leader of whose murder SS man Klaus Barbie was recently found guilty in Lyons. Moulin was *sous-prefect* in Châteaulin from 1930 to 1933; the inscription reads "mourir sans parler". Within a couple of minutes' walk upstream from the statue, and the town centre, you're on towpaths overhung by trees full of birds, with rabbits and squirrels running ahead of you on the path. For the first couple of kilometres, there are diagrams of corpulent yet energetic figures inciting you to join them in unspeakable exercises – if you can resist that temptation, you'll soon find yourself ambling in peace past the locks and weirs that climb towards the *Montagnes Noires*. If you're walking the canal seriously, Pont Coblant and Pleyben may look just ten kilometres distant on the map, but be warned the meanders make it a hike of several hours. Pick your side of the water, too; there are no bridges between Châteaulin and Pont Coblant.

Pont Coblant and Pleyben

PONT COBLANT is the first point at which you can **hire boats** (either canoes or houseboats; see "Travel Details" at the end of this chapter, or ring ☎98.73.34.69). A small village, it also has a very basic (and cheap) forty-bed unofficial **youth hostel** (contact the *Moulin de Pont Coblant*, 29190 Pleyben, ☎98.73.34.40 to reserve a bed) and a **campsite** (June–Sept; ☎98.73.31.22).

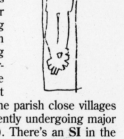

PLEYBEN, four kilometres to the north, is renowned for its **parish close** (see p.143). On its four sides the calvary traces the life of Jesus, combining great detail with an appealing naivety. The church itself, twin-towered, with a huge ornate spire dwarfing its domed Renaissance neighbour, features an altarpiece so blackened and buckled by age as to leave only two tiny "windows" decipherable, like an Advent calendar. Pleyben is more openly prosperous than the parish close villages further north; the church is well-scrubbed, and currently undergoing major restoration (not this time due to hurricane damage). There's an **SI** in the spacious and grandiose main square, the place de Gaulle, and a hotel behind the church, *Le Gai Logis* (☎98.26.63.71).

Châteauneuf and Carhaix

CHATEAUNEUF-DU-FAOU is in similar vein to Châteaulin, sloping down to the tree-lined river. It's a little more developed, though, with a tourist complex, the *Penn ar Pont* (☎98.81.81.25), that boasts a swimming pool, gîtes, and camping as well as cycle and **boat hire**. The **canal proper** separates off from the Aulne a few kilometres to the east at Pont Triffen, staking its own path on, past Carhaix, and out of Finistère.

CARHAIX, an ancient road junction, has cafés and shops to replenish supplies, but not much to recommend it. Beyond it the canal – as far as Pontivy – is navigable only by canoe. If that's not how you're travelling, it probably makes more sense to loop round to the south, through the **Montaignes Noir**, Le Faouët and Kernascléden, before rejoining the canal at **Lac Guerlédan**. Alternatively, to the north – assuming you resisted the detour from Morlaix – there are the **Forêt de Huelgoat** and the **Monts d'Arrées**. These routes are covered in the next two sections.

South through the Montaignes Noires

The **Montaignes Noires** edge along Finistère's borders, south of Châteauneuf. Despite the name, they are really no more than escarpments, though bleak and imposing nonetheless in a harsh, exposed landscape at odds with the gentle canal path. Their highest point is the stark slate **Roc de Toullaëron**, on the road between Pont Triffen and Gourin. From its 1043ft peak, you can look west and north over miles of what seems like totally deserted countryside.

Le Faouët and St-Fiacre

If you are driving, the D769 beyond Gourin offers access to the twin churches of St-Fiacre and Kernascléden, built simultaneously, according to legend, with the aid of an angelic bridge. En route is the town of **LE FAOUET**, a secluded place (unconnected by bus or train) distinguished mainly by its wooden market hall, topped by a pinnacle turret.

The church at **ST-FIACRE**, just over two kilometres south, is notable for its rood screen, brightly polychromed and carved as intricately as lace. The original purpose of a rood screen was to separate the chancel from the congregation – the decorations of this 1480 masterpiece go rather further than that. They depict scenes from the Old and New Testaments as well as a dramatic series on the wages of sin. Drunkenness is demonstrated by a man somehow vomiting a fox; theft by a peasant stealing apples; and so on.

Kernascléden

At the ornate and gargoyle-coated church at **KERNASCLEDEN**, fifteen kilometres southeast along the D782, the focus turns from carving to frescoes. The themes, however, contemporary with St-Fiacre, are equally gruesome. In a Dance of Death, a faded cousin to that at Kermaria (see p.127), the souls of the damned are boiled and minced in Hell.

The Monts d'Arrée

A broad swathe of the more desolate regions of Finistère, stretching east from the Crozon peninsula to the edge of Finistère, is designated as the *Parc Régional d'Armorique*. The park, in theory at least, is an area of conservation and of rural regeneration along traditional lines; in reality, lack of funding creates rather less impact. The **Monts d'Arrée**, however, which cut north-east across Finistère from the Aulne estuary, are something of a nature sanctuary; kestrels circle high above the bleak hilltops, sharing the skies with pippits, curlews, and great black crows. And although the ancient woods of the **Forêt de Huelgoat**, over to the east, are but a pale shadow of their former selves, the lakeside village of Huelgoat itself is still worth a detour.

East across the Monts d'Arrée

The administrative centre of the Parc d'Armorique is at **MENEZ-MEUR**, off the D342 near the Forêt de Cranou – just inland from the Brest–Quimper motorway. Menez is an official **animal reserve** with wild boar and deer roaming free (June–Sept every day 10.30am–7pm). At the reserve gate you can pick up a wealth of detail on the park and all its various activities (☎98.68.81.71).

The Moulins de Kerouat

To the north, at **SIZUN**, there's a research station, **aquarium** and fishing exhibition (daily June 15–Oct 15, 10.30am–7pm; public holidays only for the rest of the year). East of here, three kilometres along the D764 to Commana, is the abandoned hamlet of **MOULINS DE KEROUAT** (*Milin Kerroch* in Breton – and on the Michelin map), which has recently been restored as an **Eco-Musée** (March–June 2–6pm, July–Aug 11am–7pm, Sept–Oct weekends only). Kérouat's last inhabitant died in 1967 and like many a place in the Breton interior it might have crumbled into indiscernible ruins. However, the idea of eco-museums is big in France at present – they are usually excellent – and one of the hamlet's watermills has been restored to motion, and its houses repaired and refurnished. The largest belonged in the last century to the mayor of Commana, who also controlled the mills, and its furnishings are therefore those of a rich family.

The highest point of the Monts d'Arrée is the **ridge** which curves from the **Réservoir de St-Michel** (also known as the Lac de Brennilis) to Menez Kaldor. It is visible as a stark silhouette from the underused **campsite** at **NESTAVEL-BRAZ** on the eastern shore of the lake. From this deceptively tranquil vantage point, the army's antennae near **Roc Trévezel** to the north are obscured, as are those of the navy at Menez-Meur to the west. Right behind you, however, is the Brennilis nuclear power station. In a rare manifestation of separatist terrorism, Breton nationalists attacked this in 1975 with a rocket-launcher; it survived. In 1987, the British SAS conducted an astonishingly offensive exercise in this area, when they were invited by the French government to subdue a simulated Breton uprising, and in the process managed to run over a local inhabitant.

Perhaps appropriately, across the lake where the tree-lined fields around the villages end, is **Yeun Elez**, one of the legendary "holes to hell". You can walk around the lake – gorse and brambles permitting; be very careful not to stray from the paths into the surrounding peat bogs. The ridge itself is followed most of the way by a road but in places it still feels as if miles from any habitation.

The Forêt de Huelgoat

The **FORET DE HUELGOAT** spreads out to the north and east of the village of Huelgoat, the halfway point between Morlaix and Carhaix on the minor road D769 and served by the four daily buses that connect the two towns.

It's hard now to appreciate quite how special Huelgoat used to be. While there may be doubt as to whether the *Argoat*, the great forest supposed to have stretched the length of prehistoric inland Brittany, ever existed, the antiquity of Huelgoat cannot be questioned. It was a staggering, almost impossible landscape, of trees, giant boulders and waterfalls tangled together in primeval chaos. Just how delicate it really was, just how miraculous had been its long survival, was demonstrated by the hurricane of October 1987, which smashed it to smithereens in the space of fifteen minutes.

Now the few trees left standing on the hillsides are stripped of most of their branches, while the rest lie decaying in an impenetrable tangle of dead wood that it would be unrealistic to expect the village of Huelgoat ever to have the resources to clear. It is still possible to walk along most of the forest paths shown on the map over the page; in fact they're far wider than they ever were, having been bulldozed to let the lumber lorries in. If you never saw Huelgoat in its prime, you might even think it a pleasant enough stroll; but the elements that made it unique have gone.

At the **Mare aux Sangliers**, a waterfall deep in the woods, a solitary pine tree used to cling to a massive boulder, its exposed roots wrapped around the stone like tentacles. The hurricane brought it and all its neighbours down, smashing the footbridges; the topsoil ripped up with all the trees has washed down into the rock pool and completely silted it up. The **Camp d'Arthus**, the Gallo-Roman *oppidum*, or hill-fort, large enough to be a settlement for a whole community rather than just a military encampment – and the spitting image of Asterix the Gaul's fictional village – is no longer recognisable. There's just a muddy wasteland dotted with stacks of timber.

Few of the many spots in the forest where metaphorical names were attached to the natural chaos – the *Cooking Pots*, the *Horseshoe*, and so on – survive, although the **Grotte du Diable** right next to the village is still there. Here you can make a somewhat perilous descent, between the rocks, to a subterranean stream. The local story is that a Revolutionary soldier, fleeing from the *chouans*, hid in the cave, lighting a fire to keep warm; when his pursuers saw him by the red glow, brandishing a pitchfork to defend himself, they thought they'd found the Devil.

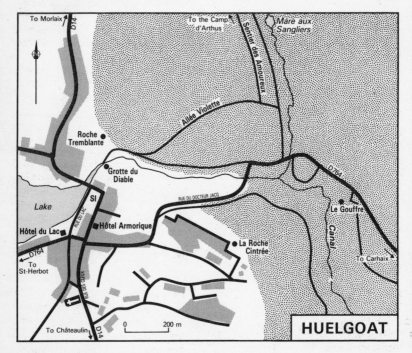

HUELGOAT

Practical details

For all the destruction, the village of **HUELGOAT** is still quite a pleasant place to stay, next to its own small **lake** (on which they hold aquatic Citroën 2CV championships each July – and have the photographs to prove it). The

SI is a bit too despondent to offer much constructive help, but the *Hôtel du Lac* (☎98.99.71.14), beside the lake, has very basic **rooms** and good food. Alternative **accommodation** includes the economically priced *Hôtel Armorique* (1 place Aristide Briand; ☎98.99.71.24), or there's a summer-only **campsite** (☎98.99.78.80), complete with swimming-pool, on the lakeside road towards Brest. **Bikes** are hired out at the garage at 1 rue du Lac.

A walk out from Huelgoat that avoids the heart of the forest is along the **canal** to the east. This stretch – not linked to any of the main Nantes–Brest waterways – was originally built to serve the old lead and silver mines, worked here from Roman times right up to this century. **LE GOUFFRE** is close by (at the junction where the road out from Huelgoat joins the D769 between Morlaix and Carhaix), worth the walk for its deep cave and, more so, for an exceptionally good (and cheap) *Routiers* **restaurant**.

Back to the Canal

Although between Carhaix and Pontivy the **Nantes–Brest canal** is limited to canoeists, it's worth some effort to follow on land, particularly for the scenery along the middle stretch from Gouarec to Mur-de-Bretagne. At the centre trails the artificial **Lac de Guerlédan**, backed to the south by the **Forêt de Quénécan**.

Approaching by road, the canal path is easiest joined at Gouarec, covered by the five daily buses between Carhaix and Loudéac. En'route, you pass the rather subdued (and unmemorable) **ROSTRENEN**, whose old facades are given a little life at the Tuesday market.

Gouarec

At **GOUAREC** the river Blavet and the canal meet in a confusing swirl of water that shoots off, edged by footpaths, in the most unlikely directions. The old schist houses of the town are barely disturbed by traffic or development, nor are there great numbers of tourists. For a comfortable overnight stop, the 2-star **hotel**, *du Blavet* (☎96.24.90.03), is in an ideal waterside position; its restaurant is principally aimed at gourmets prepared to spend several hundred francs on a single bottle of wine, but they're quite happy to serve you with the same excellent food on their cheapest menu with no wine. **Camping**, there's a well-positioned municipal site (☎96.24.90.22), next to the canal and away from the main road.

Lac Guerlédan

For the fifteen kilometres between Gouarec and Mur-de-Bretagne, the **N164** skirts the edge of the **Forêt de Quénécan**, within which is the series of artificial lakes created when the Barrage de Guerlédan was completed in 1928. The forest itself suffered severe damage in the hurricane, but this remains a beautiful stretch of river, a little overpopular with British camper-caravanners but peaceful enough nonetheless. The best bases to stay are just off the road, past the villages of St-Gelven and Caurel. At the former, you can walk down to Lac Guerlédan and the **campsite** at **KERMANEC**. From just before Caurel, the brief loop of the D111 leads to tiny sandy beaches – a bit too tiny in season – with **campsites** *Les Pins* (☎96.28.52.22) and *Les Pommiers* (☎96.28.52.35). At the spot known, justifiably, as **BEAU RIVAGE** is a complex containing a campsite, hotel, restaurant, snackbar and 140-seat glass-topped cruise-boat.

MUR-DE-BRETAGNE is set back from the eastern end of the lake, a lively place with a wide and colourful pedestrianised zone around its church. It's the nearest town to the barrage – just two kilometres distant – and has a **campsite**, the *Rond-Point du Lac* (☎96.26.01.90), with facilities for windsurfing and horse-riding. There's also a **youth hostel** a short way further along the N164 at **ST-GUEN** (☎96.28.54.34) – take the Loudéac bus and get off at *Bourg de St-Guen*.

LOUDEAC, useful for changing buses, is in itself unmemorable. Travelling on from Mur-de-Bretagne under your own steam, you'd do better to take the D767 instead and follow the Blavet south.

The Central Canal : Pontivy and around

PONTIVY is the central junction of the Nantes–Brest canal, where the course of the canal breaks off once more from the Blavet and you can again take **barges** – all the way to the Loire. The town owes much of its appearance, and its size, to the canal. When the waterway opened, the small medieval centre was expanded, re-designed, and given broad avenues to fit its new role. It was even re-named Napoléonville for a time, in honour of the instigator of its new prosperity. These days it is a bright market town, its twisting old streets contrasting with the stately riverside promenades. At the north end of the town, occupying a commanding hillside site, is the **Château de Rohan**, built by the lord of Josselin in the fifteenth century. Open to visitors, and used for low-key cultural events, the castle still belongs to the Josselin family, who are slowly restoring it. At the moment, one impressive facade, complete with deep moat and two forbidding towers, looks out over the river – behind that, the structure rather peters out. If you're looking for a place to stop over, Pontivy has several **hotels**, among them the low-priced *Martin* (☎97.25.02.04) and *Robic* (☎97.25.11.80), as well as a very spartan **youth hostel** (☎97.25.58.27; 2km from the station on the Ile des Recollets).

Rohan and Bréhan

Immediately beyond Pontivy, the **course of the canal** veers north for a while, away from the Blavet. As it curves back, the stretch from St-Maudan to Rohan is wide and smooth-flowing, with picnic and play areas but without a road or towpath you can follow for any distance. **ROHAN** looks prominent on the map but it's little more than a strip of houses by the canalside. To the northeast, **LA CHEZE** has a tiny and private lake, with an equally diminutive **campsite** (☎96.26.70.99). **LA TRINITE PORHOET**, beyond, also has a **campsite**, *Saint Yves* (☎97.93.92.00), on the long wooded slopes of the valley of the Ninian – otherwise scattered with stone farms and manor houses.

Southeast from Rohan, continuing along the canal towards Josselin, is the Cistercian **Abbaie de Timadeuc**, founded as recently as 1841. You can enter only to attend mass, but it's beautiful anyway from the outside, with its front walls and main gate covered in flowers at the end of an avenue of old pines. The abbey also provides an excuse to stay at **BREHAN** a couple of kilometres away, a quiet little village whose **hotel**, the *Cremaillère* (☎97.51.52.09), must be the best value anywhere in the province. A double room with separate luxurious bathroom costs 80 francs, and the set menu at around 45 francs can include a full seafood platter of oysters, crayfish and crabs, with the meringue-in-caramel dessert *îles flottantes*.

West from Pontivy: along the Blavet

If you choose to follow the **river Blavet** west from Pontivy towards Lorient – rather than the canal – take the time to go by the smaller roads along the valley itself. The Blavet connects the canal with the sea, and once linked Lorient to the other two great ports of Brittany, Brest and Nantes.

The D159 to **QUISTINIC** passes through lush green countryside, its hedgerows full of flowers, where by June there's already been one harvest and grass is growing up around the fresh haystacks. The ivy-clad church of **St-Mathurin** in Quistinic is the scene of a *pardon* (in the second week of May) that dates from Roman times. The devotion to the saint is strongly evident on the village's war memorial, too, his name that of almost half the victims. You can **camp** near the river at the *Ile de Menazen* (☎97.39.70.99).

The Venus de Quinipily

The main reason to go on to **BAUD**, a major road junction just to the east of the river, is to see the **Venus de Quinipily** – signposted off the Hennebont road, two kilometres out of town. The Venus is a crude statue that at first glance looks Egyptian. Once known as the "Iron Lady", it is of unknown but ancient origin. It stands on, or rather nestles its ample buttocks against, a high plinth above a kind of sarcophagus, commanding the valley in the gardens of what was once a château. Behind its stiff pose and dress, the statue has an odd informality, a half-smile on the impassive face. It used to be the object of "impure rites" and was at least twice thrown into the Blavet by Christian authorities, only to be fished out by locals eager to re-indulge. It may itself have been in some way "improper" before it was re-carved, perhaps literally "dressed", some time in the eighteenth century. The **gardens** around the statue, despite being next to a dry and dusty quarry, are luxuriantly fertile. To visit, you pay a small fee to a woman at the gatehouse, who matter-of-factly maintains that "pagans" still come to worship.

CAMORS, just south of Baud, has a smart square-towered church, with a weathercock on top and a little megalith set in the wall. There's a **campsite** (☎97.39.22.06) at one end of the series of forests that grow bleaker and harsher eastward to become the Lanvaux Moors.

Heading east from Baud, to rejoin the canal at Josselin, you pass through **LOCMINE**, another one of those towns reduced to piping rock music in its lifeless streets on summer afternoons in a desperate attempt to draw visitors.

Josselin and around

The **Château de Rohan** at **JOSSELIN** is the canal's most impressive sight: its three Rapunzel towers embedded in a vast sheet of stone above the water. It in fact turns out to be a façade. The building behind it was built in the last century, the bulk of the original castle having been demolished by Richelieu in 1629 in punishment for Henri de Rohan's leadership of the Huguenots. The Rohan family, still in possession, used to own a third of Brittany, though the present incumbent contents himself with the position of local mayor. Tours of the pompous apartments of the ducal residence are not very compelling, even if it does contain the table on which the Edict of Nantes was signed in 1598. But the duchess's collection of **dolls**, housed in the *Musée des Poupées*, behind the castle, is something special. (Hours for the château are July–Aug 10am–noon and 2–6pm daily; June & Sept 2–6pm only; Feb–May, and Oct–mid-Nov, 2–6pm on Wed, Sun and holidays only; closed mid-Nov–Jan; hours for the doll museum the same, but open mornings in June & Sept as well).

The **town** is full of medieval splendours, from the gargoyles of the Basilica to the castle ramparts, and the half-timbered houses in between (of which one of the finest is the **SI** in the place de la Congrégation). It has a history to match. One of the most famous episodes of late chivalry, the Battle of the Thirty, took place nearby in 1351. Rivalry between the French garrison at Josselin and the English at Ploërmel led to a challenge being issued to settle differences in a combat of thirty unmounted knights from each side. The French won, killing the English leader Bemborough. The actual battlesite is now isolated between the two carriageways of the N24 from Josselin to Ploërmel. More accessible is the basilica of **Notre-Dame-du-Roncier**, built on the spot where in the ninth century a peasant supposedly found a statue of the Virgin under a bramble bush. The statue was burned during the Revolution but an important *pardon* is held each year on September 8. As ever, the religious procession and open-air services are solemn in the extreme, but there's a lot else going on to keep you entertained.

Staying at Josselin, there's a *gîte d'étape* right below the castle walls, where you can also hire **canoes**. Alternatively, the *Hôtel du Commerce* (rue Beaumanoir; ☎97.22.22.08) is reasonable.

Guehenno

At **GUEHENNO**, south of Josselin on the D123, is one of the largest and best of the Breton calvaries. Built in 1550, the figures include the cock that crowed to expose Peter's denials, Mary Magdalene with the shroud, and a recumbent Christ in the crypt. Its appeal is enhanced by the naivety of its amateur restoration. After damage caused by Revolutionary soldiers in 1794 – who amused themselves by playing *boules* with the heads of the statues – all the sculptors approached for the work demanded exorbitant fees, so the parish priest and his assistant decided to undertake the task themselves.

Kerguéhennec Sculpture Park

Another unusual sculptural endeavour, this time contemporary, is taking place at the **DOMAINE DE KERGUEHENNEC**, which is signposted a short way off the D11 near St Jean-Brévelay. This innovatory **sculpture park** (April–Oct, 10am–7pm; ☎97.60.21.19) has plans to build up a permanent international collection, and if the first pieces to be installed are anything to go by it should be an increasingly compelling stop. Its setting is the lawns, woods and lake of an early eighteenth century château; studios and indoor workshops are being set up in the outbuildings for visiting artists.

Lizio

Over to the east, off the D151, **LIZIO** has also set itself up as a centre for arts and crafts, with ceramic and weaving workshops its speciality. A *Festival Artisanal* takes place on the second Sunday in August, along with street theatre (and pancakes). There are several **gîtes** (information on ☎97.74.83.03) in the town, and a **campsite**.

Ploërmel

PLOERMEL, defeated by Josselin in the fourteenth century, is still not quite a match for its rival. It's not on the canal, although it is on the railway line. Attractions are the artificial **Etang au Duc**, well stocked with fish, two kilometres to the north, and an interesting array of houses: James II is said to have spent a few days of his exile in one on rue Francs-Bourgeois, while the **Maison des Marmosets** on rue Beaumanoir has some elaborate carvings. The **hotels** *Saint Marc* (☎97.74.00.01) or *Cobh* (☎97.74.00.49) could be good bases for venturing further away from the canal, up into Paimpont forest.

The Forêt de Paimpont

The **FORET DE PAIMPONT** has a definite magic about it. Though now just forty square kilometres in extent, it seems to retain secrets of a forest once much larger and everywhere recalls legends of the vanished *Argoat*, the great primeval forest of Brittany. The one French claimant to an Arthurian past that carries any real conviction, it is just as frequently known by its Arthurian name of *Brocéliande*.

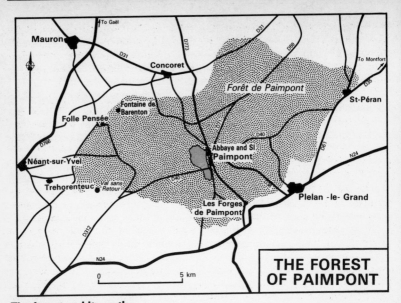

THE FOREST OF PAIMPONT

The forest and its myths

Medieval Breton minstrels, like their Welsh counterparts, set the tales of King Arthur and the Holy Grail both in *Grande Bretagne* and here in *Petite Bretagne*. The particular significance of Brocéliande was as Merlin's forest – some say that he is still here, in "Merlin's stone" where he was imprisoned by the enchantress Viviane.

The stone is next to the **Fontaine de Barenton**, a lonely spot high in the woods. Finding it is not easy. First turn off the road from Concoret at La Saudrais and you will come to the village of Folle Pensée. Go past the few farmhouses, rather than up the hill, and you arrive at a small car park. A foot-path leads up to the right, running through pine and gorse. At a junction of forest tracks, continue straight ahead for about two hundred metres, then veer left along an unobvious (and unmarked) path which leads into the woods, turning back to the north to the spring – walled in mossy stone in the roots of a mighty tree, and filled with the most delicious water imaginable.

Chrétien de Troyes sang of the fountain in the early Middle Ages:

> *You will see the spring which bubbles*
> *Though its water is colder than marble.*
> *It is shaded by the most beautiful tree*
> *That Nature ever made,*
> *For its foliage is evergreen*
> *And a basin of iron hangs from it,*
> *By a chain long enough*
> *To reach the spring;*
> *And beside the spring you will find*
> *A slab of stone which you will recognise -*
> *I cannot describe it*
> *For I have never seen one like it.*

Legend has it that if after drinking you splash water on to the stone slab, you instantly summon a mighty storm, together with roaring lions and a horseman in black armour. This story dates back at least to the fifth century and is recounted, somewhat sceptically, in Robert Wace's *Romance of the Rose*, written around 1160:

> *Hunters repair (to the fountain) in sultry weather; and drawing water with their horns, they sprinkle the stone for the purposes of having rain, which is then wont to fall, they say, throughout the forest around; but why I know not. There too fairies are to be seen (if the Bretons tell truth), and many other wonders happen. I went thither on purpose to see these marvels. I saw the forest and the land, and I sought for the marvels, but I found none. I went like a fool, and so I came back. I sought after folly, and found myself a fool for my pains.*

The parish priest of Concoret and his congregation are reported nonetheless to have successfully ended a drought by this means in 1835, and a procession endorsed by the church went to the spring as recently as 1925.

At Barenton, you are at the very spot where Merlin first set eyes on Viviane, although you are not at the Fountain of Eternal Youth, which is hidden somewhere nearby. The enchantress is supposed to have been born at the château at Comper, at the northern edge of the forest by Concoret – a village notable for having once had the Devil as its rector. Her rival, Morgane le Fay, ruled over the **Val sans Retour** (Valley of No Return) on the western edge of the forest. The valley is situated just off the footpath GR37 from Tréhorenteuc to La Guette. Follow the path that leads out from the D141 south of Tréhorenteuc to a steep valley from which exits are barred by thickets of gorse and giant furze on the rocks above. At one point it skirts past an overgrown table of rock, the **Rocher des Faux Amants**, from which the seductress Morgane enticed unwary and faithless youths.

Paimpont village and other forest bases

PAIMPONT village is the most obvious and enjoyable base for exploring the forest. It's right at the centre of the woods, backs on to a marshy lake full of wild mushrooms (*cèpes*), and has some excellent accommodation. Pick from two **campsites**, a *gîte d'étape* (c/o M & Mme Grosset; ☎99.07.81.40), a **youth hostel** (☎97.22.76.75; a couple of kilometres out on the Concoret road) and the **hotel** *Relais de Brocéliande* (☎99.07.81.07) where you can stuff yourself in the restaurant under the gaze of stuffed animal heads, and a live parrot whose one note sounds like a submarine. Next to the abbey is an **SI**.

Alternative bases – if the Paimpont hotels are full – include Les Forges and Plélan-le-Grand, at the southern edge of the forest, Mauron at the north, and, further out to the east, Montfort-sur-Meu.

The forges that gave **LES FORGES** its name, and once smelted iron from the surrounding forest, have long since disappeared. Now it's just a rural hamlet, set by a calm lake and disturbed only by the dogs in the hunting kennels. Among the houses coated with red ivy is a *gîte d'étape* (keys held by Mme Farcy; ☎97.06.93.46).

PLÉLAN-LE-GRAND, at the other end of the lake, has more affordable **hotels** in the *Orée de la Forêt* (☎99.06.81.15) and the *Bruyères* (☎99.06.81.38), while just outside the village is the *Manoir du Tertre* (☎99.07.81.02; closed

Tues, and all Feb), a very grand old country house, preserved with all its furnishings and operating, with high but not outrageous prices, as a superb hotel/restaurant. A tiny place, Plélan has an oddly dramatic history. In the ninth century it was the capital of one of Brittany's early kings, Solomon; its appeal presumably lay in its inaccessibity to Norse or other raiders. Later, in the sixteenth century, it was a part of the short-lived independent republic of Thélin, awarded to the local people after they had paid the ransom of their liegelord. And finally, after the Revolution, Plélan served as the headquarters of Puisaye, the Breton *chouan* leader.

If you continue south you come to **BELLEVUE-COETQUIDAN**, dominated by a large military camp; its hotels, full of the anxious relatives of soldiers, aren't the most attractive resting places. Beyond is **GUER**, a gentle little town containing not much more than a rusty ideas box placed in the main square and a heated covered swimming pool. From here, the D776 rolls and tumbles through further woods until it reaches the canal at Malestroit.

At the **northern** edge of the forest, the nearest rooms are at **MAURON**. A rambling country town, this has quite a charm – and a reasonable **hotel**, the *Brambily* (☎97.22.61.67) in the town centre. It too has a swimming pool, on the small side but still more than welcome after a hot day in the forest.

East: Montfort-sur-Meu

If you've been seduced by the Paimpont forest, **MONTFORT-SUR-MEU** has an **Eco-Musée** that should provide some fascination. Set in the one surviving tower of what in the fourteenth century was a complete walled town, it appears at first the usual small-town museum assortment – costumed dolls and the like. But don't be put off. Upstairs there is a detailed comparison between the forests of Paimpont and Trémelin, proving the somewhat shocking fact that the former is artificially planted (and therefore a poor candidate really to be Brocéliande). And, of more tangible appeal, there's a remarkable display of the area's quarries and stone – exhibited along with modern sculptures exploring their texture or building techniques. From the top of the tower the view takes in some of the still-visible quarries. The museum also runs workshops, where children are taught traditional crafts with materials such as cowdung, and where sculptors explain their work to casual visitors. Opening hours are 2–6pm, daily except Monday (10am–noon, too, July–Sept).

Montfort is on the railway, with a reasonable **hotel**, the *Relais de la Cane* (☎99.09.00.07), close by the **gare SNCF**. By train it is only a few minutes away from Rennes and so is a possible point from which to set out if you're coming to Paimpont from the north. You can hire **bikes** at the station, as ever. And if you've a bike problem, or you're into the machines for their own sake, you should certainly make your way to the shed marked *Atelier 2000* at no. 9 place de la Tribunal. There, ex-racing cyclist J-C Andrieux has an incredible collection of battered bikes – and any number of cycling tales. He collects old British bikes, bicycles with wooden wheels, motorised tricycles, and so on, without any apparent idea of restoring them: there's just a huge pile stacked away in the garage. One day, it'll probably be the famous Montfort cycle museum; for the moment it's fun, with only one bike, bizarrely welded into a giant fireman's helmet, in any kind of working order.

Malestroit and Rochefort

Not a lot happens in **MALESTROIT**, which was a thousand years old in 1987. But the town is full of unexpected and enjoyable corners. As you come in to the main square, the **place du Bouffay** in front of the church, the houses are covered with unlikely carvings – an anxious bagpipe-playing hare looking over its shoulder at a dragon's head on one beam, while an oblivious sow in a blue buckled belt threads her distaff on another. The **church** itself is decorated with drunkards and acrobats outside, torturing demons and erupting towers within; whilst each night the display is completed by the sullen parade of metal-festooned youth that weaves in and out of the *Vieille Auberge* bar opposite. The only ancient walls without adornment are the ruins of the **Chapelle de la Madeleine**, where one of the many temporary truces of the Hundred Years War was signed.

Beside the grey canal, the matching grey slate tiles on the turreted rooftops bulge and dip, while on its central island overgrown houses stand next to the stern walls of an old mill. If you arrive by barge (this is a good stretch to travel), you'll moor very near the town centre, so you can lurch across to the only – fortunately cheap – **hotel** and restaurant, the *Aigle d'Or* (1 rue des Ecoles; ☎97.75.20.10).

The **gare routière**, served by buses to Vannes and Rennes, is on the main bd du Pont Neuf; there's the *Dufresne* **campsite** (☎97.75.13.33) below the main bridge, and a **gîte d'étape** up at the canal lock (c/o M. Halier; ☎97.75.11.66). The **SI** is also on bd du Pont Neuf, and has details of **canoe and boat hire**; **bikes** can be hired from the *Aigle d'Or*.

The Musée de la Résistance Bretonne

Two kilometres west of Malestroit (and with no bus connection), the village of **ST-MARCEL** hosts a **Musée de la Résistance Bretonne** (June–Sept 10am–7pm, otherwise 10am–noon and 2–6pm). The museum is on the site of a June 1944 battle in which the Breton *maquis*, joined by Free French forces parachuted in from England, successfully diverted the local German troops from the main Normandy invasion movements. Its strongest feature is the presentation of the pressures that made the majority of French collaborate: the reconstructed street corner from which all life has been jerked out by the occupiers; the big colourful propaganda posters offering work in Germany, announcing executions of *maquis*, equating resistance with aiding US and British big business; and against these the low budget, flimsily printed Resistance pamphlets.

If you are not on the canal, which at this stage is the river Oust, the D764 on the south bank, or the D147/149 on the north, will keep you parallel for much of its course towards Redon. Along the way there are two worthwhile detours: south of the canal to Rochefort-en-Terre, north to La Gacilly.

Rochefort-en-Terre

ROCHEFORT-EN-TERRE has a commanding site – the high end of a gorge that is followed by the D774 (and at its end by the connecting D777). Its most imposing face is occupied, predictably enough, by a **château**. Less expected, however, is the castle's appearance. Once the property of the American painter Alfred Klots, it is a jigsaw of a building, knocked together early this century from stone pieces of other local houses. Visits feature startling terrace views and a fairly standard collection of furniture, paintings, and tapestries. It is open 10.30am until noon and 2 to 6.30pm (July–Sept 15, every day; May–June & Sept 16–30, holidays and weekends only).

The rest of the town is a prettified and polished version of Malestroit, something of a tourist trap with little antique shops and expensive restaurants. A curiosity is the Black Virgin in the church of **Notre-Dame de Tronchaye**, which was found hidden from Norman invaders in a hollow tree in the twelfth century, and is the object of a pilgrimage on the first Sunday after August 15. More interesting, though, is the **Lac Bleu**, just south of the town, where there are ancient **slate quarries**, whose deep galleries are the home of blind butterflies and long-eared bats.

Unusually for Brittany, there are no hotels in Rochefort-en-Terre, although the **SI** in the main street displays a list of rather expensive *chambres d'hôte* in the neighbourhood. There is also a **campsite**, *Le Chemin de Bogeais* (☎97.43.32.81). And at the village of **ST-VINCENT-SUR-OUST**, on the D764 towards Redon, there's a **youth hostel**, *Ti Kendalc'h* (☎99.91.28.55), which serves as a centre for Breton music and dance.

La Gacilly

Fourteen kilometres north of the canal, **LA GACILLY** makes a good base for walking trips in search of megaliths, sleepy villages and countryside. The town itself has prospered recently thanks to the creation of a beauty products industry based on the abundantly proliferating flowers in the Aff valley. It is, too, a centre for many active craftsworkers. The luxurious *chambres d'hôte* (☎99.70.04.79) in the nearby château de Trégaret in **SIXT-SUR-AFF** provide ideal countryside accommodation.

Redon

Junction of the rivers Oust and Vilaine, the Nantes–Brest canal, railways to Rennes, Vannes and Nantes, and six major roads, **REDON** is not a place it's easy to avoid. And you shouldn't try to, either. A wonderful mess of water and locks – the canal manages to cross the Vilaine at right angles in one of the more complex links – the town has history, charm and life. It's arguably the best stop along the whole course of the canal.

Up until the First World War, Redon was the seaport for Rennes. Its industrial docks – or what remains of them – are therefore on the Vilaine, while the canal, even in the very centre of town, is almost totally rural, its towpaths shaded avenues. Ship-owners' houses from the seventeenth and eighteenth centuries can be seen in the port area – walk via quai Jean Bart next to the bassin as far as the **Croix des Marins**, returning along quai Duguay-Truin beside the river. A rusted wrought-iron workbridge, equipped with a crane rolling on tracks, still crosses the river, but the main users of the port now are cruise ships. These head down to the Arzal dam, which is as close as they can get to the sea, past La Roche-Bernard.

Redon was once also a religious centre, its first abbey founded in 832 by Saint Conwoion. The most prominent church today is **St-Sauveur**, with its Gothic tower, entirely separated from the main building by a fire, and unique four-storeyed Romanesque belfry. The belfry is squat, almost obscured by later roofs and the high choir, and is best seen from the adjacent cloisters. Inside the church, you'll find the tomb of the judge who tried the legendary Bluebeard – Joan of Arc's friend, Gilles de Rais.

Practical details

Most of the town's **hotels** are near the station – and it's a small enough place for this to be no drawback. Good choices are the *de Bretagne* (place de la Gare; ☎99.77.00.42) and *de l'Ouest* (14 rue des Douves; ☎99.71.10.91) which also has a decent buffet. The *Hôtel de la Gare* (10 rue de la Gare; ☎99.71.02.04) has a reputation for gourmet **food**. There's also one of the province's rare **vegetarian** restaurants – the somewhat bizarre *Lavomagic* (18 rue du Port; ☎99.72.21.08), its frontage designed like a launderette – and a surprisingly dynamic **music bar**, *Le Trombone à Coulisse* (14 rue du Plessis).

A very large and sprawling Monday **market** is centred on the modern *halles*, where you can buy superb crêpes. The **SI** is based there too, for information on the hire of boats and gîtes; in summer they have an additional annex in the port to serve the needs of what the notices in English call the "Pleasure People". Every Friday and Saturday from the end of June to the end of July, Redon puts on a large-scale *son et lumière* re-enactment of ten of the earliest years of its history, 835–845AD.

Nantes

NANTES, the former capital of Brittany, is no longer officially a part of the province. However, such bureaucracy is not taken overseriously in the city and its history – though it is not immediately apparent amid the modern urban sprawl – is closely bound up with Breton fortunes. A considerable medieval centre, it later achieved great wealth from colonial expeditions, slave trading and shipbuilding – activities in turn surpassed by more recent industrial growth.

It is not these days an attractive place. The Loire, foundation of its site and riches, has dwindled from the centre. As recently as the 1930s the river crossed the city in seven separate channels, but German labour as part of reparations for World War I filled in five of them. What are still called the "islands" in the centre are now surrounded, and isolated, not by water but by traffic-choked dual carriageways. Even the castle is no longer on the waterfront – which instead is lined with tower blocks. Nonetheless, if you have time and energy there are things to see – chief among them the Château des Ducs and Beaux Arts museum – and the river Erdre, the vineyards of the Loire and the remarkable Italianate town of Clisson are all within reach.

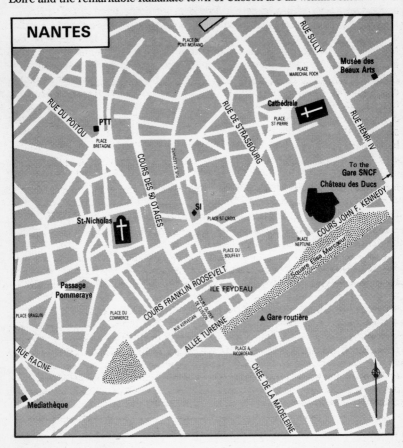

The Château des Ducs

The **Château des Ducs** is one of the country's major historic sites and has been preserved largely in the form in which it was built by the last Breton duke, François II, and his daughter Duchess Anne. As well as the trial and public burning of Bluebeard in 1440, it saw the imprisonment of John Knox as a galley-slave in 1547–49, and the departure of Bonnie Prince Charlie heading for Culloden in 1745. The Edict of Nantes, granting a certain degree of toleration to the Protestants and thereby ending the Wars of Religion, was signed in the castle by Henry IV on April 20 1598. To its credit the city refrained from indulging in the otherwise general massacre of the Huguenots subsequent to its revocation by Louis XIV in 1685.

The castle remains impressive, its walls low but very solid. You can walk into the courtyard and up onto the ramparts for nothing, but there are three museums within the precincts that are worth visiting; all are open 10am–noon and 2–6pm (closed Tues, except in July & August, and holidays). The first – housed in the old prison of the Tour de la Boulangerie, on the graffitied walls of which a sort of dolls' house has been carved by bored inmates – is the **Musée des Arts Populaires**, a good introduction to Breton history and folklore, which is depicted in a series of murals and dioramas. The **Musée des Arts Decoratifs**, in the Governor's Palace nearby, displays a refreshingly contemporary selection of textile work. The **Musée des Salorges** is devoted to trade, with a good collection of figureheads and model ships. You can also contrast the pitiful trinkets, beads and bracelets, traded for West African slaves, and the accounts and diagrams of the voyages, with the pomp of the barge used for Napoleon's ball in Nantes in August 1808 – an occasion when *epée et habit français* were compulsory attire. By the end of the eighteenth century, Nantes was the principal port of France, with huge fortunes being made on the "ebony" (slave) trade – which brought in as much as 200 percent profit per ship. The abolition of slavery coincided with an increased use of domestic French sugar beet as against Antillais sugar cane, the port began to silt up and heavy industry and wine-growing became more important.

The rest of the city

In 1800 the Spaniards Tower, the castle's arsenal, exploded, shattering the stained glass of the **Cathédrale de St-Pierre et St-Paul** over 200m away. It was just one of many disasters that have befallen the church. It was used as a barn during the Revolution; bombed during the Second World War; and damaged by a fire in 1971, just when things seemed sorted out again. Restored and finally re-opened, the clean white stone makes the building seem especially light and soaring. Its masterpiece is the tomb of François II and his wife Margaret, the parents of Duchess Anne with its somewhat grating symbols of Power, Strength and Justice for him and Fidelity, Prudence and Temperance for her.

The **Musée des Beaux Arts** in rue Clemenceau has a respectable collection of paintings displayed in excellent new galleries – and is well worth checking for its temporary exhibitions. Not all its Renaissance and contemporary works are on view at any one time, but you should be able to take in works ranging from Italian miniatures to a gorgeous "David Triumphant" by Delaunay. It also contains the remarkable spectacle of two huge Rubens canvases dominating the damp and squalid basement toilets, and is open 9.15am–noon and 1–6pm, Sunday 11am–5pm, closed Tuesday and holidays.

The **Musée d'Histoire Naturelle**, in rue Voltaire, centres on a vivarium, whose miserable animals are not for the squeamish (the soft-shelled turtle in particular tugs at the heartstrings). But don't let this put you off the eccentric assortment of oddities of its museum collection: rhinoceros toenails, a coelecanth and an aepyornis egg, and slightly tatty stuffed specimens of virtually every bird and animal imaginable. There is an Egyptian mummy, too, as well as a shrunken Maori head and a complete tanned human skin – taken in 1793 from the body of a soldier whose dying wish was to made into a drum. Hours are 10am to noon and 2 to 6pm, closed Sunday morning, Monday and holidays. Also in rue Voltaire you'll find the **Palais Dobrée**, a nineteenth-century mansion given over to two museums, one of which features Duchess Anne's heart in a box.

If you have time to kill, take the tram to the **Médiathèque** stop, where you'll find a superb modern library with bookshops and facilities to watch any of an eclectic selection of videos – Sir Alf Ramsey and the Battle of Iwo Jima side by side. From there, you can walk along quai de la Fosse to the point where the two remaining branches of the Loire meet up, with a good view of the port.

Practical details: Food, Drink and Accommodation

Very few medieval buildings survive in Nantes and, as ever, the best is now the **SI** – in the **place du Change**. This area is largely pedestrian and contains several good value **restaurants**, such as the *P'tit Bistrot* at 14 rue de la Juiverie. Otherwise, the best restaurant area – try the *Salt and Pepper* – is among the former ship-builders' houses on rue Kervegan on the **Ile Feydeau**. Jules Verne was born on the île and has a museum (10am–12.30pm & 2–5pm, closed Tues) dedicated to him at 3 rue de l'Hermitage; it's more of an amusement for the fans of his stories than a source of any serious information about the man. In place Graslin, behind the city theatre, are a couple of large cinemas, together with a smattering of arty **cafés**; and *La Cigale* at no. 4 is a well-preserved turn-of-the-century brasserie serving excellent meals, with fish as a speciality. A spectacular nineteenth-century multi-level shopping centre, the **Passage Pommeraye**, is on nearby rue Crébillon.

The easiest way to **get around** in Nantes is on the rubber-wheeled trams that run along the old riverfront. These pass by both the **gare SNCF** and the **gare routière**, which are on the south side of the boulevard a short way east of the castle. The flat fare you pay for the tram gives you a ticket for an hour rather than just one journey.

As for **places to stay**, try the *Centre Jean Macé* (90 rue du Prefet Bonnefoy; ☎40.74.55.74), or the hotels *de l'Océan* (11 rue de Maréchal-de-Lattre-de-Tassigny, between Place Graslin and the Médiathèque; ☎40.69.73.51), *Trianon* (43 bd Victor Hugo; ☎40.47.82.00), *Sanitat* (18 Rue d'Alger; ☎40.73.25.57) or *Grand Monarque* (36, rue du Marechal Joffre; ☎40.74.02.40). Of the three **youth hostels**, that at 2 place de la Manu (☎40.20.57.25) is easiest to reach, by taking Tramway 1 towards Malachère and getting off at *Manufacture*. The other two have accommodation for non-members as well, at 1 rue Porte Neuve (☎40.20.00.80) and at 9 bd Vincent Gache (☎40.47.91.64).

Within reach of Nantes

Immediately **upstream from Nantes** you are into the Loire wine-growing country that produces the two classic dry white wines, *Gros-Plant* and *Muscadet*. Any **vineyard** should be happy to give you a *dégustation*. Most operate on a very small scale. The largest, however, the **Chasseloir vineyard** (☎40.54.81.15) at **ST-FIACRE-SUR-MAINE**, is perhaps the most interesting. This occupies the grounds of a former château, with fifty acres of vines – some a century old. The vineyard sells mostly within the catering trade but anyone is welcome to visit their cellars, which are decorated with painted Rabelaisian carvings and candelabra made from vineroots. Like so many of the vineyards in this region, the grapes are now picked and pressed by machines. The old tradition of employing seasonal migrant labour on the harvest is a thing of the past.

To explore the **last section of the Nantes–Brest canal**, you can take a river cruise from quai des Versailles at the end of Cours des 50 Otages in the centre of Nantes. These cruises run up the Erdre as far as the point where it is joined by the canal coming from Redon. They thrive mainly because the Loire is not at present navigable by this sort of boat (although there are plans to change that) but the Erdre is itself beautiful and wide, with a fine selection of châteaux along its banks, chief among them **La Gacherie**. At least two boats run every day in high season, one of them with a top-class restaurant on board – contact *Lebert-Buisson* (24 quai des Versailles; ☎40.20.24.50) for reservations.

Clisson

To the south, at the point where the Sèvre meets the Maine, and the crossroads of the three ancient duchies of Brittany, Anjou and Poitou, is the town of **CLISSON**. This was re-modelled by two French architects in the last century into a close approximation of an Italian hill town. The fact that they already had the raw material of a ruined fortress, a covered market hall and a magnificent situation makes it a sight not to be missed. The best **place to stay** is the *Hôtel de la Gare* (place Gare; ☎40.36.16.55).

travel details

Trains

No railway line cuts across central Brittany; however, certain towns mentioned in this chapter can be reached by train.

Châteaulin is on the line from Brest to Quimper.
Carhaix is served by 4 trains daily from Guingamp, with connecting buses to the south coast.
Pontivy and **Loudéac** are served by 3–4 trains daily from St-Brieuc (1hr 30min/1hr), again with connecting buses running south.

Redon is on the main Rennes to Nantes line, and is the junction for trains coming from Brest, Quimper and Vannes.
Nantes connects directly with Paris (3hr), Rennes, Quimper, Brest and the South.

Buses

From Carhaix to Châteaulin (5 daily; 30min), Loudéac (5 daily; 1hr), Quimper (4 daily; 1hr) and Morlaix (hourly; 1hr).
From Vannes to Rennes (8 daily; 2hr) via Josselin (1hr) and St-Jean Brévelay (45min); to Malestroit (4 daily; 45 min).

Boats

Barges with accommodation, which can be available with bicycles and even caravans on board, can be hired from the following places:

Pont Coblant near Pleyben. Contact *Crabing-Loisirs*, M. Mercier, 20 Rue de Frout, 29000 Quimper (☎98.95.14.02).

Châteauneuf du Faou. *S.B.D.M. Nautique*, Port de Plaisance de Pen ar Pont, 29119 Châteauneuf du Faou (☎98.73.25.34) or 107 avenue de Ty Bos, 29000 Quimper (☎98.53.30.04).

Rohan. *Ecluse de Rohan* 56580 (☎97.38. 98.66) or contact M. Quenderf, Bd Victor Etienne, 22600 Loudéac (☎96.28.14.95).

Baud (on the Blavet). *Au File De L'Eau*, Ecluse de la Couard, St-Nicolas-des-Eaux, Plumeliau, 56150 Baud.

Josselin. *Le Ray Loisirs*, 14 rue Caradec B.P. 49, 56120 Josselin (☎97.75.60.98) and at 44000 Nantes (☎40.89.22.42).

Roc St-André. *Plasmor*, M. Bourçois, Z.A. 56460 Serent (☎97.75.95.70).

Malestroit. *Heron Cruisers*, M. David Chin, La Daufresne, 56140 Malestroit, (☎97.75.19.57).

La Gacilly. *Flotte Vacances* Glenac 56200 La Gacilly.

Redon. *France Bleue*, 2 Quai Surcouf, 35600 Redon (☎99.71.47.06). *Comptoir Nautique de Redon*, M. Megret, 2 Quai Surcouf 35600 Redon (☎99.71.46.03). *Bretagne Plaisance*, Quai Jean Bart 35600 Redon (☎99.72.15.80).

Plesse. *Gîtes Nautiques Bretons*, La Cour 44630 Plesse (☎40.51.90.77).

Suce-sur-Erdre. *Flotte Vacances*, Base Nautique B.P. 3, 44240 Suce-sur-Erdre, (☎40.25.18.87).

Nantes. *Le Grand Large*, M. Bonami, Quai de Versailles, le Pont-Morand, 44000 Nantes, (☎40.35.44.37) and 254, route de Vannes 447000 Nantes-Orvault (☎40.63.37.87).

For **general information** contact the *Comité de Promotion Touristique des Canaux Bretons*, 3 rue des Portes Mordelaises, 35000 Rennes (☎99.79.36.26).

CHAPTER SEVEN

THE SOUTHERN COAST

Brittany's **southern coast** takes in the province's most famous sites and offers its warmest swimming. Not surprising, then, that it is popular: around the **Gulf of Morbihan** and especially to the south at **La Baule**, you can be hard pushed to find a room in summer – or to escape the crowds.

Not that this should discourage a visit. For the whole coast is a succession of wonders, of both natural and human creation. If you have any interest in Brittany's prehistory, or even if you just enjoy ruins, then the concentration of **megaliths** around the **Morbihan** should prove irresistible. At **Carnac**, the most important site and possibly Europe's oldest settlement, there are over two thousand menhirs – laid out in alignments that are both dramatic and intriguing. **Locmariaquer**, too, has a gigantic ancient stone, which some theories hold to be the key to a prehistoric observatory. And, most beautifully sited of all, there is the great tumulus on **Gavrinis**, one of the fifty or so islets scattered in chaos around the Morbihan's inland sea.

As to more hedonistic pastimes, the south's beaches are best of all at **La Baule** – though this unfortunately is also the one resort in Brittany that's affected and overpriced. But there are excellent, lower-keyed, alternatives, throughout the region: close by La Baule at **Le Croisic**; at the megalith centres of **Carnac** and **Locmariaquer**; at **Quiberon**; and out on the **islands** of **Groix** and **Belle-Ile**. The largest Breton island, Belle-Ile is a perfect microcosm of the province – a beautiful place with grand countryside and a couple of lively towns.

The south coast is also host to Brittany's most compelling **festival**, a ten day **Inter-Celtic** gathering at Lorient in August. The same month sees a **jazz festival** at the main Morbihan town, Vannes.

Lorient and its Estuary

LORIENT, Brittany's fourth largest city, is an immense natural harbour – protected from the ocean by the Ile de Groix and strategically located at the junction of the rivers Scorff, Ter and Blavet. A functional, rather depressing port today, it was once a key base for French colonialism, founded in the mid-seventeenth century (in what its charter called a "vague, vain, and useless place") for trading operations by the *Compagnie des Indes*. The company – an equivalent of the English East India Company – was responsible for the port's name, originally *L'Orient* ("The East"). Little else, however, remains to suggest the exotic wealth that once arrived here, avoiding the English piracy that had preyed upon the company's previous base at Le Havre. During the

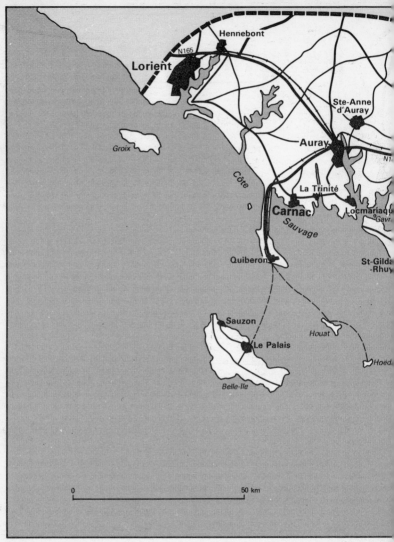

last war, Lorient was a major target for the Allies; the Germans held out until May 1945, by which time the city was almost completely destroyed. The only substantial remains were the U-boat pens – subsequently greatly expanded by the French for their nuclear submarines.

There are a few relics of Lorient's exploitative past across the estuary in Port Louis at the **Musée de la Compagnie des Indes** (10am–7pm, June–Sept, winter 10am–noon & 2–5pm – and closed all November). But this is a somewhat dismal temple to imperialism and if you do end up stopping in the

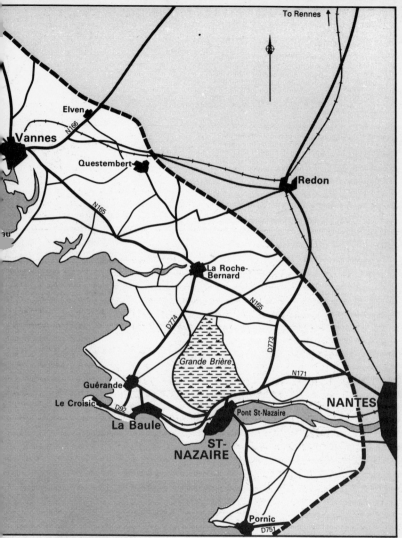

city, time would probably be more enjoyably spent on a boat trip, either up
the estuary towards Hennebont or out to the Ile de Groix (see over page).

Lorient Practicalities

Other than at festival time, Lorient offers a huge choice of **hotels**, with among
the best value the *Armor Hôtel* (☎97.21.73.87), the *Saint-Michel Hôtel*
(☎97.21.17.53) and the *d'Arvor* (104 rue Lazare Carnot; ☎97.21.07.55). The
youth hostel is at 41 rue Victor Schoelcher, three kilometres out on bus line

#C from the gare SNCF, next to the river Ter (☎97.37.11.65, closed Dec 20–Feb). There's also an *Oeuvres Sociales* hostel at 12 rue Colbert (☎97.21.42.80), which was especially designed for the **physically handicapped**. For **meals** in Lorient, your best bets are the *Restaurant de la Liberté* at 26 rue Poissonière, and *Chez Le Gallo* on rue Florient-Laporte.

THE INTER-CELTIC FESTIVAL

Each year, any of Lorient's shortcomings become quite irrelevant alongside the backdrop of the **Inter-Celtic Festival**, which is held for ten days from the first Friday to the second Sunday in August. This is the biggest Celtic event in Brittany, or anywhere else for that matter, with representation from all seven Celtic countries – the Pogues holding up the Irish camp in recent years. In a genuine popular celebration of cultural solidarity, as many as a quarter of a million people come to a hundred and fifty different shows; five languages mingle; and Scotch and Guinness flow with the French and Spanish wines and ciders. There is a certain competitive element, with championships in various categories, but the feeling of mutual enthusiasm and conviviality is more important. Most of the activities – which embrace music, dance and literature – take place around the central place Jules Ferry, and this is where most people end up sleeping, too, as accommodation is pushed to the limits.

For schedules of the festival, and further details of temporary accommodation, contact the *Office du Tourisme de Pays de Lorient*, place Jules Ferry, 56100 Lorient (☎97.21.07.84), bearing in mind that the festival programme is not finalised before May. For certain specific events, you need to reserve tickets well in advance.

The Ile de Groix

The coast immediately around Lorient is unenticing, plagued with thick drifts of weed, but straight out to sea is the eight-kilometre-long steep-sided rock of the **ILE DE GROIX**. It takes forty-five minutes to get there by boat (4–8 sailings daily depending on the season; ☎97.21.03.97) from the south quay of Lorient's new port. The island's main interest is to geologists, who come to study its peculiar rock formations, and to bird-watchers, though there are also beaches and even megaliths.

The boat docks at Port-Tudy, about five hundred metres downhill from the eponymous capital of **GROIX**. **Bicycles** are for hire at the port, well worth it if you want to get away from the crowds. Groix itself does however have the island's only facilities – a summer-only **youth hostel** (☎97.05.81.38), a **campsite** (☎97.05.53.08), and the **hotel/restaurant** *de la Marine* (☎97.05.80.05).

Hennebont

A few kilometres upstream from Lorient, at the point where the river Blavet first starts to widen into the estuary, is the old walled town of **HENNEBONT**. The fortifications, and especially the main gate, the Porte Broerec'h, are imposing, and walking around the top of the ramparts there are wide views of the river below. What you see of the old city within, however, is entirely residential – an assortment of washing-lines, budgies and garden sheds. All its public buildings were destroyed in the war and now not even a bar (or rented room) is to be found in the former centre.

The one time Hennebont comes alive is at the **Thursday market**, held below the ramparts and through the squares by the church. It's one of the largest in the region, with a heady mix of good fresh food, crêpes and Vietnamese delicacies, alongside livestock, flowers, carpets and clothes. On other days, the only places where you'll find any activity are along the **place Maréchal Foch** (in front of the Basilica) and the **quai du Pont Neuf** beside the river. If you're **staying** – and few people do – the *Hôtel de France* at 17 av de la Libération (☎97.36.21.82) is good value near the town centre; the *Toul-Douar* (☎97.36.24.04) takes a bit of finding, on the edge of town nearest Lorient across the river, but is closer to the **gare SNCF**. The town's **campsite**, *Camping Municipal de St-Caradec* (☎97.36.20.14), has a prime site on the river bank opposite the fortifications, but opens only from June to September. You can hire **bicycles** at 5 av de la République and at 87 rue Maréchal Joffre, and take **boat trips** either up the Blavet towards the Nantes–Brest canal (see Chapter 6) or out into the estuary around Lorient.

Lochrist

At **LOCHRIST**, just north of Hennebont, the great chimneys of the town's **ironworks** still stand, smokeless and silent, looking down on the Blavet. Strikes and demonstrations failed to prevent the foundry's closure in 1966, and the only work since then has been to convert it into the **Musée Forges d'Hennebont** (daily 9am–noon & 2–6pm, low season 9am–noon & 2–4pm; always closed Saturday, Sunday and Monday morning) which documents its 100-year history from the workers' point of view. Some of the men put on the dole contributed their memories and tools; for others turning their workplace into a museum was adding insult to injury. It is in fact excellent, both in contents and presentation, though in view of the joyful pictures of successful strikes in the 1930s its very existence seems a sad defeat. If it's on your route it's worth a stop: the bus station is just opposite on the other side of the river.

The Quiberon Peninsula

The **Presqu'Ile de Quiberon**, once an island, is joined to the mainland by a long strip of sand – as narrow as fifty metres in places. In the past it was always a strategic military location. The English held the peninsula for eight bloody days in 1746; *chouans* and royalists landed here in 1795 in the hope of destroying the Revolution, only to be sealed in and slaughtered; and part of the defoliation that threatens the dunes today is the result of German fortifications constructed during the last war. The peninsula is now, in the summer, packed with tourists. They come not so much to visit the towns, which other than Quiberon itself are generally featureless, but to use them as a base for trips out to Belle-Ile or around the contrasting coastline.

The mainland coast here has two quite distinct characters. The **Côte Sauvage**, facing the Atlantic to the west, is a bleak rocky heathland, lashed by heavy seas. It is the scene of innumerable drownings – the official tourist brochure contains a chilling description of just why it is absolutely impossible for *un imprudent* to swim back to land having once strayed beyond a certain distance. The sheltered eastern side, however, the **Baie de Quiberon**, contains safe sandy beaches, as well as yet another Thalassotherapy Institute.

On to the peninsula

At the very start of the peninsula, as the D768 curves around from **PLOUHARNEL**, you can't fail to notice a reconstructed **Spanish galleon**, standing in about three inches of water. This is an obsessive shell museum and shop, with dioramas, created entirely from shells, of eighteenth-century street scenes in Venice and in China, of Donald Duck and his friends, Sioux Indians and flamenco dancers. Across the road and the railway line, there's a rather uninspiring **waxwork museum** of *Chouannerie* (Mar 25–Sept 15), with displays of the 1795 fighting.

At **PORTIVY**, tucked into the only real shelter along the Côte Sauvage, windsurfers tend to congregate. If you want to join them, you can hire boards in Port Haliguen, near Quiberon town, at 16 rue des Corlis (☎97.50.25.03). There is a **campsite** just outside Portivy, *Camping de Port Blanc* on the Route du Port Blanc (☎97.30.91.30). Others nearby include the *Camping Municipal de Penthièvre* (☎97.52.33.86) and the *Camping Municipal de Kerhostin* (☎97.30.95.25). For provisions, try the morning **markets** at Kerhostin on Wednesday, St-Pierre-Quiberon on Thursday and Quiberon on Saturday.

Quiberon

QUIBERON is a lively place, centred on a crazy golf course surrounded by bars and pizzerias, clothes and antique shops (surprisingly good) and some fairly cheap hotels. The cafés by the sea are enjoyable; so too is the old-fashioned *Café du Marché* next to the PTT. There's a long bathing beach, from which windsurfing is forbidden. **Port Maria**, the fishing harbour, is the most active part of town, alongside the Gare Maritime from which boats leave for Belle-Ile. This is where the most promising **hotels** are concentrated – try *de l'Océan* (quai de l'Océan; ☎97.50.07.58) or *de la Mer* (quai de Houat; ☎97.50.09.05). The **youth hostel**, *Les Filets Bleus*, 45 rue du Roch Priol 56170 Quiberon (open all year, no age limit; ☎97.50.15.54), is set back from the sea but near the station.

A vast array of **fish restaurants** lines the seafront. It's fun to walk around browsing through the menus, but there's really no question as to which is the best, both for quality and value. This has to be *Au Bon Accueil* on the quai de Houat – its fish soup, with all the trimmings, and *assiette de fruits de mer* are total gastronomic sensations.

The **SI** (7 rue de Verdun; ☎97.50.07.84) down hill and to the left from the **gare SNCF**, has timetables for boats to Belle-Ile and the smaller islands of Houat and Hoëdic. The rail link between Quiberon and Auray (known as the *Tire-Bouchon* or Corkscrew) only operates in July and August, when there's a frequent service. Buses run to Auray and Vannes, intermittently but approximately to connect with the Belle-Ile boats.

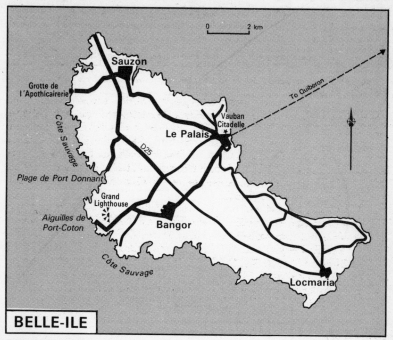

BELLE-ILE

Belle-Ile

BELLE-ILE, 45 minutes by ferry from Quiberon, mirrors Brittany in its make-up. On the landward side it is rich and fertile, interrupted by deep estuaries with tiny ports; facing the ocean, along its own *Côte Sauvage*, sparse heather-covered cliffs trail rocky crags out into the sea. You need to be able to cross and re-cross the island to appreciate these contrasts, so some kind of transport is essential – even just for a day trip. This is no great problem: bikes are available in profusion at the island port of Le Palais, and small cars are taken over on the ferries for a relatively low charge.

The island once belonged to the monks of Redon; then to the ambitious Nicholas Fouquet, Louis XIV's minister; later to the English, who in 1761 swapped it for Minorca in an unrepeatable bargain deal. Along the way it has seen a fair number of distinguished exiles. The citadel prison at Le Palais, closed only in 1961, having numbered amongst its inmates an astonishing succession of revolutionary heroes – including the son of Toussaint L'Ouverture of Haiti, Ben Bella of Algeria, and even, for a brief period after 1848, Karl Marx. Less involuntarily, creative talents of the stature of Monet, Matisse, Dali, Flaubert, Proust and Sarah Bernhardt all stayed for periods on the island, too.

Le Palais

Docking at **LE PALAIS**, the abrupt star-shaped fortifications of the **Citadelle** are the first thing you see. Built along stylish and ordered lines by the great fortress builder Vauban, early in the eighteenth century, it is startling in size – filled with doorways leading to mysterious cellars and underground passages, endless sequences of rooms and dungeons and deserted cells. Though derelict, the structure is quite sound: large signs – *DON'T BE AFRAID* – are scattered about the place, exhorting visitors to explore the abandoned shell. An informative, if over-literary museum documents the island's history, including its entanglement in Dumas' tales of *The Three Musketeers* (which feature an account of the death of Porthos on the island).

Accommodation in Le Palais includes the reasonably priced *Hôtel du Commerce* (place Hôtel de Ville; ☎97.31.81.71), campsite *Les Glacis* (☎97.31.41.76) or a **youth hostel** (phone reservations as for Quiberon, ☎97.50.15.54; a short way out of town along the clifftops from the Citadel, at Haute Boulogne).

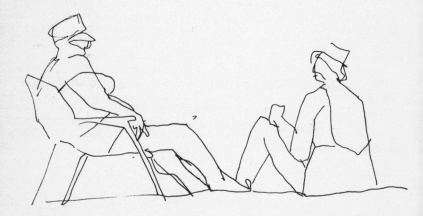

Sauzon

SAUZON, Belle-Ile's second town, is set at the mouth of a long estuary six kilometres to the west. If you're staying any length of time, and you've got your own transport, it's probably a better place to base yourself. There's a good, cheap **hotel**, the *du Phare* (☎97.31.60.36), or two **campsites**, *Pen Prad* (☎97.31.62.79) and *Prad Stivell*. On the road towards these campsites is a **vegetarian restaurant**, *le Zenith*.

Around the Island

For exploring the island, a coastal footpath runs on bare soil the length of the **Côte Sauvage**. Starting at the **Grand Lighthouse**, (which is open in the summer 9.30am–12.30pm and 2–6pm), you can see the **Aiguilles de Port-Coton**, where a savage sea foams in the pinnacles of rock, and the delicate beach of **Port-Donnant**, where bathing (despite appearances) is dangerous.

At the village of BANGOR, nearby, is an incongruous row of huge and very expensive hotels. Eventually you come to the **Grotte de l'Apothicairerie**, so called because it was once full of the nests of cormorants, arranged like the jars on a chemist's shelves. It's reached by descending a slippery flight of steps cut into the rock: take care, most years at least one person falls – and drowns – from these stairs.

The **D30 inland** from the cave leads along a miniature tree-lined valley sheltered from the Atlantic winds. If you take the **D25** back towards Le Palais you pass the two **menhirs**, Jean and Jeanne, said to be lovers petrified as punishment for wanting to meet before their marriage. Another larger menhir used to lie near these two; it was broken up to help construct the road that separates them.

Houat and Hoëdic

The islands of **HOUAT** and **HOEDIC** can be reached from Quiberon-Port Maria (90 minutes, daily except Tuesday – check return times) or from Vannes (a longer journey through the Morbihan). You can't take your car (not that there would be any point anyway) to these two very much smaller versions of Belle-Ile. Both have a feeling of being left behind by the passing centuries, although the younger fishermen of Houat have revived the island's fortunes by establishing a successful fishing co-operative. There's a story that in the eighteenth century the rector of Hoëdic lost not only his sense of time but also his calendar, and ended up reducing Lent from forty days down to a more manageable three.

HOUAT in particular has excellent **beaches** – as ever on its sheltered (eastern) side – that fill up with campers in the summer. Camping is not strictly legal here; Hoëdic on the other hand has a large municipal **campsite** (☎97.30.63.32). There is a small and not particularly cheap **hotel** on each island; on Houat it's *des Iles* (☎97.30.68.02, Easter–Sept only) and on Hoëdic *les Cardinaux* (☎97.30.68.31). It's also possible to rent **gîtes** on Hoëdic – contact ☎97.56.52.60.

Carnac

CARNAC is the most important prehistoric site in Europe. Its alignments of two thousand or so menhirs stretch over four kilometres, great burial tumuli dotted amidst them. The site, in use since at least 5700 BC, long predates Knossos, the Pyramids, Stonehenge or the great Egyptian temples of the same name at Karnak.

The town of Carnac is split into two distinct halves – the popular seaside resort of Carnac-Plage, and further inland Carnac-Ville with its alignments. It's an amalgam that can verge on the ridiculous with rows of shops named *Supermarché des Druides* and the like; but for all that, Carnac is a relaxed and attractive place, and any commercialisation doesn't intrude on the megaliths themselves. Fortunately, the ancient builders had the admirable foresight to construct their monuments well back from the sea.

The alignments

All sorts of conjectures have been advanced about the **Carnac megaliths**. One of the oldest stories was that they were Roman soldiers turned to stone as they pursued Pope Cornély; one of the most recent, the alleged belief of US soldiers in the last war, that they were German anti-tank obstructions. The general consensus today is for a religious significance connected with their use as some sort of astronomical observatory. Professor Thom, the best-known writer on the alignments, sees them – and most of the megaliths of the Morbihan – as part of a unified system for recording such phenomena as the extreme points of the lunar and solar cycles. According to this theory, the Carnac stones provided a grid system – a kind of neolithic graph paper for plotting heavenly movements and hence to determine the siting of other stones (see the further account, together with map, on p.220).

However, it's hard to see any real consistency in the size or the shape of the stones, or enough regularity in the lines to pinpoint their direction. Local tradition has it that new stones were added to the lines, illuminated by fire, each June. An annual ceremony in which willing participants set up one stone does sound more plausible than a vast programme of slave labour to erect them all at once. And in any case, the physical aspect and orientation of the stones may have been subsidiary to their metaphysical significance. It's quite possible that no practical purpose was involved nor a precise pattern, and that their importance was entirely symbolic.

The way you see them today cannot be said to be authentic. They were used for generations as a source of ready quarried stone, and then surreptitiously removed by farmers attempting to prevent the influx of academics and tourists damaging precious crops. Not only is it impossible to say how many of the stones have disappeared, but those that remain are not necessarily in their original positions – small holes filled with pink concrete at the base of the stones denote that they have been restored or re-erected.

The **menhirs** range in size from mere stumps to 22-metre-high blocks; they stand alone, in circles known as *cromlechs*, or in approximate lines. In addition there are **dolmens**, groups of standing stones roofed with further stones laid across the top, that are generally assumed to be burial chambers. And there are tumuli – most notably the **Tumulus de St-Michel**, near the town centre, a vast artificial mound containing rudimentary graves. You can scramble through subterranean passages and tunnels beneath the mound to view little stone cairns and piles of charred bones; the tunnels are, however, again not authentic, being the recent creation of archaeologists.

Taken all together, the stones make up three distinct major alignments, running roughly in the same northeast–southwest direction but each with a slightly separate orientation. They are the **Alignements de Menec**, "the place of stones" or "place of remembrance", with 1169 stones in eleven rows; the **Alignements de Kermario**, "the place of the dead", with 1029 menhirs in ten rows; and the **Alignements de Kerlescan**, "the place of burning", with 555 menhirs in thirteen lines. All three are sited parallel to the sea alongside the "Route des Alignements", a kilometre or so to the north of Carnac-Ville.

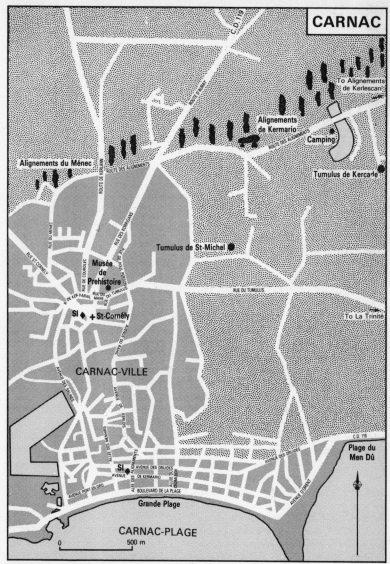

The museum of Prehistory

The **Musée de Préhistoire** – recently redesigned – documents and examines the various megalithic theories in great and entertaining depth. It's refreshing to find a museum combining serious scholarship with large blowups of Asterix cartoons. The history of the area is traced from earliest times, about 450,000 years ago, up to and beyond the Romans. There are both authentic physical relics, such as the original "twisted dolmen" of Luffang, with a carving of an octopus-like divinity guaranteed to chill the blood of any devotee of H. P. Lovecraft, and reproductions and casts of the carvings at Locmariaquer. The museum also attempts to provide some account of the social culture that existed at the time the megaliths were erected – whilst acknowledging that much of this is more or less pure speculation.

Hours for the museum are: July to mid-September, 10am to noon and 2 to 6.30pm daily; rest of the year, 10am to noon and 2 until 5pm, closed Tuesday.

Close to the museum in the centre of Carnac is the church of **St-Cornély**, built in the seventeenth century in honour of the patron saint of horned animals. Archaeological discoveries suggest that the custom of bringing diseased cattle to Carnac to be cured, still honoured at least in theory at the saint's *pardon* on the second Sunday in September, dates back as far as the Romans.

The Romans also had heated sea-water baths here; today the **Thalassotherapy Centre** is an ultra-modern building where among other things they treat *maladies de civilisation*.

Getting around Carnac

The permanent **SI** for Carnac is at 74 av des Druides in Carnac-Plage (☎97.52.13.52), although there's an annex open in the church square of Carnac-Ville in summer. Both provide fully comprehensive maps and details.

The obvious way to explore the alignments is to spend a day walking, cycling, or riding around them. You can hire **cycles** at *Lorcy*, 6 rue de Cordiec, Carnac-Ville (☎97.52.09.73), at *Cyclo-Loisirs*, 62 av des Druides, Carnac-Plage (☎97.52.02.33), or at *BMX*, 20 av des Druides, Carnac-Plage. **Horses** are available from the *Centre Equestre des Menhirs*, which in summer is based at the *Camping de la Grande Métairie* (☎97.55.71.47), near the Kercado Tumulus, and in winter may be contacted in Le Manio (☎97.55.73.45).

However, it's clear that by far the best way to see the alignments would be from the air, which, if you split the costs three or four ways, it's possible to do for not much more than a good meal. At the **Aérodrome de Quiberon**, near the tip of the Quiberon peninsula, two companies operate short flights over the peninsula and the Morbihan: the *Quiberon Air Club* (year round except Jan), and *Thalass Air* (to the left of the Air Club building; July–Sept with a reservation the same day, ☎97.30.40.00).

Beaches and Accommodation

The best of Carnac's many **beaches** is probably the smallest, the **Men Dû** on the road towards La Trinité. If you want to **camp** by the sea, go to *L'Océan* (☎97.52.02.71) or *Men Dû* (☎97.52.04.23) – otherwise, the best·site is *La Grande Métairie* (see above), near the Kermario alignments, with tennis, horse-riding and a swimming pool.

Among the innumerable **hotels**, the *Hoty* (15 av de Kermario; ☎97.52.11.12) is the best value near the beach; in town, try the small *Le Râtelier* (4 chemin Douët; ☎97.52.05.04) or *Chez Nous* (2 rue Poul Person; ☎97.52.07.28). The *Hôtel du Commerce* (☎97.55.72.36) in **LA TRINITE**, a couple of miles along the coast, is excellent value, but the town itself is uninteresting – just an up-market yacht harbour without a proper beach. The nearest **youth hostel** is in Quiberon (see p.196), only within reach if you have a car.

There are **markets** in Carnac each Wednesday and Sunday. Elsewhere in the region at Locmariaquer on Tuesday and Saturday; in La Trinité on Tuesday and Friday; and in Auray on Monday.

Auray

There's something slightly dull about **AURAY**, with its twee, over-restored old quarter – but it's a lot less crowded than Vannes, a lot cheaper than Quiberon town, and usefully poised for exploring Carnac, the peninsula and the Gulf. Paris–Quimper trains make a stop here (the *Tire-Bouchon* rail connection with Quiberon runs only in the summer) and you can hire bikes at the station.

Since the station is a good twenty minutes walk from the central place de la République, you'll be glad of some sort of transport. The **SI** is in the *place* and has the usual local maps; or if you're making for the islands, you can pick up comprehensive details at the *Iles du Ponant Promotional Association* at 11 place du Joffre. The town's most remarkable building is close by, a vast Gothic church which was dissolved by Louis XIV and is now let out to clubs, with stray cats and the odd wrecked car keeping an eye on the gargoyles.

From high on the promenade du Loch on the east bank of the Auray river you can look across to the town's showpiece **Quartier St-Goustan**, focussed on a diminutive bridge. The setting is fine enough, although once you've clambered down the hill, or coasted around by the rue du Château, you may find that what St-Goustan lacks in feel and interest, it doesn't quite make up for with its plethora of expensive restaurants. The **quay**, downstream to the left of the square, is named after Benjamin Franklin, who landed here in an unscheduled detou,r having been blown off-course from Nantes, on his way to negotiate the first-ever alliance between the still-rebel US colonies and France in 1776. (Auray was also the last place Julius Caesar reached in his conquest of Gaul.)

If you want to stay in Auray, **hotels** at fairly average prices include the *Hôtel de la Mairie* (26 pl de la Mairie; ☎97.24.04.65; closed first three weeks Oct, first two weeks Jan, and Sat night & Sun in low season), *Armoric* (rue St-Goustan; ☎97.24.10.36), and *Belvédère* (2 rue du Belvédère).

North of Auray

A short way north of the station – and thus quite a long way out from the town, on the Pontivy road – is the imposing and evocative **Abbaye de Chartreuse** (10am–noon & 2–5.30pm). This houses a David d'Angers mausoleum of black and white marble commemorating the failed *chouan* landing at Quiberon in 1795 (see p.195). For Bretons the event was something more than an attempt at a Royalist restoration, with strong undertones of a struggle for independence. Another gloomy piece of Counter-Revolutionary history is recalled by the nearby **Champ des Martyrs**, where 350 of the *chouans* were executed. It's located on the right of the D120, going out of town.

Two kilometres further along the D120, towards Brech, you come to the **EcoMusée St-Degan** (July to mid-Sept only, 2–6pm), a group of reconstructed farm buildings, representing the local peasant life at the beginning of this century. It's a bit determinedly rustic and charming but a good attempt to break away from the glass cases and wax models of most folk museums. In **BRECH** itself there's a fine parish church with a weatherbeaten and faded calvary in its yard; a nice café, *des Bretons*; and a **gîte d'étape** – not a very eventful place to stay, perhaps, but a peaceful one.

Ste-Anne d'Auray

Should you be in this area around July 26, one of the largest of the Breton *pardons* takes place on that day at **STE-ANNE D'AURAY**. Some 25,000 pilgrims gather for the occasion to hear mass in the church, mount the *scala sancta* on their knees and buy trinkets and snacks from the street stalls. The origin of this **pardon**, typical of many, was the discovery in 1623 of a statue of Ste Anne by a local peasant, one Nicolazic. He claimed that the saint directed him to the spot where the statue had been buried for over nine hundred years and instructed him to build a church. Twenty years later, on his deathbed, Nicolazic was still being interrogated by the ecclesiastical authorities as to the truth of his story but the church had been constructed and already become a place of pilgrimage. Nicolazic was an illiterate peasant who spoke no French; it is a testimony to his obduracy that his claims were eventually accepted against the opposition of sceptical clergy and nobility. The continuing campaign for his canonisation is polarised along similar lines today. Nicolazic's supporters see him as a representative of the downtrodden classes, and as a symbol of Breton independence – the wealthy Church establishment continue to oppose him.

As a major centre for pilgrimage, Ste-Anne was chosen as the site for the vast **Monument aux Morts** erected by public subscription as a memorial to the 250,000 Breton dead of the Great War. One in fourteen of the population died, the highest proportion of losses of any region involved. The monument, a crypt topped by a dome with a granite altar, is surrounded by a wall that must be 200m long, covered with inscriptions to the dead; and yet even that huge and sombre wall does not contain room to list them all by name, often just cataloguing the horrific death tallies of tiny and obscure villages. A short distance north on the D102 is a National Necropolis, with dead from all wars since 1870–71.

Ste-Anne is a sad and solemn place. The town, away from the spacious promenades for the pilgrims, is small, low, and drab; not really a place for a long·stay, although there is no particular shortage of **hotels**, among them *Le Moderne* (☎97.57.66.55) and *La Croix Blanche* (25 rue de Vannes; ☎97.57.64.44, closed all of January, and Sunday night and Monday out of season).

Locmariaquer

LOCMARIAQUER, easily accessible from Auray or Carnac, stands right at the mouth of the Gulf of Morbihan – its cape separated by only a few hundred metres from the tip of the Rhuys Peninsula. On the ocean side, it has a long but not very sandy beach, more popular for scavenging shellfish than for bathing; on the Gulf side, a small tidal port. **Boat trips** run in all directions, for which tickets are bought in the town centre or at the port, although the boats themselves leave from further down towards the narrow straits. As well as trips around the Gulf and up the Auray river, there is an intermittent ferry service to the island of Gavrinis (see p.210), which is more usually (and more easily) reached from Larmor-Baden.

Menhirs and Dolmens

The **Grand Menhir Brise** at Locmariaquer is supposed to have been the crucial central point of the megalithic observatory of the Morbihan (see p.220). Before being floored by an earthquake in 1722, it was by far the largest known menhir – 66ft high and weighing rather more than a full Jumbo Jet at 347 tons. It now lies on the ground in four pieces, with a possible fifth missing. Alongside is the **Table des Marchands**, a dolmen once exposed but now reburied for its protection under a tumulus. It is currently being excavated, though you can still go inside, along a narrow passage, and stand beneath its huge carved roof, on which carvings seem to depict ploughing. It has recently been discovered that this roof is part of the same stone as that on the tumulus at Gavrinis, and on another local dolmen – the carvings match like a jigsaw. This is another mystery for the archaeologists, possibly suggesting that the builders did not revere the stones in themselves, as most theories had previously implied.

Both the Grand Menhir and the Table des Marchands are fenced off, and closed for lunch 12.30–2.30pm. The rest of the megaliths of Locmariaquer are open at all times – open to the weather as well, so watch out for muddy and water-logged underground passages and take a torch if you want to explore them thoroughly. The most interesting are the **Dolmen des Pierres Plates**, at the end of the town beach, with an octopus divinity deep in its long chamber, and the **Dolmen de Mané Rethual**, a long covered tunnel leading to a burial chamber capped with a huge rock, reached along a narrow footpath that starts behind the phone boxes next to the Mairie/SI. At a third dolmen, the **Mané-Lud**, a horse's skull was found on top of each stone during excavations.

Locmariaquer accommodation

There are are a couple of reasonable small **hotels** in Locmariaquer, the *Lautram* (place Eglise; ☎97.57.31.32, closed Oct–March) and *L'Escale* (☎97.57.32.51, open June–Sept 19 only); several campsites, too, including the excellent *La Ferme Fleurie* (☎97.57.34.06) one kilometre towards Kerinis.

Vannes

It was from **VANNES** that the great Breton hero Nominoé set out to unify Brittany at the start of the ninth century; he beat the hell out of the Franks, and pushed the borders past Nantes and Rennes to where they were to remain up until the French Revolution nearly a millennium later. Here too, the Breton *Etats* assembled in 1532 to ratify the Act of Union with France, in the building known as *La Cohue*.

Vieux Vannes, the medieval walled town, still exists – its chaotic network of streets crammed around the cathedral. It is about 10 minutes walk from the bus and railway stations – out to the north – and bordered by a new administrative centre, constructed in the last century's craze for urbanisation around the **place de la République**. In refreshing contrast to the somewhat insane road system around the modern parts of the city, most of the inner area is pedestrianised.

Exploring Vannes

La Cohue, which fills a block between rue des Halles and the place du Cathédrale, is a good initial point to make for. It has recently reverted to its original use as a market-place, having served at various times over the past 750 years as high court and assembly room, prison, revolutionary tribunal and theatre. These days the stalls downstairs sell various arts and crafts, while upstairs is the local **Beaux Arts** museum.

Twisting to either side of La Cohue are cobbled streets of skew-windowed and half-timbered houses – most overhanging and witch-hatted, some tumbling down, some newly propped-up and painted. To the east of the quarter, around what used to be the castle moat, is an old slate-roofed washing place. Close by is the city's excellent **fish-market**, active in the covered hall on place de la Poissonerie each Wednesday, Friday and Saturday, with a general market spreading slightly higher up on the streets towards the Cathedral on Wednesday and Saturday.

The **Cathédrale St-Pierre** is a rather forbidding place, with its stern main altar almost imprisoned by four solemn grey pillars. The light, purple through the new stained glass, spears in to illuminate the finger of the Blessed Pierre Rogue, who was guillotined in the main square on March 3 1796. Opposite this desiccated digit is the black-lidded sarcophagus that marks the current site of the tomb of the fifteenth-century Spanish Dominican preacher Saint Vincent Ferrier (which has meandered around the Cathedral for centuries). For a small fee, you can in summer examine the assorted **treasure** in the chapter-house, which includes a twelfth-century wedding-chest, brightly decorated with enigmatic scenes of romantic chivalry.

The city's other two museums are probably best left to the committed. The **Musée Archaeologie**, in what remains of the Château Gaillard on rue Noé, is reputed to have one of the world's finest collections of prehistoric artefacts. But unlike the excellent display at Carnac (which anyone intrigued by the megaliths should see) it's all pretty lifeless – some elegant stone axes, more recent Oceanic exhibits by way of context, but nothing very illuminating. Further collections of fossils, shells and stuffed birds, equally traditional in their display, are on show around the corner in the **Hôtel de Roscannec** at 19 Rue des Halles. (Both museums open June–Sept 9.30am–noon & 2.30–6pm.)

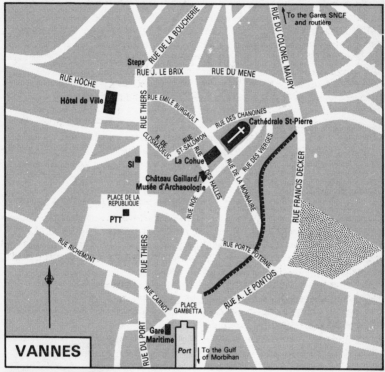

Vannes practicalities

More rewarding than the museums are the open spaces of Vieux Vannes, particularly around place Gambetta. All over the quarter there are restaurants, crêperies, ice-cream parlours and patisseries. *Le Brick* at 25 rue Ferdinand-le-Dressay, on the left quay of the port, is one of the best value **restaurants**, with a good bar downstairs as well, while *Le Richemond* opposite the railway station is a bit more up-market. For a **late night bar** (open until 1am) with a friendly atmosphere and Irish folk bands, hunt out *Le Pandémonium* on rue de la Boucherie, just north of the Hôtel de Ville – down some steps from the main road. And if you're visiting in the first week of August, the open-air concerts of the **Vannes Jazz Festival** take place in the Théâtre de Verdure.

There are some cheap **hotels** on rue Olivier de Clisson, near the bus and train stations; the *Clisson* (no. 11; ☎97.54.13.94) is a good standby here. But, so long as you can find rooms, it's a lot nicer staying in Vieux Vannes. Among quite a number of possibilities, the *Moderne* (2 rue de la Boucherie; ☎97.47.40.78; no restaurant) is noteworthy for the utterly kitsch undersea dioramas in its lobby; the *Bretagne* (34 rue du Mène; ☎97.47.20.21) is reasonable; or there are rooms above the *Voile d'Or* (☎97.42.71.81) in place Gambetta, at the end of the canalised port. The best **campsite** nearby is the *Vannes-Conleau* at 188 av du Maréchal-Juin (April–Sept only; ☎97.63.13.88).

If you have any problems, you'll find the **SI** with its free maps and the usual bundles of information behind the Théâtre de Verdure at 1 rue Thiers (☎97.47.24.34). They can also give you the fullest details on **boat trips** around the Morbihan islands, to Auray (via Le Bono), or out to Belle-Ile, Houat and Hoëdic. The main boat company, the SNCF's *Vedettes Vertes*, leave from a terminal next to the modern aquarium on the promenade de la Rabbine – about 150m from the town centre. **Buses** to the alternative ports of Larmor-Baden (via Baden) and Port Navalo run from the main **gare routière**.

East of Vannes

Whilst Gavrinis and the other Morbihan islands (see the following section) are the most exciting excursions from Vannes, there are a number of sights inland, to the east of the city, that can fill a good day's round trip. Vannes' **traffic system** will do its damnedest to prevent you leaving the city in any direction, however, so you can't be too choosy about where you end up.

The Château de Largoët
If you follow the **N166** 10km towards Elven, and then turn off to the left about four kilometers short, you come to the ruins of the **CHATEAU DE LARGOET**, perched on an eminence in the small forest. The castle consists mainly of two granite towers. The *donjon* proper is topped by a finger-like watch tower, one of the highest in the country at over 150ft, where from 1474–76 the Breton Duke Francis imprisoned the future English king, Henry VII. At that time simply Henry Tudor, Duke of Richmond – a title traditionally awarded to royal bastards or English nobility with Breton connections – he had fled to Brittany after the Battle of Tewkesbury, in which Lancastrian ambitions in the Wars of the Roses were defeated. François welcomed Henry as a guest, then realised his value and held him for ransom. The castle is also known by the name *Elven Towers* and under that name puts on *son-et-lumière* costume spectacles of unsurpassed tackiness, combining Henry's drama with the site's spurious claim to Arthurian authenticity as the home of Sir Lancelot of the Lake. The show takes place sporadically through June (at 11pm) and on Friday and Saturday in July and August (at 10.30pm) – far too late at night to be much use to most holiday-makers, certainly those with families.

Le Gorvello and Questembert
There's little point going to **ELVEN** itself, though if you've always wondered where René Descartes grew up you can find the answer en route at the

manor-house of Kerleau. More rewarding is to head south, to the beautiful village of **LE GORVELLO**, at a crossroads with the D7. Bedecked with potted geraniums and huge azaleas, it has at its centre a perfect roadside cross. Beyond, the D7 leads on into **QUESTEMBERT**, where the low-roofed wooden market hall from 1675 makes a very classy cycle park. What's reputed to be one of the best restaurants in France is in this little town, the ivy-coated *Hôtel du Bretagne* (☎97.26.11.12). Its sumptuous menus start at 150F, while room prices are astronomical.

If you continue east or north from Questembert you come to the **Nantes–Brest canal** at Malestroit (see p.183) or Redon (see p.184).

The Morbihan Islands

By popular tradition the scattered islands of the **Golfe de Morbihan** ("little sea" in Breton) used to number the days of the year. For centuries, though, the waters have been rising and there is now about one for each week. Of these, some thirty are owned by film stars and the like; while two – the **Ile des Moines** and **Ile d'Arz** – have regular ferry services and permanent populations, and end up extremely crowded in summer. The rest are the best, and a **boat tour** around them, or at least a trip out to **Gavrinis**, near the mouth of the gulf, is one of the most compelling attractions of Southern Brittany. As the boats thread their way through the baffling muddle of channels you lose track of which is island and which is mainland; and everywhere there are megalithic ruins, stone circles disappearing beneath the water, and solitary menhirs on small hillocks. Flaubert evocatively described Celtic mercenaries far off in Carthage pining for the Morbihan – "*Les Celtes regrettaient trois pierres brutes, sous un ciel plouvieux, dans un golfe remple d'îlots*" – not that the Celts actually set up the stones in the first place.

In season, there are dozens of different **gulf tours** available, leaving from Vannes, Port Navalo and Larmor-Baden. Full details are available from the Vannes SI but briefly the options are these. **From Vannes**, there are SNCF-run *vedettes*, quite a deluxe service offering any combination of island and gulf visits; **from Port Navalo** much the same applies (mid-March to mid-September), though under the auspices of *TCVP*; whilst **from Larmor-Baden** (connected by a daily bus from Vannes) there's a regular run to Gavrinis only.

Larmor Baden and Le Bono

Making your own way to Larmor-Baden, the best route is along the main road down the Auray estuary, the D17. This crosses the river Bono on a high bridge; visible way below it to the left is a beautiful iron bridge. A side turning before the river leads across that bridge into **LE BONO**, a harbour village that looks almost ludicrously idyllic seen from one of the *vedettes* out in the gulf. There is nowhere to stay but it makes a tempting stop-over for a meal or picnic.

LARMOR-BADEN itself is a subdued little town lying at the bottom of a long slope of fields of dazzling sunflowers. The port looks out on the tangle of islands in the Gulf of Morbihan, which at this point is so narrow that **ARZON** on the Rhuys peninsula appears to be on just another nearby island. It is not really an inspiring place to stay – not properly a resort or town – but there's a functional **campsite**, the *Ker Eden* (☎97.57.05.23), and a fair number of hotels including the *Auberge Parc Fétan* (☎97.57.04.38) and the *du Centre* (☎97.57.04.68).

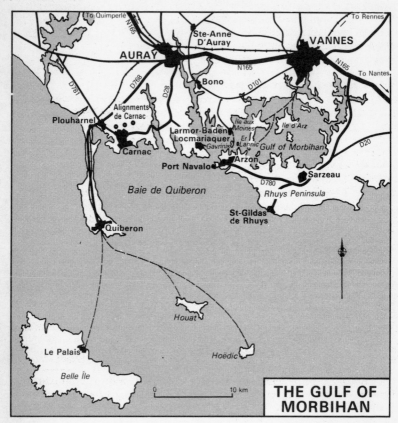

Gavrinis

The reason to visit the island of **GAVRINIS** is its megalithic site. The most impressive and remarkable in Brittany, it would be memorable just for its location. But it really is extraordinary as a structure, standing comparison with Newgrange in Ireland and – in shape as well as size and age – with the earliest pyramids of Egypt.

It is essentially a **tumulus**, an earth mound covering a stone cairn and "passage grave". However in 1981 half of the mound was peeled back and, using the original stones around the entrance as a basis, the side of the cairn

that faces the water was reconstructed to make a facade resem-
bling a step-pyramid. Inside,
every stone of the passageway
and chamber is covered in carvings, with a restricted "alphabet"
of fingerprint whorls, axeheads,
and other conventional signs,
including the spirals familiar in
Ireland but seen only here in
Brittany. It has been thought for
a long time that the stones were
brought at least the few kilo-

metres from Locmariaquer; and this view received dramatic confirmation
when in 1984 the roof was shown to be made from the self-same piece of
carved stone as covers the Merchant's Table there (see p.205).

One mystery has consistently eluded explanation; the purpose of the three
holes leading to a recessed niche in one of the walls of the chamber. Some
medieval monks were buried in the mound, but the cairn itself seems never
to have been a grave.

Erosion since the site was opened has so rapidly damaged the tumulus that
it may well soon be barred to visitors altogether; conceivably a replica will be
built. For the moment, however, you can still scramble to the top, and look
across to the half-submerged stone circle on the tiny island of **Er Lanic**,
which rests on its skirt of mud like an abandoned hovercraft.

Gavrinis is a 15-minute **ferry** ride from Larmor-Baden. Boats run 9.30–11.30am and
1.30–5pm, leaving the town on the hour and returning from the island on the half-
hour. Don't forget to take money with you: the ferry trip doesn't include the admission charge to look round the island.

Southern Morbihan: The Rhuys Peninsula

The **Presqu'île de Rhuys** marks a distinctly southwards shift in climate.
The *Côte Sauvage* is lost and in its wake appear pomegranates, fig trees,
camellias, even vineyards (Rhuys produces the only Breton wine), along with
cultivated oysters down below in the mud.

There are, unfortunately, fierce currents in the gulf – which all the way
along here is very unsafe for swimming. The **ocean beaches**, however, have
potential. They break out intermittently to either side of St-Gildas de Rhuys,
amidst the glittering gold and silver coloured rocks.

Arzon

If you're spending any length of time on the peninsula, **ARZON** is probably
the nicest of its towns; stay at the *Hôtel de Rhuys* (☎97.41.20.01) or either of
the two big campsites, *Le Tindio* (☎97.41.25.59) or *Port Sable* (☎97.41.21.98).
You are well-poised here for the less crowded beaches east of St-Gildas. And

at the tip of the peninsula, an islet-view filled walk, there is the **Tumulus de Thumiac**, from the top of which Julius Caesar is supposed to have watched the sea battle in which the Romans defeated the Veneti – their only naval victory on the ocean, away from the Mediterranean. **PORT NAVALO**, with a couple of hotels and its ferries to the islands, is on the next cape.

St-Gildas de Rhuys

At **ST-GILDAS DE RHUYS**, Pierre Abélard, the theologian lover of Héloïse, was abbot for a period from 1126, having been exiled from Paris. "I live in a wild country where every day brings new perils", he wrote to Héloïse, eventually fleeing after his brother monks – hedonists unimpressed by his stern scholasticism – attempted to poison him. By the beaches round about the village are a handful of **campsites**, among them *Le Menhir* (☎97.45.22.88) and *Les Govelins* (☎97.45.21.67); there's also an average-priced **hotel**, the *Giquel* (☎97.45.23.12).

Near **SARZEAU**, which also has accommodation if you're stuck, is the most impressive local sight, the **Château de Suscinio**. This fourteenth-century castle, once a hunting-lodge of the Dukes of Brittany, is almost completely moated, set in isolation amidst marsh and sandy plain, and has a sagging but still vivid mosaic floor. You can take a precarious stroll around the high ramparts (April–Sept only, 9.30am–noon & 2–6.30pm, closed Wed morning; evening concerts and performances Aug 5–20).

The *Grande-Brière*

South of the **Vilaine** river at La Roche-Bernard you leave the Morbihan – and technically you leave Brittany as well, entering the *département* of Loire Atlantique. The roads veer firmly east and west – to Nantes and La Baule respectively. Inland between them, as you approach the wide Loire estuary, are the other-worldly marshes of the **Grande-Brière**.

These 20,000 acres of peat bog have for centuries been deemed to be the common property of all who lived in them. The scattered population, the *Brièroise*, made and make their living by fishing for eels in the streams, gathering reeds, and – on the nine days permitted each year – cutting the peat. Tourism has arrived only recently, and is resented. The touted attraction is **hiring a punt**, known as a "*chaland*" or a "*blain*". This activity seems to be promoted with the unstated intention of getting you lost for a few hours with your pole tangled in the rushes.

Nonetheless, it can be quite a captivating region for unhurried exploration. Much of it is a **bird sanctuary**, obviously mostly for waterfowl, and it is filled with lilies and irises. The few villages are known as *îles*, being hard granite outcrops in the boggy wastes. Most of them consist of a circular road around the inside of a ring of thatched cottages – slightly raised above the waters on to which they back. The chief of these villages, the **ILE DE FEDRUN**, has a couple of exhibitions of local customs, and traditional dwellings, but nowhere to stay.

Guérande

On the edge of the marshes, just before you come to the sea, is the walled town of **GUERANDE**. The moat around the thick ramparts, long since filled, forms a spacious promenade around the old city, whose best feature is a market round by the church. It's quite a metropolis by Brière standards, though not one likely to delay you overlong.

There are further marshes between Guérande and the sea. This time, however, they are salt, a "white country" of bizarre-looking *oeillets* – pens 70 to 80 square metres in extent, in which the sea water, since Roman times, has been collected and evaporated.

The Coast at the mouth of the Loire

There is something very surreal about emerging from the Brière to the coast at La Baule. For this is Brittany's most up-market pocket – an imposing, moneyed landscape where the dunes are bonded together no longer with scrub and pines but with massive apartment blocks and luxury hotels.

La Baule

LA BAULE certainly is a place apart from its rival Breton resorts, which can seem rustic and amateur by comparison. Sited on the long stretch of dunes that link the former island of Le Croisic to the mainland, it owes its existence to a violent storm in 1779 that engulfed the old town of Escoublac in silt from the Loire, and thereby created a wonderful crescent of sandy beach.

For the moment, though, La Baule's permanence seems in little doubt. As, for that matter, is its affluence. This is a resort that very firmly imagines itself in the South of France: around the crab-shaped bay, bronzed nymphettes and would-be Clint Eastwoods ride across the sands into the sunset against a backdrop of cruising lifeguards, horse-dung removers and fantastically priced cocktails. It can be fun if you feel like a break from the more subdued Breton attractions.

Be warned, however, that none of this chic comes cheap. What **campsites** there are charge what you'd normally pay for hotels; the **hotels** (at their most extreme in the £150 a night *Hermitage*) what you might pay for your whole holiday. At the cheapest hotels – *Violettas* (44 av Georges Clemenceau; ☎40.60.32.16) and the *Almadies* (☎40.60.79.05) – you're likely to find intense competition for rooms. Still, the resort's beach is undeniably impressive; there is a brilliant ice-cream shop, *A Manuel*, on the corner of the promenade; and, a little out of character, the excellent **bookshop** *Breizh* (at 9 av du Général-de-Gaulle) specialises in Breton culture, language, and politics.

Le Croisic

The small port of **LE CROISIC**, sheltering from the ocean around the corner of the headland, is probably a more realistic (and to many perceptions, more attractive) place to stay. These days it's basically a pleasure port, but fishing boats do still sail from its harbour and there's a modern **fish market**, near the long Tréhic jetty, where you can go to see the day's catch auctioned. The hills on either side of the harbour, Mont Lenigo and Mont Esprit, are not natural; they are formed from the ballast left by the ships of the salt trade. If you are staying, choose between the **hotels** *Les Nids* (83, bd Général-Leclerc; ☎40.23.00.63) or *l'Estacade* (4 quai Lénigo; ☎40.23.03.77).

Close by, all around the rocky sea coast known as the **Grande Côte**, are a whole range of **campsites**. Just outside Le Croisic itself is the *Océan* (☎40.23.07.69); at Batz, another former island, is the *Casse Cailloux* (☎40.23. 91.71). For equally good beaches and a chance of cheaper **hotel** accommodation, you could alternatively go east from La Baule to **PORNICHET** (though preferably keeping away from the plush marina) or to the tiny **ST-MARC**, where in 1953 Jacques Tati filmed "Monsieur Hulot's Holiday".

St-Nazaire

The best sandy coves in the region, bizarrely enough, are to be found on the outskirts of **ST-NAZAIRE**: just off to the west, they are linked by wooded paths and almost deserted. But it's a gloomy city – bombed to extinction in the last war, its shipyards, in more or less continuous operation since they built Julius Caesar's fleet, are closing all around it. The one reason you might want to stay is the relative ease of finding inexpensive **hotel** space – so elusive in this area in summer. Options include the *Normandy* (35 rue de la Paix), the *Touraine* (4 av de la République; ☎40.22.47.56) and the *Windsor* (53 av de la République); or the **hostel**, the *Foyer du Travailleur*, at 30 rue Soleil Levant.

South of the Loire

From St-Nazaire you can cross the mouth of the Loire via an inspired piece of engineering, the **Pont St-Nazaire**. This is a great elongated S-curve of a suspension bridge, its lines only visible at an acute angle at either end. A hefty toll is demanded for the privilege of driving across its 3km length, but bikes go over for free.

From this high viewpoint (up to 131m), you can see that **the Loire** is a definite climatic dividing line (a point regularly confirmed by French television weather bulletins). To the north of the river, the houses have steep grey slate roofs against the storms; to the south, in the *Pays de Retz*, the roofs are flat and red tiled. Nonetheless the vast deposits of Loire silt have affected both banks of the huge estuary – they buried the ancient town of Montoise on the southern side just as they did Escoublac to the north.

As you continue **south** along the coast, Brittany begins to slip away. Dolmens stand above the ocean, and the rocky coast is interspersed with bathing beaches, but the climate, the architecture, the countryside, and most obvious of all the vineyards make it clear that this is the start of the South.

Pornic

The **Pays de Retz** coast is developed for most of its length – an almost unbroken line of holiday flats, *pepsi*, *frites*, and *crêpes* stands. **PORNIC** is the nicest of the resorts, with a still-functional fishing port and one of Bluebeard Gilles de Retz's many castles. It is a small place: you can walk beyond the harbour and along the cliffs to a tiny beach where the rock walls glitter from phosphorescent seawater. The **hotels** in town are not cheap, though better value than those of La Baule. The *Relais Saint Gilles* (☎40.82.02.25), just down the road from the post office, is the most reasonable, with a menu to match.

Inland, towards Nantes, the countryside is once more marshy, although richer than that of the Brière, with some scenic lakes and waterways. The largest of the lakes, the **Grand-Lieu**, contains two drowned villages, Murin and Langon. Along the **estuary** itself, the towns are depressed and depressing, their traditional industries struck hard by unemployment.

For **NANTES** itself, see Chapter 6.

travel details

Trains

Redon–Quimper/Brest 5 times daily service, stopping at Questembert (25min), Vannes (45min), Auray (1hr) and Lorient (1hr 30min).

Auray–Quiberon July and August only service, the *Tire Bouchon*. 3 times daily (40min), stopping at Plouharnel (20min) with connecting buses to Carnac and La Trinité.

La Baule/St-Nazaire Trains can only be caught from Nantes (5 daily; 30min/1hr).

Buses

From Vannes to Rennes via Josselin; to Nantes via La Roche Bernard; to Quiberon via Auray; and to Larmor-Baden via Arradon: all run by *TTO*, (☎97.47.29.64.)

From Vannes to Arzon; to Pontivy; and to Ploërmel: operated by *CTM* from the place de la Gare, (☎97.47.21.64.)

From Vannes to Port-Blanc (for the Ile de Moines), *Transport Cautru*, 26 rue Hoche, (☎97.47.22.86.)

From Auray From the *SNCF*: 4 daily to Quiberon (1hr) via Carnac (30min); 4 daily to Vannes (30min); both services operated by *Transports Le Bayon*, (☎97.57.31.31.)

From Lorient From the *SNCF*: 4 daily to Pontivy (1hr); 2 daily to Carnac (1hr).

Ferries

● Groix

From Lorient: 8 per day July–Aug, 3 per day rest of year; 45min, 40/60F. (☎97.21.03.97.)

From Concarneau: Day trips leave Wed & Sun 8.45am, July–Aug only, 120F. (☎98.97.10.31.)

● Lorient

Shuttle service to Port-Louis, 20 per day. (☎97.33.40.55.)

● Belle Ile

From Quiberon, 45min, 10 per day July–8 Sept, 2 to 4 per day rest of year, 58F. (☎97.31.80.01.)

From La Trinité, day trips, 2hr crossing, leave 9.00 Tues & Fri in summer, 81F. (☎97.33.40.55.)

From Vannes, day trips, 2hr 30min, leave 7.45am every day in summer, Sunday all year, 85F. (☎97.63.79.99.)

● Gulf of Morbihan

Various tours leave from **Vannes**, **Locmariaquer**, **Auray**, **Port-Navalo**, Easter–Sept. (☎97.63.79.99.)

● Ile de Moines

From Port-Blanc, 5min every half-hour, 7F. (☎97.26.31.45.)

From Vannes, 1hr, 2 trips daily Easter–Sept, 38F. (☎97.63.79.99.)

From La-Trinité, July–Sept 8, not Tues or Fri. Leave 2pm, 2hr on island, 52F. (☎97.33.40.55.)

● Gavrinis

From Larmor-Baden, 15min, every half-hour in season.

● Houat and Hoëdic

From Quiberon, 1hr, 4 daily July–Aug, 1 daily rest of year, 59F. (☎97.50.06.90.)

From Vannes, **La Trinité**, July–Aug. Houat every day, Hoëdic Mon & Thur, 59F+. (☎97.63 .79.99.)

Air

From Lorient direct flights to **Paris**, twice daily from Easter–Oct. Contact Lorient (☎97.82.32.93) or Vannes (☎97.60.78.79).

From Quiberon aerodrome (☎97.31.83.09 or ☎97.30.40.00), Easter–Oct, trips around Gulf of Morbihan, over Carnac, and to Belle-Ile.

PART FOUR

THE
CONTEXTS

THE HISTORICAL FRAMEWORK

Brittany and Normandy – the western provinces – have belonged to the French State for over 450 years, but they have been distinct entities throughout recorded history and their traditions and interests remain separate.

Brittany, for most of the five millennia during which its past can be traced, took its cultural links and influences not inland, from the rest of France, but from the Atlantic seaboard. Isolated both by the difficulty of its marsh and moorland terrain, and its sheer distance from the heartland of Europe, it was at the centre of a sophisticated prehistoric culture intimately connected with those of Britain and Ireland. It is populated today by the descendants of the Celtic immigrants who arrived from Britain and Ireland at around the time that the Romans were leaving. The "golden age" of Brittany came in the fifteenth century, when it was ruled as an independent Duchy – but it was eventually absorbed into France after centuries of military and dynastic struggles with the English. The economic decline of the province in recent centuries is attributed by Breton nationalists wholly to the union with France. There were inevitably other factors at play, but the rulers of France did often ignore or oppress their westernmost region, and even now the current revival of Brittany's fortunes is largely due to the conscious attempt to revive the old pan-Celtic trading routes.

Normandy has no equivalent prehistoric remains, and only very briefly did it possess the identity of an independent nation. Its founders were Scandinavian, the Vikings who raided along the Seine in the ninth century. These Northmen gave the region its name, and were the warriors who brought it military glory in the great Norman age of the eleventh century, when William conquered England and his nobles controlled swathes of land as far afield as Sicily and the Near East. They were also responsible for the cathedrals, castles and monasteries that are the most enduring monuments of Normandy's past.

The Normans blended into the general mass of the population, both in France and in England, and Normandy itself was formally surrendered to Louis IX by Henry III of England in 1259. After the fluctuations of the Hundred Years War, the province was firmly integrated into France, and all but disappears from history until the Allied invasion of 1944. There are Normans today – a handful – who regard Queen Elizabeth II as the true Duchess of Normandy, a title she does in fact bear. The majority of contemporary Normans, however, put their faith in the industrial and agricultural wealth of the province, and take pride in their individualism and conservatism.

THE MEGALITHS OF BRITTANY

Megalithic sites exist around the Mediterranean, notably in Malta and Sardinia, and along the Atlantic seaboard from Spain to Scandinavia. The most significant include Newgrange in Ireland, Stonehenge in England and the Ring of Brodgar in the Orkneys. However, the megalith-building culture is no longer thought to have originated in the Mediterranean and spread out to the "barbarian" outposts of Europe. In fact, the tumuli, alignments and single standing stones of Brittany are of pre-eminent importance. The very words used for the megaliths are Breton: *menhir* (long stone), *dolmen* (flat stone), *cromlech* (stone circle). And, dated at 5700 BC, the tumulus of Kercado at **Carnac**, in southern Brittany, appears to be the earliest stone construction of Europe, predating the Egyptian pyramids and the palace of Knossos on Crete.

Each megalithic centre seems to have had its own distinct styles and traditions. In Brittany, there are fewer stone circles and a greater proportion of free-standing stones; fewer burials, and more evidence of ritual fires; different styles of carving; and, uniquely, the sheer complexity of the Carnac alignments, which may be an astronomical observatory. (The fact that so many megalithic remains are on bleak seaside heathland sites may just be because these were the most likely to survive; those at Rétiers and Fougères do not fit the stereotype.)

Little is known of the **people** who erected the megaliths. Only rarely have skeletons been found in the graves, but what few there have been seem to indicate a short, dark, hairy race with a life expectancy of no more than the mid-30s. Legends speak of shambling subhuman giants who served as their slaves, who assisted Merlin in bringing the slabs of Stonehenge from Wales, and who built the Giant's Causeway on the coast of Antrim. What is certain is that the civilisation was a long-lasting one. The earliest and the latest constructions at Carnac are over five thousand years apart.

As for the actual **purpose of the stones**, there are numerous theories and few definite conclusions. Flaubert commented "those who like mythology see them as the Pillars of Hercules; those who like natural history see here a symbol of the Python ... lovers of astronomy see a zodiac". In the eighteenth century, for example, enthusiasts managed to see snakes in everything, and declared the megalithic sites to be remnants of some Druidic serpent cult. In fact, the stones were already ancient before the Druids appeared. Innumerable theses have wandered off into considerations of "Lost Atlantis", water-divining, mysterious psychic energies and extra-terrestrial assistance.

The **theories** gaining most popular acceptance these days see the megaliths as part of a vast system of **astronomical measurement**, record-keeping, and prediction. Precise measurements of sites all over Europe suggest that they share a standard measure of length, the "megalithic yard" (2.72 modern feet). In Brittany, the argument goes, the now fallen

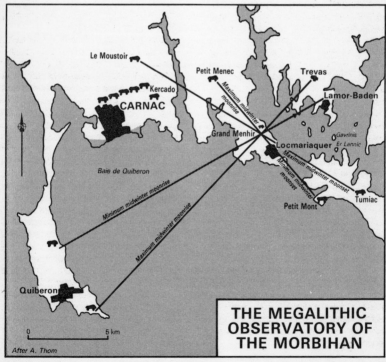

THE MEGALITHIC OBSERVATORY OF THE MORBIHAN

After A. Thom

Grand Menhir of Locmariaquer was erected, using this prehistoric calibration, as a "universal lunar foresight". Its alignments with eight other sites are said to correspond to the eight extreme points of the rising and setting of the moon during its 18.61-year cycle. The Golfe de Morbihan was the ideal place for such a marking stone – set on a lagoon surrounded by low peninsulas, the menhir was visible from all directions. Once the need for the Grand Menhir was decided upon, it would then have taken hundreds of years of careful observation of the moon to fix the exact spot for it. It is thought that this was done by lighting fires on the top of high poles at trial points on the crucial nights every nine years. The alignments of Carnac are thus explained as the graph paper, as it were, on which the lunar movements were plotted.

This "megalithic observatory" explanation, researched in great detail by Professor Thom, despite being hindered by occasional "encounters with irate peasants" and most clearly expounded in his *Megalithic Remains in Britain and Brittany* (1978), is certainly appealing. However, **rival experts** have come up with damning counter-evidence. To quote from Aubrey Burl's authoritative *Megalithic Brittany* (1985): "of the eight proposed backsights, three do not exist, and of the five others the Carnac mound at Tumiac is not accurately placed, the Goulvarch menhir, the stone at Kerran, the Carnac mound of Le Moustoir with its menhir, and the passage grave of Petit-Mont, are too dissimilar in architecture and date to be convincing purpose-built Neolithic viewing-stations." Doubts are even cast as to whether the Grand Menhir ever stood, and the measurements are accused of ignoring the difference in sea-level 5000 years ago.

In any case, the stones at Carnac have been so greatly eroded that perhaps it is little more than wishful thinking to imagine that their original size, shape, and orientation can be accurately determined. They have been knocked down and pulled out by peasants trying to cultivate the land; they have been quarried for use in making roads; they have been removed by landowners angry at the trespass of tourists and scientists; nineteenth-century pseudo-scientists have tampered with them, re-erecting some and shifting others; and what may have gone on in much earlier periods is anyone's guess.

An alternative approach is more sociological. This argues that the stones date from the great period of transition when humankind was changing from a predatory role to a producing one, and that they can only have been erected by the co-ordinated efforts of a large and stable **community**. In 1979 an experiment was carried out in which it took 260 people, using rollers, to set up a 32,000 kilogram stone, as well as a large number of others to provide food and shelter. The united physical exertion created very much a festival atmosphere, and the participants described the event as a "bonding" experience. Those who originally and perhaps unwillingly dragged the Carnac stones into place might feel that to be a trifle sentimental. Even so, it does make some sense to imagine the act of setting up a menhir as serving a valuable social purpose, both as an achievement and as a celebration. The annual or occasional setting-up of a new stone is easier to envisage than the vast effort required to erect them all at once. In which case the social significance of constructing these lines, mounds and circles, could have been of greater importance than any physical characteristics of the arrangements themselves.

For all the pervasive legends, the megaliths cannot be attributed to the Celts. Even so, theological parallels have been drawn between ancient and modern **Breton beliefs**. It is argued that there is a uniquely Breton attitude to death, dating back thousands of years, in which the living are in everyday communication with the dead. The phenomenon of the "parish close" is said to mirror the design of the ancient passage graves, with the Christian ossuary serving the same function as the buried passageways of the old tombs – a link between the place of the dead and the place of the living.

True or false, the popular significance of the prehistoric sites was something about which later Christian authorities were somewhat ambivalent. They felt it necessary to place crosses on the top of many menhirs, or even to destroy them altogether. There are reports of the "Indecent Stone" at Reguiny being "cut down and made harmless" in 1825, and of steps being taken to stop naked couples sliding down the Grand Menhir on May Day as a fertility rite, or rubbing against the "protuberances" of the Kerloas menhir.

CELTS AND ROMANS

Both the Bretons and the Normans make their first appearance in recorded history as traders in **tin and copper**. Small trading ports emerged all along the Atlantic coast, and the routes went up the rivers Loire and Seine. Iron Age forts, traces of one of which remain in the forest of Huelgoat, show evidence of large-scale stable communities even far inland. The tin itself was mostly mined in Cornwall, and the Seine became important as the "Tin Road", the most direct means for the metals to be transported towards the heart of Europe.

That was why the **Romans'** top priority, when they came to Gaul centuries later, was to secure control of the Seine valley and tie the province firmly into the network of empire. Brittany, less accessible to the invading armies, was able to put up a more spirited resistance, although sadly there was no such last-ditch rebel stronghold as Asterix's fictional village. The **Breton Gauls**, descendants of a first influx of Celts, were divided into five major tribes, each of which controlled an area roughly corresponding to the modern *départements*.

The most powerful of these tribes were the **Veneti**, based in the Morbihan with what is now Vannes as their capital. The decisive sea battle in which they were defeated in 56 BC took place around the Golfe de Morbihan and was the only major naval battle the Romans ever won outside the Mediterranean. Seafaring was not one of the Romans' strong points, hence their predilection for roads and foot-slogging, but on this occasion their galleys, built somewhere near St-Nazaire, had far superior mobility to the leather-sailed ships of the Veneti. The cost of defeat for the tribes was severe; those who were not killed were sold into slavery, and their children mutilated. Julius Caesar was there to see the battle; he went no further than Auray, but the whole Breton peninsula was swiftly conquered, and incorporated with much of Normandy into the province of Armorica.

Roman Armorica experienced five hundred years of peace, though without the benefit of any great prosperity. The Roman-built roads were the first efficient means of land communication, but served mainly to channel wealth away towards the centre of their empire. Walled cities were founded, such as Rennes, Vannes, Rouen and Caen, but little was done to change, let alone improve, the lives of the native population.

What civilising effect the Romans had had disappeared in any case during the **barbarian invasions** as the Empire disintegrated at the start of the fifth century. The one thread of continuity was provided by the Christian church. The first **Christians** had already arrived in Normandy during Roman rule and at Rouen the bishopric had been established by Saint Mellon as early as AD 300. They were followed in the fifth and sixth centuries by waves of Celtic immigrants crossing from Britain to Brittany. Traditional history considered these to be "Dark Ages" of terror and chaos throughout Europe, with the immigrants as no more than panic-stricken refugees. However, recent evidence of stable diplomatic and trading contact across the Channel suggests that there was a much more ordered process of movement and interchange.

The vigorous Welsh and Irish missionaries named their new lands **Little Britain**, and their Christianity supplanted the old Celtic and Roman gods. The era is characterised by great legendary confrontations of elemental forces – the Devil grappling with the Archangel Michael from Dol to Mont St-Michel, Saint Pol driving out the "laidley worm" from the Ile de Batz – symbolising the forcible expulsion of paganism. Often the changes were little more than superficial; crosses were erected on top of menhirs, mystical springs and wells became the sites of churches, Christian processions such as *pardons* followed circuits of megalithic sites, and ancient tales of magic and witchcraft were retold as stories of Jesus and the saints. The names of innumerable Celtic religious leaders – Malo, Brieuc, Pol – have survived in place names, even if the Church has never officially recognised them as saints.

The cultural links with Britain and Ireland meant that Brittany played an important role in many of the **Arthurian legends**. Breton minstrels, like their Welsh counterparts, did much to popularise the tales in the Middle Ages. None of the local claimants to Arthur's Camelot carry much conviction, although Tristan who loved Iseult came from Brittany (the lovers may have hidden at Trémazan castle in Finistère – see p.147), as did King Ban and his son Lancelot. Sir Galahad found the Holy Grail somewhere in Brocéliande Forest, which was also the home of such diverse residents as Merlin, Morgan le Fay, and the Fisher King.

Such legends reflect the fact that for all this time, central Brittany was an almost impenetrable wilderness, and the region as a whole was split into two separate petty monarchies, Dumnonia in the north and Cornubia (the basis of Cornuaille) in the south. Charlemagne amalgamated the two by force under **Frankish control** in 799, after they had consistently failed to pay tribute. When the Frankish Empire began to fall apart, their appointee as governor, **Nominoë**, seized the opportunity to become the first leader of an independent Brittany, by defeating Charles the Bald in the battle of Redon (near modern La Bataille) in 845. He has taken on the status of a prototype independent leader in Breton history.

Without Celtic immigration on anything like the same scale, it took longer for **Normandy** to become fully Christianised. It was only when it too came under the control of Charlemagne's **Merovingian** dynasty that the newly founded monasteries of Jumièges and St-Wandrille became pre-eminent. As the Franks' authority weakened over the succeeding centuries, there were repeated Viking raids along the Seine. Major incursions took place in the second half of the ninth century, interspersed with attempts to conquer England. They came more often and for longer, until in 911 King Charles the Simple acknowledged the inevitable and granted their leader **Rollo** formal title to the **Duchy of Normandy**.

THE NORMANS

In the eleventh century **the Normans** became one of the most significant forces in Europe. Not only did the Dukes of Normandy invade and conquer England, but Norman mercenaries and adventurers fought to gain lands for themselves wherever they found the opportunity. They insinuated themselves into the wars of Italy, individually acquiring control of Aversa, Apulia and Calabria, and most of Sicily, their greatest prize. They took part in the church's wars, too, fighting in campaigns in Greece against Byzantium, and in the First Crusade – which in 1098 saw the Norman leader Bohemond take Antioch.

In their adopted French homeland, the pagan Scandinavians had so rapidly adopted the culture, language and religion of their new subjects that spoken Norse had died out in Rouen by the time of Rollo's grandson, Duke Richard I. Yet they were still seen as a race apart – and not a very pleasant one at that. One authority describes them as without exception physically repellent, cruel and unscrupulous.

Duke William's **invasion of England** is portrayed by the Bayeux Tapestry as a just struggle: the result solely of William's conviction that he was the rightful heir to Edward the Confessor, a succession acknowledged under oath by Harold. Be that as it may, the sheer speed of what proved to be such a permanent conquest indicates the extent of Norman power at the time. Having crossed the Channel to defeat the usurper Harold in September 1066, the Conqueror was crowned King in Westminster Abbey on Christmas Day, and by the next Easter was secure enough to be able to return to Normandy. The Battle of Hastings was a decisive moment in the balance of Europe. Almost paradoxically, the Norsemen from France finally freed England from the threat of invasion from Scandinavia, which had existed for centuries up until 1070. English attention was thus re-orientated towards the mainland of Europe – a shift which was to have a major impact on history.

It was the Norman capacity for **organisation** that was primarily responsible not just for the military triumphs but also the consolidation of power and wealth which followed. The Domesday Book which catalogued the riches of England was paralleled by a similar undertaking in Sicily, the *Catalogus Baronum*. William's son Henry introduced trial by jury in the King's Courts – justice that had to be paid for. Henry II established the Exchequer to collect royal revenue. **Intellectually**, too, the Normans were dominant; the Abbey of Bec-Hellouin was a renowned centre of learning, inspired first by Lanfranc and then by the theologian Anselm, each of whom moved on to become Archbishop of Canterbury. And **architecturally**, the wealth and technical expertise of the Normans made possible the construction of such lasting monuments as the cathedrals of Bayeux, Coutances, and Durham, and the monasteries of Mont St-Michel, Jumièges and Caen.

The twelfth-century "**Anglo-Normans**" who invaded Ireland were recognisably descended from the army of the Conqueror, and Norman French remained the legal and administrative language of England until 1400. Elsewhere the mark of the conquerors was less distinct. The Norman Kings of Sicily did not style themselves Normans, and ruled over a cosmopolitan society dependent largely on the skills of Moslem craftsmen. Their architecture barely resembles what is thought of today as "Norman"; and the Norman bloodline soon vanished into the general population of Sicily.

But for the duchy and the kingdom on either side of the Channel, the shared rulers made close connections inevitable. The Norman lords in England required luxury items to be imported. Flemish weavers were encouraged to settle in London and East Anglia, and gradually the centre of affluence and importance shifted away from Normandy. By the time Henry II, great-grandson of William the Conqueror, inherited the throne, England was a major power and the seeds of the Hundred Years War had been sown. Fifteen years later Chateau Gaillard on the Seine was taken by **Phillipe Auguste** and Normandy for the first time became part of France.

THE HUNDRED YEARS WAR

While Normandy was at the height of its power, the Bretons lived in constant fear of invasion by their belligerent neighbours. Although their own leaders had managed to prevent a parallel Viking takeover of **Brittany**, it was at the price of numerous **warlords** setting up their own private strongholds. Their emergence seriously weakened the authority of Nominoë's successors, and the resultant anarchy devastated the Breton economy. Frequent power bids by the Norman English and the kings of France – the **Hundred Years War** – hardly helped the situation.

Bertrand du Guesclin, born in 1321 at Broons, an unprepossessing place south of Dinan, was the outstanding military genius of the Middle Ages. After an ignominious start when his father disowned him because of his extraordinary ugliness, he practised his novel tactics as an outlaw chief in the heart of Brittany. With little truck for chivalric conventions, he simplified the chaotic feudal map and in a bewildering succession of French and Spanish campaigns earned the command of the French army. He taught the French to fight dirty – in medieval terms. Nobles were forced to dismount and fight on foot; his soldiers were paid so that they did not alienate the peasantry by plundering. The use of gunpowder and new assault techniques that devastated the strongest fortresses were developed by this formidable man who refused pre-arranged battles in favour of ambush and general guerilla tactics.

The net result of du Guesclin's strategies was that by 1377 the English had been driven almost completely out of France. Virtually every town and castle in Brittany and Normandy seems to have some du Guesclin connection; not only did he live, besiege or fight almost everywhere, but after his death in 1380, parts of his body were buried in no less than four different cities. Yet despite all his myriad intrigues and battles, Brittany benefited very little from his activities.

The **Hundred Years War** resurfaced after du Guesclin's death, with much of the fighting taking place in Normandy. Henry V recaptured the province step by step, until by 1420 he was in a position to demand recognition of his claim to the French throne. Eight years later, the French were defending their last significant stronghold, Orléans on the Loire. It was here that the extraordinary figure of **Jeanne d'Arc** appeared on the scene and relieved the siege of the city. In a very different way to du Guesclin she ensured that the mass of ordinary, miserable peasants, not to mention the demoralised soldiers of the French army, made the enemy occupation untenable. Within two astonishing years, the Dauphin, not Henry, had been crowned. Jeanne herself was captured by the Burgundian allies of the occupiers, tried by

a French bishop and an English commander, and burnt at the stake as a witch on place Vieux-Marché in Rouen. But in 1449 her king, Charles VII, was able to make a triumphal entry into the regional capital. Within twelve months this latest thirty-two-year English occupation of Normandy was at an end.

THE DUCHY OF BRITTANY

Breton involvement in the opening stages of the second phase of the Hundred Years War was minimal and from 1399–1442 **Duc Jean V** took a neutral stand, allowing the economy of the province to prosper. Fishing, ship-building and sail manufacture developed, accompanied by a flowering of the arts. It was in this period that the Kreisker chapel and the church of Folgoët were built.

Although involvement in the Anglo-French conflict was inevitable, Jean's heirs for a time continued to rule over a successful and **independent duchy**. Arthur III, duke in the mid-fifteenth century, had fought alongside Jeanne d'Arc but used his connections with the French army to protect Breton autonomy. His successor, however, Duc François II, was less astute. Brittany, the last large region of present-day France to resist agglomeration, was a very desirable prize for King Louis XI. To resist encroachment, François needed allies beyond France; and in looking for those allies he antagonised and alarmed the French. A pretext was eventually found for the royal army to invade Brittany, where the Breton army was defeated at the battle of St-Aubin-du-Cormier in 1488. Duc François was forced to concede to the French King the right to determine his own daughter's marriage, and died of shame, so the story goes, within a few weeks.

François' heiress, **Duchess Anne**, was to be the last ruler of an independent Brittany. Having once been engaged to the Prince of Wales, she then married by proxy Maximilian of Austria in the hope of a strong alliance against the French. Charles VIII of France (who was himself in theory married to Maximilian's daughter) demanded adherence to the treaty of 1488, captured Nantes, advanced north and west and proposed to Anne.

By and large the population prefered a Royal wedding to death by starvation or massacre. Anne bemoaned "Must I thus be so unfortunate and friendless as to have to enter into marriage with a man who has so ill-treated me?" – and then, to the amazement of all, the couple actually fell in love with each other. Despite the marriage, the Duchy remained independent – but Anne was contractually obliged to marry Charles' successor should he die before they produced an heir. Charles did bump his head and die in 1498 whereupon the next King, Louis XII, divorced his wife and married Anne. This time Anne's position was considerably stronger and in the contract she laid down certain conditions which were to be a source of Breton pride and frustration for many centuries. The three main clauses stipulated that no taxes could be imposed without the consent of the Breton *Etats*; conscripts were only to fight for the defence of Brittany; and Bretons could only be tried in their own courts. When Anne died, Bretons mourned – all records show that she was a genuinely loved leader.

In 1514, the still independent Duchy passed to Anne's daughter Claude, whom the future François I of France married with every intention of incorporating Brittany into his kingdom. This he did and the permanent **union of Brittany and France** was endorsed by the Breton *Etats* at Vannes in 1532. In theory, the act confirmed Anne's stipulations that all the rights and privileges of Brittany would be observed and safeguaded as inviolable. But it was rarely honoured and their subsequent violation by successive French kings and governments has been the source of conflict ever since.

THE ANCIEN REGIME

As the French crown gradually consolidated its power and began to centralise its economy, the ports of the two western provinces developed, serving the **colonial interests** of the state. In fact as early as 1364 sailors from Dieppe had established the city of Petit Dieppe in what is now Sierra Leone. Le Havre was founded in 1517 to be France's premier Atlantic port and, between intermittent attacks and takeovers by the English, became a centre for the coffee and cotton markets. Sailors from Granville, Dieppe and Cherbourg set up colonies in Brazil, Canada, Florida and Louisiana.

In Brittany St-Malo and Lorient were the two top trading ports, with the latter benefiting

every time the English decided to harass Channel ports and shipping. **Jacques Cartier** of St-Malo sailed up the St Lawrence river and added Canada to the possession of the French crown. Nantes too was an important base for trade with the Americas, India and the Middle East, with **slaves** one of the most profitable "commodities". Though the business of exploitation and battles with rival foreign ships was motivated by private profit, the net result was very much to the advantage of the state.

The early contact with England, and the cosmopolitan nature of its Channel ports, meant that Normandy became one of the main Protestant centres of France, with Caen and its university having very active Huguenot populations. The region was therefore in the frontline during the **Wars of Religion** which flared up in 1561–3, and again in 1574–6. When the Edict of Nantes with its Protestant privileges and immunities was revoked, large-scale Huguenot emigration took place, seriously damaging the local textile industry.

Brittany on the other hand was an area of minimal Protestant presence, and the Wars of Religion were only significant as a cover for a brief attempt to win back independence. Breton linen manufacture had taken advantage of the lack of French tolls and customs dues and declined much later – when England, post-industrial revolution, was flooding the market with mass-produced textiles.

Although the power of the French kings increased over the centuries, practical considerations meant that outlying regions were not always completely under royal control. The rural nobles were persistently lawless, and intermittent **peasant revolts** took place, such as that of the dispossessed *nu-pieds* in 1639. In 1675 came the most serious rebellion against the Crown, when Louis XIV's finance minister put a tax on tobacco, pewter and all legal documents to raise money for the war with Holland. This "Stamped Paper" revolt, which started with riots in Nantes, Rennes and Guingamp soon spread to the country with the peasants making demands very similar in their content to those of the revolutionaries over a hundred years later. The aristocracy took great delight in brutally crushing the uprising, pillaging several towns and stringing up insurgents and bystanders from every tree.

The reign of **Louis XIV** saw numerous infringements of Breton liberties, including the uprooting of vines throughout the province on the royal grounds that the people were all drunkards. If the Bretons could not get revenge they could at least be entertained by court scandals. In 1650 Louis' Superintendent of Finance, **Nicolas Fouquet**, bought the entire island of Belle-Ile and fortified it as his own private kingdom. The alarmed King had to send D'Artagnan and the Three Musketeers to arrest him before his ambitious plans went any further.

While taxes on Brittany increased in the early eighteenth century, Normandy found new prosperity from the closeness of Paris for its edible produce. Lace-making became a major regional industry and several abbeys, closed during the Wars of Religion, were revitalised. But by 1763 France had lost Canada and given up all pretensions to India. The ports declined and trade fell off as England became the workshop of the world.

THE REVOLUTION

The people of both Brittany and Normandy at first welcomed the **Revolution**. Breton representatives at the *Etats Généraux* in Paris seized the opportunity to air all Brittany's grievances and the "Club Breton" they formed was the basis of the **Jacobins**. Caen, meanwhile, became the centre of the bourgeois **Girondist** faction. In August of 1789 it was a Breton *député* who proposed the abolition of privileges. However, under the Convention it became clear that the price to be paid for the elimination of the *ancien régime* was further reductions in local autonomy and the suppression of the Breton language.

Neither province was sympathetic to the execution of the King – in Rouen 30,000 people took to the streets to express their opposition. The Girondins came out worst in the factional infighting at the Convention, having opposed the abolition of the monarchy and supported the disastrous war in the Netherlands. Some Girondist deputies managed to flee the edict of June 2 1793 which ordered their arrest, but the army they organised to march on Paris was defeated at Pacy-sur-Eure. The final major Norman contribution to Revolutionary history

was provided on that same day by **Charlotte Corday** of Caen, when she stabbed Jean-Paul Marat in his bath.

The concerted attack on religion and the clergy was not happily received, particularly in Brittany where the church was closely bound up with the region's independent identity. The attempt to conscript an army of 300,000 Bretons was deeply resented as an infringement of the Act of Union. The popular image of the Revolution in Brittany, where the riots and disturbances of 1787 had been crucial, was now further damaged by the brief **reign of terror** in 1793 of Carrier, the Convention's representative in Nantes. Under the slogan "all the rich, all the merchants are counter-revolutionaries" he killed perhaps 13,000 people in three months, by such methods as throwing prisoners into the Loire tied together in pairs. This was done without Tribunal sanction or approval, and Carrier was himself guillotined before the end of the year.

All this made Brittany an inevitable focal point for the Royalist **counter-revolution** known as the *Chouannerie*, which also had adherents in a few outlying areas of Normandy. A vast invasion force of exiled and foreign nobility, backed by the English, was supposed to sweep through France rallying all dissenters to the Royalist flag. In the event only 8000 landed at Quiberon in 1795, and were not even capable of escaping from the self-imposed trap of the peninsula. They devastated what little they could before themselves being brutally massacred. Much of the local support was motivated by the age-old desire to win back independence but the Breton *chouans* ("screech owls") fighting elsewhere ended up being tarred with the same aristocratic brush and then abandoned to years of quixotic and doomed guerilla warfare.

A rebel army continued to fight sporadically in the Cotentin and the Bocage until 1800 while in Brittany another **royalist revolt** in 1799 was easily crushed. In 1804, Cadoudal, "the last *chouan*", was captured and executed in Paris, where he had gone to kidnap Napoleon – having refused the emperor's offer of a generalship if he surrendered. The rebel movement lingered on until 1832, when the Duchess of Berry failed to interest anyone in the restoration of the *ancien régime*.

THE NINETEENTH CENTURY

Normandy, at the beginning of the nineteenth century, remained a wealthy region despite the crippling of its ports by the blockade imposed by the European coalition against Napoleon. It had proportionally five times as many people eligible, as property owners, to vote as the impoverished mountain areas of the south. Its agriculture accounted for 11 percent of France's produce on 6 percent of its land, while industry remained relatively unadvanced.

When protectionist tariffs were removed from grain in 1828 and Normandy was forced to compete with other producers, widespread **rural arson and tax riots** ensued. But when the revolution of 1848 offered the prospect of socialism, the deeply conservative Catholic peasantry showed little enthusiasm for change. Even the re-emergence of a rural textile industry in the 1840s, relying on outworkers brutally exploited by the Rouen capitalists, added no radical impetus.

The advent of the **railways** and the patronage of the imperial court encouraged the development of Normandy's resorts while along the Seine, water mills provided the power for the major spinning centres at Louviers, Evreux and Elbeuf. Serious decline did not come until the 1880s, when **rural depopulation** was brought on by emigration combined with a low birth-rate – and a high death-rate in which excessive drinking played a part.

Nineteenth-century Brittany was no longer an official entity, save as five *départements* of France. The railways were of negative benefit, submitting the province to competition from more heavily industrialised regions, while the Nantes–Brest canal did not achieve the expected success, and **emigration** increased. Culturally, the century witnessed a revival of the language, customs and folklore but the initiative came from intellectuals, not the mainly illiterate masses.

Around the turn of the **twentieth century** both provinces experienced a surge of artistic creativity, with painters such as Gauguin in Pont-Aven and Monet in Giverny, and such writers as Proust in Normandy and Pierre Loti in Brittany. As everywhere in Europe, this idyll was shattered by the **Great War**; although removed from the actual battlefields, both Brittany and Normandy were dramatically affected. Brittany, for its size, suffered the heaviest death toll of anywhere in the world. The vast memorial at Ste-Anne-d'Auray is testimony to the extent of the loss, while a parallel spiritual grief can be seen in the dramatic growth in Normandy of the cult of the recently-dead Thérèse of Lisieux. Symbols of a changing world are the two leading aristocratic families of the regions; the heir to the Rohans of Josselin was killed on the Somme, while Prince Louis de Broglie became the first physicist to question the solidity of matter.

WORLD WAR II AND THE BATTLE OF NORMANDY

That the **beaches of Normandy** were chosen as the site of the Allied invasion of Europe in June 1944 was by no means inevitable. Far from the major disputed areas and communication routes of Europe, Normandy had seen almost no military activity since the Hundred Years War. But in that blazing summer, six armies and millions of men fought bloody battles across the placid Norman countryside. A whole swathe of the province was laid in ruins before Hitler's defensive line was broken and the road to Paris cleared.

France, under **Marshal Pétain**, had surrendered to the Germans in 1940. A year later, the fascist armies turned east to invade the Soviet Union – America and Britain declaring full support for the Soviets but resisting Stalin's demand for a second front. In 1942 the two western powers promised a landing in northern France but all that ensued was an abortive commando raid on Dieppe. By the time the second front materialised the tide of the war had already been turned at Stalingrad.

The Germans had meanwhile fortified the whole northwest seaboard of Europe. They expected the attack to come, however, at the Channel's narrowest point, across the Straits of Dover. The **D-Day invasion** of June 6 1944, was presaged by months of intensive aerial bombardment across Europe, without concentrating too obviously on the chosen landing sites. In the event, the Nazis vastly overestimated the Allied resources – two weeks after D-Day Rommel still thought the Normandy landings might be no more than a preliminary diversion to a larger-scale assault around Calais.

A photographic survey of the whole Norman coast had been prepared in Britain, using every

possible source including prewar holiday snaps. The landing forces actually took their own "Mulberry" harbours with them. The basic plan was for the British and Commonwealth forces under Montgomery to strike for Caen, the pivot around which the Americans (whose General Eisenhower was in overall command) were to swing following their own landings further west.

Not everything went smoothly. There are appalling stories of armoured cars full of men plunging straight to the bottom of the sea as they rolled off landing craft unable to get near enough to the shore. Many of the early objectives took much longer to capture than was originally envisaged – the British took weeks rather than hours to reach Caen, while American hopes of a rapid seizure of the deepwater port at Cherbourg were thwarted. Most notorious of all, the opportunity of capturing the bulk of the German army, which was all but surrounded in the "Falaise pocket", was lost.

Military historians say that man for man the German Army was the more effective fighting force; but with their sheer weight of resources the Allies achieved a fairly rapid victory. There was never a significant German air presence over Normandy since it was all concentrated on the Eastern Front. Parachutists, reconnaissance

flights and air support for ground troops were all able to operate virtually unimpeded, as too were the bombing raids on Norman towns and on every bridge across the Seine west of Paris. Furthermore, the muddled enemy command, in which generals at the front were obliged to follow broad directives from Berlin, caused an American general to comment, "one's imagination boggled at what the German army might have done to us without Hitler working so effectively for our side".

Within a few days of D-Day, **De Gaulle** was able to return to Free France, making an emotional first speech at Bayeux, while a seasick Winston Churchill sailed up to Deauville in a destroyer and "took a plug at the Hun". At the end of July, General Patton's Third Army broke out across Brittany from Avranches with the aid of 30,000 **French Resistance** fighters, and on August 25 Allied divisions entered Paris, where the German garrison had already been routed by the Resistance. In the east the Red Army were sweeping back the Axis powers. Though the war in Europe still had several bloody months to run, with Hitler coming very close to smashing the Western front in December 1944, the road to Berlin was finally opening up.

POSTWAR: THE BRETON RESURGENCE

The war left most of Normandy in ruins; while it remained a relatively prosperous area in terms of its produce, decades of reconstruction were required. The development of private transport also meant that Normandy became ever more filled with the second homes of the rich. This has often been resented – the film actor Jean Gabin, for example, was literally besieged in his new country house by hundreds of peasants insisting that he had "too much land", and was obliged to sell some of it off.

Meanwhile, there was very little happening in **postwar Brittany** save migration from the countryside to the main towns and from there, often, out of the province all together. By the 1950s some 300,000 Bretons lived in Paris, industry was almost exclusively limited to the Loire estuary, and agriculture was dogged by archaic marketing and distribution.

But since the late 1960s Brittany has experienced considerable economic advance, due in part to the initiatives of **Alexis Gourvennec**. He first came to prominence at the age of 24, in 1961, when he led a group of fellow farmers into Morlaix to occupy the government's regional offices in an effective (if violent) protest at exploitation by middlemen. The act set the pace for his lifetime's concern – to obtain the best possible price for Breton agricultural produce. To this end he lobbied Paris for a deep water port at Roscoff, and once that was built, his farmers' co-operative set up *Brittany Ferries* to carry Breton artichokes and cabbages to English markets. The company was an explicit move to re-establish the old trading links of the Atlantic seaboard, independent of Paris and central French authority.

Brittany Ferries has prospered, thanks to the British and Irish entry to the EC upon which Gourvennec had gambled. And it has proved that Brittany's future economic fortunes are more closely linked to its old Celtic connections than to the French state. Yet despite Gourvennec's enthusiasm for his Celtic cousins there have been several instances of ugly right-wing **protectionism** – attacking British lorries importing meat, violently breaking up strikes in Brittany, and forcibly preventing *Townsend Thoresen* from starting a rival ferry service to St-Malo.

In 1973 a semi-decentralised **regional administration** was set up to provide an intermediate level between the *départements* and the state. Normandy, being rich, became two regions – *Basse* and *Maine* – while Brittany, with the Loire-Atlantique *département* around Nantes lopped off, was a single entity. The new boundaries had no impact on people's perception of the provinces, though they did start to have some practical consequence when the Socialist government increased regional powers in 1981.

The traditional industrial centres on the Loire estuary, like the ship-building town of St-Nazaire, no longer come under Breton planning – perhaps just as well given the recession. Fishing and agriculture are still the mainstay of the Breton economy, though the former has never benefited from an equivalent to Gourvennec. The socialist policy of **decentralisation** brought certain industries to the region – such as a *Citroën* plant at Rennes and *Renault* in Lorient – but it is still industrially backward compared to most of France. Its isolation has long made it a favourite location for nuclear power stations, despite local opposition which, on occasion (as at Plogoff), has made world headline news.

A decade ago hopes of new riches were raised by drilling for offshore oil in Finistère. If oil is discovered, it would create interesting parallels with the situation in Scotland. As yet, however, these remain pipe dreams and Brittany's experience of oil has been at the receiving end of major disasters – the *Torrey Canyon* in March 1967 and the *Amoco Cadiz* in 1978 both polluting hundreds of miles of coastline.

Towards the end of the 1980s leading Breton economic figures began to prepare themselves for a future in which it may not be possible for the province to depend so heavily on its agriculture. They earmarked the development of the city of Brest as being the best way forward. The **Brest Charter**, drawn up in 1987 and approved by the French government in February 1988, plans for large-scale investment in the city area, partly on higher education and research facilities, and partly on upgrading the harbour and airport to cope with international traffic. The ultra-fast Paris–Brest *TGV* rail link, inaugurated in 1989, should also make a big difference.

Politically, Bretons consistently provide an above-average proportion of the conservative vote. Almost three-quarters of the population supported De Gaulle in the 1960s, and in 1981 the majority voted against Mitterand. The most traditional, rural, areas are the most conservative of all. Perhaps for that reason the **separatist movement**, as a positive celebration of the Breton nation rather than a reactionary throwback, has never been all that powerful. In 1932 a bomb in Rennes destroyed the monument to Franco-Breton unity, and since 1966 the Front de Libération de Bretagne has intermittently attacked such targets as the nuclear power station in the Monts d'Arrée, and the Hall of Mirrors at the palace of Versailles in 1978. The emphasis for most Breton activists these days, however, is on cultural pride rather than militancy. The idea is to establish a clear and vital sense of national identity – to create, as one leader put it, "the spiritual basis for a new political thrust". Although overall use of the Breton language may be declining, great stress has been placed on its historical and artistic significance. And notable victories have been won on the question of its official status.

AN HISTORICAL CHRONOLOGY

BC

c450,000 Evidence of Paleolithic activity at St Columban

c5700 Earliest megalithic site – tumulus of Kercado

c4600 Tomb containing antlers and shells, Hoëdic island

up to 1800 Megalithic Age; construction of Carnac alignments

2500 on Seine becomes the "Tin Road"

6thC First wave of Celts arrive, the Gauls

56 Julius Caesar's fleet defeats Veneti

AD

up to 476 Roman occupation of Armorica

497 Franks arrive in Normandy; Clovis occupies Rouen

5th–6th C Celts fleeing from Britain rename Brittany

6thC First monasteries founded, Brittany and Normandy

Saint Pol kills 'laidley-worm' on island of Batz

709 Mont-St-Michel consecrated by bishop of Avranches

799 Charlemagne controls all Brittany

8th–9th C Forest of Scissy drowns to form Mont-St-Michel Bay

Viking expeditions against Normandy

845 Battle of Redon, Nominoë first Duke of Brittany

911 Rollo becomes first Duke of Normandy, capital Rouen

9th–10th C Repeated Norman invasions of Brittany

1035 Birth of William 'The Bastard' at Falaise

1064 Harold and William together at Battle of Brittany (Dol)

1066 William invades and conquers England

1067 Abbey of Jumièges consecrated

1077 Bishop Odo dedicates Bayeux cathedral, with Tapestry

11thC Golden age of Abbey of Bec – Lanfranc and Anselm

1120 William, heir to the English throne, drowns at Barfleur

1136 Pierre Abelard abbot of St Gildas

1162 Eleanor of Aquitaine born at Domfront

12th C Romanesque cloister of Abbey of Daoulas

1160 Robert Wace visits Broceliande forest "like a fool"

1171 Henry II, in Argentan, hears news of Becket's murder

1172 Henry does public penance at Avranches

1195 Richard the Lionheart builds Château Gaillard

1204 Normandy reunited with French throne

1211–28 Building of *La Merveille* at Mont-St-Michel

1218 Construction of Cathedral at Coutances

1303 Saint Yves dies, Tréguier

1351 "Combat of the Thirty" between Josselin and Ploermel

1359 Du Guesclin fights single combat at Dinan

1375 Building of Kreisker belfry at St-Pol

1420 Henry V of England King of France, after Agincourt

1431 Joan of Arc's trial and execution (May 30) at Rouen

1437 John the Baptist's finger arrives at St-Jean-du-Doigt

1440 "Bluebeard" burnt at stake in Nantes

1450 Normandy finally recovered by France

1450 Frescoes at Kermaria-an-Isquit

1469 Locronan starts its ascendancy in the linen trade

1474–6 Henry Tudor, England's future king, prisoner at Elven

1491 Duchess Anne of Brittany becomes Queen of France

1499 Duchess Anne becomes Queen of France again

1510 Monk, Vincelli, invents Benedictine liqueur

1517 Construction of Le Havre

1526 Aître de St-Maclou, charnel-house, built at Rouen

1532 Vannes Parliament ratifies Brittany-France Union

1548 Mary Queen of Scots at Morlaix

1550–1750 Rival Breton towns build the "parish closes"

1562	Rouen sacked by Protestants
1598	Henry IV signs Edict of Nantes
1608	Champlain sails from Honfleur to found Quebec
1661	Three Musketeers end Fouquet's ownership of Belle-Ile
1668	10,000 die of plague in Dieppe
1675	"Stamped Paper" peasant revolt in Brittany
1693	English "infernal machine" devastates St Malo
1698	Gouin de Beauchère of St-Malo colonises the Falklands
1722	Dec 22; Drunken carpenter burns down most of Rennes
1745	Bonnie Prince Charlie sails from Nantes
1758	Duke of Marlborough attacks St Malo with 15,000 men
1776	Benjamin Franklin lands at Auray (by mistake)
1789	Revolution makes no concessions to Breton autonomy
1793	Carrier kills thousands in "marriages" at Nantes
1794	Soldiers play boules with heads from Guéhenno Calvary
1795	Royalist and exile *chouans* land at Quiberon
1801	Robert Fulton tests first submarine at Camaret
1808	Napoleon arrives by barge for his ball at Nantes
c1810	Marie Herel invents Camembert
1821	Flaubert born at Rouen
1836	Opening of the Nantes–Brest Canal
1843	Victor Hugo's daughter drowns in Seine
1852	First major Icelandic fishery expedition from Paimpol
1866	Composer Erik Satie born in Honfleur
1873	Thérèse Martin born, Lisieux; died 1897, sainted 1925
1881	Young Marcel Proust pays his first visit to Combourg

1883–1926	Monet paints waterlilies in his garden at Giverny
1888	Gauguin at Pont-Aven
1896	*Drummond Castle* goes down off Ouessant
1899	Second trial of Dreyfus at Rennes
1905	France secularised, although Brittany votes against
1927	Nungesser and Coli disappear over Etretat attempting first transatlantic flight
1928	Amundsen's air-rescue flight from Caudebec disappears
1932	Bomb destroys Rennes monument to Franco-Breton unity
1930s	Nauseous Jean-Paul Sartre teaches philosophy in Le Havre
1940	All the men of Sein join De Gaulle in England
1942	March 28; British commando raid on St-Nazaire
1942	August: 1000 Canadians die in commando raid on Dieppe
1944	June 6; D-Day – Battle of Normandy
1954	Consecration of Basilica of St Thérèse at Lisieux
1962	First Telstar transatlantic signals at Pleumeur-Bodou
1966	Tidal power dam built across the Rance estuary
1967	*Torrey Canyon* disaster; oil slicks hit Brittany
1972	Loire-Atlantique no longer officially in Brittany
1980	*Rainbow Warrior* pursues nuclear-dumping vessel into Cherbourg; anti-nuclear riots at Plogoff
1984	40th anniversary of D-Day; Thatcher and Reagan visit
1987	Oct 15; Hurricane causes extensive damage in Finistère
1988	Brest Charter on Brittany's economic future approved by French govt.

BOOKS

PREHISTORY AND MEGALITHS

Aubrey Burl *Megalithic Brittany* (Thames & Hudson 1985). Detailed guide to all the prehistoric sites of Brittany, area by area. Very precise on how to find each site, and what you see when you get there, but with little historical or theoretical overview. It is not intended as a practical guide-book for anything other than ancient stones – no details of towns, hotels, or anything else.

John Michell *Megalithomania* (Thames & Hudson 1982). More popular general work about megaliths everywhere, with a lot of entertaining descriptions of how modern visitors have reacted to them.

A. Thom & A. S. Thom *Megalithic Remains in Britain and Brittany* (Clarendon Press, 1978). A scientific rather than anecdotal account of the Thoms' extensive analysis. The mathematics and astronomy can be a bit over-powering, without necessarily convincing you of anything.

Uderzo and Goscinny *Asterix the Gaul* (Hodder Dargaud). Breton history mixed together in a magic cauldron.

HISTORY AND POLITICS

David C. Douglas *The Norman Achievement 1050–1100* (Eyre & Spottiswoode, 1969). Comprehensive and readable assessment of the Norman Conquerors.

Barbara Tuchman *Distant Mirror* (Penguin, £3.50). A history of the fourteenth century as experienced by a French nobleman. Makes sense of the human complexities of the Hundred Years War.

Theodore Zeldin *France 1845–1945* (OUP, £3.95 each book). Five thematic volumes on aspects of French history.

Alfred Cobban *A History of Modern France* (Penguin, three vols, £2.25–2.75). Very complete political history from Louis XIV to de Gaulle.

John Ardagh *France in the 1980s* (Pelican, 1982, £5.50). Detailed journalistic survey of modern France, with an interesting and relevant section on "Brittany's revival".

Morvan Lebesque *Comment Peut-on Etre Breton?* (Editions du Seuil, 1970, 27F). A classic of Breton separatism, taking a psychological and sociological approach rather than a political one. He argues that awareness of one's cultural identity is vital for participation in the international community.

Kendalc'h *Breiz Hor Bro* (Editions Breiz, 1976) Produced by a Breton youth association in French, this militant pamphlet covers history, language, literature, and folklore, never losing an opportunity to take a swipe at the age old oppressors of Brittany.

THE NORMANDY LANDINGS

Max Hastings *Overlord* (Michael Joseph, 1984). Detailed history of D-Day and its aftermath by a man who for his sins is now editor of the *Daily Telegraph*. Surprisingly balanced and objective; he distances himself thoroughly from propaganda and myth-making.

John Keegan *Six Armies in Normandy* (Penguin, 1982, £4.50). Military history combining the personal and the public to original effect.

Donald Horne *The Great Museum: the Representation of History* (Pluto, £5.50). A stimulating analysis of how history is presented to the tourist. Particularly interesting for its treatment of the D-Day landing sites.

Studs Turkel *The Good War* (Ballantine, 1984). Excellent collection of interviews with participants of every rank and nation, including civilians, in World War II.

ART AND ARCHITECTURE

Henry Adams *Mont St-Michel and Chartres* (1904, Penguin Classics, £4.95). Extraordinary, idiosyncratic account of the two medieval masterpieces, attempting through prayer, song, and sheer imagination to understand the society and the people which created them. A tribute to Norman wisdom.

John Ardagh *Writers' France* (Hamish Hamilton, 1989, £18) Entertaining anecdotes about most of the writers mentioned in this book, with colour photos.

Christina Björk *Linnea in Monet's Garden* (Ragged Bears, Andover £6.95). A Swedish book for children which tells the story of a young girl achieving her unlikely lifetime's dream of visiting Monet's home in Giverny. Well illustrated, providing a good first introduction to the Impressionists.

Alfonso Castelao *Les Croix de Pierre en Bretagne* (available by post for 59F from the *Comité Bretagne-Galice*, BP66A, 35031 Rennes) A real collector's item; a pocket-sized collection of sketches of Breton calvaries made by the influential Gallego writer and illustrator during a visit in the 1920s. Includes an obsessive series of studies of Christ's ribcage. For more on Castelao, see the *Rough Guide to Spain*.

Claire Joyes *Monet at Giverny* (Matthews Millar Dunbar, 1975). Large-format account of Monet's years at Giverny, combining biography with good reproductions of the famous waterlilies.

BRITTANY IN FICTION

Honoré de Balzac *The Chouans* (Penguin Classics, £3.99). A hectic and crazily romantic story of the royalist *chouan* rebellion shortly after the Revolution, set mainly in Fougères.

Alexandre Dumas *The Three Musketeers* (Penguin Classics, £2.95). Brilliant swashbuckling romance with peripheral Breton scenes on Ouessant and elsewhere.

Victor Hugo *Ninety-Three* (Penguin Classics, £2.95). Rather more restrained but still compelling *chouan* novel.

Jack Kerouac *Satori in Paris* (Quartet, £2.50) . . . and in Brittany. Typically inconsequential Kerouac anecdotes.

Pierre Loti *Pecheur d'Islande* (Livre de Poche, 45F). Novel (on which the film was based) of the whaling fleets that sailed from Paimpol. Not available in translation.

NORMANDY IN FICTION

Julian Barnes *Flaubert's Parrot* (Picador, £3.95). A lightweight novel which rambles around the life of Flaubert, with much of the action taking place in Rouen and along the Seine.

Gustave Flaubert *Madame Bovary* (Penguin Classics, £2.50). "The first modern novel", by the Rouennais writer. It contains little that is specifically Norman, however.

Gustave Flaubert *Bouvard and Pécuchet* (Penguin Classics, £3.50). Two petty-bourgeois retire to a village between Caen and Falaise and attempt to practise every science of the time. Very funny or dead boring, according to taste.

Marcel Proust *In Remembrance of Things Past* (Penguin, 3 vols, £9.95 each). Dense autobiographical trilogy evocative of almost everything except the places in Normandy and Brittany that his memories take him back to.

Jean-Paul Sartre *Nausea* (Penguin Modern Classics, £3.50). Sartre's relentlessly gloomy description of how unpleasant it is to drag out one's existence – as it happens, materially speaking, in Le Havre (or "Bouville") in the 1930s.

BRETON MYTH AND FOLKTALES

Pierre-Jakez Hélias *The Horse of Pride* (Yale University Press). That account of a childhood in the Bigouden district earlier this century sold two million copies in France is probably because of, rather than despite, it's being deeply reactionary and sentimental.

Prof Anatole Le Braz *La Legende du Mort* (Editions Jeanne Laffitte, 1982). The definitive French text on Breton myths centred on Ankou and the prescience of death.

F. M. Luzel *Celtic Folk-Tales from Armorica* (Llanerch Enterprises, Lampeter, Wales 1985, £2.95). A collection of Breton fairy stories translated into English, with commentaries.

W. Y. Evans Wentz *The Fairy Faith in Celtic Countries* (first published 1911, Colin Smythe 1977, £4.95). Utterly bizarre survey of similarities and differences in folk beliefs and religion between Celtic nations, with extensive details about Brittany.

LANGUAGE

Although Breton does remain a living language, in both Brittany and Normandy every encounter you are likely to have with the local people will be conducted in French. This is of course a lot more familiar than Breton, sharing numerous words with English, but it's not a particularly easy language to pick up.

The bare essentials of French, though, are not difficult, and make all the difference. Even just saying "Bonjour Madame/Monsieur" when you go into a shop, and then pointing, will usually get you a smile and helpful service. People working in hotels, restaurants, and tourist offices almost always speak some English, and tend to use it even if you're trying in French – be grateful not insulted.

Breton is one of the Celtic family of languages, with an especially strong oral tradition ranging from medieval minstrels to modern singers and musicians. If you have a familiarity with Welsh or Gaelic, you should find yourself understanding, and being understood, in it.

Current estimates put the number of Breton speakers at between 400,000 and 800,000, but you are only likely to find it spoken as a first, day-to-day language either amongst the old, or in the more remote parts of Finistère. For centuries it was discouraged by the State; its use was forbidden for official and legal purposes, and even Breton-speaking parents would seek to enhance their children's prospects by bringing them up to speak French. Although it is now taught in schools once again, learning Breton is not really a viable prospect for visitors who do not already have a grounding in another Celtic language. However, as you travel through the province, it's interesting to note the roots of Breton place names, many of which have a simple meaning in the language. The box below lists some of the most common.

A GLOSSARY OF BRETON PLACE-NAMES

Aber	estuary	*Lann*	heath
Avel	wind	*Lech*	flat stone
Bihan	little	*Men*	stone
Bran	hill	*Menz*	mountain
Braz	big	*Mario*	dead
Creach	height	*Menhir*	long stone
Cromlech	stone circle	*Meur*	big
Dol	table	*Mor*	sea
Du	black	*Nevez*	new
Gavre	goat	*Parc*	field
Goat	forest	*Penn*	end, head
Goaz	stream	*Plou*	parish
Guen	white	*Pors*	port, farmyard
Hen	old	*Roch*	stone
Heol	sun	*Ster*	river
Hir	long	*Stivel*	fountain, spring
Inis	island	*Trez*	sand, beach
Ker	town or house	*Trou*	valley
Koz	old	*Ty*	house
Lan	church	*Wrach*	witch

A BRIEF GUIDE TO SPEAKING FRENCH

PRONUNCIATION

One easy rule to remember is that **consonants** at the ends of words are usually silent. *Pas plus tard* (not later) is thus pronounced pa-plu-tarr. But when the following word begins with a vowel, you run the two together : *pas après* (not after) becomes pazapre.

Vowels are the hardest sounds to get right. Roughly:

a	as in h**a**t		*i*	as in mach**i**ne
e	as in g**e**t		*o*	as in h**o**t
é	between g**e**t and g**a**te		*o, au*	as in **o**ver
è	between g**e**t and g**u**t		*ou*	as in f**oo**d
eu	like the **u** in h**u**rt		*u*	as in a pursed-lip version of **u**se

More awkward are the **combinations** in/im, en/em, an/am. on/om, un/um at the ends of words, or followed by consonants other than n or m. Again, roughly:

in/im	like the **an** in **an**xious		*on/om*	like the **don** in **Don**caster said by
an/am, en/em	like the **don** in **Don**caster when			someone with a heavy cold
	said with a nasal accent		*un/um*	like the **u** in **u**nderstand

Consonants are much as in English, except that: ch is always sh, c is s, h is silent, th is the same as t, ll is like the y in yes, w is v, and r is growled (or rolled).

BASIC WORDS AND PHRASES

French nouns are divided into masculine and feminine. This causes difficulties with adjectives, whose endings have to change to suit the gender of the nouns they qualify. If you know some grammar, you will know what to do. If not, stick to the masculine form, which is the simplest – it's what we have done in this glossary.

today	*aujourd'hui*	that one	*celà*
yesterday	*hier*	open	*ouvert*
tomorrow	*demain*	closed *	*fermé*
in the morning	*le matin*	big	*grand*
in the afternoon	*l'après-midi*	small	*petit*
in the evening	*le soir*	more	*plus*
now	*maintenant*	less	*moins*
later	*plus tard*	a little	*un peu*
at one o'clock	*à une heure*	a lot	*beaucoup*
at three o'clock	*à trois heures*	cheap	*bon marché*
at ten-thirty	*à dix heures et demie*	expensive	*cher*
at midday	*à midi*	good	*bon*
man	*un homme*	bad	*mauvais*
woman	*une femme*	hot	*chaud*
here	*ici*	cold	*froid*
there	*là*	with	*avec*
this one	*ceci*	without	*sans*

TALKING TO PEOPLE

When addressing people you should always use *Monsieur* for a man, *Madame* for a woman, *Mademoiselle* for a girl. Plain *bonjour* by itself is not enough. This isn't as formal as it seems, and it has its uses when you've forgotten someone's name or want to attract someone's attention.

Excuse me	*Pardon*	please	*s'il vous plaît*
Do you speak English ?	*Vous parlez anglais ?*	thank you	*merci*
		hello	*bonjour*
How do you say it in French ?	*Comment ça se dit en Français ?*	goodbye	*au revoir*
		good morning/ afternoon	*bonjour*
What's your name ?	*Comment vous appelez-vous ?*	good evening	*bonsoir*
My name is . . .	*Je m'appelle . . .*	good night	*bonne nuit*
I'm English/	*Je suis anglais[e]/*	How are you ?	*Comment allez-vous ?/ Ça va ?*
Irish/Scottish	*irlandais[e]/écossais[e]/*	Fine, thanks	*Très bien, merci*
Welsh/American/	*gallois[e]/américain[e]/*	I don't know	*Je ne sais pas*
Australian/	*australien[ne]/*	Let's go	*Allons-y*
Canadian/	*canadien[ne]/*	See you tomorrow	*à demain*
a New Zealander	*néo-zélandais[e]*	See you soon	*à bientôt*
yes	*oui*	Sorry	*Pardon, Madame/ je m'excuse*
no	*non*		
I understand	*Je comprends*		
I don't understand	*Je ne comprends pas*	Leave me alone (aggressive)	*Fichez-moi la paix!*
Can you speak slower ?	*s'il vous plaît, parlez moins vite*	Please help me	*Aidez-moi, s'il vous plaît*
OK/agreed	*d'accord*		

FINDING THE WAY

bus	*autobus, bus, car*	hitch-hiking	*autostop*
bus station	*gare routière*	on foot	*à pied*
bus stop	*arrêt*	Where are you going ?	*Vous allez où ?*
car	*voiture*		
train/taxi/ferry	*train/taxi/ferry*	I'm going to . . .	*Je vais à . . .*
boat	*bâteau*	I want to get off at . . .	*Je voudrais descendre à . . .*
plane	*avion*		
railway station	*gare*	the road to . . .	*la route pour . . .*
platform	*quai*	near	*près/pas loin*
What time does it leave ?	*Il part à quelle heure ?*	far	*loin*
		left	*à gauche*
What time does it arrive ?	*Il arrive à quelle heure ?*	right	*à droite*
		straight on	*tout droit*
a ticket to . . .	*un billet pour . . .*	on the other side of	*l'autre côté de*
single ticket	*aller simple*	on the corner of	*à l'angle de*
return ticket	*aller retour*	next to	*à côté de*
validate your ticket	*compostez votre billet*	behind	*derrière*
		in front of	*devant*
valid for	*valable pour*	before	*avant*
ticket office	*vente de billets*	after	*après*
how many kilometres ?	*combien de kilomètres ?*	under	*sous*
		to cross	*traverser*
how many hours ?	*combien d'heures ?*	bridge	*pont*

QUESTIONS AND REQUESTS

The simplest way of asking a question is to start with *s'il vous plaît* (please), then name the thing you want in an interrogative tone of voice. For example:

Where is there a bakery ?	*S'il vous plaît, la boulangerie ?*
Which way is it to Caen ?	*S'il vous plaît, la route pour Caen ?*

Similarly with requests:

We'd like a room for two	*S'il vous plaît, une chambre pour deux*
Can I have a kilo of oranges	*S'il vous plaît, un kilo d'oranges*

Question words

Where ?	*où ?*	When ?	*quand ?*
How ?	*comment ?*	Why ?	*pourquoi ?*
How many/	*combien ?*	At what time ?	*à quelle heure ?*
how much ?		What is/which is ?	*quel est ?*

ACCOMMODATION

a room for one/two people	*une chambre pour une/deux personnes*	do laundry	*faire la lessive*
a double bed	*un lit double*	sheets	*draps*
a room with a shower	*une chambre avec douche*	blankets	*couvertures*
		quiet	*calme*
a room with a bath	*une chambre avec salle de bain*	noisy	*bruyant*
		hot water	*eau chaude*
For one/two/three nights	*Pour une/deux/trois nuits*	cold water	*eau froide*
		Is breakfast included ?	*Est-ce que le petit déjeuner est compris ?*
Can I see it ?	*Je peux la voir ?*	I would like breakfast	*Je voudrais prendre le petit déjeuner*
a room on the courtyard	*une chambre sur la cour*	I don't want breakfast	*Je ne veux pas le petit déjeuner*
a room over the street	*une chambre sur la rue*	Can we camp here ?	*On peut camper ici ?*
first floor	*premier étage*	campsite	*un camping/terrain de camping*
second floor	*deuxième étage*		
with a view	*avec vue*	tent	*une tente*
key	*clef*	tent space	*un emplacement*
to iron	*repasser*	youth hostel	*auberge de jeunesse*

CARS

garage	*garage*	put air in the tyres	*gonfler les pneus*
service	*service*	battery	*batterie*
to park the car	*garer la voiture*	the battery is dead	*la batterie est morte*
car park	*un parking*	plugs	*bougies*
no parking	*défense de stationner/ stationnement interdit*	to break down	*tomber en panne*
		petrol can	*bidon*
petrol station	*poste d'essence*	insurance	*assurance*
petrol	*essence*	green card	*carte verte*
fill 'er up	*faire le plein*	traffic lights	*feux*
oil	*huile*	red light	*feu rouge*
air line	*ligne à air*	green light	*feu vert*

HEALTH MATTERS

doctor	*médecin*	stomach ache	*mal à l'estomac*
I don't feel well	*Je ne me sens pas bien*	period	*règles*
medicines	*médicaments*	pain	*douleur*
prescription	*ordonnance*	it hurts	*ça fait mal*
I feel sick	*Je suis malade*	chemist	*pharmacie*
headache	*J'ai mal à la tête*	hospital	*hôpital*

OTHER NEEDS

bakery	*boulangerie*	bank	*banque*
food shop	*alimentation*	money	*argent*
supermarket	*supermarché*	toilets	*toilettes*
to eat	*manger*	police	*police*
to drink	*boire*	telephone	*téléphone*
camping gas	*camping gaz*	cinema	*cinéma*
tobacconist	*tabac*	theatre	*théâtre*
stamps	*timbres*	to reserve/book	*réserver*

NUMBERS

1	*un*	11	*onze*	21	*vingt-et-un*	95	*quatre-vingt-quinze*
2	*deux*	12	*douze*	22	*vingt-deux*	100	*cent*
3	*trois*	13	*treize*	30	*trente*	101	*cent-et-un*
4	*quatre*	14	*quatorze*	40	*quarante*	200	*deux cents*
5	*cinq*	15	*quinze*	50	*cinquante*	300	*trois cents*
6	*six*	16	*seize*	60	*soixante*	500	*cinq cents*
7	*sept*	17	*dix-sept*	70	*soixante-dix*	1000	*mille*
8	*huit*	18	*dix-huit*	75	*soixante-quinze*	2000	*deux milles*
9	*neuf*	19	*dix-neuf*	80	*quatre-vingts*	5000	*cinq milles*
10	*dix*	20	*vingt*	90	*quatre-vingt-dix*	1,000,000	*un million*

DAYS AND DATES

January	*janvier*	November	*novembre*	August 1	*le premier août*
February	*février*	December	*décembre*	March 2	*le deux mars*
March	*mars*			July 14	*le quatorze juillet*
April	*avril*	Sunday	*dimanche*	November 23	*le vingt-trois*
May	*mai*	Monday	*lundi*		*novembre*
June	*juin*	Tuesday	*mardi*		
July	*juillet*	Wednesday	*mercredi*	1990	*dix-neuf-cent-*
August	*août*	Thursday	*jeudi*		*quatre-vingt-dix*
September	*septembre*	Friday	*vendredi*	1991	*dix-neuf-cent-*
October	*octobre*	Saturday	*samedi*		*quatre-vingt-onze*

DICTIONARIES AND PHRASEBOOKS

Harrap's French Phrase Book (Harrap, £1.95). Good pocket reference – with useful contemporary phrases and a 5000-word dictionary of terms.

Mini French Dictionary (Harrap, £1.95). French–English and English–French, plus a brief grammar and pronunciation guide.

Breakthrough French (Pan; book and two cassettes). Excellent teach-yourself course.

French and English Slang Dictionary (Harrap, £9.95); **Dictionary of Modern Colloquial French** (Routledge, £15). Both volumes are a bit large to carry, but they are the key to all you ever wanted to understand.

A Vous La France; Franc Extra; Franc-Parler (BBC Publications; each has a book and two cassettes). BBC radio courses, running from beginners' to fairly advanced language.

GLOSSARY OF FRENCH TERMS

ABBAYE abbey

ABER estuary

ACCUEIL reception

ARRET bus stop

ASSEMBLEE NATIONALE the French parliament

AUBERGE DE JEUNESSE (AJ) youth hostel

AUTOBUS city bus

BANQUE bank

BEAUX ARTS Fine Arts school (and often museum)

BESSIN harbour basin

BIBLIOTHEQUE library

BISTRO small restaurant or bar

BOIS wood

BOULANGERIE baker

BRASSERIE café/restaurant

BUREAU DE CHANGE money exchange

CAR coach, bus

CAVE (wine) cellar

CHARCUTERIE delicatessen

CHASSE, CHASSE GARDEE hunting grounds (beware)

CHATEAU castle or mansion

CIMETIERE cemetery

CITADELLE fortified city

CLOITRE cloister

CODENE French CND

CONSIGNE left luggage

COUVENT monastery

CREPERIE pancake restaurant

DEGUSTATION tasting

DEPARTEMENT county equivalent

DOLMEN megalithic stone "table"

DONJON castle keep

EGLISE church

ENCLOS group of church buildings

ENTREE entrance

FERMETURE closing time/period

FORET forest

FOUILLES archaeological excavations

GARE ROUTIERE bus station

GARE SNCF train station

GITE D'ETAPE countryside hostel

GROTTE cave

HALLES covered market

HLM publicly subsidised housing

HOPITAL hospital

HOTEL hotel – but also used for an aristocratic townhouse or mansion

HOTEL DE VILLE town hall

ILE island

JOURS FERIES public holidays

MAIRIE town hall

MAISON literally a house – can also be an office or base of an organisation

MARCHE market

MENHIR single megalithic stone

OFFICE DU TOURISME (OT) tourist office

OUVERTURE opening time/period

PATISSERIE pastry shop

PHARMACIE chemist

PLACE square

PLAGE beach

PORTE gate

POSTE post office

PRESQU'ILE peninsula

PRIVE private

PTT post office

QUARTIER quarter of a town

RELAIS ROUTIER truck-stop restaurant

REZ DE CHAUSSEE ground floor

RN route nationale (main road)

SALON DE THE tea room

SI tourist office (see below)

SNCF French railways

SYNDICAT D'INITIATIVE (SI) tourist office

TABAC bar or shop selling stamps, cigarettes, etc.

TOUR tower

VAUBAN seventeenth-century military architect

ZONE BLEUE parking zone

ZONE PIETONNE pedestrian zone

INDEX